Children Living With D

Children Living
With Domestic Violence:

Putting Men's Abuse of Women
on the Child Care Agenda

Edited by

Audrey Mullender and Rebecca Morley

Whiting & Birch Ltd

MCMXCIV

Published by Whiting & Birch Ltd, PO Box 872, Forest Hill, London SE23 3HL, England.
USA: Paul & Co, Publishers' Consortium Inc, PO Box 442, Concord, MA 01742.

British Library Cataloguing in Publication Data.
A CIP catalogue record is available from the British Library

ISBN 1 871177 71 5 (cased)
ISBN 1 871177 72 3 (limp)

Fourth Impression, 1998
Printed by Watkiss Studios, England

Cover illustration: 'Punch and Judy' is a traditional English puppet entertainment for children, performed in a booth at the seaside and latterly at children's parties, in which Mr Punch kills Judy (his wife), their baby and a number of other characters. It is played as a comedy. Not only does the story depict violence by a man towards the woman and child with whom he lives, but it has formed part of the fabric of childhood in Britain for many generations. It therefore seemed highly appropriate as an illustration for this book.

DEDICATION

To our nieces
Mary and Honey Bee

Contents

SECTION I

Introduction

1

Context and Content
of a New Agenda

Audrey Mullender and Rebecca Morley

Domestic violence concerns men's violence to their woman partners[1]. Despite an upsurge of public attention in Britain (see below), it is still largely a hidden problem surrounded by myths and misconceptions. Its impact on children living in households where the violence occurs has, until recently, been even more neglected than the impact on women themselves, yet it is of major proportions both in scope and severity. This book aims to bring the issue out into the open and to explore positive responses for children. It is our central contention that positive support for mothers subject to abuse is typically the most positive response for children. Moreover, any direct work undertaken with the children themselves needs to build on models developed specifically in contexts where the abuse of women is best understood: for example in refuges and other settings by Women's Aid, and in domestic violence programmes here and overseas.

The majority of adult women who suffer physical, emotional and sexual attacks from their partners have children. Their children witness[2] or hear the abuse, including much that their parents believe has been kept hidden. The trauma and distress this causes can lead to a range of emotional, behavioural and other difficulties. It is rarely possible to conceal abuse from children or to prevent their being frightened and confused by it. Any professional working with children may observe the results of living with domestic violence but will typically be equipped with little idea of how to respond: the teacher or classroom aide who cannot seem to help an aggressive or withdrawn child to concentrate in class; the health visitor or doctor seeing unexplained aches and pains, insomnia or bed-wetting; child psychologists and speech therapists who meet children in distress on a daily basis; the social worker who notices that the children in a particular family always look frightened or cling to their mother - any of these may fail to recognise what is causing the difficulties or, even when aware of the problems at home, may feel powerless to help. Indeed, few such professionals even have a tenable model for understanding the prevalence, severity or nature of men's abuse of women, let alone a clear view of how best to help either the children or their mothers - they are far more likely to cite the unsubstantiated 'cycle of violence' as their chief concern for the children.

This book springs from the firm conviction that child care professionals urgently need to increase their levels of knowledge in this area and to learn about good practice which they may be able to emulate or support. They need to know about the risks to children who intervene to help their mothers, the frequent co-existence of domestic violence and child abuse, what to do when a child discloses they are living with abuse, the positive role of groupwork in teaching children how to understand what has happened to them and how to protect themselves, and the enormous potential for preventive work in schools. They need to learn to take the impact of domestic violence more seriously without rushing in to remove children from non-abusive mothers. All these areas will be explored in later chapters. They need to remember, too, that the children living with violence may be white or Black; affluent or poor; healthy, sick or disabled. There is not one stereotypical group who can be targeted for help, so professionals must be consistently alert for signs and symptoms that something is wrong.

THE TERMS OF THE DEBATE

These issues, and others, are beginning to be discussed in Britain but have yet to be drawn together into a coherent debate, let alone to influence the mainstream policy and practice agenda in the field of child care. There is little political will to hear about the impact on children of men's abusive behaviour during 1994, the European 'Year of the Family', at a time when we are being encouraged to believe that a return to traditional family values would be the salvation of the nation. Nothing is more traditional than male abuse, of course, but it is not politically popular to recognise that fact.

So successfully has the debate been kept off the child care agenda that this is the first basic text dealing specifically with children and domestic violence to appear in Britain. Up to now, there have been only conference reports: one from the London Borough of Hackney (1993) called *The Links Between Domestic Violence and Child Abuse: Developing Services*, and another from Hammersmith and Fulham called *Suffering in Silence: Children and Young People Who Witness Domestic Violence* (Holder et al., 1994). These events were largely the domain of women's activists and children's workers in refuges, although the link with child abuse has begun to attract attention from the child protection professions.

Looking further afield, the only specialist book available has been the Canadian one, *Children of Battered Women* by Peter Jaffe et al. (1990). Its clinically orientated, individualistic model has never fitted well with typical British approaches - especially in refuges where the major work with children escaping violence here has taken place. A further North American book is due (Peled et al., forthcoming 1994) which combines much useful material from US and Canadian practitioners and researchers. It is unfortunate that, judging from its title: *Ending the*

Cycle of Violence, it appears to accept this 'cycle' as its raison d'être (see Morley and Mullender, this volume). It includes material on trauma therapy, system and individual advocacy, child protection, groupwork of various kinds, and school-based work. In Canada, training packs are now beginning to appear such as one on disclosure called *Make a Difference* (the text of which is reproduced in this volume). Another, *ASAP*, on school-based anti-violence work, is discussed in the chapter on that theme by Mullender (this volume). There is also material available from the USA. From Duluth, one of the most respected centres of co-ordinated work on combating woman abuse, a manual entitled *What About the Kids?* (Pence et al., n.d.) mainly concerns parents' groups, a visitation (contact) centre, and groupwork with young people who are already violent. Naturally, these sources cast no light on British legal or practice dilemmas which have begun to spawn a number of interesting articles and as yet incomplete research studies (see chapter by Morley and Mullender, this volume) as well as the conferences mentioned above.

As can be seen from this, interventive work with children exposed to the abuse of their mothers is considerably further advanced in North America than here, though patchily so. There, as here, women's organisations work unstintingly and are the repositories of much expertise and skill. The chief difference is the existence in certain locations like London Ontario, Duluth, and Minneapolis Minnesota of co-ordinated programmes of work - within and across agencies - which mean that work with children can both develop over time and operate against a background of effective support for women and of challenge to their male abusers. Where child care professionals such as social workers, teachers, psychologists and child psychiatrists are drawn into or employed within this orbit, their practice is far more likely to be based on an understanding of the nature and impact of woman abuse. Britain and North America have in common, though, large numbers of child care professionals who continue to intervene as if the last twenty years of research and practice in the field of work with abused women had never happened. This book demonstrates that we can learn from North America, though not uncritically, and that we can also build on strengths here, notably in Women's Aid's long history of responding to children's needs.

Currently emerging concerns in Britain, both theoretical and practice-based, which will be considered in the chapters to follow include the need:

1. to provide a child's eye view, both current and retrospective, of the issues and the experiences;
2. to begin to consider the particular issues encountered by Black and Asian children;
3. to highlight the impact on children of the abuse of their mothers;
4. to draw out the links between the abuse of women in the home and

the abuse of children, including in circumstances where children have died;

5. to identify any adverse consequences of recent legislation - notably the 1989 Children Act, the 1991 Child Support Act, and existing and proposed legislation on housing and homelessness - on women's ability to protect themselves and their children;

6. to pay particular attention to the attitudes and decisions of courts and court welfare officers;

7. to question received truths such as the cycle of violence (the idea of automatic intergenerational transmission) and the stance that all families benefit from the involvement of fathers, whether or not they demonstrate active concern for their children;

8. to explore good practice with children who are living with or who have escaped the abuse: in refuges in Britain, in the children's groups and children's advocacy developed in North America, in the disclosure work and primary prevention in schools also well developed there;

9. to help generate a research agenda to tackle the unanswered questions and gaps in current knowledge.

In order to approach these issues with a viable level of understanding, we need to begin by considering the abusive context in which so many children are living. Although it is not routinely taught to child care professionals, we now have considerable knowledge in this area.

THE CONTEXT: DOMESTIC VIOLENCE AGAINST WOMEN

Domestic violence against women is the most common form of family violence worldwide, even more common than physical punishment of children (Levinson, 1989, pp.28, 31). Although its true extent is unknown, recent British evidence attests to its widespread existence. The single largest category of assaults uncovered by the most recent British Crime Survey was 'domestic violence'[3] and 80 per cent of these assaults were against women[4]; nonetheless, the authors caution that because 'the survey is likely to undercount many such incidents [against women], this figure should be regarded as a minimum' (Mayhew et al., 1993, p.83). UK figures indicate that between 40 and 60 per cent of separated or divorced women experienced violence in their relationships (Borkowski et al., 1983, p.26; Evason, 1982, p.17; Painter, 1991, p.44). Each year from 1983 to 1992, between 42 and 49 per cent of all female homicide victims in England and Wales were killed by current or former partners or lovers, in contrast to between 7 and 11 per cent of male victims; and for most years during that period, about one fifth of all homicide victims were women killed by male partners/lovers (calculated from Home Office, 1993, pp.78-9, Table 4.4). A high proportion of the women referred to above are likely to have children.

Perhaps the best estimates we have concerning the prevalence and frequency of domestic violence in Britain come from a methodologically sophisticated[5] random-sample survey of approximately 1,000 men and women in North London (Mooney, 1994) though the author cautions that, due to the very sensitive nature of the subject, the figures undoubtedly represent the 'bottom line' (p.24). Thirty per cent of women admitted suffering physical violence 'more severe' than being grabbed, pushed or shaken from a current or former partner or boyfriend at some time during their adult lives; 27 per cent had been injured (i.e. about 90 per cent of those who had been physically attacked); 27 per cent had been threatened with violence; 23 per cent had been raped; and 37 per cent had suffered mental cruelty (Table 5). Twelve per cent of women had suffered physical violence in the last twelve months and 30 per cent of these women had experienced 6 or more attacks during this time (Tables 6 and 7). Again, the majority of these women most probably have children. Only small differences were found in prevalence of domestic violence by class or ethnicity (Tables 11 and 13). The men in this study were presented with vignettes detailing a number of 'stereotypical conflict situations' between partners: only 37 per cent said they would never use physical violence in any of these situations, about half said they would do so in up to two of the vignettes, and 17 per cent said they would do so in every example. Nineteen per cent of men said they actually had used physical violence against their partner in at least one of the range of situations described (p.63). The percentage of men who admitted using violence did not differ appreciably by class (Table 22; ethnicity was not reported).

Domestic violence is rarely a one-off event; moreover, attacks tend to escalate in frequency and severity over time (e.g. Hanmer and Stanko, 1985, p.366; Andrews and Brown, 1988, p.308). Homicide may be the end result of long-term, escalating domestic violence. When men kill their partners it is typically the final violent act of many; when women kill it is typically after years of suffering abuse (e.g. Browne, 1987, p.10, Ewing, 1987, p.23).

Although we normally think of domestic violence as physical, commonly the physical is but one aspect of a pattern of abuse which also includes sexual, emotional, and material abuses. As the Women's Aid Federation England (WAFE) states:

> Domestic violence may, and often does, include a range of abusive behaviours, not all of which are, in themselves, inherently 'violent'. Violence can mean, among other things: threats, intimidation, manipulation, isolation, keeping [a] woman without money, locked in, deprived of food, or using (and abusing) her children in various ways to frighten her or enforce compliance. It can also include systematic criticism and belittling comments (e.g. 'You're so stupid and ugly no one else would want you'). Sometimes the abuser's behaviour fluctuates wildly; he may offer 'rewards' on certain

conditions, or in an attempt to persuade his partner that the abuse will never happen again. (Barron et al. 1992, para 2.2)

This gross mistreatment establishes a climate in the home which cannot be hidden from children and which therefore cannot fail to be distressing for them. Interviews with children (Jaffe et al., 1990, p.20) have revealed that the majority could describe in detail assaults their parents were unaware they had witnessed.

Work by feminist activists and researchers has produced strong evidence that the roots of domestic violence lie not in pathology, stress, or family conflicts but in men's domination and control over women (see, for example, Dobash and Dobash, 1980, 1992; Schechter, 1982; Kelly, 1988; Kirkwood, 1993). The abusive behaviours characteristic of men in violent relationships are best described as control tactics, ways of instilling fear and coercing compliance. These tactics are part of the language of the relationship which women become highly skilled at interpreting. Violent men often give out very subtle, verbal and non-verbal, signals of their threats and intentions - signals which would be unrecognisable to anyone except those they are abusing. Behaviours not obviously abusive to an outsider can signal extreme danger to the woman on the receiving end, and hence terrorise her; indeed, violence does not have to be continuous or physical for her to be terrified that she could be harmed at any moment. A lack of understanding of these features of violent relationships, along with the difficulties women have in naming and/or disclosing the violence[6] (see, for example, Kelly, 1988), may partly explain why professionals often underestimate or disregard the seriousness of the situation, to the detriment of women's and children's safety. (See, for example, Hester et al., this volume, for a discussion of professional disregard for the dangers facing women and their children in the context of arranging contact after divorce where there has been violence.)

The question most frequently asked by outsiders is almost certainly 'Why does she stay?'. This question not only implies culpability or failing on the part of women in abusive relationships, but also shifts the focus away from the abusers; indeed, it is of fundamental significance that this question, rather than 'Why is he brutal towards someone he supposedly loves?', is widely viewed as appropriate. Moreover, it is in many respects misplaced. The first violent incident usually occurs only after the relationship has become serious and committed, often after marriage. It is rarely an unambiguous event, signalling a need to end the relationship. Women react initially with shock and disbelief, wanting to forget and believing the violence to be an isolated event caused by stress or other trauma. Men often initially beg forgiveness and promise it will not happen again. Women may blame themselves and promise to do better. A violent relationship unfolds in time - it is only in retrospect that the first incident(s) can be identified as the beginning of a pattern. Given the investment which women often have in their relationship - including feelings of love for their partner and responsibility for their children - and, given that there are usually initially positive aspects to the relationship, it is totally inappropriate to ask at this stage: 'Why does she stay?'. (For research bearing on these issues see, for example, Dobash and Dobash, 1980; Browne 1987; NiCarthy, 1987; Hoff, 1990.) Finally, although we do not have precise data, it is clear that very many women, if not most, *do* leave violent relationships eventually - but the process of leaving is often a long and painful one.

Without underestimating the damaging psychological impact of living with abuse (e.g. Kirkwood, 1993), it is possible to see past the stereotypes of the passive 'victim' suffering from 'learned helplessness'[7] and the like, and state that women do not submissively accept their situation. Studies (e.g. Browne, 1987; Kelly, 1988; Hoff, 1990) have documented numerous strategies which women use to cope and resist: for example, trying to talk to their partner about the abuse; refusing to obey the abuser's orders, often in the context of defending the interests of their children; talking to relatives and friends; calling the police; seeking counselling or legal advice; and, indeed, leaving. In fact, attempts to seek help appear to *increase* rather than decrease over time (e.g. Dobash and Dobash, 1980; Bowker, 1983; Kelly, 1988). Denying and minimising the abuse have also been analysed as coping strategies, allowing women at least a short escape from the pain and trauma of violence (e.g. Kelly, 1988). Another aspect of their coping is that women go to great lengths to protect their children by trying to conceal what is happening (Hoff, 1990, p.204). Most recognise that the abuse they personally suffer has an unavoidably adverse impact on their children; they are greatly worried both by the short-term and longer-lasting effects of this (Evason, 1982, p.45). Such concerns are a significant factor in women's eventual decisions to end their relationships (Evason, op. cit.; Pahl, 1982, p.529; 1985, p.50), often after trying to stay together 'for the sake of the children'.

Yet, for many women violence does not stop at the point of leaving. Of the women in the North London survey (Mooney, 1994) experiencing 'more severe' physical violence during their adult lives, 34 per cent were no longer living with their partners when the last incident occurred (p.38, Table 10) and in 6 per cent of cases the violence only started after the breakdown of the relationship (p.39). Figures for England and Wales in 1986 and 1987 show that, in 30 per cent of incidents where men killed women spouses, the couple were no longer living together (in Edwards, 1989, p.200). Indeed, it is increasingly acknowledged that women are at greatest risk of harm from their partners when they are attempting to leave the relationship or seeking outside help (e.g. Pence, 1989, p.345; Browne and Williams, 1989). Men sometimes go to great lengths to find their ex-partners, and frequently use contact with children as a means to continue their violence (see chapter by Hester et al., this volume). As one US researcher states:

For many battered women, leaving their mates and living in constant fear of reprisal or death seems more intolerable than remaining, despite their fears of further harm. Women in hiding relate how they are afraid to go into their apartment when they get home; to go to work in the morning or to leave at night; to approach their car in a parking lot; to visit friends . . . . Every sound in the night, every step in the hall, every pair of headlights pulling up behind them might be him. Accomplishing daily tasks against this wall of fear becomes exhausting (Browne, 1987, p.115).

Historically, helping professionals - including police, lawyers, social workers, housing officials, doctors, and the like - have reacted unsympathetically and ineffectively to women's calls for help, often blaming them for 'provoking' the violence (see, for example, Dobash and Dobash, 1980; Pahl, 1985; Mama, 1989). Indeed, it has been argued (Gondolf, 1988, p.22) that it is those from whom women seek help who suffer from 'learned helplessness'. Thus these professionals and their agencies have been centrally implicated in the very construction and perpetuation of violent relationships. Only Women's Aid refuges and support services have been consistently rated highly by women, and they have remained largely unsupported and underfunded (e.g. Binney et al., 1981; Borkowski et al., 1983; Homer et al., 1984; Pahl, 1985; Barron et al., 1992, Appendix 2).

Recently however, domestic violence has (again[8]) been put on the public agenda. All police forces in England and Wales have produced policy statements on domestic violence[9], and local initiatives are rapidly developing in an increasing number of directions - besides policing, most notably inter-agency working and programmes for violent men. At national level, recent developments include: two Law Commission reports - one on marital rape (1992a), the other on measures to protect women under the civil law (1992b); a Victim Support (1992) national inter-agency working party report on domestic violence; a number of notable Appeal Court decisions (see, for example, *The Guardian*, 3 April 1992, 26 September 1992, 30 October 1992) resulting in the release of women imprisoned for killing violent partners; an Association of Chief Officers of Probation position statement (ACOP, 1992); a Home Affairs Committee inquiry (1993a and 1993b) into domestic violence, and a governmental response (Cm 2269, 1993); and the formation of a ministerial group on domestic violence, headed by the Home Office - the newly appointed 'lead' department for co-ordinating work nationally - which is currently producing an inter-agency circular on domestic violence, planning a public awareness campaign (first phase to take place in late September 1994), and developing good practice guidelines for key professionals.

However, the impact of these developments on women's ability to extricate themselves and their children from violent relationships may be negligible, at least in the shorter term. Changes in practice are much more difficult to achieve than legal or policy change. Moreover, although the Home Affairs Committee recommended that 'the first priority for Government action on domestic violence should be the establishment of a central, coordinated policy for refuge provision throughout the country' (1993a, para.130), this was rejected by the Government. Finally, the potential for positive change is undermined by a wider framework of legislation, policy, and economic realities damaging to women's interests including reductions in legal aid, changes in family law, proposed changes in housing law, public spending cuts, immigration legislation, and increased poverty among women generally and lone mothers in particular (see Morley, 1993; some of these issues are discussed in later chapters in this volume).

CONCLUSION

Women and men are not equal in British society. A woman who has been persistently and terrifyingly abused may not have the power or the options to protect her children's interests as she would wish without help. No legal, medical or welfare judgement which ignores that fact can be regarded as sound. But nor can any judgement which fails to differentiate between the lives children live while their mother's abuser is present or closely involved, on the one hand, and the lives their mother would make for them if she and they were safe and had access to adequate services, on the other.

This is not a naïve book. We recognise throughout that women's and children's interests may conflict but, except where this is demonstrably and irresolvably the case, the most effective and cost effective way to help children is to understand what is happening to their mothers and to work in alliance with them.

This volume draws together the state of our knowledge about children living with domestic violence. The parameters of the debate in Britain are not yet clear, but levels of interest are growing and the grounds for concern are sufficiently established for this collection of papers to make what we hope will be a powerful impact. It attempts to build a crucial bridge between, on the one hand, those who are primarily involved in helping women and who have come to an understanding of children's needs through that route and, on the other, the child care establishment which has more resources but not yet the clear awareness that children are at risk when their mothers are at risk - and that both can best be helped together in the vast majority of instances. In attempting to map current theoretical concerns and outline positive practice responses, we hope to open both to wide and urgent discussion.

The subject of this book deals with inequalities in power. It attempts to do so in a way which recognises not only gender inequalities but also those which result from the social structuring of race, sexuality, disability and class. In a book on children, we need to remember that age, too, is a basis of oppressive attitudes and policies. As the WAFE children's rights policy recognises (see Debbonaire, this volume), children have no vote and often no voice in what happens to them.

Since our subject is concern about children, we begin in the next chapter with the personal accounts of children who have been living with domestic violence. These reveal something of what they undergo and how their needs can best be met.

Notes

1. The term 'domestic violence' is used in this book to denote men's abuse of their female partners and ex-partners because it is the expression most easily recognised by professionals and by the general public for the phenomenon in question; nevertheless it is important to recognise that it has been criticised on several grounds.

   The word 'domestic' is challenged for its links with the trivialisation of the problem and its connotations of the police, in particular, not responding on the same level to an assault they see as 'just a domestic' as to an assault in a public place. (The official policy is now that both are equally serious.) The term 'domestic' is also inaccurate in this context for three reasons. Firstly, there are other crimes in the home, such as child abuse, which are not encompassed by it in common parlance (though see note 3, below). Secondly, the abuser and the abused woman may have had a continuing relationship but need not actually have lived together. Thirdly, harassment and violence often continue after the woman has attempted to end the relationship and either she or her partner has left. The word 'violence' also conveys an incomplete impression since, in fact, men's ill-treatment of women takes many forms which combine together into a pattern of intimidation and attacks encompassing physical violence, pyschological intimidation, emotional and sexual abuse. Economic domination and abuse of male privilege also feature, as does using the children against the woman in a range of ways. Finally, domestic violence is not a term which places the blame where it should really lie: with the man. Its vagueness is exploited by those who choose to overlook the gender power dynamic involved and to talk about 'warring' or 'violent families'. The North American term 'woman abuse' is clearer but still puts the survivor rather than the perpetrator in the frame and is also less readily recognisable to a British audience. The phrase 'men's abuse of women in intimate relationships' would perhaps offer the clearest description. 'Domestic violence' should be regarded throughout the book as a shorthand term for this.

2. Dobash and Dobash (1984, p.279) found that almost half the incidents of domestic violence they analysed took place in front of observers, by far the largest group of whom (58 per cent) were the couple's children; i.e. almost three out of ten attacks were witnessed by at least one child.

3. 'Domestic violence' was defined as 'incidents involving partners, ex-partners, household members and other relatives, irrespective of location' (Mayhew et al., 1993, p.82). The other assault categories measured were

'home based' - incidents in and immediately around the home not involving those included in domestic violence; 'street'; 'pubs/clubs'; 'work-based'; 'mugging'; and 'other assaults' including 'incidents at sporting events, schools, shops and leisure centres' (p.83).

4. While the vast majority of domestic assaults on women were from current or former (heterosexual) partners and boyfriends, only a minority of domestic attacks on men were from comparable people (Mayhew et al., 1993, p.88). This confirms previous findings that most assaults between partners are perpetrated by men. For example, Dobash and Dobash's (1980) examination of records in selected police areas in Edinburgh and Glasgow showed that 98.5 per cent of violence between partners was men's violence to women (calculated from Table 5, p.247).

5. The strength of this study lies both in its sampling and its data collection methods. Most of the statistics we have on domestic violence come from non-representative samples of women: women who have come to the attention of welfare or legal agencies or, more infrequently, women who have volunteered as a result of advertising. The North London study achieved a random sample of all residents in Islington, using the Post Office Address File as its sampling frame (the File is updated every three months and avoids under-representation of minority groups, the unemployed, those in rented accommodation, and poll tax evaders). Random sampling allows us to generalise to the population from which the sample was selected; the sample should reflect, within known statistical limits, the correct proportion of people according to gender, race, class, employment status, and the like. Findings concerning prevalence and incidence of domestic violence should also reflect their true proportions in North London. To the extent that North London is representative of other urban areas in Britain, it can be argued that the findings are further generalisable.

Appropriate data collection methods are crucial to the success of a survey asking questions about such a very sensitive topic. The North London interviewers were highly experienced and chosen for their understanding and commitment to the issue of domestic violence. Respondents were interviewed on their own to minimise inhibitions and maintain safety. Detailed information from women was gained from self-complete questionnaires which the interviewer left with the respondents. This allowed maximum anonymity and time for reflection. (See Mooney, 1994, ch.3, for further details of the methodology.)

6. The North London survey, for example, found that 38 per cent of women who had endured violence at some time during their adult lives and 45 per cent during the last twelve months had told no one about their experiences (Mooney, 1984, p.60). This study, along with many others, found fear of punitive agency responses to be a key reason for women not disclosing violence to professionals - women fear not being taken seriously, being blamed, being forced to take legal action, having their children taken into care, having their safety compromised, and the like.

7. Learned helplessness' is a theoretical concept originally developed through experiments with dogs who were caged and given random shocks which they could not control; eventually they stopped responding, even when escape became possible, because they had learned that their behaviour had no effect on what happened to them - they became 'depressed' (see Seligman, 1975).

    The theory was first used with 'battered women' by American psychologist, Lenore Walker (1979; see also 1984), who argued that repeated non-controllable battering leads women over time to become passive and submissive. She hypothesised that:

    > ...early social influences on women facilitate [this] psychological condition called 'learned helplessness'. . . which causes women to feel powerless to effect positive control over their lives. . . . 'learned helplessness' is responsible for the apparent emotional, cognitive, and behavioral deficits observed in the battered woman, which negatively influence her from leaving a relationship after the battering occurs (Walker, 1984, p.2).

    She further suggested that 'battered women are *more* rigidly socialised into the female sex role stereotype' (1984, p.2, emphasis added). Crudely, this suggests that abused women are in, and stay in, their abusive relationships because of psychological or personality deficits.

    Despite research evidence contradicting the theory from Walker herself (e.g. 1984, pp.148-51), as well as from many others, she remains attached to its importance - though she does acknowledge that things may be more complicated than she originally postulated. The theory is still widely accepted, including by Barnett and LaViolette (1993) who, in a recent book, argue that learned helplessness is one among other 'learning theory' factors explaining 'why battered women stay'. Walker also coined the term 'battered woman syndrome' to refer to the psychological 'condition' which results from battering. In North America, the syndrome is used in expert testimony in defence of women who kill violent partners, and it has recently been imported into British courts (see Morley, 1993, pp.190-92).

8. The issue earlier came to public prominence in the mid nineteenth century (see, for example, May, 1978).

9. The history to this was that, influenced by research and policy in North America, the Metropolitan Police issued a working party report in 1986, a force order in 1987, and best practice guidelines in 1990. Similar advances were being made in West Yorkshire. These were followed by Home Office Circular 60/1990 (and equivalent guidelines in Scotland and Northern Ireland) urging a comprehensive national shift in policing policy towards a far greater use of existing powers of arrest, the establishment of domestic violence units, and involvement in inter-agency forums (see Morley and Mullender, 1992; also Morley and Mullender, 1994, for a review of police initiatives in the context of broader prevention strategies).

References

Andrews, B. and Brown, G.W. (1988) 'Marital violence in the community: a biographical approach', *British Journal of Psychiatry*, 153, pp.305-312.

Association of Chief Officers of Probation (1992) *Association of Chief Officers of Probation Position Statement on Domestic Violence*. London: ACOP. Drafted by David Sleightholm.

Barron, J., Harwin, N. and Singh, T. (1992) *Women's Aid Federation England Written Evidence to the House of Commons Home Affairs Committee Inquiry into Domestic Violence*. October, Bristol: Women's Aid Federation England. (Also published as Memorandum 22, submitted by Women's Aid Federation England, in Home Affairs Committee, 1993b, see below.)

Barnett, O.W. and LaViolette, A.D. (1993) *It Could Happen to Anyone: Why Battered Women Stay*. Newbury Park, California: Sage.

Binney, V., Harkell, G., and Nixon, J. (1981) *Leaving Violent Men: A Study of Refuges and Housing for Battered Women*. Leeds: Women's Aid Federation England.

Borkowski, M., Murch, M., and Walker, V. (1983) *Marital Violence: the Community Response*. London: Tavistock.

Bowker, L.H. (1983) *Beating Wife-Beating*. Lexington, Massachusetts: D. C. Heath and Company.

Browne, A. (1987) *When Battered Women Kill*. New York: The Free Press.

Browne, A. and Williams, K.R. (1989) 'Exploring the effect of resource availability and the likelihood of female-precipitated homicides', *Law and Society Review*, 23(1), pp.75-94.

Children's Subcommittee of the London Coordinating Committee to End Woman Abuse (1994) *Make a Difference: How to Respond to Child Witnesses of Woman Abuse*. London, Ontario, Canada: London Coordinating Committee to End Woman Abuse. (Training pack with video and manual. Available from: Children's Aid Society of London and Middlesex (Attention Larry Marshall), PO Box 6010, Depot 1, London, Ontario, Canada N5W 5RD. Video needs to be adapted for UK use.)

Dobash, R.E. and Dobash, R. (1980) *Violence Against Wives: a Case Against the Patriarchy*. Shepton Mallet, Somerset: Open Books.

Dobash, R.E. and Dobash, R.P. (1984) 'The nature and antecedents of violent events', *British Journal of Criminology*, 24(3), July, pp.269-288

Edwards, S.S.M. (1989) *Policing 'Domestic' Violence: Women, the Law and the State*. London: Sage.

Evason, E. (1982) *Hidden Violence: Battered Women in Northern Ireland*. Belfast: Farset Co-operative Press.

Ewing, C.P. (1987) *Battered Women Who Kill: Psychological Self-Defense as Legal Justification*. Lexington, Massachusetts: D. C. Heath and Co.

Gondolf, E.W. (1988) *Battered Women as Survivors: an Alternative to Treating Learned Helplessness*. Lexington, Kentucky: Lexington.

Hanmer, J. and Stanko, E.A. (1985) 'Stripping away the rhetoric of protection: violence to women, law and the state in Britain and the U.S.A', *International Journal of the Sociology of Law*, 13, pp.357-74.

Hoff, L.A. (1990) *Battered Women as Survivors*. London: Routledge.

Holder, R., Kelly, L. and Singh, T. (1994) *Suffering in Silence: Children and Young People Who Witness Domestic Violence*. London: Hammersmith and Fulham Domestic Violence Forum. (Available from Community Safety Unit, Hammersmith Town Hall, King Street, London W6 9JU.)

Home Affairs Committee (1993a) *Domestic Violence*, Vol.I. Report together with the Proceedings of the Committee, House of Commons, Session 1992-93. London: HMSO.

Home Affairs Committee (1993b) *Domestic Violence*, Vol.II. Memoranda of Evidence, Minutes of Evidence and Appendices, House of Commons, Session 1992-93. London: HMSO.

Home Office (1993) *Criminal Statistics: England and Wales 1992*. London: HMSO.

Homer, M., Leonard, A. E., and Taylor, M. P. (1984) *Private Violence - Public Shame: A Report on the Circumstances of Women Leaving Domestic Violence in Cleveland*. Middlesbrough: Cleveland Refuge and Aid for Women and Children.

Kelly, L. (1988) *Surviving Sexual Violence*. Cambridge: Polity Press.

Kirkwood, C. (1993) *Leaving Abusive Partners: From the Scars of Survival to the Wisdom for Change*. London: Sage.

Law Commission (1992a) *Criminal Law: Rape Within Marriage*. Law Com. No.205. London: HMSO.

Law Commission (1992b) *Family Law: Domestic Violence and Occupation of the Family Home*. Law Com. No.207. London: HMSO.

Levinson, D. (1989) *Family Violence in Cross-Cultural Perspective*. Newbury Park, California: Sage.

London Borough of Hackney (1993) *The Links Between Domestic Violence and Child Abuse: Developing Services*. London: London Borough of Hackney. (Available from the Women's Unit.)

Mama, A. (1989) *The Hidden Struggle: Statutory and Voluntary Sector Responses to Violence Against Black Women in the Home*. London: London Race and Housing Research Unit.

May, M. (1978) 'Violence in the family: an historical perspective' in Martin, J.P. (ed.) *Violence and the Family*. Chichester: John Wiley and Sons.

Mayhew, P., Maung, N.A., and Mirrlees-Black, C. (1993) *The 1992 British Crime Survey*. Home Office Research Study No. 132. London: HMSO.

Mooney, J. (1994) *The Hidden Figure: Domestic Violence in North London*. London: Islington Police and Crime Prevention Unit.

Morley, R. (1993) 'Recent responses to domestic violence against women: a feminist critique' in Page, R. and Baldock, J. (eds.) *Social Policy Review 5: the Evolving State of Welfare*. Canterbury: Social Policy Association.

Morley, R. and Mullender, A. (1992) 'Hype or hope? The importation of pro-arrest policies and batterers' programmes from North America to Britain as key measures for preventing violence against women in the home', *International Journal of Law and the Family*, 6, pp.265-288.

Morley, R. and Mullender, A. (1994) *Preventing Domestic Violence to Women*.

London: Home Office. Police Research Group, Crime Prevention Unit Series, Paper 48.

NiCarthy, G. (1987) *The Ones Who Got Away: Women Who Left Abusive Partners.* Seattle, Washington: Seal Press.

Pahl, J. (ed.) (1985) *Private Violence and Public Policy: The Needs of Battered Women and the Responses of the Public Services.* London: Routledge and Kegan Paul.

Painter, K. (1991) *Wife Rape, Marriage and the Law. Survey Report: Key Findings and Recommendations.* Faculty of Economic and Social Studies University of Manchester, Department of Social Policy and Social Work.

Peled, E., Shapell, B., Jaffe, P.G. and Edleson, J.L. (forthcoming 1994) *Ending the Cycle of Violence: Community Responses to Children of Battered Women.* Newbury Park, California: Sage.

Pence, E. (1989) *The Justice System's Response to Domestic Assault Cases: a Guide for Policy Development.* Duluth, Minnesota: Minnesota Program Development Inc.

Pence, E., Hardesty, L., Steil, K., Soderberg, J. and Ottman, L. (n.d.) *What About the Kids? Community Intervention in Domestic Assault Cases - A Focus on Children.* Duluty, Minnesota, USA: Duluth Domestic Abuse Intervention Project.

Seligman, M.E.P. (1975) *Helplessness: On Depression, Development and Death.* San Francisco: Freeman.

Schechter, S. (1982) *Women and Male Violence: The Visions and Struggles of the Battered Women's Movement.* Boston: Massachusetts: South End Press.

Victim Support (1992) *Domestic Violence: Report of a National Inter-Agency Working Party on Domestic Violence.* London: Victim Support.

Walker, L.E. (1979) *The Battered Woman.* New York: Harper and Row.

Walker, L.E. (1984) *The Battered Woman Syndrome.* New York: Springer.

2

Children's Accounts

gathered by Gina Higgins

These first-hand accounts were gathered by a children's worker in a Women's Aid refuge who was approached by the editors. Her method of working was as follows.

After obtaining the agreement of the local Women's Aid collective, the childworker showed the editors' letter individually to the mothers of a number of children with whom she had built up trust over a period of time; it would not have felt appropriate to do this work with children who had just arrived, or who had been in the refuge for less than about two months. All the mothers readily agreed because they knew and had confidence in the childworker.

In accordance with the normal, participative style of the children's work, the worker then called a children's meeting with the children concerned (both resident and ex-resident) at which she read out the letter about the book and told the children their mothers had given permission if they wanted to be involved. The meeting discussed how best to record the personal accounts. No one wanted to go away and write down their own thoughts, so Gina suggested that she could ask questions and write down the replies. The children wanted to know what the questions would be and the following were agreed: what it had been like for them at home; how they had felt about coming into the refuge initially, and about living as a family in one room; how well the young person was now getting on with their mother, and brothers and sisters; what school was like; whether they had made friends in the new school. For ex-residents, there would be additional questions covering how they felt about where they were living now, and how well they were getting on with their family.

Only one child did not want to participate: a thirteen-year old who did not want the workers to work with him at all. In addition, one of the ex-residents was going through a sensitive time over contact with his father so it seemed best not to interview him.

The childworker made a separate appointment with each child and used the quiet room, with an arrangement not to be disturbed. She asked the agreed questions and told the children she would write down exactly what came out of their mouths, then read it back to them for them to agree with what had been written. This was duly done. The children's mothers then asked to see the accounts, and the children and young people individually agreed to this. After a volunteer had typed them up, one copy was given to the child concerned, one to their mother, and one was sent off for the book. No other copy was kept in the refuge, either on paper or on the computer. Everyone was assured that no names or addresses would appear in the book, so that no child or family would be identifiable. One boy had been worried about that, but everyone felt safe to work within the agreed groundrules.

When the mothers read their children's accounts, none disagreed with anything she saw and several commented on how real it felt. One mother had not known how great an impact the violence had had on her child and was pleased that the child had opened up to the childworker in this way. The woman now realised how right she had been to leave home and come into the refuge.

The childworker's strongest impression from doing this work for the book was that it confirmed how, although people often do not talk to children about their experiences and even try to stop them thinking about what they have been through, children benefit enormously from talking to someone they can trust. They often feel caught in the middle between their parents so can find it difficult to talk to either of them. Given the chance to talk to a childworker in a refuge - who is there just for them and who will listen to them and support them - they make tremendous progress and are helped to work on their feelings of anger and sadness.

Thus the work of gathering these accounts actually fed into the work being undertaken with the children and had some positive results, both for them and their mothers.

PERSONAL ACCOUNTS BY CHILDREN WHO ARE LIVING IN, OR WHO HAVE RECENTLY LIVED IN REFUGES

Boy aged 12, white, ex-resident:

> When I lived in the refuge I had to share one room with my brother and Mum. It was OK, I didn't mind, you get what you are given. The workers couldn't afford a bigger house. I can't remember much because I was four and a half and now I'm twelve years old.
>
> I keep in touch with the refuge and sometimes I go when there is a workshop on for us. The best one was about Malcolm X, it was about race awareness. I thought it was interesting and I could write my own thing about him.
>
> I now live with my Mum and I like it. My Mum has a girlfriend and I like her as well. I like living here. My brother is sixteen and lives now with my Dad - I don't mind. I like my school and I have been chosen by my class to be their council representative. I don't see my Dad much; I see him when I want - every two months. My Mum has helped me a lot, she talks to me about racism and sexism and about sexuality and keeping safe.

Boy aged 14, Chinese, resident:

Not my Dad - Mum's boyfriend. He argued and shouted a lot; didn't like it much. I told him to shut up but he doesn't listen. He never talked to me, I ignored him. It is domestic violence - not very good. No contact with Dad or Mum's boyfriend.

In the refuge there's not much privacy. There's a lot of stuff I can't do myself like if I was at home. Run about a lot and make some noise. I usually don't venture out of my room, I stay and read and do homework. I don't go in my room at eight thirty, I come home pretty late and go straight in my room. I didn't have many friends so it hasn't affected me, being in the refuge. School didn't affect me because I came from Australia anyway, I was waiting for one then we came in the refuge.

School is good: make friends, have Chinese lessons, learn about my culture. Kept up with my friends: written, 'phoned. I contact them - I say I'm still moving around; hasn't affected me. I'm a bit lazy; I'm quiet, gentle. I'm shy - Mum doesn't like it. Mum wants me to be more outgoing.

I want a home.

Girl aged 12, white, resident:

I thought my stepdad hitting us, me and my Mum and my brother, was bad. He hit us on hands and across the face and that. He gave us chores to do and we had two Rottweiler puppies and we had to take it in turns to wash the dishes. We had to clean the dogs out and hoover before we went to school. One day I didn't do it: hoover under the cushions. (We had to call him 'Dad'.) Dad came over - he said: 'Put your hands out' and he hit me and hit me and hit me. I thought it was out of order. I was very frightened, I tried to stay out of his way. I don't remember my real father. Sometimes it bothers me not being able to see him.

Sometimes I get very angry with Mum: we have arguments, I shout at her. My brother annoys me because he butts in. I'm OK with my baby sister.

I like it in the refuge. The workers are friendlier than the other refuge. I thought it would be a big hall - queue up for food and women sleep on the floor. We go on outings. I don't like living in one room.

School is all right - I miss my friends. I feel sad. I've made new friends - I keep refuge a secret. I don't tell people; I make an excuse where I live.

Boy aged 14, Asian/Caribbean, ex-resident:

My Dad cut my Mum with a knife; children left and went to Auntie. I was there - I used to hear arguments and shouting about drinking ('Alcoholic !').

Unhappy I felt - I'd go in my room and play, I was ten years. Domestic violence is horrible - not worth it, people getting hurt. I never see my Dad - I saw him once one year ago, walking down the street; we just walked on. I don't feel anything for Dad. Relationship better with Mum and me. Relationship all right - we fight a bit, me and my brother, and hurt each other. I play a lot with my baby brother. In the refuge I liked the playroom and everything - I felt safe.

Changed school six times - I get worried: start all over again making friends. School now all right, I know everyone there. I've been there one and a half years, feel better at school - I've friends. Temporary accommodation, we've been accepted for a three bedroom house - feel great ! Auntie helped us.

Watch violent films and start acting them out. It gets out of order: one gets hurt and angry, then we hit each other harder. Family therapy might help us all. We are now going there as a family.

Boy aged 6, Asian, resident:

He says he loves my Mum but he lies. He tells Mum to do everything at home. He never gave Mum any money. He hit my Mum, I saw it. I tried to look happy but I wasn't inside. He never played with me - I felt lonely. I feel sad for my Dad, he's an idiot. I do not like my Dad. My Dad hit my sister with a plate and she started bleeding on her head. She was red everywhere.

I feel happy now 'cos I'm away from my Dad; he can't find us now because he doesn't know the way.

I saw my Dad yesterday in a car at my Nan's, shouting 'Us Salaam Alaikum'[1]. I was really frightened. I don't feel happy at new school - no friends. We kids make a mess and Mum cleans it up. We're OK now.

My Dad really wants to kill us and shoot us. He will lock us in a room and we will never get out and have nothing to eat. I must look after my Mum, my Dad is really bad.

When I am big, I could be Batman and go and kill my Dad and throw him in a dustbin.

I like the refuge because if children do something wrong you see the workers and then it's all right.

I am scared when I have to see my Dad sometimes, that he will hurt me and shoot me. He said lots of times he would do that to all of us.

Boy aged 13, Asian/Caribbean, ex-resident:

My Dad attacked my Mum with a knife. My Dad cut my Mum's toe. He fell asleep. I was at Auntie's. I saw my Mum and I fainted. He used to hit my brother and me. Felt pretty sad. Domestic violence: I think it's bad that it should happen. Go where they can get help. Dad is abusive, needs mental help. I help Mum so she doesn't get bad memories and my baby brother is OK.

We arranged to see Dad but he didn't turn up. I felt disappointed.

It was fun in the refuge. Good for my Mum 'cos other women were in similar situations.

Relationship is going good, some bad points. I don't listen to her - she gets angry. I try to listen to her now and help her. We fight a lot and we play too.

Dad hit my brother a lot and I think my brother takes it out on me 'cos he thought my Dad liked me better. We are in temporary accommodation at the moment. We will be getting a home soon.

School: I'm doing good, sometimes I don't concentrate. Some friends are a bad influence. Family therapy is helping to stop hitting. I call my brother names so he will hit me. I don't know why I do it. It is abuse as well as my Dad hitting us.

Girl aged 7, mixed parentage, ex-resident:

I was really upset sometimes because my Dad: sometimes he hit my Mum and he hit me and my brother, sometimes he could be really nice and we could have lots of fun. It made me feel very unhappy when he hit me, and it hurt. We left and went into a refuge because he was hitting my Mum.

I was scared coming to the refuge at first, but when I met most of the children and played, I was then happy. I liked everything in the refuge. I now live with my Mum and my brother, and my Godmother comes and stays with us sometimes. I feel fine that my Godmother is with us because she is really nice. It's happy in my house now, and Mum and Godmother really understand me most of the time. Me and my brother get on fine; sometimes I can get quite annoyed with him - when we play wrestling he can hurt me, but then he says sorry so that's OK.

I'm doing very well and I get lots of congratulations for my school work.

At my Dad's, I wet my knickers by accident and Daddy hit me. I felt scared and unhappy. Sometimes I did not want to see my Dad. I haven't seen my Dad for six weeks now; I feel unhappy because I haven't seen him.

Sometimes my Dad still threatens my Mum - it makes me feel unhappy. Most of the time they talk about access visits.

I think no one should do domestic violence *ever* , even in heaven, because if you go to war you could get hurt or end up dead yourself.

Girl aged 15, white, ex-resident:

Me and my Mam and the rest of us left the North and went to live in the refuge. I'm glad my Mam left - it was horrible living at home.

When we lived in the refuge, I remember the other kids used to take the mick out of my accent. It was OK after, though, because we all had a children's meeting and we were all talking about racism and it came up about languages and accents. I liked the meetings and workshops - all of us learned a lot.

The room was really small with us all living in it. I was glad when we got our own place. I didn't like it travelling to school, though, but I had no choice as I didn't want to leave another school.

I'm OK about everything now, but my brother had a hard time of it when we moved to our house. He kept bunking off school - he said he was being bullied at school. He's OK now, I think!

I'm glad my Mam left and I'm glad I was in the refuge. I have a new life now and new friends.

It was wrong for us to live in that situation. I didn't like it when my Mam got hurt and cried. My Da needs help, like a doctor or someone.

I am happy now. I have a few problems now, but only little ones. I hope that when I'm older, I won't let a man push me around. My Mam is happy now, and so are we. We never see me Da now, I like it.

Note
1. A traditional greeting - the equivalent of 'Hello!'

SECTION II

Researching the Impact on Children
of Men's Abuse of Women
and the Links With Child Abuse

3

Domestic Violence and Children: What Do We Know From Research?

Rebecca Morley and Audrey Mullender

INTRODUCTION

This chapter explores the existing research pertaining to the ways in which domestic violence against women relates to children. Broadly, this research examines three areas:

1. the impacts on children of living with domestic violence;
2. the links between domestic violence and child abuse;
3. the hypothesis that children who live with violence grow up to repeat the pattern in adulthood, perpetuating a 'cycle of violence'.

What is apparent from this review is that convincing evidence exists that domestic violence is highly relevant to children's present and future well-being and does overlap significantly with child abuse. However, the research is sparse and begs important conceptual and methodological issues. These issues and their implications for policy and practice are perceptively discussed in Liz Kelly's chapter which follows this one, and we suggest that the two are read together.

THE IMPACTS ON CHILDREN OF LIVING WITH DOMESTIC VIOLENCE

There is a growing body of research into the impact of domestic violence on children, both from professional and academic perspectives. The earliest work tended to rely on observation in shelter (refuge) settings, either by shelter staff or caseworkers (Jaffe et al., 1990b, pp.34-36, summarising a number of studies from the early 1980s) and showed a high incidence of emotional problems such as crying, anxiety and sadness, or eating and sleeping problems in babies. Sopp-Gilson (1980) found many children to be unsettled and anxious but she also described relief at being away from the violent home, a factor which is typically observed by British refuge workers but little remarked on in research.

An interesting review of 29 published papers on children observing violence, traced through six computer databases and chiefly of North American origin, is offered by Fantuzzo and Lindquist (1989). Of these articles, 23 were based on original data, covering 1069 children in all. The compilers looked for information on behavioural, emotional, social, intellectual and physical problems.

Externalised behaviours, such as aggression, appeared linked with exposure to violence in almost all of the studies but not consistently across all ages or both sexes (with some contradictions between studies). On the emotional side, qualitative material from case studies reported depression, suicidal behaviour, bed-wetting, insomnia, tics, and fears and phobias. Only two of the quantitative studies failed to establish negative emotional effects in the groups exposed to violence as compared with non-exposed control groups. The others all reported some impact. The smaller number of studies that considered social, intellectual or physical functioning also tended to find problems in those areas: for example, Hinchey and Gavelek (1982) did so in three out of four social skills measures. Only one study (Rosenbaum and O'Leary, 1981) found no statistically significant differences on any measure but even this (p.696) did record the children of women who experienced abuse as somewhat more disordered both in conduct and in personality than children who had not lived with violence. Two studies (Hershorn and Rosenbaum, 1985; Wolfe et al., 1985) suggested that children were reacting more to the stress their mothers were under than to the violence itself. Looking directly at Wolfe et al. (1985), witnessing abuse was found to have a negative impact over and above that caused by separation from the other parent and loss of home, friends and so on. Further analysis revealed the stress it placed on their mothers as particularly damaging for the children, as compared to the violence alone. Supporting a woman to leave or to free herself of the abuse can therefore be expected to give her children greater stability.

To add to the overview by Fantuzzo and Lindquist, attitudes have also been studied. Exposed children condoned violence to resolve relationship conflict more readily than controls, and older children who had experienced extreme violence and other negative life events had some tendency to hold themselves responsible (Jaffe et al., 1988).

Fantuzzo and Lindquist identify a range of methodological criticisms of the studies they reviewed which mean that more questions remain unanswered than resolved. These include biased (as opposed to generalisable) samples taken mainly from shelter residents, and possible bias in rating women as abused; inadequate matching of control groups, particularly on demographic and distress variables; economic and ethnic status too rarely considered; a wide reliance on self-report or maternal ratings (for unknown reasons mothers in a number of these studies tended to rate their own children more negatively than did other measures); and a failure by the majority of authors to define the nature, frequency or extent of violence, or of the child's exposure to it. Indeed, fewer than half even state clearly that the children had directly witnessed the violence. Too few sources of data are used and too few aspects of the child's life and functioning are considered. There are no longitudinal studies and no follow-ups so we do not know whether negative effects fade, under what circumstances, or how quickly. Few studies distinguish between the effects of the violence itself and the impact of other family stresses, and those which do suggest that the impact of all these may be confused in the results. Only a quarter take into account child abuse and neglect which have their own negative effects and which overlap heavily with domestic violence. In short, we know enough to be concerned but very little that is clear cut. We can only say for certain that there is a great deal more to learn. Jaffe et al. (1990b, ch.2) also provide an overview of available research in this field which shows inconsistent findings at the level of detail but, nevertheless, clear grounds for concern.

A worrying methodological bias in much of the empirical work has been the stereotypically gendered model adopted. Researchers have tended to look for externalised behaviours in boys modelled on their fathers' aggression, and internalised distress in girls modelled on their mothers' supposedly passive suffering. This gender difference has not been consistently borne out (see above) and is specifically refuted now by practitioners in North America (personal communications), including children's advocates and groupworkers who find age differences more important in offering appropriate intervention (see chapters by Loosley and Mullender, this volume). Both boys and girls, as one might expect, exhibit confusion, anger and depression whilst girls as well as boys may become troublesome at school or at home.

Highly publicised findings of gender difference were probably overstated. They tended to be based on quite small samples: for example, Jaffe et al. (1986) had only 36 boys and 22 girls in the 'violent families' group in a study of 6 to 11-year olds which concluded that: 'These findings support previous research which suggests that boys are more vulnerable to parental discord than are girls' (p.76). Less well publicised was the comment in the same study which showed that the findings were not conclusive:

> *A significant Group by Sex interaction was not found on any of the three factors, which suggests that the problems shown by both sexes were comparable* . . . however, the differences between boys from violent and nonviolent homes were more marked than those for girls, especially in reference to externalising behavior problems (p.75, emphasis added).

Another way of reading the results is that the girls from nonviolent homes had more internalised *and* externalised behaviour problems than the boys, making the contrast with the girls from violent homes less marked. One might speculate about the general problems of being female in contemporary society, or about differing expectations of boys and girls in the research measurement.

Further studies have continued to appear since those included in

Fantuzzo and Lindquist's survey and they show increasing methodological sophistication. Hughes (1988) introduced child physical abuse as a separate variable, sub-divided her sample of children by age, sought both mother and child reports, included a control group, and utilised a range of standardised scales. As expected, children who were both abused and had witnessed violence showed the most distress, particularly the preschoolers, followed by non-abused witnesses (p.83). The latter group were most affected in relation to anxiety and self-esteem (p.85), but not significantly in behaviour. Holden and Ritchie (1991) also found negative effects, particularly psychological problems such as difficult temperaments, in the 2 to 8-year old children of 37 shelter residents (direct abuse was not considered here) as compared with a same-sized comparison group of children whose mothers had not been abused. The researchers combined maternal self-report with mother-child observation. Maternal stress was again linked with the children's problems, as was paternal anger - which was reported as far more marked than amongst the control group. Violent fathers were also less involved in bringing up the children and more physically punitive than the non-violent fathers of the comparison group. (It is interesting that so few of the other studies have collected data about fathers or their behaviour. It is as if the perpetrators are invisible.) Parenting was less consistent than in other families, perhaps because mothers changed their behaviour to protect their children against their partners and/or were prevented by abuse from maintaining their desired standards of care. This study therefore appears to provide further grounds for seeing mothers as able to provide a better environment for their children once free of their violent partners.

No research has been traced on the additional difficulties faced by Black and Asian children, when they not only live with violence but experience racist hostility in their own lives and from officials responding to their parents, or by the children of travelling women who may find help particularly hard to reach. No research mentions children with disabilities, even though we might expect a higher proportion to be living with violence given the risk of damage to the foetus from violence during pregnancy and the direct attacks on children (see below). The samples in research, because so much of it has focused on shelter residents, have tended to be biased towards the lower socioeconomic classes. So, although we know that domestic violence occurs across all classes (see chapter by Mullender and Morley, this volume), we do not know whether it has the same impact on children living in different circumstances or whether other factors have more effect, such as the length of time children live with violence or their own resilience and survival strategies.

It is important to remember that some children remain perfectly well adjusted despite living with abuse (26 per cent in Wolfe et al., 1985, for example) and that a majority survive within non-clinical or 'normal' limits of functioning (two thirds of the boys and four fifths of the girls in the same study). Practitioners therefore need a heightened awareness of possible problems but can never assume pathology.

Children can also recover from adverse effects. Wolfe et al. (1986) conducted a study which compared current and former shelter residents aged 4 to 13 with a control group (total sample: 63). Despite the fact that the ex-residents were suffering the most social disadvantage, they resembled the control group on emotional and behavioural measures. The authors conclude (p.102):

> . . . it appears plausible that children can recover from the impact of parental conflict and separation, provided that the violence is eliminated and proper supports and opportunities for recovery are provided.

This is a clarion call to all the relevant services to do far more to make women safe as the best way of helping their children. It also means that we need more research which examines protective and healing factors in children's experiences and reactions, as well as more longitudinal studies. Anecdotal evidence and common sense suggest that children's potential for, and speed of recovery will vary. Evason (1982, p.45) cites women remarking, on the one hand: 'Mentally they suffered - they were very nervous and still have nightmares. They calmed down, but not to be normal children - sometimes I wonder if the wee girl will ever come out of it' and, on the other: 'Their nerves were shattered and I had to leave for their sakes - they're settled now'.

To summarise this overview of research on the impact on children living with domestic violence, there is not one typical reaction, but a range of behavioural and/or emotional difficulties *have* been observed as children respond to their own and their mother's distress and draw on whatever survival resources they have - from intervening to withdrawing - dependent on their age, personality and experiences. Any rigid conclusions about male or female responses should be mistrusted. The important thing is to learn how each individual child has suffered, responded and coped. Factors to be considered in any subsequent work with the child will include whether he or she has been abused directly; what relationship he or she has with each parent; what feelings, reactions, emotional or behavioural difficulties may respond to positive help; and what coping capacities and mechanisms the child has drawn on and whether these could continue to be useful or could get in the way of the child's own development - for example, extreme sensitivity to parental moods or being taken over by the role of substitute parent to younger children. Above all, it is crucial to ensure that both mother and child have access to the necessary assistance so that the woman can meet her own child's needs in safety.

THE CONNECTIONS BETWEEN ABUSE OF MOTHERS AND ABUSE OF CHILDREN

Growing understanding of the negative impacts on children of living with domestic violence, as outlined in the preceding section, has led some commentators to suggest that this experience, in and of itself, may be abusive (e.g. Stark and Flitcraft, 1988, p.102; Jaffe et al., 1990a, p.469).

A small number of North American studies, notably Stark and Flitcraft (1985; 1988) and Bowker et al. (1988), have systematically examined the relationship between direct abuse of children and abuse of mothers where these abuses are defined or understood as separate phenomena. Bowker et al.'s data come from self reports of a volunteer (non-representative) sample of 1,000 women throughout the USA, contacted through advertisements in the media and in *Women's Day* magazine, who identified themselves as experiencing 'wife beating'. Of women with children, 70 per cent reported that their abusing husbands also physically abused their children: 41 per cent slapped (as opposed to spanked); 16 per cent kicked, hit, or punched; 4 per cent 'thoroughly beat up'; and 9 per cent used weapons (Bowker et al., 1988, pp.162-63).

Generally, the child abuse was less severe than the wife abuse - 'batterers were five times more likely to beat up thoroughly or use weapons against their wives than to inflict these levels of abuse upon their children' (pp.162-63) - though 'the worse the wife beating, the worse the child abuse' (p.164). Child abuse was found most likely to occur where the husband's dominance in the family was high (p.164). Where child abuse was present, the mother's level of help-seeking was higher than where child abuse was absent, suggesting that mothers who are abused attempt to protect their children; however, 'the effectiveness of these help-sources was generally inversely related to child abuse' (p.164). The authors argue that their results show not only that child abuse by fathers is very high in families where abuse of mothers is present, but also that it is linked to men's efforts to control women and children and to maintain dominance in the family.

While indicative, this study suffers from a number of methodological shortcomings (which the authors largely acknowledge): for example, the sample was not a representative one, so we have no statistical grounds for extrapolating the percentages produced to the general population of mothers subject to domestic violence; the women contacted through *Women's Day* sent in written questionnaires, so there was no opportunity to negotiate the meanings of responses - what does it mean, for example, for a child to be 'slapped' as opposed to 'spanked'; a limited range of variables was measured and these lacked precision; and the level of detail provided in the report was limited - for example, we are told that men *as opposed to* women in these families physically abused the children and that men's abuse of children is likely to have different roots from women's (dominance in the case of men; stress, poverty, and the like in the case of women), but we are given no explicit empirical evidence for these assertions.

Some of these shortcomings are overcome in Stark and Flitcraft's study (1985; 1988) which constitutes the most methodologically sophisticated and informative research on the links between child abuse and domestic violence to date. The research was a controlled study based on official records, it distinguished between physical abuse and non-physical 'neglect' of children, and compared abuse of children by fathers with abuse by mothers. Rather than examining the likelihood of abused mothers having abused children, as did Bowker et al., Stark and Flitcraft began by examining the reverse: the likelihood of abused children having abused mothers. The researchers analysed the reports of *all* children who had been registered[1] for suspected child abuse - classified as either physical abuse or neglect - at a large hospital in a metropolitan area of the USA during a 12 month period. These reports were matched with the hospital medical records of the children's mothers (totalling 116), who were classified according to the likelihood of their having been physically assaulted by their partners[2]. Other information concerning the mothers - for example, the existence of alcohol misuse, suicide attempts, violence and/or disorganisation in the family of origin - was obtained from social services notes contained in the medical files and from the files kept on the registered children.

Use of official records to identify violence and abuse has obvious shortcomings. In the case of mothers, identification by physical assault recorded via hospital visits results in an extremely conservative definition of domestic violence. On the other hand, defining child abuse through registration provides a good indication of society's concern. Moreover, while this method allows no first-hand accounts from women or children, access to case notes provides a wealth of information concerning the ways in which professionals construe and deal with child abuse and mothers subject to abuse.

Examination of the data showed that 45 per cent of the 116 mothers whose children were registered had a medical history indicative of assaults by their partners (hereafter, 'domestic violence'), while another five per cent had a history of 'marital conflict' although there was not enough evidence to tell if physical violence had occurred (1988, p.104). The rate of domestic violence was almost two and a half times higher among this group of 116 women than among a sample of women who had presented injuries to the hospital, and twice as high as among women attending the hospital prenatal clinic (1988, p.104). While only a minority of the children had been registered for documented *physical* abuse, children of mothers with a positive history of domestic violence were twice as likely as children of mothers without such a history to have been registered for physical abuse (1988, p.105). Where mothers were subject to domestic violence, the father was more than three times as likely to be the child's abuser than in families where mothers were not being physically abused (1988, p.106). Mothers suffering domestic violence typically did not come from 'multi-problem' families of origin, and were no more likely than non-abused mothers to have come from violent families (1988, p.105). Finally, the researchers examined the dispositions of child abuse cases *excluding* those registered for documented physical abuse (as opposed to non-physical 'neglect' or 'mother needs support'), finding that children were far more likely to be removed from the homes of mothers experiencing domestic violence than those of mothers without this experience (1988, p.106), even though domestic violence was rarely noted in the case files (1988, p.105&107).

These results indicate the following key points regarding the relationship between child abuse and domestic violence:

1. where there is child abuse - and most especially physical child abuse - the likelihood is very high that the mother is being physically abused; indeed, Stark and Flitcraft argue that child abuse is the 'highest at risk site thus far identified' for domestic violence (1985, p.161);
2. where there is domestic violence, the child abuse is much more likely to be physical (as opposed to non-physical) than where domestic violence is not occurring;
3. where there is domestic violence, the father is typically also the child's abuser;
4. abused mothers of abused children do not usually come from disorganised or violent families of origin, casting doubt on the commonly held notion that family history predisposes women to domestic violence and to child abuse (see 'A cycle of violence?' below);
5. mothers experiencing domestic violence are more punitively treated (i.e. their children are removed) than mothers not experiencing domestic violence, even when the child abuse is *not* physical;
6. professionals fail to acknowledge the existence of domestic violence at the same time as they blame women for the abuse of their children.

Stark and Flitcraft argue that domestic violence provides the typical context in which child abuse develops: 'in all probability, [woman] battering is the single most important context for child abuse. It also appears that child abuse is an intermediary point in an unfolding history of battering' (1985, p.165). Like Bowker et al., they argue that abuse of women and abuse of children have a common source in male control (1988, p.100); and they suggest that, instead of engaging in typical professional practices which serve to exacerbate the situation - such as ignoring the domestic violence, emphasising 'the mother's failure to fulfill [sic] her feminine role' (1988, p.107), and removing children from their mothers:

> . . . *case-workers and clinicians would do well to look toward advocacy and protection of battered mothers as the best available means to prevent current child abuse as well as child abuse in the future* (1985, p.168, emphasis added).

Little research on the links between domestic violence and child abuse has been done in the UK. However, a study by the Social Services

Department of the London Borough of Hackney indicated that at least one third of children on the Child Protection Register had mothers who were experiencing domestic violence (in London Borough of Hackney, 1993, p.7); and in a study of women with children who had used refuges in Dublin, 28 per cent said their children had been severely beaten by their partner (Casey, 1987, in O'Hara, 1993, p.20). Recent enquiries into child deaths from physical abuse by fathers or step-fathers indicate that in many cases the father or step-father was also physically abusing the mother (see chapter by O'Hara, this volume).

Much less research attention has focused specifically on child *sexual* abuse. However there exists evidence, scattered among several small-scale US studies (e.g. Browning and Boatman, 1977; Dietz and Craft, 1980; Truesdell et al., 1986), that domestic violence is very high in families where fathers or step-fathers are sexually abusing their children. Truesdell et al. (1986), for example, found that 73 per cent of 30 women attending a mothers' group of an incest treatment programme at a child welfare department had experienced some form of physical and psychological abuse from their partner and 23 per cent had suffered 'life threatening' violence; these figures were considerably higher than corresponding figures for the general population. Similarly, a Scottish Office funded study of 20 women in Strathclyde (whose children had been sexually abused by their partner and had been through the child protection system) found domestic violence in *all* cases, only three of which did not involve physical violence (Forman, n.d., p.20). Thirty per cent of the women in Casey's Dublin study (1987, in O'Hara, 1993, p.20) knew of or suspected sexual abuse of their children by their partners. Of course, not all mothers know about the sexual abuse; first disclosure in the safety of a refuge is not uncommon (see chapter by Debbonaire, this volume).

While the physical abuse of children as defined and understood in the studies summarised above does not normally occur at the same time as abuse of mothers, children may become targets - intended or unintended - during domestic violence incidents. A recent study in Toronto, Canada, found that children were assaulted in over 12 per cent of domestic violence incidents at which they were present (in Ministers Responsible for the Status of Women, 1991, p.4). Children had intervened in one third of incidents reported by women in a study in West Yorkshire; the main reason children did not try to protect their mothers was that they were too young, although in one case a two year old ' "picked up a shoe and hit him with it" ' (Hanmer, 1990, p.26). Some children have themselves killed the abuser (Jaffe et al., 1990b).

Domestic violence also threatens unborn children, since women who are abused are frequently battered during pregnancy, often in the abdomen. American studies suggest this happens in between 40 and 60 per cent of domestic violence cases (McFarlane, 1991, pp.136-38). An Islington community study of a representative sample of 286 married working class mothers and single mothers of all classes found that many women who experienced domestic violence reported more severe violence while pregnant than at other times, and that women who had experienced violence were more than twice as likely as women with no such experience to have had a miscarriage or stillbirth (Andrews and Brown, 1988, p.311).

Attacks on children during domestic violence incidents and on pregnant women constitute examples of the way in which the abuse of women and children may be inextricably intertwined. Additionally, children are frequently used and abused by violent men as a vehicle to manipulate, control and physically abuse their partners during the relationship and after separation. 'Abuse of women often includes threats to abuse children, destroying children's toys or possessions, hurting and even killing pets' (Women's Aid Federation England, 1993). It also includes making women feel guilty about their children, using children to relay messages, and threatening to take children away (Pence and Paymar, 1990, p.6, Figure 2, the 'Power and Control Wheel'). Men often use contact with children as a means to further their abuse of ex-partners. The women interviewed for a study of domestic violence and contact arrangements reported:

> . . . a variety of incidents and tactics, including physical and verbal abuse of the mother or others at 'hand over' time, abduction and use of a child as a hostage in an effort to secure the mother's return to the marriage, grilling children for information about their mothers, and manipulating legal procedures relating to childcare in an effort to involve the courts and the law in continued harassment (Hester and Radford, 1992, p.61).

Moreover, the children were themselves at risk of physical, sexual and mental abuse: 'our study has confirmed that children of women who experience domestic violence are at risk from abuse themselves during contact visits' (see chapter by Hester et al., this volume). And just as men may use children as a vehicle to abuse mothers, so they may abuse mothers as a means of gaining access to and abusing children. The Strathclyde study of child sexual abuse, for example, found evidence that men abuse mothers to hide their sexual abuse - by isolating and/or otherwise incapacitating the mother so that she is not available to the child as a source of help (Forman, n.d., p.30).

A 'CYCLE OF VIOLENCE'?

It is very commonly asserted by academics, professionals, and lay persons alike that people who grow up in violent families engage in violent adult family relationships (as perpetrator or victim) and/or abuse their children. This assertion[3] (often termed the 'cycle of violence'[4] or 'intergenerational transmission of violence') is accepted by most as received truth - beyond debate - and 'ending the cycle of violence' becomes a primary motive for professional intervention.

There are in fact a number of inexactly formulated versions of the assertion, notably: children who witness domestic violence grow up to become perpetrators or victims of such violence; children who are abused by parents grow up to abuse, or be abused by, their partners; and, more elaborately, men abused as children beat their wives who in turn abuse their children. Additionally, the assertion comes in two strengths. The weaker one is that *relatively* more people from violent homes are violent adults than people from non-violent homes; conversely that *relatively* more violent adults come from violent homes than non-violent adults. The stronger statement suggests absolute certainty: 'violence breeds violence'. It is this stronger version which dominates both professional and popular discourse. Much of this discourse also takes a learning theory approach to understanding the cycle, assuming that children both model and learn the meaning and appropriateness of aggressive behaviours through experiences in the family (e.g. Straus et al., 1980).

A large literature (much of it North American) exists addressing the cycle of violence in some fashion: many writers simply assert its existence with no support at all; some make reference to authority (that is, similar assertions from other writers); some use data from their own or other studies. The following is a brief summary of key findings from these studies[5] (for more detailed reviews of cycle of violence research, see Pagelow, 1984: ch.7; Straus and Flitcraft, 1985, pp.151-158; Okun, 1986, pp.59-63, 110-112; Kaufman and Zigler, 1987; Widom, 1989):

1. Percentages of adult perpetrators or victims of domestic violence found to have had violent childhoods vary enormously from study to study. They are virtually never 100 per cent and very often less than 50 per cent. Thus, in many studies, the *majority* of current abusers and victims come from backgrounds defined as non-violent. This is especially the case when currently abused women, as opposed to abusive men, are examined.

2. Studies comparing adult perpetrators or victims with non perpetrators or victims very often find differences in the predicted direction - relatively more adult perpetrators or victims have come from violent families of origin than non perpetrators or victims. However, the percentage differences between the two groups are usually small.

3. Most, but not all, studies suggest that transmission is gender related - boys become aggressors, girls victims. However, the percentages given for violent men with abusive childhoods are almost always considerably higher than those for women victims with abusive childhoods; indeed, as mentioned above, the figures for women are almost always less than 50 per cent. Thus, those writers who support the cycle of violence idea often argue that it applies to men but not to women.

These findings suggest that there may be some merit in the cycle of violence hypothesis, though clearly in a muted form; transmission is in no way absolute. However, the studies suffer from a number of serious methodological flaws which temper their findings further:

1. Many studies do not employ control groups of adults who are *not* perpetrators or victims of domestic violence, so the abusers and victims cannot be compared with adults not in identified violent families. It is clearly vital to know whether rates of violent childhoods are higher in these populations than in violence-free populations. As mentioned above, studies with comparison groups tend to find *small* differences in the predicted direction.

2. Most samples studied are highly selected and therefore biased: they are often clinical samples of people who have come to the attention of public agencies and which are therefore unlikely to be representative of the population at large.

3. Almost all studies are strictly correlational: they attempt to find an association or relationship between specific experiences in childhood and specific adult behaviours or experiences. It is totally inappropriate in these circumstances to suggest that the childhood experiences *cause* the adult outcomes unless all possible confounding and intervening factors are ruled out. This has not, and probably could not, be done.

4. Definitions of childhood 'abuse' and 'violence' differ enormously from study to study: for example, *experiencing* severe physical or sexual abuse, routine physical punishment, psychological abuse, physical or emotional neglect; or *witnessing* fathers assaulting mothers and/ or mothers assaulting fathers, or unspecified 'parental violence'. Often the experiences being measured are extremely vague. Gayford, for example, says the husbands of his 'battered wives' had 'disturbed or violent childhoods' (1975, in Stark and Flitcraft 1985, p.155). Most of the population might in fact find its way into at least one of the categories of childhood abuse employed in these studies.

5. The studies are overwhelmingly retrospective ones, with abusers and victims asked about their childhoods and the childhoods of their partners. However, basing evidence on retrospective accounts may be highly suspect since we interpret the past through the present; past troubles often providing convenient rationales for current behaviour. Indeed, as Widom (1989, p.5) points out, 'retrospective data are notoriously unreliable'.

There is one study addressing the cycle of violence which requires closer scrutiny: Straus et al.'s (1980) national random sample survey of family violence in the USA which was carried out in 1975. The use of scientific sampling methods means that its findings can be taken as broadly representative of the American population. It is also, quite simply, the most frequently quoted authority today on the subject of family violence. The researchers argue that their data provide 'striking evidence for the idea of social heredity in [marital] violence - that violence by parents begets violence in the next generation' (pp.112-13). In other words, theirs is the strong rather than the muted assertion.

Despite this confident statement, Straus et al.'s methodology gives grave cause for doubt. They interviewed either the man or woman in over 2,000 American couples, asking questions concerning his or her violence to spouse and spouse's violence to him or her; his or her violence to their children and their children's violence to him or her; and violence between siblings. They also asked questions concerning violence in the family of origin. To measure the use of violence by each of these family members, the authors constructed the now widely used Conflict Tactics Scales containing eighteen items depicting three different types of tactic used to resolve conflicts: reasoning, verbal aggression, and violence. Any one of eight abstracted behavioural items defined 'violence' and identified a violent individual; any one of the final five behaviours in this list defined 'abusive violence' and identified a 'wife beater', 'husband beater', or serious child abuser:

1. threw something at the other one
2. pushed, grabbed, or shoved the other one
3. slapped the other one
4. kicked, bit, or hit with a fist
5. hit, or tried to hit with something
6. beat up the other one
7. threatened with a knife or gun
8. used a knife or gun (p.256).

In this scheme, threats are equated with actual assaults, scrapes with life threatening injury. We know nothing about the specific context or meaning of these acts to the individuals who perpetrated or experienced them - for example, whether the act was an attempt at coercing compliance or an act of frustration or desperate self-defence. Nor do we know the consequences of these acts - physically, psychologically or materially. It is not entirely surprising, therefore, that the data show comparable proportions of male violence to female partners and female violence to male partners (p.36), with slightly more husband beaters than wife beaters (pp.40-41). These findings, of course, contradict the overwhelming weight of evidence from other studies and criminal statistics that the vast majority of domestic violence is men's violence to women (see chapter by Mullender and Morley, this volume; see also Dobash and Dobash, 1992, ch.8 for a detailed critique of 'family violence' research).

Leaving aside these fundamental problems with their measuring instrument, what of Straus et al.'s claim that 'violence begets violence'? Their data show that *relatively* more men (and women) whose parents were 'violent towards each other' are violent towards their partners than those with non-violent parents. Thirty-five per cent of men who had witnessed parental violence were currently violent towards their partners compared with 10.7 per cent of men whose parents were not violent (p.100), and 20 per cent of men whose parents were 'the most violent' were wife beaters compared with 2 per cent of men whose parents were not violent (p.100-101). Similarly, *relatively* more men (and women) whose parents physically punished them were violent towards their partners than those whose parents did not so punish them. Between 20 and 25 per cent of people who were 'punished the most' as teenagers were currently violent towards their partners compared with 6 per cent who were not punished (p.109), and 8 per cent of men who were punished the most as teenagers were currently wife beaters compared with 2 per cent of men who were not punished (p.109-10).

With respect to witnessing parental violence in childhood, the authors proclaim:

> . . . the sons of the most violent parents have a rate of wife-beating
> 1,000 per cent greater than that of the sons of non-violent parents (20
> per cent [compared to 2 per cent]) (p.101, original emphasis; actually
> this is 900 per cent greater).

But the significance of this and the other findings listed above is debatable for predicting or understanding domestic violence, given that the overriding majority from all the groups with violent childhoods are not now violent towards their partners - in this quoted example, 80 per cent - and the percentage differences between the groups are relatively small - in this example, 18 per cent. Further, Stark and Flitcraft (1985, p.157) demonstrate that the Straus et al. findings show that:

> . . . a current batterer is more than twice as likely to have had a 'non-
> violent' rather than a 'violent' childhood (7:3) and seven times more
> likely to have come from a 'non-violent' home than from a home
> classified as 'most violent'.

Clearly, the evidence is rather flimsy for the thesis that 'the *majority* of today's violent couples are those who were brought up by parents violent toward each other' (Straus et al., 1980, p.100, emphasis added).

In summary, the most that can be said of the Straus et al. study and others employing non-violent control groups is that *relative* differences in the predicted direction are usually found. But definitional and retrospective interviewing biases would tend to inflate these differences. Indeed, given the popularity of the 'cycle of violence' idea, empirical evidence for it may, in part, be a product of self-fulfilling prophesy: practitioners, researchers and abusers may all take it for granted that 'violence breeds violence' and find what they expect to find. Even so, many studies show only a minority of abusers to be afflicted by the 'cycle of violence' (the Straus et al., 1980 study is one example) suggesting that its predictive value is likely to be meagre. Two recent scholarly reviews of the existing research conclude that although experiencing violence in childhood *may* increase the risk of becoming a violent adult, the process is neither direct nor certain (Kaufman and Zigler, 1987; Widom, 1989).

To argue against the certainty that 'violence breeds violence' is not however to argue that children enjoy or thrive on violence, or that childhood experiences do not bear on the kinds of adults we become. But precisely what these consequences are varies enormously. Indeed, there is a great deal of evidence that many children survive violent childhoods and grow into loving and socially productive adults. Certainly some men with violent childhoods are violent to women and children; for others, that childhood experience precludes a repetition. Moreover, it may also be that the damage caused by living in violent families is internalised as depression, withdrawal or *self*-destructive behaviours (Widom, 1989, p.24).

Finally, looking for causes in a single source of past experience negates the myriad of continuing influences on our lives including those which emanate from the culture at large and, most importantly perhaps, those which concern our active intentions in the present. With respect to men's violence to women and children, this focus on childhood may amount to a negation of men's responsibility for their actions and of the social context of gender and generational politics which underpins these actions.

THE RESEARCH AGENDA

As has clearly been demonstrated above, there are huge areas of our understanding regarding children and domestic violence which have yet to be adequately researched. Moreover, most of the work reported in this chapter was undertaken in North America and would not necessarily translate in its entirety to the British policy or practice context.

There is now sufficient recognition in Britain that men's violence to women (or at least a range of stresses including or stemming from that violence) causes problems for children to generate research here. Some important beginnings are being made and a number of studies, recently commenced, are briefly outlined below.

The Women's Aid Federation (England) is funding a nationwide pilot by a research team based at the Universities of Bristol, North London and Durham. The study will explore the impact on children both of living with violence and moving to a refuge; the overlap with child abuse; the nature, impact and context of child work in refuges and beyond, and the extent of inclusion within it of agendas to combat racism, sexism, homophobia and violence. One key objective is to identify and help to disseminate best practice in direct intervention with children who have lived with violence, recognising the child work offered by local Women's Aid groups as our key national resource in this field. The same team plans more extensive research to examine children's experiences, agency responses, the connections between violence to women and violence to children, and any relevant preventative work. Another research team at Exeter University and Roehampton Institute (see chapter by Hester et al., this volume) is examining the court-related practice of a range of professionals involved in questions of contact and residence after domestic violence has split the family. The Children's Legal Centre is carrying out a national survey of the child protection policies and practices of social services departments, the police, and the court welfare side of the probation service as these relate to domestic violence. Rights of Women is conducting research, via legal practitioners, into the weaknesses of the Children Act 1989 in relation to domestic violence. A researcher at the University of Nottingham is using questionnaire data from 50 participants at a child protection seminar, primarily social workers, to analyse their knowledge and attitudes towards domestic violence and its relationship with child abuse. Finally, before the end of 1994, NCH Action for Children is due to publish the findings of a nationwide study of the views of mothers and children using its family centres which has asked about the impact of domestic violence and is aimed at providing good practice guidelines for staff, with implications also for social workers.

The findings from all these studies are awaited with interest. In a field where our ignorance certainly outweighs our knowledge, child care practitioners and policy makers - as well as children themselves and their mothers - can only benefit from well conducted studies which cast light on children's experiences and needs.

Notes

1. At the hospital concerned, 'medical records of children suspected of being abused or neglected are specifically marked or "darted" and the children are referred for investigation and disposition to a special hospital "Dart Committee" ' (Stark and Flitcraft, 1988, p.103).

2. The classification method involved using a 'trauma screen' developed in previous research (Stark et al., 1979) to identify domestic violence in a group not explicitly identified as battered. 'Each adult hospital visit prompted by trauma after the age of 16 was reviewed, and women assigned to a "battering risk group" . . .' (Stark and Flitcraft, 1988, p.103). Only one of the four risk groups was comprised of cases where assaults were explicitly attributed in the medical records to men, that is, cases where there was a recognition by medical staff of domestic violence.

3. In fact, this assertion is one of a wide range of loosely articulated hypotheses which state that being abused (or, less frequently, observing violence) in childhood leads to various forms of delinquency, violence, and criminal behaviour in later life inside and/or outside the family (see Widom, 1989, for a review of a number of specific 'cycle of violence' hypotheses). These hypotheses are, in turn, related to 'cycle of deprivation' notions which suggest that deprivation and poverty are reproduced from generation to generation through childrearing practices in the family.

4. This use of the term 'cycle of violence' should not be confused with Lenore Walker's (1979) 'cycle theory of violence' used to explain why women stay in

violent relationships when the violence escalates in frequency and severity over time. Walker hypothesises a recurring battering cycle with three phases - i. tension building, ii. the acute battering incident, iii. the honeymoon or loving contrition - the third phase allegedly acting as positive reinforcement for the woman to stay in the relationship. This theory is quite widely used in children's groups in North America to explain to children why the relationship between their parents, and the atmosphere in their home, can appear to fluctuate so widely. Walker proposed the cycle theory of violence in tandem with 'learned helplessness' (see chapter by Mullender and Morley, this volume, note 7), and it has been criticised on similar grounds: it implicates women and their alleged psychological inadequacies in the continuance of the violence and it fails accurately to convey the lived reality of women's experiences of violent relationships.

5. 'Cycle of violence' statistics are usually expressed either in terms of *percentages of adult perpetrators or victims* of family violence who experienced violent childhoods or, conversely, of *percentages of adults with violent childhoods* who grew up to become perpetrators or victims of family violence. For reasons of linguistic simplicity, the summary of key findings in this chapter employs one or other of these formulations, not both. However, in all cases, the findings also apply to the reverse.

References

Andrews, B. and Brown, G.W. (1988) 'Marital violence in the community: a biographical approach', *British Journal of Psychiatry*, 153, pp.305-12.

Bowker, L.H., Arbitell, M. and McFerron, J.R. (1988) 'On the relationship between wife beating and child abuse' in Ylló, K. and Bograd, M. (eds.) *Feminist Perspectives on Wife Abuse*. Newbury Park, California: Sage.

Browning, D.H. and Boatman, B. (1977) 'Incest: children at risk', *American Journal of Psychiatry*, 134(1), pp.69-72.

Casey, M. (1987) *Domestic Violence Against Women*. Dublin: Dublin Federation of Refuges.

Dietz, C.A. and Craft, J.L. (1980) 'Family dynamics of incest: a new perspective', *Social Casework*, 61, pp.602-609.

Dobash, R.E. and Dobash, R.P. (1992) *Women, Violence and Social Change*. London: Routledge.

Evason, E. (1982) *Hidden Violence*. Belfast: Farset Press.

Fantuzzo, J.W. and Lindquist, C.U. (1989) 'The effects of observing conjugal violence on children: a review and analysis of research methodology', *Journal of Family Violence*, 4(1), pp.77-94.

Forman, J. (no date) *Is There a Correlation Between Child Sexual Abuse and Domestic Violence? An Exploratory Study of the Links Between Child Sexual Abuse and Domestic Violence in a Sample of Intrafamilial Child Sexual Abuse Cases*. Glasgow: Women's Support Project.

Gayford, J.J. (1975) 'Battered wives', *Medicine, Science and Law*, 15(4), pp.237-45.

Hanmer, J. (1990) *Women, Violence and Crime Prevention: a Study of Changes in Police Policy and Practices in West Yorkshire*. Violence, Abuse and Gender

Relations Unit Research Paper No. 1, Bradford: Department of Applied Social Studies, University of Bradford.

Hershorn, M. and Rosenbaum, A. (1985) 'Children of marital violence: a closer look at the unintended victims', *American Journal of Orthopsychiatry*, 55, pp.260-66.

Hester, M. and Radford, L. (1992) 'Domestic violence and access arrangements for children in Denmark and Britain', *Journal of Social Welfare and Family Law*, 1, pp.57-70.

Hinchey, F.S. and Gavelek, J.R. (1982) 'Empathic responding in children of battered mothers', *Child Abuse and Neglect*, 6, pp.395-401.

Holden, G.W. and Ritchie, K.L. (1991) 'Linking extreme marital discord, child rearing and child behavior problems: evidence from battered women', *Child Development*, 62, pp.311-27.

Hughes, H.M. (1988) 'Psychological and behavioral correlates of family violence in child witnesses and victims', *American Journal of Orthopsychiatry*, 58(1), pp.77-90.

Jaffe, P.G., Hurley, D.J. and Wolfe, D. (1990a) 'Children's observations of violence: I. Critical issues in child development and intervention planning, *Canadian Journal of Psychiatry*, 36, pp.466-70.

Jaffe, P., Wilson, S.K. and Wolfe, D. (1988) 'Specific assessment and intervention strategies for children exposed to wife battering: preliminary empirical investigations', *Canadian Journal of Community Mental Health*, 7(2), Autumn, pp.157-63.

Jaffe, P.G., Wolfe, D.A. and Wilson, S.K. (1990b) *Children of Battered Women*. Newbury Park, California: Sage.

Jaffe, P.G., Wolfe, D. and Wilson, S. and Zak, L. (1986) 'Family violence and child adjustment: a comparative analysis of girls' and boys' behavioral symptoms', *American Journal of Psychiatry*, 143(1), pp.74-77.

Kaufman, J. and Zigler, E. (1987) 'Do abused children become abusive parents?', *American Journal of Orthopsychiatry*, 57(2), pp.186-92.

London Borough of Hackney (1993) *The Links between Domestic Violence and Child Abuse: Developing Services*. London: London Borough of Hackney.

McFarlane, J. (1991) 'Violence during teen pregnancy: health consequences for mother and child' in Levy, B. (ed.) *Dating Violence: Young Women in Danger*. Seattle, Washington, USA: Seal Press.

Ministers Responsible for the Status of Women (1991) *Building Blocks: Framework for a National Strategy on Violence Against Women*. 10th Annual Federal-Provincial-Territorial Conference of Ministers, Responsible for the Status of Women. St. John's, Newfoundland, Canada. June 18-20

O'Hara, M. (1993) 'Child protection and domestic violence: changing policy and practice' in London Borough of Hackney (1993) *The Links between Domestic Violence and Child Abuse: Developing Services*. London: London Borough of Hackney.

Okun, L. (1986) *Woman Abuse: Facts Replacing Myths*. New York: State University of New York Press.

Pagelow, M.D. (1984) *Family Violence*. New York: Praeger.

Pence, E. and Paymar, M. (1990) *Power and Control: Tactics of Men Who Batter. An Educational Curriculum*. Duluth, Minnesota, USA: Minnesota Program Development Inc. (Revised edition).

Rosenbaum, A. and O'Leary, K.D. (1981) 'Children: the unintended victims of marital violence', *American Journal of Orthopsychiatry*, 51(4), pp.692-99.

Sopp-Gilson, S. (1980) 'Children from violent homes', *Journal of Ontario Association of Children's Aid Societies*, 23(10), pp.1-5.

Stark, E. and Flitcraft, A. (1985) 'Woman-battering, child abuse and social heredity: what is the relationship?' in Johnson, N. (ed.) *Marital Violence*. London: Routledge and Kegan Paul.

Stark, E. and Flitcraft, A. (1988) 'Women and children at risk: a feminist perspective on child abuse', *International Journal of Health Services*, 18(1), pp.97-118.

Stark, E., Flitcraft, A. and Frazier, W. (1979) 'Medicine and patriarchal violence: the social construction of a "private" event', *International Journal of Health Services*, 9(3), pp.461-93.

Straus, M.A., Gelles, R.J. and Steinmetz, S.K. (1980) *Behind Closed Doors: Violence in the American Family*. Newbury Park, California: Sage.

Truesdell, D.L., McNeil, J.S. and Deschner, J.P. (1986) 'Incidence of wife abuse in incestuous families', *Social Work*, March-April, pp.138-40.

Walker, L.E.A. (1979) *The Battered Woman*. New York: Harper and Row.

Widom, C.S. (1989) 'Does violence beget violence? A critical examination of the literature', *Psychological Bulletin*, 106(1), pp.3-28.

Wolfe, D.A., Jaffe, P., Wilson, S.K. and Zak, L. (1985) 'Children of battered women: the relation of child behavior to family violence and maternal stress', *Journal of Consulting and Clinical Psychology*, 53(5), pp.657-65.

Wolfe, D.A., Zak, L., Wilson, S. and Jaffe, P. (1986) 'Child witnesses to violence between parents: critical issues in behavioural and social adjustment', *Journal of Abnormal Child Psychology*, 14(1), pp.95-104.

Women's Aid Federation England (1993) *Briefing Paper - Domestic Violence and Child Abuse: Some Links*. Bristol: WAFE.

4

The Interconnectedness of Domestic Violence and Child Abuse: Challenges for Research, Policy and Practice

Liz Kelly

As the issue of children's experiences of domestic violence came to public prominence in Britain in 1992, the most common responses were statements suggesting that the issue - and its links with child abuse - had hitherto been neglected, if not ignored; children were frequently referred to as the 'forgotten victims'. Whilst in many quarters this was indeed the case, Women's Aid and its sister organisations in other countries have always provided safety for women *and children*; and within immense resource limitations, refuges and shelters[1] have developed specific forms of support for children (see Section IV, this volume). The resources which do exist for working with children have originated from women's support agencies. Each national Women's Aid federation in Britain, the coalitions in the US and Canada (and no doubt elsewhere) are all working with the complex implications of applying 'no violence' rules in refuges and shelters to relationships between the children, the adults and children, and the adults who live and work there. Refuges have, therefore, a rich and diverse history of paying attention to children's realities and needs.

Moreover, for over a century, feminists have been noting the connections between abuse of women and abuse of children in households. They have pointed to the failures of professional and legal practice in protecting children and/or their mothers, and have made public the damaging implications of policy and legislation - most recently the Children Act 1989, the Child Support Act 1991, and proposals to amend the homelessness legislation - for women and children's safety (see Section III, this volume).

In developing our understanding of children's experiences, we need to guard against recreating idealised, universalistic and western-centric notions of family life and child development. Few childhoods are lived without some distress. The majority of children in the world have, at minimum, to cope with inequality, loss and deprivation; many live their childhoods in regions that are riven by civil or international conflict and/ or are struggling with dire poverty and famine. Western notions of childhood are recent constructions which on the one hand idealise and on the other impose restrictions on children's experience. If we take the global condition of children's lives as our point of departure, we are forced to recognise children's ability to survive, to fend for themselves, and to take responsibility for others at ages which many of us who live in the West would consider extremely young. In saying this, I am not suggesting that loss, war, poverty or famine are 'uplifting'. Rather, by beginning from a broader context, we can avoid constructing children as 'passive victims' and include in our developing understanding the fact that children are individuals who act and make choices, and who develop, in contexts of necessity, coping and survival strategies.

CHILDREN AND DOMESTIC VIOLENCE

Children's contact with and experience of violence towards their mother can take a range of forms. Over time most children living with violence will have had to cope with many, if not all, of the following, and frequently on repeated occasions:

- being aware of the violence as witness or overhearer;
- intervening to protect their mother - either directly, risking assault to themselves; or indirectly by seeking help such as contacting the police, a relative, or neighbour;
- being encouraged to support and/or participate in the abuse and degradation of their mother.

Children may also be being abused, either in a situation where the man rules the household by open and deliberate terrorisation of everyone, or secretly and separately from the abuse of their mother. All children have to find ways of making sense of and coping with the reality in their household and its effects on their relationships with parents or carers, siblings, relatives, and friends. There may be far reaching consequences in their lives of the abuse and their mother's struggles to end it, ranging from never feeling safe through to the disruption of leaving home and losing possessions, pets, friends, and possibly contact with one of their parents or carers.

We need to know far more about many of these areas, *from children and young people themselves* - otherwise adult-centred and impressionistic models emerge which exclude many of the complex, and at times contradictory, aspects of their experience. Whilst many commentators (see chapter by Morley and Mullender, this volume, for an overview) refer to developmental issues, such as age-related responses to the abuse, very little has been said about a range of other potential influences on children's perceptions and attempts to create meaning.

We already know that women's experiences of domestic violence - whilst having a common core - vary in many ways, and that many women do not name the abuse they are experiencing for some time (Kelly, 1988). We need to ask similar questions in relation to children. What difference does it make if abuse is described to, and/or understood by, children as 'fighting'; is this a word which is simply familiar to children, or does it contain a presumption of mutuality in conflict as opposed to unacceptable male behaviour toward women? (This is a pressing practical issue, since workbooks for children tend to use the word 'fighting' in the text. It would be an unfortunate, unintended consequence if language usage which developed to make literature accessible to children limited rather than extended their understanding.) What difference does it make to children's understandings if their mother is a woman who resists unreasonable demands and expectations, who sometimes defends herself, or who decides to break the unbearable building tension of an inevitable outburst of violence by 'picking a fight' (Kelly, 1988)? Do children make a different kind of sense if violence is frequent or infrequent, if injuries to their mother are visible or invisible, if the police have been called and responded in one way rather than another, or if visits to casualty have been necessary? Perhaps most importantly, what difference does it make if *both* parents or carers remain silent, if children have access only to the abuser's justifications, or if they have access to how their mother understands the violence?

In addition to lacking answers to these basic questions, we know very little about how age, gender, race, class, disability and sexuality influence children's experiences and understandings. How children make sense will inevitably change as they grow older, and there are some obvious questions in relation to gender and identification with parents of the same and opposite sex. Complex questions will be raised for a mixed race child where one parent is white and the other Black, as well as for children within Black families, where abusive men use the fact and reality of racism as a form of control (for example in relation to immigration) to justify abuse and/or to persuade women, and possibly children, not to call the police or not to exclude them from the home (Mama, 1989).

Economic and status issues may also become implicated in abuse where men blame their violence (and have this accepted sometimes by their partner) on unemployment, on stress at work, and/or on the woman achieving more status via education or paid employment. What is the impact of the abuser being able to claim an explanation either through his own disability or ill health or through that of the woman? What does it mean to children if the violence only emerges in relation to their mother's wish to leave a heterosexual relationship since she now defines herself as a lesbian, and what difference does it make to children if they come to know this through angry and bitter words from the abuser or from their mother?

Being able to think and ask these questions is essential if we are to develop research and practice which taps children's reality. It matters whether children are more likely to side with the abusive man if their mother remains silent through shame and guilt, or if he uses areas of disadvantage as justification for his abuse. It matters that making sense of violence often gets tied up with complex issues which will affect the child's own developing sense of identity; with how they locate each of their parents and other adults in social categories.

Simply responding to these questions as drawing on excuses, justifications or myths is not enough. They draw on powerful ideas which suffuse our culture, and we need to investigate how they affect children's and women's perceptions and actions. Otherwise we are in no position to help children unpick the confused and painful meanings they have created to make sense and cope.

THE CONNECTIONS BETWEEN DOMESTIC VIOLENCE AND CHILD ABUSE

We know that both domestic violence and child abuse are extremely common. Whilst there are no national prevalence studies in Britain of either domestic violence or physical abuse of children, the current estimates are that violence occurs in between 30 and 50 per cent of heterosexual relationships (McGibbon et al., 1989; Mooney, 1994). The use of physical punishment of children as discipline is still widely supported in this country - and in most others in the world. What is indisputable, therefore, is that a substantial proportion of children spend some part of their childhood in a household where violence is commonplace.

Just focusing on domestic violence, some studies have asked where children are during attacks - in 90 per cent of cases they are in the same or next room (Hughes, 1992). We also know that in a substantial number of cases violence increases in frequency and severity during pregnancy, and is often directed at the developing foetus (see chapter by Morley and Mullender, this volume).

Beyond this, we have very little detailed knowledge about children's contact with the violence, or how they make sense of it at the time and later. Most published research has focused on the impacts of domestic violence on children, and taken for granted that we know enough about their experience of the abuse. We do not. Impacts are linked to experience; the experience provides the context in which children try to make sense of the behaviour of adults and their own feelings and responses.

In terms of the connections between domestic violence and abuse of children there is rather more evidence. But even here we need to think in more complex ways[2]. If we begin from a recognition that domestic violence and child abuse are not necessarily separate co-existing forms of violence, it becomes possible to notice that they can occur concurrently. At the most obvious level, living with domestic violence can be defined as a form of emotional abuse of children. However, if it is defined this way in child protection guidelines, careful attention must be paid to *not* defining the perpetrator as 'the family', but as the man who is abusing the woman.

There are also particular aspects of abusive men's behaviour which defy categorisation as *either* child abuse *or* domestic violence. Part of what needs to be understood here is a double level of intentionality: that an act directed towards one individual is at the same time intended to affect another or others. Examples include the abuse or humiliation of a woman in front of her children in order to increase control over both; hitting or threatening a child in front of his or her mother in order to threaten and/or control the woman; making women watch, or possibly even participate in, the sexual abuse of a child.

An important research area involves illuminating the range of ways in which 'simultaneous abuse' of women and children occurs. We would benefit from this in a number of ways. It would enable an understanding of how women and children's experiences are intertwined and often deliberately manipulated (connections need to made here with work on the manipulation of mother/child relationships as part of sexual abuse of the child; see Hooper, 1992). The practical uses of this information encompass the following: improved professional understanding and training; better resources to enable women and children to understand abuse when it is occurring and to re-build their relationships with each other once abuse has ended; and provision of a resource to question the reasoning of judges and magistrates who believe that, in contact orders, child abuse but *not* domestic violence should be taken into account (see for example, chapter by Hester et al. this volume).

Where the connection has been studied, to date domestic violence and child abuse have been defined as separate. These studies find that, in a high proportion of cases, abuse of women and children occur in the same family; and that in these cases it is not usually women who abuse the children, but men (see chapter by Morley and Mullender, this volume, for a review of this research).

Further evidence of the connections between domestic violence and child abuse comes from recent child death enquiries in Britain (see chapter by O'Hara, this volume). In several of these, a central point made has been that the women were also being abused; and the enquiry reports note the implications of social work failure to address this in their response. Also attesting to the co-presence of abuse of women and children is the frequency with which children tell their mother about the sexual abuse they have experienced after she has decided to leave the man because of her own abuse. This is not an uncommon eventuality in refuges (see chapter by Debonnaire, this volume).

In their ground-breaking paper 'Women and children at risk: a feminist perspective on child abuse', Evan Stark and Anne Flitcraft (1988, p.97) demonstrate that '[woman] battering is the most common context for child abuse, that the battering male is the typical child abuser' (see chapter by Morley and Mullender, this volume, for a detailed account of this study). In analysing their data, they go beyond noting these connections to highlight the bitter irony that it is in fact women -

not men - who are targeted by professionals. They make the following key points:

- The child abuse establishment assigns responsibility for abuse to mothers regardless of who assaults the child, and responds punitively to women, withholding vital resources and often removing the child to foster care, if women are battered or otherwise fail to meet expectations of 'good mothering' (p.97).
- One result is that men [who are the majority of child abusers] are invisible (p.101).
- Holding women responsible and targeting their inadequacies as parents can deepen a woman's resentment of her child and constrain her to behave in gender-stereotyped ways that seriously increase her risk in a battering relationship (p.98).
- The best way to prevent child abuse is through 'female empowerment' (p.97).

Unfortunately, the current professional orthodoxy in relation to physical abuse of children is the opposite of 'female empowerment': women - not men - are targeted for intervention, and they are offered support in parenting rather than resources and protection. Where prevention focuses on mothering, an unintended consequence is that women are entrapped in what can become a spiral of escalating violence and distress.

THE IMPACTS OF DOMESTIC VIOLENCE ON CHILDREN

Our knowledge of the impacts of domestic violence on children is limited, and constrained by conceptual and methodological problems. The best known studies (e.g. Hughes and Barad, 1983; Jaffe et al., 1990; Hughes, 1992) are North American and have been done by psychologists. The children studied were all living in shelters - little attempt was made to explore whether there was a confounding (a research term meaning blurring) of the effects of domestic violence and the effects of living in a shelter. This sample source also means that there is an over-representation of children from low income families.

Many of the commonly noted stress responses in children have been recorded in these studies - problems with sleeping, eating, toileting, lower achievement at nursery or school. In studies which have used psychological testing, no higher than a third of children, and sometimes lower than that, were found to have levels and forms of distress which were defined as requiring 'therapeutic' intervention (Hughes, 1992) - there were more boys than girls in this group, which may be a reflection of the gendered valuing of male and female with respect to definitions of 'seriousness'.

Contrary to popular myth, gender differences in how children respond are not as clear cut as we like to believe. Both boys and girls in North American shelters expressed their distress in internalised and externalised ways. One study (Hughes, 1992), however, looked only at boys since the authors decided that the impacts on them were greater and worse (this echoes similar presumptions made regarding the relative impacts on boys and girls of child sexual abuse; Kelly et al., 1991). Having said that, however, what children are witnessing is male dominance and female subordination. Their own developing gender identities will be affected in some way - but *how* they will be affected is not 'given'. For example, some boys - we don't know what proportion or what accounts for this response - identify strongly with their mothers, and distance themselves from aggressive masculinity. Some girls are judgemental and blaming of their mothers, and try to distance themselves from traditional femininity. To say that simple models of gendered responses are unhelpful, however, is not to say that gender is irrelevant. Rather, what we need is a framework which takes gender as a critical factor, but which allows for differences within, as well as between, the responses of girls and boys.

A Canadian study (Jaffe et al., 1990) is the most detailed to date, and concluded that there was no common set of impacts or responses: how and in what ways children were affected depended on their adaptational responses. The researchers attempted to explain the different responses of children through examining how much violence they had witnessed and for how long. Like many researchers in this field, they relied on data which can be measured; that is, numbers which can be subjected to complicated statistical tests. Adaptational responses are ways we find to *cope*: to manage fear, anger, and confusion. No-one has yet looked in any detail at what children think they know and understand, or how this might affect their reactions to domestic violence. Investigating the questions raised earlier in this chapter would require researchers to interact directly with children over some time, gathering data which cannot easily be 'number crunched'.

One way we could begin looking at these issues differently is by focusing on the issues children have to cope with - beyond the obvious fact of the abuse. Here we could begin from the detailed work which has been done on women's responses, where minimising or denial, uncertainty and anxiety, self blame, loss, and trust are key issues (see Kelly, 1988).

Researchers have also outlined factors which either accentuate or limit the impacts of domestic violence on children. As with work on the impacts of other forms of violence against women and children (see for example Koss and Harvey, 1991, on rape), these factors tend to be divided into those which relate to the individual child and those which are associated with the context of their experience. For the individual child, age, emotional and physical development, and gender have been noted; but little work has addressed how race, class, and disability might mediate impact. Also important here is how each child makes sense of events: who, if anyone, they blame; how they cope; and whether they see violence as a way of getting their own way or their own needs met.

Within the broader context, the following factors will all contribute to a heightening or lessening of their levels of distress: the range and extent of violence they witness (from verbal abuse to murder); whether they are themselves abused and/or the household discipline is harsh and inconsistent; whether the abusive man manipulates family relationships; the health of their mother; how she responds and her children's relationship to her; and whether they have stable and positive relationships outside the family.

Overall, whilst most research has been done in the area of 'impacts' of domestic violence on children (see chapter by Morley and Mullender, this volume, for a discussion of this research), there is still relatively little of this work when set against the larger body of research on domestic violence. When children are mentioned, they tend to be defined as 'unintended victims', suffering 'secondary' impacts from the violence. This model excludes the possibility that children are themselves intentionally victimised. We currently lack studies which include a recognition of children's own experiences of victimisation and the combination of direct impacts on children both of these experiences and of living with domestic violence. Only with such studies can we unpick those consequences which are limited to witnessing the mother's abuse, and those which are inextricably entwined with abuse of the child.

For example, recent work on the connections between disability and abuse is documenting how forms of both physical and learning disabilities are *caused* by abuse (Kelly, 1992): the former being a direct outcome of violent attacks, the latter a consequence of abuse and attempts to cope with it. Where children are themselves being abused, the possibility that their physical well-being may be permanently affected has not been addressed by researchers, since the research has taken a psychological focus. We also need to know whether living in a household where violence occurs influences children's development and coping responses to the extent that it results in what could be defined as a learning difficulty[3] or a mental health problem. These connections mean that, in a proportion of cases, preventing abuse also prevents forms of disability.

CYCLE OF ABUSE

One of the most commonly mentioned reasons for doing work with children is the 'cycle of abuse': if we don't do this work, children will repeat abusive behaviour in adulthood. This denies children's need for, not to mention right to, support simply because they have been hurt or are in distress.

Quite apart from that central point, no study has yet demonstrated that there is such a 'cycle' (see chapter by Morley and Mullender, this volume). Disputing this model does not mean, however, that there are no cases where experiences of abuse are present in generations of families. Rather, it means questioning simplistic ideas about repeating learnt behaviour as if were the same as learning a nursery rhyme. Human beings are not machines - we make sense of, place ourselves in relation to, events and actions. A thinking and decision-making process is involved before we act similarly or differently to events we have witnessed or experienced.

So powerful is this 'idea', though, that even academics who recognise that most people do not 'repeat the cycle' refer to 'breaking' it. We need to ask ourselves why this notion has taken such powerful hold over public and professional thinking. The reason is simple. It has a common sense appeal. But, most importantly, it excludes more challenging explanations - those which question power relations between men and women, adults and children. Breaking cycles is much easier and safer to discuss than changing the structure of social relations.

IMPACTS ON MOTHERING

The other side of children's experience of domestic violence which is seldom discussed is how continuing abuse affects women's relationships to their children. Many women do their utmost to protect their children from abuse and from knowledge of the violence they are experiencing. Some succeed to an extraordinary degree. Hiding one's own abuse, however, has contradictory consequences and outcomes. A woman may stay 'for the sake of the children' only to discover that one or more of the children were also being abused, and/or that some or all of them knew about her abuse and longed for her to separate. Her 'silence' makes it much more difficult for her children to voice their experience and feelings. This form of 'protection' is seldom in women's or children's long-term interests, and we should encourage honesty wherever possible. Conducting a small scale evaluation of in depth work with children in a London refuge has revealed how difficult women and children find it to talk about abuse, even in a context of relative safety, and how welcome a third party who facilitates this communication can be (Kelly, 1994).

The circumstances in which women conceive, bear, and care for children seldom resemble the idealised version of motherhood. The realities of women's lives affect their ability to care - the limitations imposed by poverty, inadequate housing, and minimal social support should never be underestimated. Professional perspectives on parenting often marginalise the facts of everyday life, focusing instead on an idealised white middle class norm of what 'good enough' mothering consists of, and tending to assign primary responsibility for abuse and neglect to women. Ideologies of the family and motherhood are frequently reinforced, if not imposed, by agency intervention. Stark and Flitcraft (1988, p.110) define this as the imposition of 'patriarchal mothering'. In this process women's desire for independence, autonomy, and safety may be suppressed, creating resentment and frustration which they may connect to expectations of themselves as mothers (not unreasonably in the circumstances); and this may, in turn, sometimes be taken out on their children.

Domestic violence is an everyday reality which affects women's experience of motherhood. It can have profound and far-reaching effects on women's feelings and behaviour towards their children, as well as on their sense of identity as mothers and as women. This deserves research in its own right - so what I present here are initial thoughts which need to be developed.

For some women, bearing and caring for their children is so connected to their own abuse that it is extremely difficult if not impossible, to disconnect them. For example:

- where children were conceived as consequence of rape;
- where continual pregnancies have been used by the abusive man as a control strategy;
- when children have been encouraged, and/or have chosen, to side with the abusive man;
- where children have been drawn into in the abuse of their mother and, in the case of some boys, have chosen to replicate aspects of their father's role or behaviour after their mother has decided to leave.

In each of these situations, the child and/or the child's behaviour is a continual reminder or extension of the woman's abuse. In such circumstances she may understand and experience her mothering responsibilities as an unchosen imposition; at the very least, her feelings about motherhood will contain conflicts and contradictions. It is possible for these feelings to be self-consciously known and struggled with, to the extent that her children are totally unaware of the difficulties. It is also possible that a woman's conflictual feelings are expressed through inconsistent and even abusive behaviour towards her children, yet not understood by her as the outcome of coerced motherhood. It is also possible for elements of both these responses to be present in women's perceptions and behaviour. Regardless, women need the safety to express their ambivalences without being automatically defined as a 'risk' to their children. Challenging, not just supportive, work may need to be done with some of the children. And there may be occasions when what women need is support to choose not to care for some or all of their children, either in the shorter or longer term.

There are other impacts of domestic violence on mothering about which we need to be mindful:

- women being forced to sacrifice children or a child in order to protect themselves and/or the other children (where women's 'escape' or ability to live free of harassment is made conditional by the abuser on leaving behind one or more of the children; where the lack of housing options means women have a 'choice' either to remain and continue to be abused, or leave without their children[4]);
- women choosing to have children as the only source of positive meaning and/or identity in their lives - mothering as 'all there is'; this

may be exacerbated when enforced isolation means that a woman's children are literally her only source of company, support and nurturance[5];

- women using violence themselves - either to pre-empt harsher treatment from their partner, or as an expression of their own frustration and distress;
- women losing confidence in their ability, and/or their emotional resources, to care for her children, as a result of repeated degradation;
- women making inconsistent responses in relation to rules, boundaries or discipline - either as a result of their fear of their children 'turning out like their father' or to compensate for what they have had to endure.

Again, the space for women to openly discuss the issues and conflicts without feeling that they are judged is essential. And in some cases, supporting a woman's felt need not to have sole or even any daily care responsibilities for children may be necessary in either the shorter or longer term.

Ideologies of motherhood, women's awareness of potential punitive responses if they tell about violence, and their own ambivalence, trap women in a vicious Catch 22. Their dilemma is that they cannot protect their children unless they are themselves protected; but if they speak about the violence, they fear that their child/ren may be removed. This fear is the single most frequently cited reason for women not contacting certain organisations (other than the police) about domestic violence, or for not telling workers about its occurrence if they are in contact already (e.g. McGibbon et al., 1989). Rather than tell this dangerous truth, women try to access child protection resources by suggesting they are 'unable to cope'. It is a bitter irony that this may result in precisely what they initially feared. As Stark and Flitcraft (1988) point out, 'battered women cannot fully protect their children from the assailant. To protect themselves from child services, however, they pretend they can' (p.110). They also note, 'not only are the mothers who pose least danger to their children most likely to lose them, but they may also lose access to whatever meagre resources resulted from agency concern' (p.107).

One simple and key principle from which we can begin is that *woman protection is frequently the most effective form of child protection*. This simple philosophy could change practice fundamentally, and enable women to have more confidence in agencies. It does not prevent an acknowledgment that, in some instances, women's and children's interests and needs are not compatible, temporarily or permanently.

THE IMPLICATIONS OF TAKING COMPLEXITY SERIOUSLY

I conclude by listing some of the implications of taking seriously the connections between domestic violence and child abuse, and children's experiences of domestic violence:

- We have to begin by recognising the complexity of childhood, motherhood, the family, and the prevalence of violence in families.
- Where domestic violence or child abuse is known about, the co-presence of the other should *always* be investigated.
- *The guiding principle for policy and practice must be that safety and empowerment of women constitute the most effective form of child protection.* This principle can encompass the fact that women's and children's interests sometimes conflict, and that some women may choose or be obliged to give up the care of their children.
- Care must be taken to ensure that policy and practice which recognise the connections between woman abuse and child abuse do not develop punitive forms - for example, threatening to remove children if a woman does not get an injunction, go to a refuge, or take other steps imposed by child protection professionals; or formulating definitions of the 'abusing parent' (such as one in New York State which includes 'allows to be created a substantial risk of physical injury to the child' and is often interpreted to mean allowing a child to witness abuse of a mother; Stark and Flitcraft, 1988, p.102), which may be used to remove children who have witnessed domestic violence.
- It is essential to establish legal recognition of children's rights to see and *not* to see their parents, and to be protected from coercion and pressure during contact.
- We need to draw out connections with work on supporting mothers and children in child sexual abuse, particularly work enabling them to unpick how their relationship was manipulated as part of the abuse (Hooper, 1992). Mothers and practitioners need to be encouraged and enabled to be honest with children about events and their consequences.
- It is important to build a stronger knowledge base from children's own experiences, understandings, responses, and feelings about domestic violence.
- We need to develop advocacy services for children which provide information and options about protecting themselves and their mothers.
- It is essential to ensure that properly resourced child care and children's services exist in refuges and in bed and breakfast hostels.
- We need to develop support services for children which build in recognition of differences between them. The framework should begin by acknowledging children's strengths in coping and surviving, whilst enabling them to develop more accurate understandings and self- and other-affirming responses to their experience.
- Drawing on US models of peer support systems in school and youth work contexts would be useful.
- It is crucial to develop prevention and education work which places acquiring new interpersonal and problem-solving skills within a framework which questions the use of 'power over' others in relationships.

Notes

1. Shelters are the North American equivalents to refuges.
2. Thanks to Carol-Ann Hooper for challenging me to develop the ideas in this section.
3. Learning difficulty is a concept developed by activists to replace terms such as 'mental handicap', 'educational subnormality' and the like. It is both less pejorative and indicates a broader range of inclusion. In this instance, it refers to the possibility of both temporary and permanent disabilities which can be caused by violence directed at the child's head and/or to the disruption of relationships, emotions, sleep and concentration which living with domestic violence produces and which often affects educational attainment.
4. This dilemma is especially poignant for women with older sons, since many refuges in Britain have age limits for older boys.
5. The possibility of children caring for adults tends to be discussed critically, especially in western constructions of childhood. Rather than discuss this issue in the abstract, it would be more productive to talk about the context and the level of need and expectation. It is clearly a problem when children are required to care for siblings and/or adults, and punished for failure to do so. It is possible in principle, however, for children to give care and support when there is a reciprocity involved, when it does not tax their physical and emotional resources, and when an appreciation exists of what they have given and why. In contexts of enforced separation from others and ongoing abuse, it is an achievement of no small proportion for mothers and children to forge supportive, and at times protective, alliances with one another.

References

Hooper, C-A. (1992) *Mothers Surviving Child Sexual Abuse*. London: Routledge.

Hughes, H. (1992) 'Impact of spouse abuse on children of battered women', *Violence Update*, August, 1, pp.9-11.

Hughes, H. and Barad, S. (1983) 'Psychological functioning of children in a battered women's shelter', *American Journal of Orthopsychiatry*, 53(3), pp.525-531.

Jaffe, P.G., Wolfe, D.A. and Wilson, S.K. (1990) *Children of Battered Women*. Newbury Park, California: Sage.

Kelly, L. (1988) *Surviving Sexual Violence*. Cambridge: Polity Press.

Kelly, L. (1992) 'Disability and child abuse: a research review of the connections', *Child Abuse Review*, 1, pp.157-167.

Kelly, L. (1994) *Evaluation of Child Work in a London Refuge*. Report to Hammersmith and Fulham Safer Cities. Unpublished.

Kelly, L., Regan, L. and Burton, S. (1991) *An Exploratory Study of the Prevalence of Sexual Abuse in a Sample of 1200 16 to 21 Year Olds*. Final Report to the ESRC. London: Child Abuse Studies Unit, University of North London.

Koss, M. and Harvey, M. (1991) *The Rape Victim: Clinical and Community Interventions*. Beverly Hills, California: Sage.

Mama, A. (1989) *The Hidden Struggle: Statutory and Voluntary Sector Responses to Violence against Black Women in the Home*. London: London Race and Housing Research Unit.

McGibbon, A., Cooper, L. and Kelly, L. (1989) *'What Support?': An Exploratory Study of Council Policy and Practice and Local Support Services in the area of Domestic Violence within Hammersmith and Fulham*. London: Hammersmith and Fulham Council.

Mooney, J. (1994) *The Hidden Figure: Domestic Violence in North London*. London: Islington Police and Crime Prevention Unit.

Stark, E. and Flitcraft, A. (1988) 'Women and children at risk: a feminist perspective on child abuse', *International Journal of Health Services*, 18(1), pp.97-118.

5

Child Deaths in Contexts of Domestic Violence: Implications for Professional Practice

Maureen O'Hara

In recent years, the Department of Health has received 120 notifications annually of child deaths or incidents of serious harm to children involving 'potential major public concern' (James,1994, para.1.1)[1]. Some cases of serious injury or death lead to Area Child Protection Committee (ACPC) case reviews - known as 'section 8' reviews[2] - which are made available to the Department of Health, who on average currently receive a report on one such review each week. A smaller proportion result in inquiries by independent bodies, the results of which are made available to the general public.

Generally, those cases which lead to 'section 8' reviews and/or public inquiries involve the death of a child resulting from physical assault and/or neglect by one or both parents or step-parents. Of these, a large proportion of the parents responsible for the child's death are fathers or step-fathers who have a history of violence towards their female partners as well as towards the child concerned. In most cases, social services and/or other agencies concerned with child protection have had prior contact with the children and their families. In many cases, the professionals involved have been aware of the context of domestic violence in which the abuse or neglect of the child was taking place, but generally seem to have failed to take this context into account in their assessment of the danger or in their strategies for protecting the child.

PROFESSIONAL RELUCTANCE TO ACKNOWLEDGE DOMESTIC VIOLENCE

This failure is part of a more general failing in much child protection practice and theory to take adequate account of the power dynamics of gender and age within families, or of the ways in which these are shaped by male dominance both within the family and the wider society. This results in a tendency to treat parents as a homogeneous entity and to fail to make distinctions between abusing and non-abusing parents - a distinction which is often crucial to the development of effective child protection strategies.

Recognition of the distinction between abusing and non-abusing parents, or of the impact of a context of domestic violence on child protection, has been largely absent from child protection guidelines at both national and local levels. Yet it is clear from the research literature, and from other indicators such as the inquiry reports mentioned above, that men who beat their wives frequently also physically abuse children. For example, a study by Bowker et al. (1988) found that men who beat their wives also physically abused children in 70 per cent of cases in which children were present in the home. Other studies reviewed by Hughes *et al.* (1989) have found correlations of between 40 and 60 per cent (see the chapter by Morley and Mullender for a fuller discussion of this research evidence).

A striking example of professional reluctance to acknowledge the significance of domestic violence in children's lives occurs in a review by Reder et al. (1993) of reports of 35 inquiries into child deaths resulting from physical abuse or neglect. Many of these deaths were the result of physical attacks on children by fathers who were also physically abusing the child's mother. Only three paragraphs in a book of 191 pages make any comments which obviously relate to domestic violence, but even they do not use that term. Reder et al. note:

> Even more common than histories of aggression to children was recurrent violence between the partners, which was reported in at least half of the cases. Often it was aggression by the male partner who was known to have an unpredictable violent temper . . . There were occasional stories of apparent rages of frustration by parents who experienced events happening out of their control. The frustration was particularly pronounced when the mother and child were in hospital and it was as though the partner was *desperate for them to return home within his ambit of control* . Heidi Koseda's step-father banged his head against the wall of the hospital when told his wife's pregnancy would be induced: he had previously had a violent outburst on the ante-natal ward. Shirley Woodcock's father created a disturbance on the post-natal ward when he found his wife had discharged herself. Simon Peacock's father angrily demanded both mother and baby's discharge from hospital and Charlene Salt's father insisted on taking the mother and baby home ten hours after the birth. Later, when Charlene was in hospital on a Place of Safety Order, he refused to let her mother stay visiting alone (1993, p.44, emphasis added).

Reder et al. make no attempt to explore the relationship between the need of these men to control their partners and children, their use of physical violence in doing so, and the circumstances of the child's eventual death. They examine the need for control over children primarily in terms of the 'unmet dependency needs' of both parents, and make no reference to men's control over women except in the excerpt quoted. Their insistence on using gender neutral terms wherever possible indicates a wilful, though not uncommon, refusal to engage with questions about the significance of domestic violence in child protection, or to critically examine the significance of gender in the dynamics of violence within the families concerned.

This stance is effectively the norm within the social work and therapeutic professions and it leads in many cases to inappropriate child protection strategies and practices which fail to protect children.

THE BEGINNINGS OF PROFESSIONAL RECOGNITION?

A recent study of 30 'section 8' reviews carried out for the Department of Health does stress the importance of recognising domestic violence in child protection work (James, 1994), as does the report of the ACPCs' most recent national conference (Armstrong, 1994).

The limitations of child protection practice which fails to address the significance of domestic violence are also highlighted in the reports of inquiries into the circumstances leading to the deaths of 5-year old Sukina Hammond, who was killed by her father in 1988, and of 3-year old Toni Dales, killed by her step-father in 1993. In both cases the professionals involved with the children suspected that they were being physically abused and knew that their mothers were being subjected to violence by their partners, and in both cases there was a failure to appreciate the danger to the children represented by the men concerned.

The inquiry report into Sukina Hammond's death notes:

> . . . the family were perceived to be one in which 'domestic violence' occurred, and yet very little is recorded about the nature of 'domestic violence'. It has since transpired however, that some of the incidents when Sukina's father attacked her mother were of an appallingly vicious nature (Bridge Child Care Consultancy Service, 1991, p.85).

Only three months after a prolonged attack on their mother, Sukina and her younger sister were removed from the child protection register. A few months later, Sukina was killed. The report comments on the de-registration: 'the likelihood is that the existence of domestic violence appeared to be perceived as acceptable without seeking clarification of the details of the assault' (Bridge Child Care Consultancy Service, 1991, p.86)[3].

The National Children's Bureau report (1993) of the inquiry into the death of Toni Dales also found failure clearly to acknowledge the context of domestic violence in which she was living. It further notes that reports by neighbours about her step-father's treatment of Toni were dismissed by child protection professionals. Both reports suggest a failure on the part of the professionals concerned to perceive clear evidence of violence against women and children which was right in front of them.

In the cases of these two children, this failure may have resulted partly from stereotyped perceptions about the 'acceptability' of violence within working class communities. The perception that 'violence between adults is a way of life round here' was common among professionals involved in the cases reviewed in James' study (cited by Armstrong,1994: 18, reporting on a conference presentation by James). However, class stereotyping cannot fully explain the selective perception which seems to have occurred in these cases. Fully to perceive what was happening and to take effective action to change it would have meant challenging both men's power in general and the individual violent men concerned. In the case of Toni Dales in particular, it is clear from the inquiry report that fear of her step-father, Glenn McPherson, played a significant part in the failure of professionals to take adequate steps to protect her.

Such professional fear of violent men is a frequent theme of many of the inquiry reports into the circumstances of children's deaths. As James' work on 'section 8' reports showed:

> It is evident that some of the men in these families were so hostile and aggressive that professionals made special arrangements to meet them, often refusing to make home visits at all. Yet children were living in these homes . . . The failure of key professionals to face up to the risk to the child, their refusal to acknowledge their own fear of the violent males involved, and the failure to acknowledge the need to take difficult action, meant that cases known to the whole community went without adequate response (cited in Armstrong, 1994, pp.18-19)

IMPLICATIONS FOR CHILD PROTECTION PRACTICE

Effective child protection in contexts of domestic violence will require a fundamental change of attitudes towards men's violence and the development of a new willingness to take action against it. Recent initiatives in the voluntary and statutory sectors at both local and national level, and the recognition of the significance of domestic violence in recent Department of Health reports concerning child protection, may indicate the beginnings of important shifts in attitudes and practice in this area.

The inquiry report into the death of Toni Dales suggests that:

> The Child Protection Services need to work within an atmosphere where there is public support for their work if they are to be effective. Community leaders and public attitudes should be willing to openly challenge attitudes and ways of life which endanger women and children. Public services should be encouraged to help reduce the underlying factors which contribute to child abuse, such as domestic violence (National Children's Bureau, 1993, p.57).

Such changes clearly cannot be brought about by one agency. Nevertheless each agency - and individual workers within agencies - can contribute to the process of change by, first of all, recognising the significance of domestic violence in relation to child protection, and then developing policies and practices which effectively challenge domestic violence both at a general level and in individual instances.

Four key areas in the development of effective professional practice are: consultation with children, the formation of alliances with non-abusing mothers wherever possible, directly confronting and controlling the behaviour of violent men, and developing strategies for protecting workers as well as women and children from violence. Each of these is briefly explored below.

Consultation with children

Genuine consultation with children which is appropriate to their age, understanding and mode of communication needs to be a central principle of all child protection work. Armstrong (1994, p.20, drawing on a conference presentation by James) points out that, while children are generally seen as the prime source of information in investigations of suspected sexual abuse, in cases of suspected physical abuse or neglect investigation still relies primarily on forensic evidence.

As the inquiry reports into the deaths of Sukina Hammond and Toni Dales indicate, listening to children and taking what they say seriously needs to be seen as crucial in protecting children from all forms of abuse. There was, in fact, a failure in both cases to communicate appropriately with the children themselves. Sukina Hammond stated to her social worker and to nursery and hospital staff on many occasions that her father hurt her and that she was frightened of him. After receiving treatment for a broken arm, she told at least two professionals that her father was responsible. With the exception of one social worker, participants in child protection case conferences effectively ignored her statements, with fatal results. The National Children's Bureau report (1993) of the inquiry into the death of Toni Dales also found failure to communicate effectively with the child about her obvious fear and distress.

Alliances with non-abusing mothers

Attempting to make genuine alliances with non-abusing mothers in a manner which accords them respect is the most effective way, in most cases, to protect children who are at risk in a context of domestic violence. In many cases, the gender and ethnic background of workers will be significant factors in determining whether they are able to develop relationships of trust with children and/or their mothers and the views of children on this, as well as those of mothers, need to be taken into account and acted on where possible.

The precise nature of workers' relationships with children and with non-abusing mothers will obviously vary according to particular circumstances and to the nature of any abuse, or risk of abuse, to the child. Very different strategies will be necessary in relation to sexual abuse, in part because of the secrecy and manipulation which usually form the context in which such abuse takes place, than in relation to physical abuse, which mothers are much more likely to know about both when it first happens and if it recurs after intervention. However, in all contexts of domestic violence, child protection strategies need to be developed which will enhance the protection of children, their mothers or other endangered relatives, and child protection workers themselves, whose work will be ineffective if they are not given adequate support in trying to challenge the behaviour of violent men.

Confronting violent men

Most child protection professionals involved in face-to-face work are women, and child protection strategies aimed at controlling the behaviour of violent men need to take this into account. Workers, whether women or men, should not be expected to deal with potential violence alone, and inexperienced staff should not be allocated to cases in which domestic violence is involved. Ideally senior staff should be directly involved in such cases, to which two workers should be allocated wherever possible. At the very least, workers should not make home visits, or participate in meetings with violent men, without another worker present.

This work needs to include a range of clearly defined and concrete strategies for challenging and controlling violent men. Often these will be most effective if they are planned in consultation with the women who live with them, who know more about their patterns of violence than anyone else. Many women will have developed a range of strategies for resisting that violence (Kelly, 1988). Building on women's strengths by acknowledging those strategies can be an important aspect of developing appropriate alliances.

The historical work of Gordon (1988), and Hooper's research with non-abusing mothers whose children had been sexually abused (1992), highlight the importance of child protection agencies taking a strong and controlling stance towards violent men. Mothers interviewed in Hooper's study commented that, while social services' intervention had resulted in expectations being placed on them which they were given little support in fulfilling, and in their behaviour being monitored, little or no effective action was taken to monitor or control the behaviour of their partners. In both studies, women expressed a need for State agencies to exercise control over their partners which they themselves did not have the power or authority to exercise alone. James' study of 'section 8' reports similarly found that:

> In these reports there were areas of content where information was conspicuously sparse and unsatisfactory. Notably the reports gave a lot of attention and detailed information on mothers. Mothers were often described in very considerable detail - but where were the men? . . . It was these 'invisible' men who were usually suspected of

killing or damaging the child. Yet in several Section 47 inquiries ...
the man in the family was never properly identified much less
interviewed (Armstrong, 1994, p.17, reporting James).

Strategies for controlling men's violence should include the use of the
civil and criminal law relating to domestic violence, as well as the use of
child protection legislation where this is appropriate. Even where the
focus of work is on supporting women and children who continue to live
with violent men, it should always be made clear to the woman that the
support offered will include assistance in taking legal action to remove
an abusive man from the home, or in finding alternative accommodation
for herself and her children should she later choose this course of action.
In circumstances where women consider it helpful, this can also be made
clear to the man.

Protection strategies

In some instances where children cannot be protected from abuse within
the context of their families, decisions about their living arrangements
may ultimately be made in the course of care proceedings. In others,
older children may make their own decisions and seek the help of the
courts in changing their living arrangements by making independent
applications for residence orders where they have access to an alternative
household.

Women who are living with violent men may plan to leave at a point
where this becomes feasible for them, or may decide to leave after being
given appropriate practical and emotional support by child protection
agencies and/or voluntary sector organisations working around domestic
violence. One of the most important roles child protection agencies and
individual workers can play in the process of escaping violence is to help
widen the options open to children and non-abusing mothers. They can
do this by working with them in a spirit of consultation and partnership
wherever possible, while at the same time ensuring the maximum
possible protection for children during the processes of change and
escape.

THE RESPONSE OF THE CRIMINAL JUSTICE SYSTEM

The responses of the criminal justice system to child deaths which have
occurred in a context of domestic violence often involve a failure to
distinguish between the abusing and the non-abusing parent which
mirrors that of child protection agencies. Kennedy (1992, pp.95-96)
suggests that, in many cases where children have been killed by their
fathers, failure to take adequate account of domestic violence leads to
charges being brought precipitously against both parents when further
or more sympathetic investigation could help reveal the true
circumstances of the child's death. As a result, the possibility of bringing
murder or manslaughter charges against the person responsible is lost.

Instead, both parents may be charged with lesser offences such as cruelty. While there *are* cases of child death for which both parents are responsible, and some for which mothers are solely responsible, there is often a failure to distinguish between these cases and those in which the child's mother has played no part in the fatal assault on the child and has herself been terrorised by the man responsible.

One example of this was the imprisonment of Sally Emery, whose daughter, Chanel Hedman, died from injuries inflicted by the child's father, Brian Hedman. Hedman, who blamed Sally Emery for the child's death, was sentenced to eight years imprisonment for cruelty and assault. Emery, who was being beaten by Hedman, was acquitted of assault but was given four years detention in a young offender institution for failing to protect her daughter from Hedman. The Court of Appeal later reduced Emery's sentence to 30 months, in part because the trial jury was given insufficient evidence of the effects of Hedman's violence on her, but stated that a substantial period of imprisonment was called for. Lord Taylor, the Lord Chief Justice, commented that 'a parent's paramount duty is to protect his or her child' and that failure to do so could not be excused by a mother putting 'even her own protection . . . before the life and health of her child' (*R v. Emery* , 1992, p.394). The evidence presented in court suggested that, at the time Chanel was killed, Emery has reached a point where the only strategy she felt able to use to limit Hedman's violence was total passivity - her experience was that anything else led to more violence. Such feelings of powerlessness and inability to control events are a common response to continuous and prolonged violence, not only among women living with violent men but among those subjected to any other form of terror (Lewis Herman, 1992).

Prosecuting a parent - or any other adult - for failing to exercise a duty of care towards a child serves a purpose only where the parent is genuinely capable of exercising that duty, has the means necessary, and wilfully neglects to do so. If a parent fails to act because of terror or a genuine belief, however mistaken, that the child will come to less harm if she does nothing, prosecution is of no benefit to children. Punitive judicial practices towards mothers whose children are assaulted by their partners are likely to discourage women from seeking professional help for themselves and their children in escaping violence, and this will increase rather than reduce the risk to children.

Punishing women for their partners' violence towards their children helps to obscure, rather than clarify, the nature of the power dynamics within the family which lead to many forms of child abuse. All forms of child abuse are essentially abuses of power, and stopping abuse at either an individual or a societal level requires clarity about the nature of the power being exercised, and about who is exercising power in particular situations. If the mother can be blamed for the failure to protect the child, it is easier to avoid examining the nature of power relationships within the family which maintain domestic violence, as well as the reasons for society's failure effectively to protect women and children from that violence. Criminalising women in Sally Emery's situation helps to maintain, rather than challenge, the social relationships which lead to violence against children and women while providing an outlet for societal guilt. It is, in effect, a form of scapegoating.

The criminal justice system can play a more effective part in child protection if its agencies take into account the nature of domestic violence and its effects on women, and make clear distinctions between abusing and non-abusing parents. Such clarity would lead to better informed investigative procedures and prosecution strategies, and would therefore make it easier to bring to justice those parents of either sex who are genuinely responsible for causing death or serious injury to a child.

CONCLUSION

In conclusion, all professionals involved in responding to child abuse need to recognise the power dynamics of gender as well as age in understanding the context of that abuse. Failure to do so will mean that children continue to die what might otherwise be preventable deaths.

Notes

1. This figure includes notifications of the death from any cause of any child being looked after by a local authority and of any child who dies in residential care.
2. These reviews are carried out under Part 8 of *Working Together* (Home Office et al., 1991) but are rather confusingly known as section 8 reviews.
3. Although there is an implicit recognition in the report of the ways in which power dynamics within families are shaped by gender, this is not made explicit or critically discussed. The issue is also obscured by the use of gender-neutral terminology such as 'dangerous' families (p.85) and 'violence between adults' (p.86).

References

Armstrong, H. (1994) *Report of Area Child Protection Committees National Conference: 8 March 1994.* London: Department of Health. ACPC Series, Report No. 4.

Bowker, L. H., Arbitell, M. and McFerron, J. R. (1988) 'On the relationship between wife beating and child abuse' in Yllö, K. and Bograd, M. (eds.) *Feminist Perspectives on Wife Abuse.* Newbury Park, California: Sage.

Bridge Child Care Consultancy Service (1991) *Sukina: An Evaluation of the Circumstances Leading to her Death.* London: Bridge Child Care Consultancy Service.

Children's Legal Centre (1992) *Children and Domestic Violence: Submission to the Home Affairs Inquiry into Domestic Violence.* London: Children's Legal Centre. (Also published in House of Commons Home Affairs Committee, Session 1992-93, *Domestic Violence. Memoranda of Evidence,* volume II, Minutes of Evidence and Appendices, London: HMSO.)

Gordon, L. (1988) *Heroes of Their Own Lives:The Politics and History of Family Violence*. London: Virago.

Home Office, Department of Health, Department of Education and Science, and Welsh Office (1991) *Working Together Under the Children Act 1989: A Guide to Arrangements for Inter-Agency Cooperation for the Protection of Children from Abuse*. London: HMSO.

Hooper, C.-A. (1992) *Mothers Surviving Child Sexual Abuse*. London: Routledge.

Hughes, H. M., Parkinson, D. and Vargo, M. (1989) 'Witnessing spouse abuse and experiencing physical abuse: a 'double whammy' ?', *Journal of Family Violence*, 4(2), pp.197-209.

Jaffe, P. G., Wolfe, D. A., and Wilson, S. K., (1990) *Children of Battered Women*. Newbury Park, California: Sage.

James, G. (1994) *Discussion Report for ACPC Conference 1994: Study of Working Together 'Part 8' Reports*. London: Department of Health, ACPC Series, Report no.1.

Kelly, L. (1988) *Surviving Sexual Violence*. Cambridge: Polity Press.

Kennedy, H. (1992) *Eve Was Framed: Women and British Justice*. London: Chatto and Windus.

Lewis Herman, J. (1992) *Trauma and Recovery: From Domestic Abuse to Political Terror*. New York: Basic Books.

National Children's Bureau (1993) *Investigation into Inter-Agency Practice Following the Cleveland Area Child Protection Committee's Report Concerning the Death of Toni Dales*. London: National Children's Bureau.

O'Hara, M. (1992) 'Child protection and domestic violence: making the links', *Childright*, 88, pp.4-5.

O'Hara, M. (1992) 'A mother's duty to care: are there no limits?', *Childright*, 92, pp.5-6.

O'Hara, M. (1993) 'Child protection and domestic violence: changing policy and practice' in *The Links Between Domestic Violence and Child Abuse: Developing Services*. London: London Borough of Hackney (Women's Unit).

R v. Emery (1992) 14 Cr.App.R. (S.)

Reder, P., Duncan, S. and Gray, M. (1993) *Beyond Blame: Child Abuse Tragedies Revisited*. London: Routledge.

Section III

Families Separating as a Result of Men's Abuse of Women

6

Reinstating Patriarchy: The Politics of the Family and the New Legislation

Lynne Harne and Jill Radford

The main purpose of this chapter is to identify and question some central ideologies behind the 1989 Children Act, an Act which has been widely welcomed and heralded as the most significant piece of childcare legislation this century. At face value it is child centred, liberal legislation which emphasises children's welfare, parental responsibilities and reasonableness, rather than rights and adversarial conflict. In theory, it has the potential for quite radical decisions. For example, it acknowledges difference in family forms and accepts that parental responsibility need not be limited to biological parents; thus legal status could be accorded to a range of parenting forms outside the white, heterosexual, two parent family norm[1]. Despite this potential, however, the Act rests on some problematic assumptions and omissions which, as predicted by feminists, are seriously compromising the safety of women and children. By locating the legislation in its historical and political context, we identify and trace some of the assumptions which underpin its liberal rhetoric and re-enforce traditional patriarchal relations of male control over women and children beyond the breakdown of the family.

The Act makes two problematic assumptions: first, the unlikely notion that separating parents behave reasonably and, second, the patriarchal belief that the interests of children are best served by retaining paternal control through continuing contact with the father. Its major omission is its failure to recognise that male sexual violence, including domestic violence, is a primary factor in the breakdown of heterosexual relationships and that this violence does not necessarily end with the ending of a relationship. These features of the Act can be seen in dangerous interaction when, for example, judges routinely invite violent fathers to make Children Act applications when granting domestic violence injunctions. We question the premise that male control and male models of behaving are such desirable requirements in childhood that children need continuing contact with those fathers whose violence may have harmed them (see chapter by Hooper, this volume). Granting contact orders in these circumstances may facilitate further violence or abuse (see chapter by Hester et al., this volume).

Whilst the Act encodes new ideologies and a new language to describe children's rights, children's welfare, and parental responsibilities, we demonstrate that in practice these have become synonymous with fathers' rights. They have also converged with a government policy that is committed to conservative family values. Thus, the implementation of the Children Act has had the effect of undermining autonomous motherhood and of reinforcing traditional notions of the father as authority figure and provider.

This notion of the father figure as provider has been reinforced by another new law - the Child Support Act 1991. By legislating that lone mothers on welfare benefits must pursue biological fathers for maintenance rather than claiming from the state, this Act has aimed to undermine the financial independence of women with children from individual men within the family. A second purpose of this chapter is to argue that, by financially penalising both women and men who have not conformed to the traditional family ideal, this legislation may fuel male violence towards women and children attempting to escape abusive situations and may increase demands for contact with children from what the state defines as 'absent' fathers.

This chapter concludes by proposing that, rather than deeming 'father right' inviolable, fathers' continuing contact with children should be qualified by a requirement of 'fitness' as carers of children. This 'fitness' we suggest is ruled out by violent and abusive behaviour towards children's mothers and children themselves.

HISTORICAL OVERVIEW

To understand the current situation, it is helpful to examine the historical legal positioning of women and children in relation to men within the family. This needs to include an understanding both of the development of women's rights to live with children on separation and divorce and of the role of domestic violence as a means of social control over women and children.

Up to and during most of the nineteenth century - and deriving from the Roman legal concept of pater familias - married women and their children were considered the property of the husband, the legal ruler of the family (Cretney, 1979, p.427, note 9). Women who separated from their husbands had no legal rights of custody or access to their children. Under common law, married fathers had absolute rights of guardianship over their legitimate offspring. The historical position of unmarried mothers was different: they had the degraded position of being unmarried and therefore without any legal status. For most of the nineteenth century, a child born outside of marriage was considered under common law 'the child of no one' since only men within the married state could confer legal ownership of a child.

As an aspect of legal ownership, English common law conferred on the husband the right to 'give his wife moderate correction . . . by domestic chastisement' and to restrain her physically 'from going into society of which he disapproves or otherwise disobeying his rightfully authority' (in Radford and Russell, 1992, p.46). A father also had the legal right to inflict 'moderate and reasonable corporal punishment' on his children (Cretney, 1979, pp.434-36)).

However, as demonstrated in the work of Frances Power Cobbe (Spender, 1983, pp.429-439), feminists began to challenge the whole concept of the rule of the father and gained some very limited legal rights through statute during the nineteenth and early twentieth centuries (see, generally, Rights of Women Lesbian Custody Group, 1986, ch.11). In 1839, the Custody of Infants Act gave the Court of Chancery power to commit the custody of children to their mother up until the age of seven and access until the age of majority - provided she had not committed adultery. This constituted the beginning of the 'tender years doctrine' - a legal presumption that young children should be with their mothers. It was, however, always qualified by the 'deservingness' of the mother as defined by the patriarchal courts. The doctrine continues to the present day in competing claims between fathers and mothers concerning where children should live following divorce or separation. No equivalent concept of 'deservingness' has ever been applied to fathers' rights to children (see e.g. Rights of Women, 1994; Rights of Women Lesbian Custody Group, 1986).

The 1857 Matrimonial Causes Act, which brought about very limited grounds for divorce for the rich, stated that a husband could divorce his wife for adultery alone, 'but a wife had to have additional grounds such as cruelty and desertion' (Cretney, 1979, p.87, note 46). Vigorous campaigning by nineteenth century feminists such as Frances Power Cobbe brought about the 1878 Matrimonial Causes Act. This Act stated that wives subject to abuse could obtain separation orders to keep their husbands away from them. They were allowed to keep their children until the age of seven.

The 1886 Guardianship of Infants Act gave married women the right to contest custody of their children up to the age of 21, irrespective of whether or not they had committed adultery. It also directed the court for the first time to have regard to the welfare of the child. However, the welfare of the child and the mother's behaviour were seen by the courts as being inextricably connected. Thus, if the mother had committed adultery or had stepped outside other patriarchally-defined norms of feminine behaviour such as being involved in feminist campaigning, she was unlikely to get custody of her children (Chesler, 1987). The 1925 Guardianship of Infants Act made the welfare of the child the first and paramount consideration, and equalised the married mother's claim to custody to that of the father - if they came before a court. However, within marriage the father was still considered the child's only legal guardian. It was not until the 1971 Guardianship of Minors Act that married women were given equal rights in relation to 'the legal custody of a minor and his (*sic*) property as had previously been allowed a father' (Cretney, 1979, p.440).

Unmarried mothers gained the right to custody of their children in 1891. The House of Lords ruled that a mother had responsibility to maintain her child under the *Poor Law*, and this in turn gave her a right to custody of that child (Cretney, 1979, p.588).

During the early part of the twentieth century when divorce was made easier by the 1923 Divorce Act, married women tended to be awarded custody of young children - provided that they had behaved 'appropriately' as mothers and wives. Until the mid 1960s, the courts tended to regard a mother who committed adultery as unfit to have care of children (see Rights of Women Lesbian Custody Group, 1986, for a more detailed discussion). As one judge stated:

> This [good mothering] in itself is not always enough; one must remember that to be a good mother involves not only looking after the children, but making and keeping a home for them with their father. . . . in so far as she herself by her conduct broke up that home she is not a good mother (Re: L [infants] [1962] 3 All ER 4).

During the early 1950s, psychological theories - such as Bowlby's maternal deprivation thesis (Bowlby, 1953) - began influencing judicial decision-making in awarding custody of young children to mothers. Whilst these theories may have helped women get custody of children, it is not surprising that they were constructed during the post war period of social reconstruction when women were being encouraged to stay at home to look after children and free up paid employment for men (see Walby, 1986, for a discussion of this issue).

As this historical overview indicates, married women's rights and responsibilities towards children were always precarious in that they came to be inseparably connected with the concept of 'the welfare of the child' and its interpretation by the courts. The interpretation of the welfare principle, in turn, hinged on perceptions of the mother's behaviour and whether she was viewed as able to put the interests of her child before her own (Brophy, 1985).

The 1970s began to see challenges both to legal practices regarding child custody and to the psychological discourse on the importance of the mother to young children which, it was argued, had ignored 'paternal deprivation' (Maidment, 1981). These challenges followed changes to the divorce laws in 1969 and 1973 which made divorce accessible to many more people.

REINSTATING FATHERHOOD: 'FAMILIES NEED FATHERS'
AND THE SHIFT FROM SOLE TO JOINT CUSTODY WITH ONGOING CONTACT

A powerful challenge was mounted by 'Families Need Fathers' (FNF), a fathers' rights pressure group founded in 1974 - after married women won equal custody rights to their children in law. FNF argued vociferously that the courts were discriminating against fathers in custody disputes. They claimed that 'nine out of ten children end up in the sole custody of the mother' (Harne, 1984).

This statistic was roughly confirmed in two studies on the outcomes of custody orders on divorce in 1973 and 1974 (Maidment, 1976; Eekelaar and Clive, 1977). However, a closer examination of the studies showed that, in fact, the vast majority of cases were uncontested since fathers, apparently happy to relinquish child care responsibilities, had agreed to the mothers having sole custody. In endorsing sole custody arrangements, the courts were simply maintaining the status quo. Only six per cent of cases in both studies were contested and, in deciding these, the courts again tended to confirm the status quo, awarding custody to whoever the child was living with at the time. In only two cases, both reported in Eekelaar, did the courts overturn the status quo in transferring custody from the father to the mother - showing the complaints made by FNF to be unfounded (Maidment, 1981). Despite the lack of empirical evidence, the claims of FNF fell on fertile ground. This coincided with the publication of psychological studies which emphasised the importance of fathers to young children and the need to maintain paternal 'bonds' after divorce (Maidment, 1981).

Prior to the 1989 Children Act, the courts in divorce proceedings frequently distinguished between legal custody and the day-to-day care and control of children. Although the meaning of legal custody had been vague, it had frequently been interpreted as the right to continue to make major decisions about a child's life including where she/he goes to school. FNF's campaigning aims (see Harne, 1984; O'Hara, 1991) were for joint custody orders to become the norm, with fathers having ongoing contact with children *whatever the circumstances*. They also aimed to equalise the position of the unmarried father to that of the unmarried mother who had gained sole guardianship rights in respect of her children. FNF saw joint custody orders as a means of maintaining paternal authority and increasing fathers' rights to access, which they felt were undermined by sole custody orders to the mother (Harne, 1984).

FNF argued that fathers should always have contact with their children, despite any history of violence or sexual abuse. In fact, in their evidence to the 1974-75 Select Committee on Violence in Marriage (Harne, 1984), they drew on the threat of violence to support their case, arguing that fathers who are excluded from access may resort to 'assault, manslaughter and even murder'. Moreover, they asserted that the real problem is *women's* violence: 'we believe it fair to see much of the physical violence . . . as a final response to violence inflicted in other forms, especially by women - verbal violence'.

In 1992, they went much further than this in their evidence submitted to the Home Affairs Committee, claiming:

> The prevalence of female-instigated violence .... It has only been through my regular voluntary work with Families Need Fathers over the past four years that I have come to understand the possible extent of this problem. As an erstwhile victim of my estranged-wife's violence I have discovered that many men feel free to discuss their own experiences with me (p.53).

> A most sinister factor in the perverse-dynamic [*sic*] often arises when there are young children of the family. .... Where there is a loving and spontaneous father/child relationship in the family the violent-wife [*sic*] frequently becomes jealous of the relationship in a way that further fuels her violence (p.54) (Bruce Liddington, FNF, in Home Affairs Committee, 1993b).

In 1982, FNF outlined its own model of access arrangements for violent fathers which included the following provisions: for an infant under three, access should take place in a separate room in the mother's home several times a week and, for an older child, should comprise weekly staying access plus regular additional visits (Families Need Fathers, 1982). By 1993, FNF were still using the same arguments, but with a slight change in language - occasionally replacing the word 'father' with 'parent':

> We want equality for fathers, however unworthy the natural parent is, he is best and should be involved as much as possible . . . otherwise children will grow up unable to form stable relationships. The absence of a male role model leads to crime (*Guardian* 20 September 1993)

FNF are now beginning to avail themselves of the plethora of newly constructed psychological syndromes imported from American fathers' rights movements to support their arguments in access and custody battles. These include the 'Parental Alienation Syndrome' which alleges that mothers inflict a form of emotional abuse on children by alienating them from their fathers. FNF believe that legal recognition of the Syndrome could be instrumental in stopping mothers getting legal aid to prevent paternal contact (*Guardian* 20 September 1993). It is not inconceivable that they may also take up another syndrome currently being used by US fathers' rights movements to combat allegations of child sexual abuse in custody: the False Memory Syndrome has been used to suggest that false memories of sexual abuse have been implanted by mothers to win custody (Kelly, 1989).

The syndrome phenomenon not only attributes women with a pathological selfishness and malicious intent towards fathers, but also shifts child welfare discourses further into the province of experts in psychotherapy. As such, they are unchallengeable except by other experts of the psyche. The material realities of child sex abuse and domestic violence thus disappear. These realities are also hidden by the focus on women's violence. In their continuing focus on female pathology and violence, FNF have presumably been attempting to shift the prevailing discourse: representing both domestic violence and child sex abuse as genderless symptoms of family dysfunction (or, indeed, as fantasies of vindictive women), rather than as criminal expressions of male sexual violence against women and children as feminist research has consistently demonstrated (e.g. Dobash and Dobash, 1992; Hanmer and Maynard, l987; Kelly, 1988; Radford and Russell, l992). Whilst so far they have not been entirely successful (e.g. Home Affairs Committee l993a), their exaggerated concern to portray *women* as violent has been echoed in recent media portrayals of violent women (see e.g. 'Unspeakable Acts', Open Space, BBC2, 26 April 1993; 'Motherlove', BBC2, 29 May 94).

We do not deny that women can be violent, but we would argue that recent media emphasis on women as violent is part of a wider anti-feminist politique aimed at shifting attention away from the fact that the overwhelming incidence of domestic violence and child sexual abuse is carried out by men (see Driver and Droisen, 1989; Kelly, et al., 1991; chapter by Mullender and Morley, this volume). Attempts to claim an equivalence between the use of violence by men and by women overlooks the facts: many, if not most, 'violent' women are acting defensively to protect themselves and their children; and, for the most part, reactive violence from women to men is neither as harmful or threatening to men as is men's violence against women and children (e.g. Wilson and Daly, 1992). It is interesting to note that although several men's refuges have opened recently, each claiming to be the first, they have either closed again quickly for lack of custom or have become hostels for violent men.

Whilst FNF have been discredited to a certain extent by recent allegations that they have been encouraging divorced and separated men to abduct their children (Guardian 17 October 93), their influence has been far more extensive than their actual numbers. Their key demands have been heard and acted upon within legislation (see below), in judicial decision-making, and within the child welfare profession (see e.g. chapter by Hester et al., this volume) .

THE WELFARE OF CHILDREN

Although FNF have been preoccupied by narrow issues of fathers' legal rights, their concerns have converged with and influenced new perspectives on 'the welfare of the child'. These were also influenced by liberal lawyers and by psych-discourses which maintained that parental conflict is aggravated by adversarial divorce hearings and is consequently damaging to children (Maidment, l981; Wallerstein and Kelly, l980). These arguments were, in turn, reinforced by popular representations of 'new man as new father' - present at the child's birth, comfortable with nappies and bathing babies - as well as by psychological and psycho-analytic studies emphasising father-child bonding and a consequent need for children's continuing contact with fathers after divorce (Richards, 1982), both of which ignored the material reality that to the present the vast majority of fathers take little day to day responsibility for the actual care of children (see chapter by Hooper, this volume, for a discussion of these issues).

As Smart (1989) has pointed out, the meaning of the 'best interests of the child' has moved into the remit of the professional welfare agencies. The tender years doctrine is now less available for women to use in disputes over custody or residence of a child. As we have shown, the concept of the 'best interests' or 'welfare' of the child is not neutral, but is informed and re-defined by dominant social structures, power relationships, and discourses. The new discourses have accorded increasing power and influence in decisions around residence or contact to professional welfare experts. Experts in child care have come to interpret the 'best interests of the child' as meaning ongoing contact with fathers irrespective of their relationship to the child or involvement in child care, and despite evidence of violence, whether directed against the child or mother. Rarely does the court recognise the ways in which contact orders may be used to continue harassment of the mother (see chapter by Hester et al., this volume).

Even where the evidence is overwhelming that children themselves have experienced physical violence or sexual abuse, it is argued that it still better for children to have contact with fathers, albeit supervised. The establishment of 'contact' centres fits comfortably with this argument: the violent or abusive father is not safe to be left alone with the child but, in order for his rights to be exercised, contact must continue in a room for one or two hours each week overseen by a social worker. We question what possible benefit these 'prison visits', as we have heard them described, can be to the child concerned[2] (see chapter by Hester et al., this volume, for an alternative view of contact centres, but not of contact dangers).

From our work with women escaping violent relationships, we have learned how accepted is the ideology of continuing paternal contact at any cost. For example, women have told us they fear that if they express any reservations about continuing contact with fathers to court welfare officers they will be regarded as malicious or totally unreasonable. To express concerns for the safety of their children is now regarded as a heresy against 'father right'.

THE INFLUENCE OF THE NEW RIGHT

Paralleling the growth of FNF in the 1970s was a more macro political shift to right-wing authoritarian politics which came into its own in the mid and late eighties. The New Right's two apparently contradictory elements - traditional conservative paternalist moralism and non-interventionist economic liberalism - were both reflected in its family policy, which consequently converged with many of FNF's aims. It had economic and moral concerns about the rising divorce rate and the increase of woman-headed households. Economically, New Right monetarists were concerned with the cost to the state of legal aid, welfare benefits, and public services which were attributed to the breakdown of the heterosexual family. Morally, the New Right had focused on the demise and dilution of the traditional nuclear father-headed family which it saw as being responsible for rising crime and social disintegration.

There was a connection between the two strands at the political level, however, as it was assumed that the availability of welfare benefits to single women with children reinforced the demise of the traditional father-headed family. Thus, New Right fundamentalism identified the family as a cornerstone of the nation: playing a crucial role in maintaining social order, disciplining men and women in both economic and sexual terms, and socialising children into moral values.

This model of the family underpinning New Right philosophy is narrow and limited, drawing on white patriarchal middle-class christian ideals from a mythical vision of the golden days of Victorian England. It is a patriarchal model in which males dominate females who are treated like children. Men are controlled by familial breadwinning responsibilities, women by men, and children by two parents - socialised by full-time mothers acting under male authority and control. It is also racist. Both the extended families of Asian communities and woman-headed households in African-Caribbean communities are represented as deviant.

This is the context in which single mothers - including lesbian mothers - have been targeted and blamed for moral decline, rising crime, and social unrest. Once targeted, single mothers have been classified and subjected to particular forms of surveillance and control, both through reinstating father right and in social policy. The ideological influence of the New Right can be seen in legislative attempts to reconstruct individual male control of women within the family and to socially engineer 'responsible fatherhood', both within the Children Act and the later Child Support Act.

THE CHILD SUPPORT ACT 1991

We look first at the Child Support Act[3] which is ostensibly more limited in scope than the Children Act in being primarily concerned with the collection of maintenance payments from absent parents following divorce or separation. Its two main aims are to reduce the state's social security bill and to reinstate women's financial dependence on individual men instead of the state. Accessibility to state benefits for single mothers has meant that some women have been able to gain a relative autonomy (albeit on a very low income) from male control within the family. The number of lone parent families - the vast majority of whom are headed by women - claiming income support had increased from 330,000 in 1980 to 770,000 in 1989; the proportion of those receiving any maintenance from fathers had decreased from 50 per cent in 1981-2 to 23 per cent in 1988-89, often as a result of 'clean-break' settlements where mothers would get the house in exchange for fathers not having to pay any further maintenance (Hoggett, 1993).

The Child Support Act is ostensibly about promoting 'responsible fatherhood'. It requires 'absent parents' - who are defined as the natural or adoptive parents of the child who do not live in the same household as the child (and who are overwhelmingly fathers) - to pay child support to the 'person with care'. Absent fathers include men who have never lived with their biological children because, for example, the child was conceived through a casual sexual encounter or self insemination[4]. Assessments of how much the absent parent must pay are made by the newly created Child Support Agency.

Whilst applications for assessment are voluntary for those not on benefit, women who are claiming income support, family credit, or disability working allowance are required to cooperate with the Agency in giving information about the absent biological father so that he can be traced and an assessment made for child support. Where this assessment is the same or above the level of income support, the mother not only loses this benefit but also others - such as free school meals, free prescriptions, and dental treatment - which accompany it. Mothers who refuse to cooperate in giving information to the agency are penalised with a reduction in benefit by 20 per cent for the first six months and 10 per cent for the following year (Child Support Regulations 1992, no.36). They also lose their own rights to claim income support for themselves, as child support includes an element for the support of the person with care, effectively making them appendages of their children.

Thus the Act specifically targets woman-headed households who are amongst the worst off and most likely to be claiming income support. Moreover, it has racist implications since 51 per cent of African-Caribbean families and increasing numbers of Asian families are headed by lone mothers, a large proportion of whom are in receipt of welfare benefits (Campaign Against the Child Support Act, 1993). It also forces single heterosexual women and lesbians who have chosen to have children without fathers into financial dependence on men who have had no social relationship whatsoever with themselves or their children.

The Act operates retrospectively so that clean break settlements or previous legal agreements the mother may have made about not claiming maintenance are not recognised as reasonable grounds for failure to cooperate with the Child Support Agency in pursuance of a child support claim. The Act enables the Agency to take draconian measures to trace and extract payments from absent fathers: it may deduct earnings and, where biological paternity is disputed, can apply to a court for a declaration of parentage and the court can then order DNA testing to establish paternity.

Given such measures, the Act is unlikely to reduce any hostility the absent father may feel towards the mother or ex-partner. Indeed, fathers may renew demands for increased contact - or demand contact where they had none before - as compensation or revenge for having to pay child support (see chapter by Debbonaire, this volume). Moreover, an insidious clause reduces the amount of child support the father has to pay if he has staying contact of two or more nights per week - this may be an incentive to make demands for increased contact. All this has obvious implications for women subject to domestic violence.

Unlike the Children Act (see below), the Child Support Act *does* recognise fear of domestic and sexual violence as reasons for not giving the Agency information about the father. (The guidelines also recognise rape and the sexual abuse of children as reasonable grounds for not cooperating.) It states that the requirement to cooperate will be waived if:

... there are reasonable grounds for believing that there would be a risk of the parent with care, or any child living with her, suffering harm or undue distress as a result of authorising the Secretary of State to take action (Section 6(2) Child Support Act 1991).

However, in order to establish that there is a risk of harm, the mother is usually required to attend for an interview and convince a child support officer that her fears are reasonable. Although the guidelines state that the mother has 'the right to believed, unless what she says is inherently contradictory or implausible' and 'a fear of violence may be reasonable even where there is no history of it' (Internal Policy Guidelines to Child Support Agency Staff) accounts of women undergoing such interviews vary. Women are inevitably dependent on the subjective judgement of individual child support officers as to whether or not they are believed. Further, women who fear domestic and/or sexual violence may not be fully conversant with their rights about giving information to the Agency. They may, for example, feel under pressure to reveal information for fear they may not be believed and lose their benefit as a result. Moreover, the guidelines to the Act state that fear of renewed demands for contact is *not* grounds for non-cooperation with the Agency (Internal Policy Guidelines to Child Support Agency Staff), despite its direct relevance to violence.

As the Act has only been operational since April 1993, it is too early to assess in detail how women who fear violence or abuse are being treated by the Agency, whether women and/or children are experiencing an increased level of violence or abuse as a result of child support claims, and the degree to which absent fathers are increasing demands for contact (but see chapter by Debbonaire, this volume). However, it is interesting to note that the Government has been prepared to listen to the vocal protests from absent fathers - as orchestrated by FNF and new fathers' campaigning groups like DAD (Dads After Divorce) - about the high levels of maintenance payments. Such protests have already produced some changes to the formula to reduce the amount of maintenance fathers with second families have to pay. Further changes are predicted in the near future.

THE EMERGENCE OF THE CHILDREN ACT 1989

In apparent contrast with New Right ideology embodied in the Child Support Act, the Children Act is phrased within a liberal, child-centred discourse both in prioritising the welfare of the child and in recognising that, depending on their ages and understanding, children's wishes should be taken into account in decision making regarding their lives. Indeed, since the 1950s, the wishes of older children have been paid more attention in disputes over custody and contact. Moreover, the rights of children - perceived as independent from the rights of mothers and fathers - were foregrounded in the Gillick case in the House of Lords in 1986. This case recognised:

> . . . the older child's capacity for decision-making in the medical context where she possesses sufficient maturity and understanding.
> It was also held that a child's decision was capable of superseding any parental right or power over upbringing (Bainham, 1990).

However, the Children Act does not prioritise children's wishes over what the courts or welfare agencies define as the best interests of the child. Further, the liberal notion of children's rights suggests that these can exist outside a context of socially structured unequal gender relationships. For example, what does it mean for a child to say she wants to live or have contact with her father when this wish, in an intensely consumer society, may be influenced by what the father can purchase for the child? It further assumes that children are never subject to pressure, and rarely questions how best their wishes may be determined. The practice by court welfare officers of asking children in front of their parents about their own wishes with regards to residence and contact is not, in our view, conducive to genuinely trying to ascertain children's views and feelings, since the expression of these views in such a context can be influenced by feelings of fear or loyalty.

However, an innovation of the Act was to introduce a checklist to help the courts to interpret the welfare of the children principle as the 'paramount consideration' in making orders. The checklist tends to embody previous legal presumptions: for example, the status quo factor. Apart from emphasising the importance of the wishes of the child, by putting them at the top of the checklist, interpretation of the other items is still vague and wide open to individual judicial decisions. The checklist could have provided an opportunity for the specific recognition of domestic violence and/or child abuse as factors which would rule out a father's suitability for contact or residence and would put the mother's and child's safety at risk. But it failed to do so. On the contrary, since the Act came into force, judicial and welfare officers' decisions appear to interpret the 'physical, emotional and educational needs of the child' (one of the items in the checklist) as requiring ongoing contact with the father whatever he has done. This is in contrast to the later Child Support Act which recognises that pursuing some fathers for child support might cause 'harm' to the parent with care of a child (see above).

Another liberal premise that has accompanied the emergence of the Children Act is that conflict between mothers and fathers is aggravated by legal representatives and adversarial court hearings; thus it is assumed that replacing legal formalities by conciliation will reduce conflict and socially engineer responsible parenthood. This shift in processes has coincided with, and facilitated, liberal ideas on fathers' continuing contact. In fact, pressure from some lawyers and the court welfare service mounted throughout the eighties for conciliation to become the main way for parents to resolve disputes over children. This was greatly influenced by Wallerstein and Kelly's psychoanalytic study on children of divorced parents in the US which maintained that lack of hostility between parents was important to children's emotional adjustment after divorce (Brophy, 1989; see also chapter by Hooper, this volume).

In the 1990s, it is expected that parents will enter into joint conciliation meetings as a prelude to, or instead of, a court hearing. New proposals for divorce law reform may make such meetings compulsory with the penalty of withholding legal aid for those who refuse (Lord Chancellor's Department, 1993). It is not surprising, therefore, that many women - particularly women who have been subjected to domestic violence - feel pressured into attending and pressured within conciliation meetings. If they refuse to attend such meetings, they fear that they will be regarded as selfish and unable to put their children's interests first (see chapter by Hester et al., for further discussion of these issues). Failure to recognise the operation of gendered power relations in conciliation meetings has led to their being seen by many women as coercive. Moreover, the Women's Aid Federation, England evidence to the Home Affairs Committee inquiry into domestic violence records that many women are subjected to further violence and abuse before, during, and after conciliation meetings (Barron et al., 1992, para.9.11-9.12). In the light of research pointing to the prevalence of domestic violence and the fact that it is a contributory factor in a large number of marriage breakdowns (see chapter by Hester et al., this volume), this apparent lack of awareness by welfare professionals and policy makers is hard to explain.

Another key feature of the Act is its emphasis on joint parental responsibility after divorce. The constellation of ideologies from New Right fundamentalism, christianity, psych-discourses, welfarism, and fathers' rights lobbies was active in the campaign for reinstating fatherhood through joint custody orders. The campaign culminated in the Booth Committee report (Booth, 1985) which recommended that joint custody should be the normal order of the courts. However, by the mid 1980s, lawyers like Maidment (1984) had moved away from the concept of joint legal custody advocating instead 'parental responsibility' as a new legal concept. The shift of language from 'parental rights' to 'parental responsibility' was meant to convey a symbolic message about the continuity of fathers' responsibilities after divorce, and about the primacy of the needs of children. It was also argued that conflict would be reduced by giving fathers the same legal power and status as they had within marriage, since this would reduce their hostility towards mothers (Brophy, 1989). New Right ideologies concerning the necessity of continuing paternal responsibility to prevent juvenile crime were no doubt also responsible for a shift in emphasis. The concept of 'parental responsibility' evolved through a long series of Reports and Working Papers from the Law Society. It was defined in 1988 (Law Commission, 1988) and was finally adopted in the Children Act in 1989.

Parental responsibility and joint custody mean much the same thing to women as the usual primary carers of children. However, the concept of parental responsibility differs from the concept of joint custody in one crucial aspect: joint custody - in theory at least - conveyed the notion of consultation between parents on major decisions affecting the children. Parental responsibility, on the other hand, allows each parent to act independently of the other when the child is with him or her - for example, on a contact visit. Parental responsibility, and therefore decision-making rights, go with the physical location of the child, enabling a father to make decisions about children when they are with him which may be in opposition to the mother's wishes. The Act does allow one parent to prevent another from doing something through applying for a 'prohibited steps' order; however, this presupposes that the applicant will know what the other parent is going to do before the event. The Act also permits parents to apply for a 'specific issues' order to determine a particular issue such as the child's education if they cannot agree.

Another major principle of the Act is that courts should *not* make orders about children unless they are satisfied that the order would positively contribute to the child's welfare. This is in line with the continuing parental responsibility concept as well as with the optimistic assumption that parents should be able to work out arrangements about the children without the interference of the courts.

In recommending the legal concept of continuing parental responsibility for fathers and the allied concept of ongoing paternal contact, which as we have seen were both adopted in the Children Act, it cannot be argued that the Law Commission was unaware of the issue of domestic violence or the problems it causes for the safety of mothers and children on separation and divorce. Evidence presented to the Law

Commission by Rights of Women (Brophy, 1987) pointed out that both joint custody and access orders were used by violent fathers as a means to continue to intimidate and abuse the mother. Specifically, this evidence pointed out that the problem was compounded for some groups of women from Asian communities (see chapter by Imam, this volume) whose safety and very lives were threatened by opposition to divorce within these communities. In addition, both the Law Commission and welfare agencies chose to ignore the evidence that 'for children to witness the physical and emotional abuse of their mother is itself a form of child abuse' (Brophy 1989, see also chapters by Morley and Mullender, Kelly, this volume).

CONCLUSION

One very obvious conclusion which can be drawn with respect to the new legislation is that the state was concerned to redress the balance following the presumed freedoms won by women by the early 1970s, and to re-establish patriarchal control over women and children. This concern has taken priority over women and children's safety.

Currently, the Children Act is widely regarded as an abuser's charter, and this situation urgently needs to be rectified if the concept of 'the best interests of the child' is to continue to be meaningful. In particular, the fitness of fathers as carers of children needs to be addressed. Rather than taking it as axiomatic that fathers are good for children, policy makers and practitioners need to address material realities and ask such crucial questions as what are fathers for, and what are their actual roles as carers of children? (see Woodcraft, 1993; chapter by Hooper, this volume).

Many of the substantive issues raised in this chapter are explored in further detail in following chapters in this section. We would however like to conclude our chapter with some specific recommendations:

1. The principle that women and children have the right to live free from the threat and reality of violence and abuse must be recognised in law and written into the Children Act. This could be issued in government good practice guidelines instructing courts to be mindful of women's safety in making orders for children in their care *and* written into the welfare checklist[5].
2. The checklist should specify that domestic violence and child abuse are factors which would rule out a father's suitability for contact or residence[6].
3. Training on domestic violence awareness and its implications for women and children's safety should be made compulsory for all magistrates, judges, and court welfare officers working in family courts. Solicitors and barristers working in the area of family law could also benefit from such training.
4. More recognition and material support should be given to the child

protection and child support work developing in refuges, and to their role in providing safety for women and children. The practice of granting residence orders to fathers when women have fled with their children to refuges (Barron et al., 1992, para.9.10; see chapter by Debbonaire, this volume) should be stopped.

5. Contact centres and supervised contact should be abolished, since contact with violent and abusive fathers is unnecessary and not in the child's best interests. (Such a measure could however only be effected if the judiciary and legislators recognised domestic and sexual violence as rendering a father unfit for contact. Thus this recommendation would need to be accompanied by our other recommendations.)

Notes

1. In 1994, lesbian mothers' partners were recognised and accorded parental responsibility under the Children Act.
2. Whilst acknowledging that contact centres have been set up in order to provide paternal contact that protects the safety of women and children, we question whether paternal contact is necessary at all or is in the child's best interests in such circumstances. The father, by his own behaviour, has rendered himself unfit to have contact with a child. Present arrangements merely retain a child's contact with a man who is recognised as posing a threat to his or her safety or well-being. If due regard is given to the evidence of harm to children resulting from violence directed at their mothers (see chapters by Morley and Mullender, Kelly this volume), such visits must be recognised as controlling and possibly facilitating, rather than ending, the harm.
3. At the time of writing, the whole of the Child Support Act is under review by a House of Commons Select Committee which is expected to report in October or November 1994.
4. The only exemptions are where the biological father lives abroad or where the child was conceived through anonymous donor insemination via a licensed clinic. The Child Support Agency has already stated that men who have donated sperm for self-insemination will be pursued for maintenance, even where the mother has made an agreement that she will never claim maintenance from him (*Pink Paper*, 8 July 1994).
5. Section 1(3)(e) - 'any harm which he (sic) has suffered or is at risk of suffering' - should be extended to include explicit recognition to domestic violence as causing harm or risk of harm to the child.
6. Section 1(3)(f) - 'how capable each of his (sic) parents . . . is of meeting his (sic) needs' - should include explicit reference to domestic violence as a factor that excludes fathers from being deemed fit to parent. Additional factors need to be introduced addressing protection for the mother as primary carer.

References

Bainham, J. (1990) *Children: The New Law. The Children Act 1989*. Bristol: Family Law Publications.

Barron, J., Harwin, N. and Singh, T. (1992) *Women's Aid Federation England Written Evidence to the House of Commons Home Affairs Committee Inquiry into Domestic Violence*. October, Bristol: Women's Aid Federation England. (Also published as Memorandum 22, submitted by Women's Aid Federation England, in Home Affairs Committee, 1993b, see below).

Booth, Hon. Mrs Justice (1985) *Report of the Matrimonial Causes Procedure Committee*. London: HMSO.

Bowlby, J. (1953) *Childcare and the Growth of Love*. Harmondsworth: Penguin.

Brophy, J. (1985) 'Child care and the growth of power: the status of mothers in custody disputes' in Brophy, J. and Smart, C. (eds.) *Women in Law: Explorations in Law, Family and Sexuality*. London: Routledge and Kegan Paul.

Brophy, J. (1987) 'Co-parenting and the limits of "law": divorce and parenthood in the 1990s'. Response to the Law Commission Working Paper No 96 from Rights of Women, unpublished.

Brophy, J. (1989) 'Custody law, childcare and inequality in Britain' in Smart, C. and Sevenhuijsen, S. (eds.) *Child Custody and the Politics of Gender*. London: Routledge.

Campaign Against the Child Support Act (1993) *Dossier of DSS Illegalities. Implications of the Child Support Act*. London: Kings Cross Women's Centre.

Chesler, P. (1987) *Mothers on Trial*. Seattle, Washington: Seal Press.

Cretney, S.M. (1979) *Principles of Family Law*. Third Edition. London: Sweet and Maxwell.

Dobash, R.E. and Dobash, R.P. (1992) *Women, Violence and Social Change*. London: Routledge.

Driver, E. and Droisen, A. (eds.) (1989) *Child Sexual Abuse: Feminist Perspectives*. Houndmills: Macmillan Education Ltd.

Eekelaar, J. and Clive E. (1977) *Custody after Divorce*. Oxford: Oxford Centre for Socio-legal Studies, Wolfson College.

Families Need Fathers (1982) 'Children and family breakdown: custody and access - a code of practice', unpublished pamphlet.

Hanmer, J. and Maynard, M. (eds.) (1987) *Women, Violence and Social Control*. London: Macmillan.

Harne, L. (1984) 'Lesbian custody and the new myth of the father', *Trouble and Strife*, 4, pp.12-15.

Hoggett, B. (1993) *Parents and Children*. Fourth Edition. London: Sweet and Maxwell.

Home Affairs Committee (1993a) *Domestic Violence*. Vol.I. Report together with the Proceedings of the Committee. London: HMSO.

Home Affairs Committee (1993b) *Domestic Violence, Vol.II*. Memoranda of Evidence, Minutes of Evidence and Appendices. London: HMSO.

Kelly, L. (1988) *Surviving Sexual Violence*. Cambridge: Polity Press.

Kelly, L. (1989) 'Bitter ironies: the professionalisation of child sexual abuse', *Trouble and Strife*, 16, pp.14-21.

Kelly, L., Regan, L. and Burton, S. (1991) *An Exploratory Study of the Prevalence of Sexual Abuse in a Sample of 1200 16 to 21 Year Olds*. Final Report to the ESRC. London: Child Abuse Studies Unit, University of North London.

Law Commission (1988) *Review of Child Law: Guardianship and Custody*. Law Com No 172. London: HMSO.

Lord Chancellor's Department (1993) *Looking to the Future: Summary of a Consultation Paper on Mediation and the Ground for Divorce*. Cm.2424, London: HMSO.

Maidment, S. (1976) 'A study in child custody', *Family Law*, 6, pp.195-200, 236-41.

Maidment, S. (1981) *Child Custody: What Chance for Fathers*. London: National Council for One Parent Families.

Maidment, S. (1984) 'Law and justice: the case for family law reform', *Family Law*, 12, pp.229-32.

O'Hara, M. (1991) 'Child sex abuse and the re-assertion of fathers' rights', *Trouble and Strife*, 20, pp.28-34.

Radford, J. and Russell, D.E.H. (eds.) (1992) *Femicide: The Politics of Woman Killing*. Buckingham: Open University Press.

Richards, M. (1982) 'Foreword' in Beauil, N. and McGuire, J. (eds.) *Fathers: Psychological Perspectives*. London: Junction Books.

Rights of Women (1984) *Lesbian Mothers on Trial*. London: Rights of Women.

Rights of Women Lesbian Custody Group (1986) *Lesbian Mothers' Legal Handbook*. London: The Women's Press.

Smart, C. (1989) 'Power and the politics of child custody' in Smart, C. and Sevenhuijensen, S. (eds) *Child Custody and the Politics of Gender*. London: Routledge.

Spender, D. (1983) *Women of Ideas (And What Men Have Done to Them)*. London: Ark.

Walby, S. (1986) *Patriarchy at Work: Patriarchal and Capitalist Relations in Employment*. Minneapolis, Minnesota: University of Minnesota Press.

Wallerstein, J. and Kelly, J.B. (1980) *Surviving the Breakup*, New York: Basic Books.

Wilson, M. and Daly, M. (1992) 'Till death us do part' in Radford, J. and Russell, D.E.H. (eds.) *Femicide: The Politics of Woman Killing*. Buckingham: Open University Press.

Woodcraft, L. (1992) 'Do families need fathers?' *Critical Eye*, BBC2, Dec.

Rights of Women has produced a practitioners' *Guide to the Children Act*. £2 from Rights of Women, 52 Featherstone Street, London EC1Y 8RT.

7

Do Families Need Fathers?
The Impact of Divorce
on Children

Carol-Ann Hooper

During the 1980s it became widely argued that, as a general rule, children whose parents divorce adjust best to the situation when they retain ongoing relationships with both parents. This view influenced the Children Act 1989 (see chapter by Harne and Radford, this volume) which aimed to ensure that 'parental responsibility' would continue to be exercised by both parents after divorce. The old terms custody and access were abolished in the belief that the common practice of according one parent - usually the mother - sole custody contributed to conflict between parents and to the frequent loss of contact between children and their non-resident parent - usually the father. Amongst other matters, parents are now expected, where possible, to reach their own agreements about which parent the children will live with and about how frequently and under what conditions the other parent will see them. If they are unable to do so, the courts may make orders for residence and/or contact. Women initiating divorce proceedings are now routinely advised by solicitors that the courts assume children are best served by contact with both parents after divorce. If they consult mediators or counsellors, they are likely to receive advice based on the same assumption (see chapter by Hester et al., this volume).

Where children have experienced physical or sexual violence from a parent, exceptions are commonly made to the rule of maintaining both parental relationships where possible (e.g. Coote et al., 1990). In these circumstances, it is often recognised that children's interests may require that contact with the abusing parent cease. The evidence on the effects of domestic violence on children (see chapters by Morley and Mullender, Kelly, this volume) may justify extending that exception to cases where the child's mother has experienced domestic violence. In this chapter, however, I want to raise some questions about the rule itself. The way divorcing families are perceived affects both women abused by male partners and their children via its impact on the climate of options for all women with children. Women do not always define themselves as abused or tell others easily of their experiences of domestic violence.

Hence, they will often receive advice from professionals (and others) not tailored to their specific circumstances. Such advice, if it is based on the assumption that children need ongoing contact with their fathers above all else, may significantly affect women's perceptions of their opportunities for independence from male partners. Their sense of what alternatives to their current situation are possible may, in turn, affect their ability to define that situation as unacceptable. Thus popular beliefs, as well as policy and practice based on them, may reinforce the gendered power relations which are at the root of domestic violence itself and of the difficulties women face in escaping it. The critical examination of such beliefs is therefore an important part of addressing the needs of children living with domestic violence.

THE CONTEXT: CHILDREN, FATHERS AND THE LAW

Over the past decade, children's needs after parental divorce have increasingly been equated with ongoing relationships with their fathers. This definition of children's interests reflects the overlapping influence of the fathers' rights movement, which has sought to re-assert fathers' claims to their children, and of the New Right, which has sought to re-establish the 'traditional family' and the dependence of women and children on men (Smart, 1989; see chapter by Harne and Radford, this volume). The concern to reinforce fatherhood influenced not only the Children Act 1989, but also the Child Support Act 1991 with its re-emphasis on parenthood for life, albeit in financial form only. Fears about fatherless children were further fuelled in 1993 when the Conservative government repeatedly attacked lone mothers - scapegoating them for problems of public expenditure and youth crime - and suggested a number of possible measures to deter lone parenthood. Late in 1993, proposals to change the legal framework for divorce were announced. These proclaimed the aims, first, of reducing the incidence of divorce by requiring a 'cooling-off period' and urging increased use of mediation and, second, of facilitating arrangements for ongoing parent-child relationships after divorce, again by urging use of mediation to resolve conflicts (Lord Chancellor's Department, 1993).

At the time of writing, the extent to which recent proposals will be adopted remains uncertain, given the unpopularity of the Child Support Act 1991 and the political sensitivity of the Government's misconceived slogan 'back to basics' with which changes to the framework of family law may now be associated. Nevertheless, there is no doubt that a theme running through Conservative policy has been an attempt to shore up the traditional patriarchal family, or at least to preserve its responsibilities after divorce. 'Children's needs' are a common flag waved in support of such proposals, but there is a mixture of concerns: humanitarian, resulting from the distress which both children and adults can experience at divorce; moral, relating to the New Right's commitment to marriage and the two parent family with male breadwinner/female carer as 'natural'; and economic, emanating from concern at the costs to social security of lone parents on benefit, and at the costs of legal aid for couples divorcing. There are also contradictory aims in policy: alongside the aim of preserving the traditional family has run some increased recognition of violence against women and children within families, and of the needs of the less powerful members of families for protection from the more powerful.

Arguments for joint custody in the 1980s, for the introduction of the concept of 'parental responsibility' in the Children Act 1989, and for future reform of the divorce law, have been underpinned by the belief that law and policy could influence behaviour. Changes have been supported by the belief that the legal framework could, if not necessarily reduce the incidence of divorce significantly, at least reduce its impact on children, enable couples to agree arrangements for effective co-parenting after divorce, and hence facilitate improved father-child relationships after divorce. Brophy (1989) has argued that such a belief in the power of law is questionable. In this chapter, I examine the research on the impact of divorce on children in order to consider, first, the nature of children's needs in the context of parental divorce today; and, second, the role of ongoing parental relationships in influencing children's well-being after divorce. In doing so, my aims are to suggest a broader perspective on children's needs than that which equates them either with less divorce or with ongoing relationships with non-resident fathers after divorce; to identify the contribution to their well-being of each parent-child relationship separately; and to consider the roles of non-resident fatherhood and lone motherhood (the most common combination) within their social, not simply their legal, contexts.

CHILDREN AND DIVORCE: WHAT ARE THE EFFECTS?

Research on the effects of divorce on children has shifted over the last two decades from an initial focus on demonstrating children's distress in the short term to a concern with long-term outcomes. There is now a body of research - from both the USA and the UK - which suggests that children whose parents divorce appear to be at somewhat increased risk of later disadvantage. This is indicated by such outcomes as: lower educational achievement and qualifications; lower occupational status and income as well as higher risk of unemployment; earlier transitions to adulthood linked with age of leaving school, of leaving home, of forming partnerships, and of having children; increased own risk of divorce; and worse scores on certain measures of adult health. The UK research is reviewed by Burghes (1994), and the US research by Amato and Keith (1991) and Furstenburg and Cherlin (1991). The findings indicate wide variability in outcomes, with the impact on children being affected by the child's sex and age at the time of the divorce, and also by family size, social class, household income, and mother's education and employment. Some studies suggest the consequences are worse for boys than girls, but this may be partly the result of boys and girls expressing distress in different ways, and/or may partly correlate with the finding that children appear to do somewhat better if living with the same-sex parent which girls are more likely to do. The finding that children do best with the same-sex parent, however, is fairly tentative owing to the small number of resident fathers, a group who are likely to be unrepresentative of all divorced fathers (Furstenburg and Cherlin, 1991).

There are some cautionary notes to make about these findings. As Burghes (1994) points out, a finding of worse *average* outcomes does not predetermine the outcome for any individual child. Many of the findings come from longitudinal studies of now adult children whose parents divorced a considerable time ago when divorce was a relatively rare event. These children may have suffered from stigma and the associated isolation from peers as much as from parental separation. The effects cannot be assumed to be the same in today's context. Amato and Keith (1991) found that the more recent and the more methodologically sophisticated the study, the smaller were the apparent effects of divorce. In addition, while the effects of divorce on children currently attract more political interest, other variables such as class, race and gender may influence outcomes equally or more. For example, Richards and Elliott (in Burghes, 1994, p.32) found that the likelihood of both daughters and sons of non-manual fathers who divorced achieving educational qualifications was much the same as that of sons with fathers in manual occupations whose parents stayed together (and thus greater than that of daughters with fathers in manual occupations whose parents stayed together). Greenberg and Wolfe (1982) found that the effect of father absence on later incomes was significantly greater for white boys than for Black boys - the effect being produced by economic deprivation - and greater where income was initially higher.

Although much of the research has methodological limitations, a number of factors are clearly indicated in understanding the negative impacts of divorce on children. First, it appears to be family disruption which is more significant long term than the loss or absence of a parent per se. Children whose parents divorce do worse than children who lose a parent through death. Outcomes appear to be worse for children who move from a two parent family through divorce to a lone parent family, then through re-partnering to a stepfamily, than for those who remain in a lone parent family after parental divorce. Children who are born in a lone parent family do not necessarily benefit from later living with both natural parents (Crellin et al., 1971). It appears to be the type of disruption - both divorce and re-partnering involving more complex emotional dynamics than death - and the number of transitions children experience which bring risks. Children clearly benefit from a stable and consistent environment.

Second, parental conflict appears to be equally, if not more, significant than parental separation in causing children distress. Longitudinal studies have found that much of the difference in behaviour and academic achievement found between children in disrupted families and children in intact families existed before the separation or divorce occurred (Cherlin et al., 1991; Elliott and Richards, 1991). It is therefore not at all clear that children would benefit from making divorce more difficult, unless conflict also reduced or was managed in a way less distressing to them.

Third, many of the negative effects are significantly reduced or disappear when other factors are controlled for. Lone parent households have significantly lower average household incomes than two parent households; and social class and income appear to account for some of the difference in outcomes between children whose parents have divorced and children in intact families, at least in relation to academic achievement (Burghes, 1994; Kelly, 1991). Ferri (1976), who used receipt of free school meals as an indicator of low income, found this to be the most influential factor in the lower reading scores achieved by children from disrupted families. Furthermore, in comparing all children receiving free school meals, she found that children from fatherless families obtained higher scores than children in two parent families. At present, the positive contribution of fathers to children's well-being is in part their contribution to income.

Fourth, some of the negative outcomes are clearly cumulative. For example, reduced educational attainment and low household income both contribute to leaving school early and thence to occupational disadvantage and lower income, to higher risk of unemployment for men, and to higher risk of early partnerships and childbearing for women. Early partnerships and childbearing contribute to increased risk of divorce. There is no inevitability about this chain - its logic could be interrupted if intervention were focused at an early stage. It is possible that low educational attainment is currently exacerbated by the negative images attached to children from disrupted families and consequent low expectations from teachers.

There is a growing recognition that divorce itself, while a point of crisis which presents particular challenges to children, is a single point in ongoing family processes and may or may not be the salient factor in individual outcomes. Burghes (1994) has noted that there may be variables not yet measured or thought of which explain the differences in outcome between children. In this context, it is worth noting the curious invisibility of violence in the literature on effects of divorce. While parental or family conflict has been measured and highlighted as significant, there has been little if any attention to the overlapping but analytically distinct issues of violence and abuse - either between adults or against children.

Thinking only of one form abuse may take - child sexual abuse - there are at least three reasons for more attention to be paid to the issue in the context of divorce. First, there are parallel literatures developing, one on the long-term effects of child sexual abuse and another on the long-term effects of divorce, which link some similar outcomes in adult women - in particular measures of emotional state which include symptoms of anxiety and depression - either to parental divorce in childhood (e.g. Maclean and Kuh, 1991) or to child sexual abuse (e.g. Finkelhor, 1986), apparently without considering the possible influence of the other variable.

Second, there is evidence from the literature on child sexual abuse to suggest that there may be an association between the incidence of the two events in childhood. This is not to suggest, as have some New Right pamphlets, that child sexual abuse is a problem derived from the breakdown of the traditional family and the increase in lone parenthood and stepfamilies (e.g. Whelan, 1994). On the contrary, Russell's (1984) US study showed that, historically, the incidence of child sexual abuse was lowest at a time when families were most broken and lone parenthood most common - when men were away at war. Moreover, the finding (Thoennes and Tjaden, 1990) that a slightly higher incidence of child sexual abuse has been reported in families involved in residence and contact disputes than in the general population is partly attributable to the fact that the discovery of sexual abuse often results in separation from the abuser and partly also to women's separation from abusive men enabling children to tell of past abuse. However, there are findings (Russell, 1984; Gordon, 1989) which suggest that children may be more vulnerable to sexual abuse in the context of separation or divorce, both from their fathers and from other men, and the connection needs further exploration.

Third, the invisibility of the issue of abuse in research on divorce contributes to the unsubstantiated belief that allegations of child sexual abuse in the context of residence and contact disputes are likely to be false - weapons in the post-marital conflict rather than genuine concerns (see Hooper, 1992, p.18; see chapter by Hester et al., this volume). There is a clear need for more attention to the issues of violence and abuse, both pre- and post-divorce.

Another relatively unexplored area in the literature on effects of divorce is the possibility that, at least in some circumstances, there may be positive outcomes for children. It is likely that there is a connection between violence pre-divorce and positive outcomes post-divorce, but the possibility of positive outcomes is also a broader issue. Some studies have found that children in lone mother households display more androgynous behaviour, suggesting that they may be less pressured to conform to stereotypical gender roles than children in two parent families. This is consistent with evidence that, as Johnson (1988) has put it, 'fathers "feminize" girls and "masculinize" boys more than mothers do' (p.184). Girls have also been found to adhere less rigidly to gender stereotypes and thus have higher aspirations in lesbian mother households (Green et al., 1986). In addition, children in lone mother households may be expected to assume - and see their resident parent assuming - a wider range of responsibilities than children in two parent households, and thus to broaden their skills and competencies and their definitions of gender-appropriate behaviour. There is also some evidence that adolescents in lone parent families may acquire greater maturity (Demo and Acock, 1988). More attention is now beginning to be paid to exploring what factors contribute to children overcoming the challenges that divorce presents, enabling them to achieve positive outcomes.

It would be surprising indeed if parental divorce had no impact on children, given the emotional vulnerability of children, and the social disruption involved in divorce which may entail a period of parental conflict and consequent diminished parenting, which in turn may include: reduced parental involvement in school work; significant changes in parent-child relationships; reduced income; moves of house and school; and loss of social networks. The research is narrower in focus than it could be, owing to the ideological prism through which it is mostly conceived: the traditional family tends to be idealised, and divorce to be seen as an unwanted intrusion into the ideal. Even as it is however, it indicates both the variability of impacts - many factors mediate the impact of childhood experience on later life - and the range of children's needs: for stability, protection from exposure to parental conflict, adequate household income, and positive educational experience.

PARENTAL RELATIONSHIPS AS MEDIATING FACTORS

A great deal of emphasis is commonly placed today on the maintenance of good relationships between children and both parents as a key factor in facilitating children's adjustment to parental divorce. While there is substantial evidence that continuing good parent-child relationships do contribute to better outcomes for children, this finding is often used as a basis for arguing that, as a general rule, children do best if they maintain contact with both parents, and that this holds true even when there is continuing conflict between the parents (Burgoyne et al., 1987). Further questions need to be addressed, however, in order to help clarify the implications for contact. First, how commonly, and under what conditions, does contact with a non-resident father involve a good relationship which is beneficial to the child? Second, how commonly are parents able to separate their own conflicts from their relationships with their children post-divorce, and do legal arrangements make a difference? Finally, what is the relative significance of each parent-child relationship to children's well-being? The UK research has had little to say about these matters, the argument for contact having been based mainly on early US research. While recognising that there may be differences between the UK and US contexts, I too am drawing here on US research - both the early studies and more recent research - to discuss these questions.

How commonly is contact with non-resident fathers beneficial? A key study commonly cited in arguments for maintaining children's contact with both parents is Wallerstein and Kelly's study of 60 families in

California who were interviewed at intervals over a ten year period after divorce (Wallerstein and Kelly, 1980; Wallerstein and Corbin, 1986). This study was based on a self-selected sample who volunteered to participate in exchange for counselling; thus it has been criticised for basing its conclusions on a sample of parents who had a higher incidence of psychological problems than is found in the divorcing population as a whole (Elliott et al., 1990). Equally important, and a countervailing influence on its findings, the intervention offered by the project is likely to have had some effect on outcomes. While caution is therefore necessary concerning the generalisability of its findings, the study is still illuminating in its analysis of family processes post-divorce.

Wallerstein and Kelly (1980) noted that relationships with both parents remained emotionally central for all the children, and that most longed for more contact with their non-resident parent. However, in influencing outcomes at five years after divorce, the quality and reliability of the relationship was more significant than the simple existence and frequency of contact. Irregular, erratic visiting had a negative impact on children, who were repeatedly disappointed by their fathers' abandonment, relative absence, infrequent or irregular appearance, or general unreliability; and they suffered feelings of rejection and lowered self-esteem in consequence. In contrast, good father-child relationships, characterised by continuous frequent contact, were linked to high self-esteem and the absence of depression in children. While over 90 per cent of fathers continued in contact with their children, even with the benefit of counselling only 30 per cent of children and fathers were considered at this point to have developed good relationships - that is, relationships which were emotionally sufficient to facilitate the growth and development of the children. Improvements in visiting sometimes resolved the negative effects, but in other circumstances the children resolved them themselves at adolescence by counter-rejecting the parent in favour of more worthwhile adults.

Further studies have since sought to establish the significance of contact with fathers for children's well-being. Overall, support for the hypothesis that the level of contact with non-resident fathers is positively associated with children's well-being is weak. Amato and Keith (1991) cite six studies which found that frequent contact was associated with positive outcomes (though not always for all outcomes), a further six studies which failed to find associations between frequency of contact and children's well-being, and three others which found that contact was associated with increased problems for children. While this mixed evidence suggests that more attention to the quality of relationship is needed, the evidence on this so far is no clearer. Furstenburg et al. (1987), whose study was based on a national representative sample of children, reported that they were unable to find a set of conditions in which the quality of the children's relationships with their non-resident fathers significantly affected the children's well-being.

It is perhaps not surprising that contact with non-resident fathers after divorce is not an unproblematic boon for children. The majority of fathers still play a relatively minor part in the day-to-day care of their children when married (Lewis and O'Brien, 1987). The visiting relationship after divorce is one which presents considerable challenges, including the negotiation of a new and ambiguous role and of relationships now removed from the day-to-day intimacy and structure of co-residence. Some fathers may formerly have relied on their wives to interpret the children's needs and have little experience of doing so themselves. They may start this new relationship with their children at a time when their own emotions about the divorce are still intense and their children are still distressed by it. Children of different ages and interests are frequently visited together, in circumstances arranged to suit the convenience of adults. Contact with children may be used as a weapon in the conflicts and struggles for control between parents. For both visiting parent and children, each visit brings a new parting at its end. Wallerstein and Kelly (1980) argued that fathers who managed to maintain or create good relationships with their children after divorce required maturity, an ability to adapt to the specific demands and constraints of the visiting role, an understanding of their children's needs as individuals, and an ability to give their children's needs priority over their own. Even where positive relationships are maintained with both parents, and both parents are satisfied with the arrangements, children can feel overburdened by the demands of dividing their time between two homes (Steinman, 1981).

Clearly there are benefits to some children of ongoing contact with their fathers (although it should also be noted that children who have ongoing contact may be those who have experienced less conflict before and during the divorce). But equally clearly there may be costs as well. One reason for this is that if continued contact with children involves continued contact between parents, then increased opportunities arise for parental conflict, which has been consistently found to affect children's well-being negatively whether it occurs before, during, or after divorce.

A study by Hess and Camara (1979) is often cited to demonstrate that parents can keep their own conflicts separate from their parenting. This study, which compared 16 divorced families and 16 intact families in terms of family processes as well as family structure, demonstrated the variability of post-divorce relationships by using three case studies, one of which involved a family in which there was considerable antagonism between the parents although both had close and positive relationships with their children. This case, in which conflict between the parents did not appear to interfere with their parenting, demonstrates that such an outcome is possible; but it tells us nothing of how likely it is to occur.

More recent research suggests that many parents do not manage to separate their own conflicts from their functions as parents. In a study of nearly 1,000 families, Maccoby et al. (1990) identified three major patterns of post-divorce parenting: a disengaged pattern, in which children spent time with both parents but the parents disengaged as completely as possible from each other, managing conflict by seldom talking to each other even about the children; a cooperative pattern, in which parents attempted to keep their personal conflicts separate from their roles as parents and were able to discuss plans for or problems with the children; and a conflicted pattern, in which there was little cooperation but parents were also unable to disengage from each other and their conflicts spilled over into their parenting. About one third of all couples fell into the conflicted group at a point in time around 18 months after separation. This was the most common pattern for parents whose level of hostility towards each other was high during the first six months after separation. This suggests that a sizeable minority of parents may not be able effectively to protect their children from exposure to their own conflicts. Furthermore, the level of conflict between parents may also affect the quality of parent-child relationships after divorce: Donnelly and Finkelhor (1992) found that parents who argued with each other also had significantly higher levels of disagreement with their children.

The belief that legal arrangements can facilitate better parent-child relationships, which in the USA contributed to increased use of joint custody, has received little support from research. Maccoby et al. (1990) found that type of custody arrangement had little influence on the amount of discord between parents around 18 months after divorce. Donnelly and Finkelhor (1992) found no significant relationship between custody arrangement and parent-child relationships, and concluded that the idea that a particular type of custody protected children by minimising conflict did not appear to hold. Furstenburg and Cherlin's (1991) review of relevant research argues that joint *legal* custody has modest effects at most and appears not substantially to increase fathers' decision-making authority, involvement in child-rearing, or amount of child support; and that joint *physical* custody is not necessarily better for children than the alternatives either, and may indeed be worse if conflict continues[1]. Where less parental conflict has been found in joint custody families, such an outcome may well be the result of self-selection (Luepnitz, 1986). It seems clear that legal arrangements may sometimes facilitate, but certainly do not ensure, good parent-child relationships.

In contrast to the mixed evidence on the significance of contact with the non-resident parent, there is little if any doubt that children's relationship with their resident parent is crucial in mediating the impact of divorce. Research has consistently found that the resident parent's well-being and effectiveness, and positive relationships between resident parents and their children, are amongst the most significant factors in mitigating negative outcomes for children (Furstenberg et al., 1987; Furstenberg and Cherlin, 1991; Thiriot and Buckner, 1991; Burghes, 1994).

One recent review of children's adjustment post-divorce concluded that 'the overriding issue for satisfactory post-divorce adjustment was the extent to which custodial parents felt able to take control of their decisions and life and feel good about themselves' (Thiriot and Buckner, 1991, p.43). Yet the context in which resident parents must work out their post-divorce relationships with their children is hardly conducive to maximising this outcome. The majority of resident parents are women and are also, at least initially, lone mothers. As such, some of the difficulties they confront are the various faces of oppression. Their burden of childcare responsibilities is, for most, greater than that of mothers with live-in partners or husbands. Their participation in the labour market is correspondingly lower (at least in the UK, although not always in other EC countries, with higher levels of public childcare provision; Cohen, 1990). It is also lower than that of lone fathers (Hardey and Crow, 1991). Lone mothers' low household incomes and heavy reliance on income support constrain their options, although at the same time some may have greater control over their income than they had during their marriages (Graham, 1987). Their pre-divorce responsibilities for children are often under-valued by courts, and hence by solicitors, in considering decisions and advice about children post-divorce (Brophy, 1989). They have recently been subjected to a barrage of negative images of lone motherhood from Government ministers and media alike. In addition, recent research on domestic violence has found that lone mothers were twice as likely as other women to have experienced violence from a partner or ex-partner within the last year (Mooney and Young, 1993).

The specific context of post-divorce lone parenthood poses further challenges. Custodial parents face the demands of responding to their children's distress and increased emotional needs, establishing and maintaining a daily routine in changed circumstances, and assuming a disciplinary role to which they are often unaccustomed at a time when their own emotional resources may be short, their social networks disrupted, and their income reduced. Many mothers find exercising discipline with their children particularly difficult in these circumstances. They are not helped by relationships with abusive partners which have undermined their confidence (Wallerstein and Kelly, 1980), nor by the context of a male dominated society in which women's relationship to authority is problematised in many contexts. Lone mothers may also internalise societal negative expectations of lone parenthood, resulting in self-blame for any difficulties their children experience - whether or not those difficulties are a response to family disruption - anxiety at future possible difficulties, and further loss of self-esteem.

In this context, we need to know more about what helps resident parents to function effectively, to maintain a sense of well-being themselves, and to meet their children's needs; and more about what undermines these capacities. While lone parents are a heterogeneous group who differ, amongst other dimensions, by age, race, sexual orientation, material circumstances, age and number of children, and route into lone parenthood, there are some findings of relevance. As well as level of household income, studies have found social networks (friends more than family), an independent source of income rather than benefits or child support, social status (Thiriot and Buckner, 1991), and paid employment (Popay and Jones, 1991) to be positively related to lone mothers' well-being. Social support appears to be particularly crucial (Gladow and Ray, 1986). Help with parenting was found by Friedemann and Andrews (1990) to contribute to positive outcomes, though only if the quality of relationships between the adults involved in rearing children was good. This suggests that the positive effect of father-child relationships, where found, may work at least in part via the effects of the father's involvement on the mother. Clearly, there may be benefits to mothers as well as to children from father-child contact - in a cooperative co-parenting situation, the mother may get a break from childcare, share the responsibility of decisions and so on, mitigating some of the stresses of lone parenthood. Hetherington et al. (1978) found that the effectiveness of the resident parent related to support from the other parent in matters of discipline. In contrast, a conflicted pattern of co-parenting has been found to be associated with reduced satisfaction with parenting (Maccoby et al., 1990), and fathers' visits can be a significant source of stress to custodial mothers (Wallerstein and Kelly, 1980). In relation to the issue of contact, more attention needs to be paid to the impact of the non-resident parent-child relationship on the resident parent-child relationship. If contact with fathers undermines the resident parent's ability to control her life, to exercise discipline, and to maintain a positive relationship with her children, the children may well be worse off for it.

CONCLUSIONS

Family relationships after divorce (as before divorce) are complex. Perhaps the most important conclusion to draw from existing research is that any simple rule or formula is likely to be inadequate to the variability of different family circumstances and to the balance of conflicting and interconnected needs within any one family. Thinking on the role of non-resident fathers has swung between extremes - from the arguments of Goldstein et al. (1973) against ongoing contact as damaging for children on the one hand, to the current preference for continuity of contact on the other. Both arguments may do a disservice to children and their families if turned into general rules for all.

There is no need for one pattern of post-divorce relationships to be set up as ideal or preferable for all families. We need to know more about the circumstances in which contact with fathers is beneficial to children and the circumstances in which it is harmful, and about the conditions necessary to enable resident and non-resident parents to be effective. In the meantime, those who advise divorcing parents would do well to be critical of the assumption that contact with fathers is necessarily beneficial for children. The evidence on this is mixed and inconclusive, in contrast to the much stronger evidence that the effectiveness of the resident parent and the protection of children from exposure to parental conflict are clearly related to better outcomes for children (Furstenburg and Cherlin, 1991). The presumption in favour of contact with fathers may place mothers under pressure to deny their own needs and preferences 'for the sake of the children', when standing by their own interests may ultimately benefit the children more. The assumption that the benefits of contact with fathers are an established truth may also result in the pathologising of women who are reluctant to accede to their ex-partners' requests as unconcerned with their children's interests, whereas they may often be better attuned to them than are professionals. Some fathers may also feel under pressure to continue contact which they would prefer to relinquish. There is a need for greater openness to the possibility that for some families stopping contact may bring benefits, while for others continuing contact may do likewise; and also for a greater awareness of the various combinations of individual costs and benefits within divorcing families.

Children's needs must be detached from their current conflation with ongoing relationships with their fathers; they must be addressed in their own right. At the moment, contact too often provides a means for children to meet their fathers' needs rather than vice versa. In addition to relationships with their parents, children have other needs - for supportive relationships with adults other than their parents, for good school experiences, and for awareness of their needs by all professionals who become involved in divorce. In relation to their parents, children need preparation for parental separation and involvement in decisions about contact (Cockett and Tripp, 1994). Parents, in turn, need advice on how to help their children - how to explain the situation to them and how to handle the new roles of lone and non-resident parents. These policy issues are too often avoided by a belief that the needs can be prevented by reducing the incidence of divorce. There is little evidence, however, that policies can significantly affect trends in family structure; and policy-makers must accept that divorce, as a fairly common occurrence, is here to stay.

If conflict between parents after divorce can be reduced, children may well benefit. Considerable faith is currently placed in mediation to achieve this, despite limited evidence yet on its effectiveness. This lack of evidence is due partly to the relatively recent introduction of mediation in the UK. However, the Government's aim for the proposed system to cost less than the current legal aid bill does not inspire confidence in the extent of services likely to be offered in the future; and, in this context, caution is in order. We need to know more about the degree to which the kinds of mediation services likely to be available are apt to reduce the types of conflict liable to be harmful to children, as well as for which families they may or may not be effective; and to pay attention in the process to the impact of mediation on fathers, mothers, and children separately.

In the meantime, the most urgent priority - if children's needs are a genuine concern - must surely be to provide a more positive context for lone motherhood. If lone mothers are to be enabled to be in control of their lives and to be effective parents, there is a need for a policy framework which facilitates easier access to paid employment, provides adequate income for those without it, and offers involvement in decision making -including decisions regarding contact - and protection from violence. Lone mothers may need to be encouraged by professionals to take their own needs seriously. On a broader level, a reappraisal of the positive potential of lone mother households is needed in order to give due recognition to the strengths and resourcefulness of lone mothers and their children.

Note

1. Joint legal custody refers to an arrangement in which both parents share responsibility for important decisions, but children live with one parent; joint physical custody to an arrangement in which children live for periods of time with each parent.

References

Amato, P.R. and Keith, B. (1991) 'Parental divorce and the well-being of children: a meta-analysis', *Psychological Bulletin*, 110(1), pp.26-46.

Brophy, J. (1989) 'Custody law, child care and inequality in Britain' in Smart, C. and Sevenhuijsen, S. (eds.) *Child Custody and the Politics of Gender*. London: Routledge.

Burghes, L. (1994) *Lone Parenthood and Family Disruption: the Outcomes for Children*. London: Family Policy Studies Centre.

Burgoyne, J., Ormrod, R. and Richards, M. (1987) *Divorce Matters*. Harmondsworth: Penguin.

Cherlin, A.J., Furstenberg, F.F., Chase-Lansdale, P.L., Kiernan, K., Robins, P.K., Morrison, D.R. and Teitler, J.O. (1991) 'Longitudinal studies of effects of divorce on children in Great Britain and the United States', *Science*, 252, pp.1386-1389.

Cockett, M. and Tripp, J. (1994) *Children Living in Re-ordered Families*. Social Policy Research Findings No. 45, York: Joseph Rowntree Foundation.

Cohen, B. (1990) *Caring for Children: the 1990 Report*. London: Family Policy Studies Centre.

Coote, A., Harman, H. and Hewitt, P. (1990) *The Family Way*. Social Policy Paper No.1, London: IPPR.

Crellin, E., Kellmer Pringle, M.L., and West, P. (1971) *Born Illegitimate: a Report by the National Children's Bureau*. London: National Foundation for Educational Research.

Demo, D.H. and Acock, A.C. (1988) 'The impact of divorce on children', *Journal of Marriage and the Family*, 50, pp.619-648.

Donnelly, D. and Finkelhor, D. (1992) 'Does equality in custody arrangement improve the parent-child relationship?', *Journal of Marriage and the Family*, 54, pp.837-845.

Elliott, J., Ochiltre, G., Richards, M., Sinclair, C. and Tasker, F. (1990), 'Divorce and children: a British challenge to the Wallerstein view', *Family Law*, August, pp.309-310.

Elliott, J. and Richards, M. (1991) 'Children and divorce: educational performance and behaviour before and after parental separation', *International Journal of Law and the Family*, 5, pp.258-276.

Ferri, E. (1976) *Growing Up in a One Parent Family*. Windsor: National Foundation for Educational Research.

Finkelhor, D. (1986) *A Sourcebook on Child Sexual Abuse*. London: Sage.

Friedemann, M.L. and Andrews, M. (1990) 'Family support and child adjustment in single-parent families', *Issues in Comprehensive Pediatric Nursing*, 13, pp.289-301.

Furstenburg, F. and Cherlin, A.J. (1991) *Divided Families: What Happens to Children When Parents Part*. Cambridge, MA: Harvard University Press.

Furstenberg, F., Morgan, S.P. and Allison, P.D. (1987) 'Paternal participation and children's well-being after marital dissolution', *American Sociological Review*, 52, pp.695-701.

Gladow, N.W. and Ray, M.P. (1986) 'The impact of informal support systems on the well-being of low income single parents', *Family Relations*, 35, pp.113-123.

Goldstein, J., Solnit, A.J. and Freud, A. (1973) *Beyond the Best Interests of the Child*. New York: Free Press.

Gordon, L. (1989) *Heroes of their Own Lives: the Politics and History of Family Violence*. London: Virago Press.

Graham, H. (1987) 'Being poor: perceptions of coping strategies of lone mothers' in Brannen, J. and Wilson, G. (eds.), *Give and Take in Families*. London: Allen and Unwin.

Green, R. , Mandel, J.B., Hotvedt, M.E., Gray, J. and Smith, L. (1986) 'Lesbian mothers and their children: a comparison with solo parent heterosexual mothers and their children', *Archives of Sexual Behaviour*, 15(2), pp.167-184.

Greenberg, D. and Wolfe, P.W. (1982) 'The economic consequences of experiencing parental marital disruption', *Children and Youth Services Review*, 4, pp.141-162.

Hardey, M. and Crow, G. (eds.) (1991) *Lone Parenthood: Coping with Constraints and Making Opportunities*. London: Harvester Wheatsheaf.

Hess, R.D. and Camara, K.A. (1979) 'Post-divorce family relationships as mediating factors in the consequences of divorce for children', *Journal of Social Issues*, 35(4), pp.79-96.

Hetherington, E., Cox, M. and Cox, R. (1978) 'The aftermath of divorce' in Stevens, J.H. and Matthews, M. (eds.) *Mother-Child, Father-Child Relations*. Washington DC: National Association for the Education of Young Children.

Hooper, C-A. (1992) *Mothers Surviving Child Sexual Abuse*. London: Routledge.

Johnson, M. (1988) *Strong Mothers, Weak Wives*. Berkeley, California: University of California Press, Berkeley.

Kelly, J.B. (1991) 'Children's post-divorce adjustment: effects of conflict, parent adjustment and custody arrangement', *Family Law*, February, pp.52-56.

Lewis, C. and O'Brien, M. (eds.) (1987) *Reassessing Fatherhood*. London: Sage.

Lord Chancellor's Department (1993) *Looking to the Future: Mediation and the Ground for Divorce*. London: HMSO.

Luepnitz, D.A. (1986) 'A comparison of maternal, paternal and joint custody: understanding the varieties of post-divorce family life', *Journal of Divorce*, 9(3), pp.1-12.

Maccoby, E.E., Depner, C.E. and Mnookin, R.H. (1990) 'Coparenting in the second year after divorce', *Journal of Marriage and the Family*, 52, pp.141-155.

Maclean, M. and Kuh, D. (1991) 'The long-term effects for girls of parental divorce', in Maclean, M. and Groves, D. (eds.) *Women's Issues in Social Policy*. London: Routledge.

Mooney, J. and Young, J. (1993) 'Criminal deception', *New Statesman and Society*, 17/31 December.

Popay, J. and Jones, G. (1991) 'Patterns of health and illness amongst lone parent families' in Hardey, M. and Crow, G. (eds.) *Lone Parenthood: Coping with Constraints and Making Opportunities*. London: Harvester Wheatsheaf.

Russell, D. (1984) *Sexual Exploitation*. London: Sage.

Smart, C. (1989), 'Power and the politics of custody' in Smart, C. and Sevenhuijsen, S. (eds.) *Child Custody and the Politics of Gender*. London: Routledge.

Steinman, S. (1981) 'The experience of children in joint custody arrangement: report of a study', *American Journal of Orthopsychiatry*, 51(3), pp.403-414.

Thiriot, T.L. and Buckner, E.T. (1991) 'Multiple predictors of satisfactory post-divorce adjustment of single custodial parents', *Journal of Divorce and Remarriage*, 17(1/2), pp.27-46.

Thoennes, N. and Tjaden, P.G. (1990) 'The extent, nature and validity of sexual abuse allegations in custody/visitation disputes', *Child Abuse and Neglect*, 14, pp.151-163.

Wallerstein, J.S. and Corbin, S.B. (1986) 'Father-child relationships after divorce: child support and educational opportunity', *Family Law Quarterly*, XX(2), Summer, pp.109-128.

Wallerstein, J.S. and Kelly, J.B. (1980) *Surviving the Breakup*. London: Grant McIntyre.

Whelan, R. (1994) *Broken Homes and Battered Children*. Oxford: Family Education Trust, Oxford.

8

Domestic Violence
and Child Contact

*Marianne Hester, Julie Humphries, Chris Pearson, Khalida Qaiser,
Lorraine Radford and Kandy-Sue Woodfield*

INTRODUCTION

This chapter draws on our current research[1] into the impact of domestic
violence on the negotiation of arrangements for children after the parents
separate or divorce. We are carrying out a comprehensive qualitative
study in Britain and Denmark. The cross-national study employs
ethnographic methods and includes interviews with women who have
experienced domestic violence, with some of their children, and with
professionals and advisors who are involved in the negotiation of
childcare arrangements post-separation. Two central concerns of the
research are the safety of women who have experienced violence from
male ex-partners and the welfare of their children.

Here we examine some of the findings from our research, contrasting
the experiences of women and their children with the views and practices
of professionals. The main focus is the British aspect of our work, but we
also incorporate discussion of some of the Danish findings with respect to
children's safety (see also Hester and Radford, 1992; Hester and Pearson,
1993).

We review the impact of the Children Act 1989 upon the safety and
welfare of women and children, arguing that there is a difference
between what the Act *says* regarding child welfare and what
professionals believe that the new legislation requires them to do (see
chapter by Harne and Radford, this volume, for a discussion of the
background to, and ideologies underpinning, the Children Act). We
argue that the statute has made things more difficult for women and
children leaving violent men. There was a fundamental flaw in the pre-
Act reviews of child care law in the failure to consider the effects of
domestic violence upon the lives of women and children. The private law
aspects of the Children Act, covering arrangements for children on
separation or divorce, do not make provisions for cases involving domestic
violence, despite the fact that a great many marriages that break down
do so partly as a result of domestic violence (Borkowski et al., 1983; Koch-
Nielsen 1984). The lack of debate about violence from men to their

female partners in relation to the Act has now been identified as a problem in reports recently produced by the Home Affairs Committee and the voluntary group, Victim Support (Home Affairs Committee, 1993a, 1993b; Victim Support, 1992).

In practice, we are finding overwhelmingly that women's safety, and the links between women's and children's safety, are not being addressed by professionals involved in the process of organising contact between children and the abusive parent after separation. There is a lack of recognition that domestic violence and child welfare are linked, not only in the sense that children suffer emotionally and psychologically from having lived in a violent situation, but also in that the whole process of contact-making is inherently more complex and fraught with danger. In our research, we have found that in domestic violence cases both the children's and mother's general welfare and safety can be seriously compromised by contact taking place.

Our findings so far give cause for concern about the direction of socio-legal policy in Britain as it relates to women who are abused. Despite the rhetoric about new eras and watersheds, we have found it hard to find many examples of good practice regarding children's welfare and women's safety in contact negotiations since the implementation of the Children Act. We are inclined to agree that, in domestic violence cases, the Act is being used for 'abuse preservation' (King and Piper, 1990) rather than for the promotion of children's welfare. Of particular concern amongst the matters discussed in this paper are:

1. the lack of regard for women's safety amongst professionals and legal personnel, and the effect of this upon the welfare of women and children;
2. the misguided belief of professionals and advisors that face-to-face visiting contact with an abusive father is *always* in the best interests of a child;
3. the difficulties which professionals and advisors have in considering the actual, rather than hypothetical, needs and views of a particular child.

Our experience from this research project has convinced us that domestic violence should always be taken into account when arrangements for contact are made. Professionals and advisors must take positive steps to identify cases where violence has been a major issue in the relationship breakdown so that they can confront, rather than evade, the effect of this upon the welfare of children and the safety of women. Debate will need to take place as to whether or not it is helpful for professionals to divide the experiences of women they work with into cases of 'real' violence and ongoing abuse and cases where violence and abuse are a dead issue. We have found that the outcome is a denial that violence occurred at all or, if acknowledged, it is argued that it 'didn't matter'. Better understanding amongst professionals of the impact of abuse upon women and children will perhaps come with wider use of multi-agency training. But, without resources to ensure the safety of women and the welfare of children, it would be foolhardy to see this as a panacea.

GENERAL TRENDS IN CHILD CONTACT SINCE THE CHILDREN ACT

Violent men are now more likely to apply for child contact

It has been argued that, prior to the Children Act, the law of custody and access suffered from 'maternal preference' (Hoggett and Pearl, 1991). Courts would routinely make orders for access and custody in divorce cases involving children. Women were invariably left with responsibility for the everyday care of children, with men most often finding themselves in the position of the 'absent parent' who applied for access (now contact). Parental conflicts were allegedly whipped up by an adversarial approach which was seen as inconsistent with the needs of children.

Since the Children Act, court orders for contact are no longer routine. Courts in England and Wales in 1992 granted 149,126 divorce petitions, yet there were only 16,424 Section 8 residence and 17,470 Section 8 contact orders made (*Judicial Statistics*, 1992). The small number of court orders gives the impression that the Act has been successful in curbing interventions by courts into 'private' family affairs.

Whether or not this has led to a reduction of conflict, however, is another matter. Professionals interviewed for our research reported a rise in *applications* for contact from violent men, most resulting either in informal arrangements or in a failure to carry the application through to court. An initial increase in applications was caused by absent fathers and grandparents attracted by the publicity which accompanied the legislation. The professionals believed that publicity surrounding the Children Act gave absent fathers the impression that they had automatic or increased 'rights' to their children - although the Act does not talk about such 'rights', but about 'parental responsibility'. Fathers are therefore claiming, and being encouraged to claim, these perceived 'rights'.

Ideologically, the Children Act emphasises the value of *both* parents to the well-being of the child. Thus, more attention has been given to *men* as parents and to preserving their parental 'roles' than was previously the case. Most of the cases discussed in our study involved women with daily responsibilities for the care and residence of children and men with intermittent responsibilities for children during periods of contact. It should be noted, however, that there are cases where women leave not only violent men but their children as well. If the violent partner has residence and responsibilities for the everyday care of the children, then the woman may be applying for child contact instead. Although this situation is less common, the safety issues are similar. In domestic violence cases, we need to ask whether fathers are actually wanting to hold residence or to pursue contact with their children in order to act out a parenting 'role'; or whether they are merely using the new emphasis on parental responsibility, residence, and contact as a means of renewing their violence towards, and control over, their ex-partner. We have come across many cases of the latter, as well as an optimism amongst professionals about the parenting skills, prospective care, and motives of violent men.

Contact is now paramount

One of the major shifts in practice which has arisen since the Children Act is a commitment to the idea that contact with the absent parent should take place at all costs (see chapter by Hooper, this volume, for a critique of this idea). Prior to the Act, concerns were expressed about the welfare of children when contact with fathers breaks down (Law Commission, 1986). Research conducted between 10 and 18 years ago suggests that, for between 25 to 40 per cent of the cases of divorce and separation involving children, contact with the non-resident parent breaks down after a period of 6 months (Eekelaar and Clive, 1977; Mitchell, 1985; Richards and Dyson, 1982). Within a couple of years of separation, only about half of all non-resident parents saw their children on a regular basis (Eekelaar and Clive, 1977).

Reasons put forward in this previous research for contact breaking down make no mention of domestic violence. A review of the literature by Burgoyne et al. (1988) proposes the following reasons:

1. some men believing it is in their children's interests to disappear;
2. fathers not caring about children;
3. the belief that not seeing the children will give fathers moral grounds on which to refuse to pay for child support;
4. mothers obstructing contact;
5. children moving out of the area;
6. resentment or jealousy from a new partner;
7. contact visits being too painful for the father;
8. contact visits with the father not supported by anyone.

In the Children Act, contact with parents is viewed as a right of the child and, in most cases, it is seen to be in a child's best interests to know both parents and maintain a relationship appropriate to their needs and specific circumstances. There is a 'welfare checklist' outlined in the Act which gives professionals and courts a guide for ascertaining how a child's best interests are served. It includes reference to the wishes and feelings of the child, the specific needs of the child, and the ability of parents to parent. We are finding, however, that in practice most court welfare officers and mediators are equating the *'best interests of the child'* with *contact* with the absent parent at all costs. A professional *myth* about the paramount importance of contact appears to be developing in which issues of safety may not be taken into consideration. The notion of continued parental responsibility, and the emphasis on contact for all cases, preserves a father's relationship and responsibility towards the children, regardless of his parenting skills and capacity to care. The unsympathetic treatment which courts give to 'disappearing mums' - women forced to walk out on their children when they leave their partner because of threats to their lives - is, in comparison, particularly harsh. Women in this position have subsequently lost contact and have been denied residence orders because of a court's desire to preserve the 'status quo'.

In agreement with previous research, the experience of women and children in our study is that contact which is arranged starts to break down immediately or within a period of months. However, for cases involving domestic violence, we question the assumption that a slump in contact visits to abusive fathers within six months automatically poses a problem for the welfare of children, especially if the needs of the children had not been the father's main concern in the first place. Some of the fathers in our study used contact to maintain ties with their ex-partners rather than with their children. Unable to get access to the mothers, they voluntarily pulled the curtain themselves on their child contact visits.

Rather than resisting contact with fathers, the women in our study encouraged it but became frustrated by the problems of organising it safely, especially when the sole responsibility for safe contact arrangements rests with mothers. Once started, contact is difficult to stop: termination only seemed likely when actual physical or psychological harm to the children could be proven. Risks to the safety and well-being of women are routinely ignored.

Contact promotes abuse

Problems for the children concerning contact can broadly be placed in two categories: for some children, the issue was one of dealing with the effects of not having contact with their fathers; for others, it was the converse problem of coping with contact which was established but was proving distressing. Children may still have positive feelings for their fathers, despite the violence they have witnessed and possibly experienced directly. However, our study has confirmed fears that children of women who experience domestic violence are at risk from abuse themselves during contact visits (Brophy, 1989; Johnson, 1992). Failure to address these risks, or to make provisions for safety, meant that contact had an adverse effect upon the welfare of a substantial proportion of the children. The risks to children included kidnap or abduction overseas; hostage taking; physical, sexual and mental abuse during a contact visit; neglect arising from inadequate parenting; and witnessing or being implicated in further violence and abuse of the mother.

Women in our study complained that professionals took no account of how contact meetings might be detrimental to the child's welfare. A mother's concerns about the father's parenting abilities or about his plans for abduction seemed to be particularly harshly dealt with by professionals. Any risk to the child had to be very clearly demonstrated:

> . . . the child has to be in obvious, definite danger then they'll, you know, they ask for things proved and double proved almost (Refuge worker).

But this need for 'proof' is very problematic in cases of emotional, sexual, and psychological abuse since there may not always be visible supporting evidence or, at least, none that can be linked firmly to the father's actions. Emotional abuse is particularly likely to be overlooked or minimised. Very few of the professionals appeared to consider the long term emotional and psychological problems associated with children who have lived through domestic violence. However, even where physical or sexual abuse of the children was proven, professionals showed a worrying tendency to encourage the father's contact and to dismiss concerns about the children's reluctance, thereby seemingly legitimising further abuse. For contact to work, a degree of risk-taking was viewed as inevitable and, in the long run, in the child's best interests:

> Even where the child has been abused by the father there's still the question of whether it's better for the child to have some sort of supervised contact with this man and keep this demon under control, or just to have this whole area of fear (Solicitor).

This comment came from a solicitor acting for a father recently released from a six year term of imprisonment for sexually abusing his step-children. Within a week of his release, the father had renewed supervised contact with the children.

Some other examples of supervised contact are:

1. A case where contact was arranged with a father recently released from prison for the manslaughter of the mother. The last time the children saw their father was when he axed their mother to death.
2. A case where contact was arranged with a father recently released from prison for the attempted murder of the mother. The father repeatedly stabbed the mother in the family court welfare offices. The children witnessed this.

It seems that a man can remain a 'good enough' father even after killing a child's mother. If contact does take place, 'facing the demon' can only be practical if there are facilities for the safe supervision of contact. These facilities are very limited, as we discuss later.

There is also the problem of children themselves becoming implicated in the continued abuse of their mothers, acting in proxy for the man denied access to his victim. Examples we have found include fathers getting children to convey messages of a threatening nature to their mothers, attempting to indoctrinate children against their mothers by lying, drawing children into the general belittling of their mothers, and suggesting that children play 'pranks' or steal from their mothers. This leaves children very confused and upset after a contact visit.

Maintaining women's confidentiality was particularly problematic once solicitors and the courts became involved in contact negotiations, since there were no guarantees that addresses could be omitted from court papers or that solicitors' locations could be kept secret. Of course, even if the woman's address can be kept from the man, the children may be used in contact visits as a means of extracting information about her whereabouts. This can be done quite subtly so that the children are not aware of what is happening. There are examples in our study of women being discovered through the child's contact with the father, which led to some women having constantly to move from refuge to refuge in order to stay safe.

Women's fear of discovery is constant; and men can and do use a variety of resources to track them down:

> . . . we've had men who will hunt down women, really they'll go to schools, they'll go to any expense to find them. So, obviously, it [discovery] still is a great fear (Refuge worker).

Some of the Asian women in our study even reported that their local community had employed a 'bounty hunter' to trace absent women.

Women's experiences and concerns are minimised

Our review of the practices of solicitors, court welfare officers, and mediators indicates that many professionals believe that women should be able to put the experience of violence behind them and that, because the relationship has ended, the violence has also ended. These views are contrary to almost all research in the area, which has found that violence often continues, and may escalate, after the partners have separated (e.g. Binney et al., 1988; Evason, 1982). Nonetheless, the professionals believe that the woman is using her children to avenge her ex-partner when she attempts to raise the issue of violence to herself and of its effects on her children.

Most of the mediators, court welfare officers, and solicitors we have encountered appear to base their practices on the belief that parties to a divorce or separation are prone to exaggeration and fabrication of the truth. Working 'objectively' involves keeping an 'open mind' to any allegations made, and remembering that there will be 'another side to the story'. Thus, women may not be believed when they are relating events that have happened. We have found considerable scepticism about women's concerns over the safety of their children, especially regarding child sexual abuse. If professionals feel that women are falsifying child sexual abuse claims, and fail to evaluate these claims beyond looking for 'the other side of the story', then there are worrying consequences for children where abuse has occurred. Children's welfare will be jeopardised because of the values, attitudes, and beliefs of the professionals involved.

In Britain, child centred work has been interpreted as encouraging parents to put aside their past disagreements and to look towards the future. We have found that many court welfare officers and mediators believe that the issue of contact-making can be divorced from the history of previous violence or ongoing threats; and that the children's welfare can be considered separately from issues regarding the mother's safety (see also Hester and Pearson, 1993). Thus, the practicalities of safe contact arrangements for children are ignored and the mother's concerns minimised. These professionals argue that, sooner or later, a woman will have to learn to confront her violent ex-partner and to overcome her fears. They even argue that, by confronting the violent man and 'overcoming' her fears, she will eventually become empowered. Implicit in these arguments is the belief that, to eradicate domestic violence, women need only 'stand up for themselves' and refuse to be victims. Attention conveniently shifts from men's violence back onto the characteristics of victims.

CONTACT IN PRACTICE

In this section we outline the process of arranging contact for children, the key problem areas for women, and the effect of these upon the welfare of the children involved. We argue that, on the whole, women enter into negotiations for child contact hoping to make arrangements which work. However, practical difficulties encountered in the negotiation stage, at 'handover', and during contact visits contribute to the breakdown of contact and have an adverse effect upon the children involved.

Many refuge workers we interviewed pointed out that the issue of 'timing' is important for women in relation to contact: women found contact more problematic initially, when they were still in a state of crisis and actively needed some time away from the abusive partner, making contact especially difficult at this time. For other women, the violence they had experienced was such that they could only feel safe by 'disappearing' completely and trying to build a new life elsewhere, which obviously ruled out the possibility of any contact for the children. Other women wanted their children to have no contact in order to protect them from further emotional or physical abuse.

However, the majority of women interviewed wished to maintain the children's contact with their fathers; indeed, we have found that women go to any lengths for contact to take place and for the children to be as unaffected as possible by their parents' relationship. The reasons women wanted there to be contact between the children and their fathers varied with the specific circumstances of the case. A reason most women gave was that they felt that they should put the children's interests before their own, since they thought the children would benefit from a continued relationship with the father and possibly also his family. In other words, they thought that denying contact could be detrimental to the children.

Thus refusing it could lead to feelings of guilt and anxiety for the women, who might also have to deal with their children's anger. A conflict of interests between mothers and older children posed particular problems for some. Older children are able to make their own informal arrangements and may have views which differ from their mother concerning threats to their own or their mother's safety.

There can be clear advantages for women and children in maintaining some contact with the other parent: contact, in some cases, reduces the risk and threat of abduction; if the father comes from a different cultural or religious background, it allows these traditions to be maintained; it gives women a break from child care and some time for themselves. Additionally, the women we interviewed felt strongly that helping to maintain the links between father and child was important for their own relationships with their children.

Most contact arrangements were, at some stage, negotiated and arranged informally between parents. But the reason for the mothers' initial involvement in negotiations with the fathers varied. Some became involved when the children asked to see the father; others when the father, grandparents, or father's solicitor made an approach. Since the Children Act, grandparents have been more likely to seek contact which, for women who are also abused by their own or their partner's families, has compounded the difficulty of separation and organising safe child contact.

Women were often left to sort things out for themselves because of the uneven availability of advice and professional support. This was especially the case for Black women. It is particularly important to note here how women's access to resources and legal advice on leaving violent men is affected by institutionalised racism (Mama, 1989) which, in turn, has dire effects upon women's safety in relation to contact arrangements.

Cases which cannot be organised informally may reach mediated agreements or be subject to a court ruling. Some women in our study favoured an initial informal approach, followed by the use of formal measures if things go wrong. The use of informal measures may be more viable whilst women are in the more protected environment of the refuge and whilst the possibility of reconciliation has not totally evaporated. Certainly, several refuge workers mentioned the fact that contact became a much more difficult issue once women had left the refuge, possibly then needing court intervention. Other women, especially the Asian women interviewed, were either left without support or advice, or resorted to making their own arrangements when court orders and official interventions failed to resolve matters.

Section 8 orders for contact or residence are made only if deemed in the best interests of the child. A court has the power to make no order. The court or a solicitor may advise conciliation to help parents arrange contact, or parents may seek the help of conciliation or mediation services themselves. There are essentially two types of conciliation/

mediation - in and out of court. In-court conciliation is run by court welfare officers, on or off the court premises. Out of court services vary considerably - from voluntary groups trained and affiliated to National Family Mediation, to the privately run Mediation in Divorce, to church or religious facilities. The aim of conciliation, regardless of location, is to secure agreement which addresses the needs and interests of the child.

If parents are having problems in reaching agreement through conciliation, or if there is cause for concern about the welfare of the children, a welfare report can be ordered by the court. The welfare officer often sees the parents first to find out if an agreement is possible, and may then go on to produce a report. The report addresses the welfare checklist set out in the Act, as well as the welfare officer's assessment of the situation drawn from interviews and meetings with the parents, the child, and any other persons with relevant information. Disputed cases may return to court time and again, being subject to a series of welfare reports over a number of years. We have found that welfare officers lack awareness and understanding of domestic violence and consequently minimise problems concerning safety for both women and children (Hester and Pearson, 1993).

Since the Children Act, one major change affecting women who experience violence from male partners is that the court may consider contact at the same time as making a decision about an injunction. If any question arises in family proceedings regarding the welfare of a child, a court may choose to make a Section 8 order for contact or residence, even if no such application has been made. Orders can be made regardless of the parties' wishes. This means that a woman may have contact considered if she has applied for an injunction under the Domestic Violence and Matrimonial Proceedings Act 1976 or under Section 1 of the Matrimonial Homes Act 1983. Although it has been suggested that, because of the urgency of the case, courts will be loathe to look at contact during injunction hearings (Bromley and Lowe, 1992), we have found that this is by no means a rare event. A decision made over contact in an injunction case can create severe problems for women and children as there is little time to investigate issues of safety. The women we interviewed who had gone to court to get an injunction and who had to agree to a contact order at the same time were totally unprepared. Consequently, they felt coerced into agreeing to something about which they had given insufficient prior thought. In this respect, the Children Act has reduced even further the scope of domestic violence provisions to offer women temporary legal protection. If contact is ordered at the same time as an injunction, there is no 'cooling off' period for the abuser, and no time free from harassment for the woman and children to make decisions about the future.

Throughout the post-separation process, therefore, there is scope for professionals to encourage agreements. Whilst this may generally be a worthwhile conciliatory trend for matrimonial litigants, professionals' desires to forge agreements poses problems for women leaving violent relationships. The women we interviewed saw the continued success of such arrangements as largely dependent on the attitudes of the man and whether he was able to appreciate her desire to have no contact with him. Because of the lack of safe contact options for children, women are placed in the position of having either to compromise their own safety or to appear to deny their children's rights. We are concerned by the lack of regard to safety for women involved in contact negotiations on court premises, in court welfare offices, and in mediation service offices. Single entry and exit access to buildings, and the insistence by many professionals that women attend joint meetings with ex-partners, expose women to unacceptable risks.

There are fundamental problems with the widely held view that a mediated settlement will reduce conflict and best serve the interests of a child. Indeed, ideally mediation should not be used in situations of domestic violence (Roberts, 1988; Hart, 1990; Grillo, 1991; Landau and Sharbonneau, 1993). Research on mediation has raised questions about the difference between mutual and coerced agreements over child contact (Eekelaar and Dingwall, 1988; Davis and Roberts, 1988; Grillo, 1991). Coercion is more likely if one party is in a position of power in relation to the other. Mediation may reinforce existing power differentials. If women are unable to talk freely about abuse because their abuser is in the same room, his power and control will extend to the mediation process. By using a method of working which encourages constructive discussions about the future rather than the past, women's experiences of abuse are made into 'history' and irrelevant to the mediation focus. So, even if a woman is able to raise the issue of abuse, mediators may sweep this aside or view it as evidence of her lack of cooperation (Hester and Pearson, 1993).

The current working practices of mediation thus cast women who have experienced abuse into the role of the 'uncooperative' party, whilst the abuser appears reasonable and controlled. This stereotype is further compounded for women whose first language is not English - interpretation provisions needed to make effective negotiations are often lacking, and the (often male) interpreters available in official schemes often do more than translate, thus reinforcing 'cultural values' from the male point of view. For instance, at a court hearing for contact involving an Asian family, the interpreter put pressure on the woman to return home to the children and the violent man. She had originally left him because the husband, acting as her interpreter to medical services, had succeeded in convincing local doctors that she was in need of psychiatric care. On returning home, she was 'sectioned' under the Mental Health Act.

The Association of Chief Officers of Probation (ACOP) recently issued a position statement on domestic violence (ACOP, 1992). This includes recommendations that court welfare and probation officers:

1. take domestic violence into account by looking carefully for evidence of abuse and by asking women about their past histories;
2. advise victims of domestic violence that they have the right not to attend joint meetings;
3. employ techniques of conflict management, rather than mediation.

Regrettably, although most court welfare officers interviewed for the study had knowledge of the ACOP report, we found very little evidence that this awareness had influenced their practice.

'HANDOVER'[2]

There are numerous problems with what is termed 'handover'. Even though a woman may be supportive of a child's wishes to see the father, she may have no wish to come into direct contact with him herself. Conflict between the needs of the child and the safety of women comes to the fore where there are orders for both injunctions and contact. Contact is hard to arrange if the couple are prohibited from meeting by an injunction. Where can contact with the father take place, and how? Moreover, there is the question of *who* should physically transport the children to the point of 'handover' if the woman herself feels unable to do this, especially when there are younger children involved.

Women in our study tried a variety of informal solutions to these problems: using family or friends as intermediaries, using the homes of other family members as the drop-off point, or handing the children over either in a very public place (what one professional has dubbed the 'MacDonalds syndrome') or somewhere where they would not be alone with the man. These solutions are very difficult to arrange for women who have been in a violent relationship. For example, friends and family quickly tire of being verbally abused themselves or being asked to pass on messages and threats.

Using the family to solve handover problems can also be difficult because women invariably come into contact with their ex-partner's family, who may either be hostile or encourage reconciliation. Workers in some, but by no means all, refuges in the study became involved in 'handover' and transport issues, in one case making themselves available at a weekend to try and facilitate contact. The main proviso was that they were not prepared to put themselves or the children at risk if the man had some ulterior motive in wanting to see his children.

The success of all these different forms of arrangement appeared to us to vary; and, as with contact generally, success was dependent on the man and how much he was prepared to honour the agreements made. There were examples of 'handover' working extremely well but, equally, there were occasions when it was made difficult because the man was abusive. One woman interviewed endures death threats on handover - the man telling her that he will blow her away with a shot gun. She dreads every time she has to drop the children off. This woman did have a friend helping her with handover, but the friend became frightened when the man started shouting threats at her.

Another woman, who was recently able to get contact stopped because of the continuing abuse by her ex-husband, described what happened on one contact visit:

> Next thing he's on the doorstep drunk as a lord, he'd been in the pub all day with the two kids. And he left them with the landlady . . . and he were drinking all day. Brought the children back and starts blaming me, because he's been drinking. . . . He pushed me through the glass doors in the living room in front of my children, dragged me all over the floor by the head of the hair, made me pick every piece of glass up, he had it to me throat, this is front of his kids, and said that he were gonna kill me if I didn't pick all the glass up.

'Tactics' employed by fathers who wished to maintain some power and control over the woman included arriving late to pick up or return children, not returning them at all, or turning up early. Fathers exercised control over timing, so that women and children were kept on tenterhooks, never sure whether or not contact would take place. This made it difficult for women to make plans and to keep arrangements made for their own or the children's free time. Women found this particularly disturbing for the children who they felt needed safe, predictable, and regular contact with their fathers.

Women were also at risk of abuse at 'handovers' when they were separated from their children and applied for contact themselves. One woman in the study lost contact with her children altogether because she felt unable to face the sexual abuse which she experienced at handover.

Where accessible, contact centres were seen to be a positive way of helping to ensure safety for women and children (see chapter by Harne and Radford, this volume, for an alternative view). However, few women are able to arrange for either contact, or just the 'handover', to take place at a supervised centre. Contact centres do not offer a permanent solution. They are currently used only as a temporary measure, a stepping-stone towards unsupervised contact. Nationally, the provision of such centres is paltry - a few centres exist in London and other major cities and towns. They are available primarily for English speaking families. Resources are particularly lacking for interpretation and supervision of contact for non-English speaking families. Children from violent homes who speak two languages need contact centre supervisors who are able to understand what is being said during contact.

There are also problems for the children in using contact centres. Attending such centres can make children feel different; it can enforce the status of their relationship with their father as different from others. Moreover, the kinds of activities that children and fathers can pursue on a contact visit are inevitably limited.

CHILDREN'S VIEWS

The Children Act has placed a greater, and welcome, focus on children's own views and wishes. The 'welfare checklist' in the Act indicates that the ascertainable wishes and needs of the child should be taken into account with regard to contact. The developmental age of the child is clearly an important consideration, but there is a problem concerning *who* should make the decision about whether a child is old enough to offer an opinion. Level of comprehension can vary enormously with each individual child, and some children as young as 3 or 4 are old enough to have an understanding of what has been happening and, consequently, to know what they want.

Our research raises a number of concerns about the way children are involved in negotiations concerning contact, either informally or formally. It is important to address the following questions:

1. *How* are children 'listened to'?
2. *Which* children are listened to?
3. How are children's views *incorporated* into any decisions made?
4. To what extent *should* children's wishes influence outcomes?

Moreover, the safety of women as well as children has to be borne in mind.

Where contact by the absent parent is being pursued formally, it is assumed that professionals will talk to children aged eleven years and over, but they can also talk to and/or observe children of any age. Of the professionals surveyed in our study, however, solicitors tended not to talk directly to children about their wishes; few voluntary sector mediators did so; and childcare workers in refuges (when there was one) sometimes, but not always, did so. Court welfare officers were perhaps most likely to talk to or observe children, owing to their role in compiling welfare reports. It must be recognised however that, even though their work is regarded as a skilled specialism, welfare officers are drawn from the probation service, have probably spent most of their professional lives working with adult (largely male) offenders, and are unlikely to have a child-related background or training.

Ascertaining children's wishes may seem straightforward but it is, in fact, a highly complex task and takes time. Consideration needs to be given to what children actually say, to what they do not say, to what they indicate non-verbally, and to whether they are under any undue pressures to voice a certain opinion. Children may need some time to say what they really want. There needs also to be some reflection of the child's age and understanding. In short, the task is one that ideally should to be carried out sensitively and carefully over a period of time, so that an accurate assessment can be made of what the child truly wants in relation to contact. With regard to domestic violence, it is also important to acknowledge the experiences children have had of living in circumstances where their mother is being abused (see Christensen,

1990; chapters by Morley and Mullender, Kelly, this volume). We have found that, where professionals do talk with or observe children, there are great variations in the way this material is interpreted or the extent to which it is incorporated into decisions about contact. For instance, professionals may feel that the parents are best able to articulate the views of their children, and that what children say cannot be taken at face value. There is an assumption that parents will speak for the benefit of their children and defend them from abuse. This may not be the case. Children are not always listened to as separate individuals, and professionals' own value judgments and beliefs may take precedence.

Welfare officers compiling welfare reports for the courts will tend to see the children only once or twice before making a report. It might take some children quite a long time to be able to trust another adult enough to be open about what has been happening and what they want. One worker had experienced this with some children in the refuge:

> ... when the welfare officer went to speak to them they wouldn't say anything, so access was granted ... and then little by little it started coming out and eventually they stopped the access (Refuge worker).

Many children, despite violence to their mothers or themselves, wish to see their fathers; but some children do not. It is often difficult, however, for children to say that they do *not* want this contact. On the one hand, the dynamics of parent-child relationships are such that it may be very difficult for children to express a wish not to see their father; on the other hand, professionals may dismiss or ignore children's views. We have found that mediators and, in particular, solicitors and court welfare officers often dismiss children's claims that they do not want to see their fathers, seeing the children as being unduly influenced by their mothers. As a result, contact may be established even when children do not want it, or when it is not in the children's best interests.

Once the assessment has been made, an additional issue as to how much weight should be given to the child's wishes is not unproblematic. The Children Act indicates that the wishes of children should be heard and considered, but this is not meant to imply that children become the final decision makers in these matters. A distinction is drawn between what a child says s/he wants and what professionals see as being her/his needs. This distinction is particularly important for women in refuges, especially if children make choices which might be unsafe. While the Children Act does not give children ultimate decision-making power, it has nevertheless been interpreted by some mothers, children, and professionals as giving children more *rights* than before. Perhaps this is partly due to the publicity surrounding children having the right to their own legal representation and 'divorcing' their parents. We have found that the sense of increased rights for children sometimes puts women under greater pressure to return to the abusive situation because children, especially older children, see this option as their rightful choice.

Clearly, there is a need to address the problem that the needs and/or interests of the child may at times conflict with those of the mother, and that the safety of *both* children *and* women must be taken into account. Similarly, if welfare officers lack understanding about the effects of domestic violence upon children, they may be unaware that the father may be exercising control over the child's decisions about contact or residence.

Where listening to children is concerned, our research in Denmark has produced some very interesting findings with direct implications for Britain. In Denmark, when parents do not agree about arrangements for contact after separation they are expected to attend a form of mediation involving advice counselling. This is free, funded by the state, and carried out by child-related professionals 'on loan' to the state from child psychology, child psychiatry, child guidance, or child social work (see Hester and Radford, 1992, for further details of the Danish legislation and discussion of practice).

Some of the Danish advice counsellors have developed a practice of seeing the children separately over a period of time, especially if it becomes apparent that there has been a history of domestic violence and/ or child abuse. These advice counsellors feel that seeing the children in this way serves two important purposes: first, the children can talk about their experiences of living in abusive situations and have these experiences acknowledged and taken seriously; second, the advice counsellors have time to ascertain from the children what contact arrangements they would prefer, and to discuss what options are actually possible. Especially interesting is our finding that the more these professionals focus on the children - seeing them separately and discussing their experiences - the greater the likelihood that restrictions on contact with the violent father will be recommended.

CONCLUSION

In this chapter, we have documented some of the major problems faced by children and their mothers experiencing domestic violence in the wake of the Children Act. The emphasis on the welfare of the child in the Act is, of course, welcome; but it tends to be interpreted by professionals and advisors so that contact, rather than safety, is paramount. The link between mothers' and children's safety also tends to be ignored. The whole issue as to where the needs of parents and the welfare of children coincide or conflict is a difficult and, ultimately, moral dilemma. Let us hope that some of the ideas raised in this book and in this chapter will inspire further debate amongst academics, policy makers, and practitioners. Positive changes could, given the political will, be made now to deal more adequately with the safety problems which women and children face.

We have identified the following, as some of the priorities for contact cases where there has been a history of domestic violence.

Accessibility of advice and services

In order to facilitate informal decisions and the continuation of contact where this is what women and children want, women and children affected by violence or abuse should have sufficient information on the support available to help them make contact work, and on what to do if things go wrong. Particular attention should be given to the accessibility and appropriateness of advice and services for Black parents and children, and parents and/or children for whom English is not the main language. The availability of advice and information could be improved with better funding for refuges, in order to offer comprehensive outreach and inter-agency work for women. To date, few groups or inter-agency projects in the UK have become involved in child contact. We have yet to see an advice manual or leaflet which addresses the pros and cons of contact arrangements for women leaving violent men.

Practical help with making arrangements

Depending on women's wishes and needs, this should include help with reaching and negotiating an agreement, plans for the development of safe contact between the father and children, and scope for review.

Provisions for safety

Safety should be the starting point wherever meetings of ex-partners may take place, such as courts and court welfare office premises, and from arrival to departure and beyond. Ex-partners should *always* be seen separately in the first instance to ascertain any history of violence. Professionals need to think about the timing of meetings and additional problems of holding meetings in the winter and after dark. The introduction of basic measures such as *safer access* into buildings, *entry phones*, *separate waiting rooms*, and the installation of *panic buttons* would improve the safety for staff and clients in premises. Adequate independent interpretation services are a crucial safety measure for women whose first language is not English. Contact should take place in an environment which is safe for the woman and the child. Consideration should be given to the safety of children in premises, including in contact centres.

Listening to mothers and children

Mediators and welfare officers, especially, should look into ways in which they could give women scope to express their fears for safety. Firm statements to separating couples that domestic violence is a crime and is by no means irrelevant or condoned, backed up by positive efforts to screen out and identify cases of abuse, have already been piloted with success in Canada and the USA (Sun and Woods, 1989). A separate initial meeting should always be the starting point. There is a need for further debate about the value of mediation and conflict management, and for clearer guidelines for mediators on empowering work with vulnerable people. Professionals involved with talking to and interviewing children should be trained in child-centred work. This should include specific, post-qualifying training on domestic violence.

Welfare report writing

Domestic violence should always be taken into account when welfare reports are prepared. There should be awareness of domestic violence and its detrimental effects on both children and their mothers. Awareness of the impact of abuse should allow professionals to consider whether or not contact should happen at all and whether or not it will best serve the interests of a child. Reports should give attention to the practicalities of contact arrangements. Delays in welfare report writing can, of course, cause problems for children, parents, and the courts. Further research is required into the problems and benefits of delaying report writing in order to allow consideration of safety issues for women and children leaving violent men.

Help with handover

This is essential in cases where the father is subject to an injunction, especially to an exclusion order, as well as whenever the mother feels under threat from further violence. Handover should not be left to relatives.

Contact problems

When contact problems arise, there should be a quick and sympathetic response from professionals. If appropriate, speedy police intervention to recover snatched children could prevent long periods of separation from the mother and abduction overseas. Welfare officers should be prepared to advise that contact stop when problems arise, rather than allowing them to continue until clear evidence of harm to a child can be produced.

More contact centres

More centres for supervised contact are needed. Centres should be staffed by more than one individual trained to deal with both subtle and overt abuse to children. Contact centre workers and volunteers need to be aware of the specific problems faced by women and children leaving violent men. There should be further reviews of safety on premises for women, children and staff. There should be wider availability of independent interpretation facilities for families in need of this service.

All of the above can only be effective in promoting the safety of women and children if the professionals involved are first willing to accept the prevalence and seriousness of violence from men to their female partners, and if they are able to develop ways of working which can ensure that domestic violence is identified early on in the negotiations.

Notes

1. The Research is funded by the Rowntree Foundation and the Nuffield Foundation but it does not necessarily reflect their views. It involves in-depth interviews with 50 professionals and advisors in Britain (mostly court welfare officers, voluntary sector mediators, solicitors and refuge workers, although we have also interviewed others concerned such as domestic violence unit officers, contact centre workers, etc.) and 25 equivalent professionals/advisors in Denmark; a series of interviews with 70 women in Britain and 30 women in Denmark; a small number of children in both countries; observations and analysis of relevant case notes and documentation. In Britain, one fifth of our sample of women were Black and Asian women. We began the work in 1990, carrying out a pilot study before the implementation of the Children Act and commencing the main study in 1992. The main study will be completed in 1995.
2. We dislike the term 'handover' with its implication that the child is merely baggage, but have not as yet come up with an alternative.

References

Association of Chief Officers of Probation (1992) *Association of Chief Officers of Probation Position Statement on Domestic Violence*. London: ACOP. Drafted by David Sleightholm.

Binney, V. Harkell, G. and Nixon, J. (1981) *Leaving Violent Men*. Bristol: Women's Aid Federation.

Borkowski, V. Murch, and Walker, J. (1983) *Marital Violence: The Community Response*. London: Tavistock.

Bromley, P. and Lowe, N. (1992) *Bromley's Family Law*. 8th Edition, London: Butterworth.

Brophy, J. (1989) 'Custody law, child care and inequality in Britain' in Smart, C. and Sevenhuijsen, S. (eds.) *Child Custody and the Politics of Gender*. London: Routledge.

Burgoyne, J. Ormrod, R. and Richards, M. (1988) *Divorce Matters*. Harmondsworth: Penguin.

Christensen, E. (1990) 'Children's living conditions: an investigation into disregard of care in relation to children and teenagers in families of wife maltreatment', *Nordisk Psychologi*, 42, Monograph no.31, pp.161-232.

Davis, G. and Roberts, M. (1988) *Access to Agreement*. Milton Keynes: Open University Press.

Eekelar, J. and Clive, E. (1977) *Custody After Divorce*. Oxford: SSRC Centre For Socio-Legal Studies, Wolfson College.

Eekelar, J. and Dingwall, R. (1988) (eds.) *Divorce Mediation and the Legal Process*. Oxford: Clarendon Press.

Evason, E. (1982) *Hidden Violence: Battered Women in Northern Ireland*. Belfast: Farset Cooperative Press.

Grillo, T. (1991) 'The mediation alternative: process dangers for women', *The Yale Law Journal*, 100, pp.1545-1610.

Hart, B. (1990) 'The further endangerment of battered women and children in custody mediation', *Mediation Quarterly*, 7(3), pp.278-291.

Hester, M. and Pearson, C. (1993) 'Domestic violence, mediation and child contact arrangements: issues from current research', *Family Mediation*, 3(2), pp.3-6.

Hester, M. and Radford, L. (1992) 'Domestic violence and access arrangements for children in Denmark and Britain', *Journal of Social Welfare and Family Law*, 1, pp.57-70.

Hoggett, B. and Pearl, D. (1991) *Family, Law and Society: Cases and Materials*. London: Butterworths.

Home Affairs Committee (1993a) *Domestic Violence*. Vol.I, Report together with the Proceedings of the Committee, London: HMSO.

Home Affairs Committee (1993b) *Domestic Violence*. Vol.II, Memoranda of Evidence, Minutes of Evidence and Appendices, London: HMSO.

Johnson, J. (1992) *High Conflict and Violent Divorcing Families: Findings on Children's Adjustment and Proposed Guidelines for the Resolution of Disputed Custody and Visitation: Report of the Project*. California: Centre for the Family in Transition.

Judicial Statistics (1992) London: HMSO.

King, M. and Piper, C. (1990) *How the Law 'Thinks' about Children*. Aldershot: Gower.

Koch-Nielsen, I. (1984) 'Vold i oploste parfold' in Koch-Nielsen, I and Moxnes, K. (eds.) *Vold I Parforhold*, Copenhagen: Nordisk Ministeraad.

Landau, B. and Sharbonneau, P. (eds.) (1993) *Report from the Toronto Forum on Woman Abuse and Mediation*. Toronto: Toronto Forum on Woman Abuse and Mediation.

Law Commission (1986) *Review of Child Law: Custody*. Working Paper No.96. London: HMSO.

Mama, A. (1989a) *The Hidden Struggle: Statutory and Voluntary Sector Responses to Violence Against Black Women in the Home*. London: London Race and Housing Research Unit.

Mitchell, A. (1985) *Children in the Middle: Living through Divorce*. London: Tavistock.

Richards, M. and Dyson, M. (1982) *Separation, Divorce and the Development of Children: A Review*. Cambridge: Child Care and Development Group, University of Cambridge.

Roberts, M. (1988) *Mediation in Family Disputes*. Aldershot: Wildewood House.

Sun, M. and Woods, L. (1989) *A Mediator's Guide to Domestic Abuse*. New York: National Center on Women and Family Law.

Victim Support (1992) *Domestic Violence: Report of a National Inter-Agency Working Party on Domestic Violence*. London: Victim Support.

9

Children, Domestic Violence and Housing: The Impact of Homelessness

Gill Hague and Ellen Malos

Overwhelmingly, it is women and children - and not men - who are forced to leave their homes and become homeless due to domestic violence. It is women and children - and not men - who because of domestic violence may face months or years of housing uncertainty, often in inadequate or overcrowded temporary accommodation, dependent on shrinking and heavily rationed public sector housing. Many domestic violence survivors, activists and researchers have pointed out that the most important need of women and children leaving home as a result of male violence is for somewhere safe to go: in other words, for permanent housing options of a decent standard which offer security and safety. This chapter is about the increasingly difficult search for rehousing which women and children have to undertake, and the effects on children of becoming homeless due to the abuse of their mothers by male partners.

On a general level, domestic violence has been in the public eye and the subject of official interest to an unprecedented degree in the last few years (e.g. Victim Support, 1992; Home Affairs Committee, 1993a, 1993b). Police attitudes and working practices in some parts of the country are improving, there are moves afoot to overhaul the legal protection available to women and children, and local inter-agency projects on domestic violence are being established in various areas (see Home Office, 1990; Law Commission, 1992; Hague and Malos, 1993, ch.8; Morley, 1993). Within this general concern, issues for children have been very far from the top of the agenda, as highlighted throughout this book, and children's basic needs frequently remain overlooked.

Vitally needed emergency housing for abused women and children is still in short supply. The Women's Aid federations, which have now been campaigning against domestic violence and publicising the issue for 20 years, report that there is still less than one third of the refuge provision recommended back in 1975 by the Select Committee on Violence in Marriage (Barron et al., 1992, p.35). Specialist refuges for Black women and children, and for women and children from minority ethnic communities, at least in London, are frequently even more severely under-resourced than general refuges in the same locality (Mama, 1989; Russell, 1989). And almost all existing services are hard-pressed to survive, facing recurrent funding crises and dependent on the good will of dedicated and usually over-worked staff.

HOUSING AND HOMELESSNESS

The picture with regard to permanent housing is no better and children suffer as a result. Women and children who leave home to escape domestic abuse are frequently reliant on access to public sector housing. Some women will be able to become owner occupiers, although often only after a property settlement involving the former home, which usually means housing insecurity or homelessness in between. However, many do not have access to the financial resources to pursue this route. As recently documented by Jenny Muir and Mandy Ross of the London Housing Unit, the continued economic disadvantage which women suffer in comparison to men means that women are still massively discriminated against in achieving independent housing on the private market. They report that only 15 per cent of women, as compared to 49 per cent of men, in their study earned enough to afford a mortgage on a one-bedroomed flat in London (Muir and Ross, 1993). Housing is often cheaper outside London, but women still face considerable housing difficulties in terms of owner occupation throughout the country.

Renting from a private landlord can be an alternative route to rehousing. The government favours this housing option over public sector housing, but suitable private rented accommodation is hard to come by for abused women. In many areas, it is in short supply and is often either prohibitively expensive or, alternatively, of very poor quality with little comfort or security. Even private accommodation at the cheap end of the market may cost more than most women can afford (although of course housing benefit can be of help). In their study, Muir and Ross found that only 19 per cent of women could afford to rent a private bedsit in the capital, as opposed to 57 per cent of men.

These difficulties are much more severe when women are financially responsible for dependent children. They are often then caught in a Catch-22 position of needing larger accommodation but, at the same time, being less able to work full-time to pay for such accommodation owing to childcare responsibilities. In this situation, obtaining and financially supporting a mortgage is even harder than it is for other women. And, despite government promotion of privately rented housing as a housing option for the homeless, a great deal of it has rules against taking children even though, if a woman has children, she has priority need status under current homelessness law. Thus for abused women with children, financial and housing difficulties are compounded with the result that children suffer further disadvantage and hardship.

COUNCIL AND HOUSING ASSOCIATION HOUSING

From the above discussion it can be seen that - for children to live safe, abuse-free lives in secure, decent housing conditions - access to public sector housing is of vital importance. The present and previous Conservative governments, however, have been intent on decreasing this housing option over the last fifteen years in favour of owner occupation and private renting. The sale of council flats and houses, coupled with funding and spending restrictions placed on local housing authorities, has led to a huge decrease in public sector housing. As regards 'social' rented housing, the housing association movement is being promoted by the Government as an alternative to local authority housing and, in many areas, innovative housing initiatives and projects, often developed jointly between the local council and housing associations, are taking place.

But it is clear to everyone in the field of public housing that there is just not enough public sector housing to go round. Homelessness has increased substantially over recent years, although this is not always revealed in official figures, and the country faces a housing crisis which the Government is keen to play down (Greve, 1991; CHICL/London Housing Unit, 1992; Shelter, 1991). Shelter, the national housing advice and campaigning agency, has produced an emergency contingency plan to attempt to halt the decline; and it estimates, along with other housing experts, that at least 100,000 additional homes are needed per year in the social rented sector even to begin to meet current and projected housing needs. What this shortage means (although the Government does not like to put it this way, preferring to stigmatise the homeless as demanding, irresponsible queue-jumpers) is large increases in the numbers of homeless children without anywhere permanent to live, through no fault of their own.

THE EFFECTS ON CHILDREN OF HOMELESSNESS
AND LIVING IN TEMPORARY ACCOMMODATION

The disastrous effects on children of being homeless and of living for long periods in various types of temporary accommodation have been well-documented (see, for example, Malos, 1993). Children's lives are totally disrupted by becoming homeless. They lose their home, their friends and sometimes their family and relatives. They often lose all their possessions. They lose their school or playgroup, their security, their social circle - everything. In the case of domestic violence, they generally also lose their father. In other words, the fabric of their lives can be destroyed by the homeless experience. For the children of abused women, this change may happen quickly - with little or no warning - and often as a result of a highly distressing incidence of violence to their mothers so that extreme shock, fear, and sometimes terror are added to the experience.

Moving into temporary accommodation has a very negative influence on children's schooling, as documented by a survey of the education of children living in temporary accommodation conducted in 1989 by the Department of Education and Science HMI (published 1990). This report recommends some useful changes which schools catering for transient or homeless children can implement. But, however positive such measures are, they cannot compensate for the enormous dislocation which homelessness causes, the almost inevitable stigma associated with being identifiable in the school community as homeless, and the disruption to education caused by frequent moves from school to school. The HMI report concludes that sustainable academic achievement is often beyond the reach of children in temporary accommodation due to the dependence of the school system on regular and consistent attendance over a lengthy period (Malos, 1993, p.55).

Many homeless children still live in bed and breakfast hotels despite central and local government commitments to reducing the use of this expensive and unsatisfactory option in favour of other sorts of temporary accommodation, for example clusters of self-contained units. Surveys of life in such hotels make painful reading (see Miller, 1990; Murie and Jeffers, eds, 1987). Overcrowding, lack of facilities for children, lack of safety features, lack of security, rules in some hotels to vacate the premises during the day - the problems are multiple. Many reports have expressed concern at the high level of accidents involving children, often caused by unsatisfactory safety precautions. Inadequate access to cooking facilities means that children are frequently malnourished, and many research studies and reports have noted how the poor conditions in temporary accommodation can contribute to children suffering emotionally, physically and cognitively. These reports:

> . . . showed a high incidence of depression, disturbed sleep, poor eating, over-activity, bed-wetting and soiling, toilet-training problems, temper tantrums and aggression. Up to 40% of children in bed and breakfast accommodation in a Bayswater study had behavioural problems (Stearn, *Roof,* 1986). Overcrowded bedrooms and lack of play space affected development of motor skills and speech development in young children and made it difficult for older children to do homework. Other problems were linked with overcrowding, poor sanitation and lack of basic amenities. Infectious diseases were common and easily spread. The high incidence of diarrhoea and vomiting was thought to be linked with poor water supply and shared sanitation. Children often suffered upper respiratory tract infections. . . (Health Visitors Association and General Medical Services Committee, 1989, summarised in Malos, 1993, pp.39-40)

Many of these problems occur in other types of temporary housing as well as bed and breakfast, although perhaps less severely. While some local authorities and housing associations run excellent temporary accommodation projects with good facilities for children, the overall picture as regards homeless children is not good. There is evidence, for example, that children of homeless families are less likely to have access to doctors, health care, and medical facilities. Under the Children Act 1989, local authorities are required to provide preventative services to assist children in need. However relatively few authorities classify homeless children in this category (see, for example, Tunstill and Aldgate, 1994).

PARTICULAR PROBLEMS FOR FAMILIES HOMELESS BECAUSE OF DOMESTIC VIOLENCE

In addition to the general problems of homelessness, women and their children who are homeless because of abuse experience special problems because of the violence itself. Both women and children describe living in constant fear and anxiety that they will be found and that the violence will begin again. Often, they are literally in hiding. Many women report that their children's health and/or mental well-being has been affected by the violence which they have experienced or witnessed; and homelessness then compounds their difficulties. Frequently, abused women also face a greater uncertainty than some other applicants under the homelessness legislation (see below) about whether the local authority they apply to will accept them for rehousing because of the difficulty of proving the violence, and this will apply especially if they have suffered psychological or sexual rather than physical violence. Another difference is that women and children escaping violence are frequently forced to move to a new area where they do not know anyone and have no friends or support networks. This stressful life situation may be exacerbated by fears that they will not be accepted for rehousing because they lack a local connection (see below).

Many women and children escaping from violence in the home make use of refuges rather than other types of temporary accommodation. Some of the worst aspects of most types of temporary housing may therefore be avoided as, at their best, refuges provide a supportive environment, safe and secure, in which women and children are provided with counselling, advocacy, support, and assistance. Working with children is a priority for Women's Aid, as described elsewhere in this book, and many refuges have children's workers on the staff and innovatory programmes of support work for children in operation (see Section IV, this volume).

However, refuges are crowded, and under-funding means that conditions are not always as good as they could be. Living in a refuge, however supportive, can become difficult over extended periods of time. Facilities are shared between several families, and a woman and her children will almost certainly have to share a room, often a small one. Specific equipment and play facilities for children may be rudimentary or non-existent. In addition, women and children often have to move from one refuge to another to escape the violent perpetrator, with resultant disruption of children's schooling and friendships, which perhaps have only just been established.

THE HOMELESSNESS LEGISLATION

The homelessness legislation is currently contained in Part III of the 1985 Housing Act and is accompanied by a government Code of Guidance (Department of Environment, 1991). Fairly generous at present, this gives advice on how the legislation, which is brief and open to a very wide range of interpretations, should be operated. The Act gives local housing authorities the duty to secure accommodation, initially temporary and then permanent, for homeless applicants who satisfy various criteria and 'tests': applicants must be homeless as defined in the Act, be in priority need, and not have become homeless intentionally. Domestic violence is included as a reason for homelessness. An applicant is in priority need if he or she has dependent children (though this term is not defined in the Act) or is pregnant; is homeless in an emergency; or is vulnerable through old age, mental illness or handicap, or for 'other special reasons'. The Code of Guidance states that anyone made homeless by violence who does not have dependent children should also be given priority status 'wherever possible'.

Normally, the duty to provide long term housing only applies if there is a local connection with a borough or no local connection elsewhere. But, in the case of applicants escaping domestic violence in another local authority area, the duty applies if there is a danger that they would experience violence or the threat of violence if they returned there or if they applied to another local authority where they did have a local connection. The authority must conduct investigations to establish whether applicants pass these tests and are eligible for rehousing, although they have a discretion to be more generous than the law demands.

We recently completed a study, supported by the Joseph Rowntree Foundation, of housing options available to abused women and their children (Malos and Hague, 1993). Like other researchers on homelessness (for example, Bull, 1993), we found that there were great variations between authorities in the way that they interpreted their duties under the homelessness legislation. There were also differences in practice between individual officers within the same authority, and sometimes between an authority's stated and agreed policy - which might be quite progressive - and the practices described to us in our interviews (Malos and Hague, 1993, pp.i-ii, 40-41).

HOMELESSNESS INTERVIEWS AND INVESTIGATIONS OF 'PROOF' OF VIOLENCE

The Code of Guidance states that it is not good practice for local councils to carry out elaborate enquiries to ascertain whether or not someone is eligible for rehousing, pointing out that a long period of uncertainty is bad for the applicant and may cost the authority money if they are keeping people in temporary accommodation. The Code also reminds authorities that, in situations involving violence, applicants may be in distress. In our research study, this advice seems generally to have been followed in many areas, but practice did differ between individual officers in the same authority. Many councils do everything that they can to treat women and children who have experienced domestic violence in a 'believing' and supportive manner.

In domestic violence situations, however, 'proof' or even tangible evidence is difficult to provide, and much rests on the woman's own testimony. Authorities vary as to how much detail they request of the violence that women have experienced. Some require very little evidence beyond the woman's statements in interview, but others adopt an antagonistic attitude. In a London authority where we interviewed women, for example, the provision of a great deal of supporting evidence was essential if applicants were to stand any chance of success. Women described their interviews as being combative and distressing. They talked of leaving the interview in tears, even when they had gone with the support of a refuge or advice worker, or of being called back for interview after interview. Children were present on many of these distressing occasions. Almost inevitably, traumatic housing negotiations of this kind adversely affect the children involved.

Authorities which adopt punitive attitudes to homeless women and children do so either because of acute housing shortages, or political will, or both. Such attitudes can have a strong deterrent effect on women either making or persevering with homelessness applications. Many women and children in our study returned home purely because of this deterrent effect in terms of the difficulty of achieving rehousing. Several of these women were abused again as a result, and children also experienced further violence. For example, a woman with four children returned home in desperation because of the unsympathetic way in which her housing application was treated and the deterrent effect of the lack of housing. She immediately suffered further violence and abuse. She and her children felt - and were - hopelessly trapped in a life of violence due to housing issues. This woman then lost her teenage daughter who broke contact with the family and moved away to become homeless herself rather than stay in the violent situation.

LOCAL CONNECTION

As indicated above, homelessness law says that in cases of domestic violence women should not need to have a local connection with the authority they apply to unless they can be safely referred to another authority where they do have such a connection. While very many councils are careful to abide by the legislation in this respect, some still expect women and their children to return to their previous area or to move somewhere else (Malos and Hague, 1993, pp.32-34). There can be lengthy delays while enquiries are made to see if another local authority will accept the family. This means that women and children wait in uncertainty, not even knowing which area of the country they might be living in the near future. Women's and children's own fears or, indeed, certainties that they will be in danger in other areas are sometimes ignored.

In our study, women in some London boroughs, for example, described being 'batted backwards and forwards' between authorities. One woman we talked with, who applied to a borough where she had no local connection, was only accepted for rehousing after one and a half years of protracted negotiations with the two authorities involved, during which time she had strong legal representation. Throughout, she waited in a women's refuge, living in one very small, single room with her four children, the eldest a teenager and the youngest a baby. Another woman was refused any consideration by the authority she applied to since she had no local connection. She and her children faced an almost hopeless housing situation:

> You just get pushed in the gutter, that's how I feel, as though you're nothing. I just feel desperate about it. . . . I can't go on any longer fighting them . . . . I've just given up really. I'm getting counselling now because I was taking it out on the kids. It's the housing - if I could get that sorted out, I could sort out the kids and sort out college and start my own business. It's just the housing holding us back. We've been here a year. You wait and wait and you get depressed and the kids are always saying, 'when can we leave?', 'Can we get our own home now?', 'When are we going to get a flat?'. And I'm just sitting here with my eyes blurred, I can't see, it all flashes in front of my eyes and I say to them, 'I'm trying, I'm trying, I'm trying'. What can I do? (Black woman with two children in temporary accommodation)

Such difficulties can be a particular problem in hard-pressed inner-city London authorities and also in rural areas with little council housing left. Many women return to their original boroughs as a result, and may then be quite likely to be found by their violent partner. One woman with five children whom we interviewed gave up her attempt to be rehoused in a safe rural borough, due to the housing shortage, and was referred back to, and rehoused, in her original area. Her violent partner traced the family as a result, and within weeks she was homeless again due to violence; she and her children were quickly back in bed and breakfast accommodation. Her older children, by that time, had gone through at least five changes in school over a short period, with more to come. The youngest children had spent their whole lives in one sort of temporary accommodation after another. Disturbing chains of events of this type are very familiar to refuge staff and activists. One can only speculate about the damage done to such children by the lack of permanent housing in safe areas and by their treatment in local authorities where they do not have a local connection.

Our study uncovered disturbing examples of women and children finding it extremely difficult, if not impossible, to be rehoused in some areas. In some authorities, especially in London and in rural districts, few women and children are accepted for rehousing and many wait in temporary accommodation for very long periods. This wait for rehousing could amount to years, often spent in fear and uncertainty about the final outcome:

> I don't know what the heck's happening to be honest with you. You've just got to sit and wait. 15 months so far. I know some who have waited longer. It's just a question of holding on until it's your turn to be plucked. [My son] has a behavioural problem and it's not being helped by all this. It's getting worse. He sees a specialist. He needs his own surroundings . . . something you could call home. But he can't do that at the Homeless Centre. We live out of bags because there is no room to put anything. So we're just stuck there really . . . (White woman with one child in a rural authority).

Some women in our study were forced to move desperately from place to place in the search for housing with resulting traumatic effects on both the woman concerned and any children with her. Forced transience of this nature or seemingly endless periods in temporary accommodation sometimes led, as for the children in the accounts above and below, to otherwise unnecessary intervention by child care professionals and other agencies:

> It's very restricted here. He's in child guidance now, because of it. It feels like an uphill struggle - as if there is no light at the end of the tunnel. And I can't help him sort out his problems at the moment because of all the other children here . . . (White woman with one son in temporary accommodation in London).

In this sort of situation, it is solely the difficulties in getting rehoused that lead to women and children experiencing continued homelessness and being forced to be transient. This in turn, leads to the children experiencing behavioural and emotional difficulties which they would not otherwise have had to contend with.

THE USE OF LEGAL REMEDIES

Increasing numbers of housing authorities have policies which demand that abused women applicants seek advice about taking legal action to remove the violent perpetrator from the former home or about providing legal protection to allow the woman to return to the relationship. It is well known, however, that legal injunctions are very frequently ineffective in protecting abused women and children adequately; furthermore they are normally only issued for a short time (Barron, 1990; Law Commission, 1992). The Lord Chancellor has announced that the draft bill to improve civil law remedies produced by the Law Commission (1992) will probably be introduced into Parliament in the near future, but such remedies will still be time-limited, in the main, and will be of use in only some cases. For very large numbers of women and children escaping domestic violence, the only way to achieve a safe and secure life is to leave the violent perpetrator completely and begin again somewhere else.

In our study, however, we collected evidence that women and children attempting to escape violence and seeking rehousing in various local authorities were refused any further assistance from the council once they had obtained a legal order against the violent perpetrator. In some cases, their temporary accommodation was terminated as soon as the order came through. For example, one woman's bed and breakfast placement was cancelled without notice when the power of arrest attached to her injunction was renewed, despite the fact that the man had not attended court and that the social services department had real concerns about the safety of the children:

> They arrested him and, because he was bailed, the next morning social services said, 'She's got to be moved or the children will be classed in our books as at risk'. They (the housing department) put me in Bed and Breakfast . . . The Power of Arrest expired on my injunction. . . We re-applied for an extension, and it was because of that, because I renewed my Power of Arrest, they said I could go back, even though by this time he'd skipped bail. . . They said, 'Right, you can go back' (White woman with children in a London borough).

Another woman had this to say:

> They said I'd have to go back. . . But it would be too dangerous. It wouldn't be safe to go back there . . . They just said get an injunction. So I did go for an injunction with a Power of Arrest. But then with the kids being so stressed and I was thinking of him getting his own back. And the idea of the kids seeing him being arrested and put into a police van. I decided I couldn't go through with the Power of Arrest - for my kid's sake and for his sake. But the Council said, 'OK, you've got an injunction, you can go home' (Black woman with three children in a refuge).

It does appear that some women can be successful in challenging the use of legal remedies in this way to force them back into their original accommodation against their will. They may be able, for example, to prove special circumstances (such as obvious danger to a baby) or they may have sufficient evidence, stamina, and support to convince the relevant council that returning with an injunction would lead to them and their children being further abused. In other cases, it seems that local councils refuse to accept what they may regard as the 'subjective feelings' of the woman and children concerned.

Some women, of course, want the use of legal remedies to oust the violent partner from the joint home. Also, some activists against male violence regard this option as something to be worked towards in the future. But, for women and children to be safe and secure in this situation, there will need to be an as yet unachieved level of effective legal protection and enforcement, accompanied by multi-layered support within the community and community intolerance of domestic violence. At the moment, this is not the situation in this country, and many women and children escaping violence in the home do not wish, under any circumstances, to return to their former home. To force an abused woman, made homeless due to violence, to return to the former property or to her partner against her will can hardly be regarded as a satisfactory application of the homelessness law. Children involved may suffer otherwise preventable abuse and are likely to be confused, insecure, and distressed.

In cases where abused women and children are having trouble with their housing applications, refuge staff, social workers, lawyers, and voluntary sector organisations can sometimes assist. But we found examples in our study where, even with the strongest social services support coupled with legal representation and backing from refuges and voluntary sector agencies, women and children were still refused rehousing. Such families then faced a desperate housing future. While many housing associations will accept families for rehousing independent of local authority nominations, and some have special 'quotas' for women and children in refuges refused rehousing elsewhere, these tenancies are rather like gold-dust. Otherwise, women and children remain homeless, possibly moving constantly from one temporary address to another. The future for children living under such conditions for long periods is clearly likely to be a traumatic one.

Of course, the lack of public sector housing is at the root of these difficulties. Housing associations are unable to fill the gap left by the drastic decrease in council housing, and women and children who have experienced violence are among those badly affected as a result.

RACISM AND IMMIGRATION ISSUES

The children of Black women, and of women from minority ethnic communities, forced to leave home because of violence can face particular housing difficulties. The existence of racism in the delivery of housing services has been documented (Mama, 1989), although some housing authorities and associations are making efforts to improve their anti-racist practice. In general, however, the provision of interpreting and other specialised services is inadequate. In our own study, it was the opinion of some voluntary sector and refuge workers that Black families escaping violence often wait longer for rehousing than white families in the same borough. In addition, women and children from minority ethnic communities may need to be particularly careful about where they accept rehousing offers, due to the pervading racism of British society. Some Asian and other women and their children who come from extended family networks who are fleeing violence may also need to take extreme care over housing on grounds of safety and security. Such issues inevitably affect the children involved.

Immigration and nationality matters should not get tangled up with housing, but inevitably they do. In some housing authorities, women and children with properties in other countries or who are considered to have a home abroad may face being classified as intentionally homeless if they do not return there. And women whose immigration status is dependent on that of their husbands can be in a particularly dangerous and difficult position, especially if extensive housing enquiries are carried out. Under immigration law, applying as homeless under the 1985 Act counts as having 'recourse to public funds', which is proscribed during the first twelve months in the UK (see chapter by Debbonaire, this volume); thus abused women and children whose immigration status is in doubt pending enquiries or appeals may be particularly vulnerable if made homeless by violence. On a general level, women who are either themselves immigrants or whose partners are, or who come from minority ethnic communities, may be very reluctant to involve the authorities (including housing agencies) in their affairs. This is because of the possibility of experiencing harassment and discriminatory practices and because of their own solidarity with their particular communities in the face of the far reaching racism of British society as a whole. Thus homeless children of Black, minority ethnic, or immigrant families face an especially difficult and complex situation.

SPECIFIC IMPACTS ON CHILDREN AND YOUNG PEOPLE

It is increasingly being realised that children who witness or experience violence in the home may suffer from complex and quite severe psychological and emotional stresses as a result (see chapters by Morley and Mullender, Kelly, this volume). As we have described, children's distress is then likely to be increased unnecessarily by their experiences when the family applies for rehousing, especially if they are refused help or spend long periods waiting in uncertainty.

One particular problem concerns older children. The Code of Guidance only includes dependent children up to the age of 18 years if in full-time education, or 16 years if not, unless there are special circumstances. Dependent young people who are 18 years old are therefore not accepted as in priority need for rehousing. We met one woman living with her 18 year old son who was not in work. This was a mutually supportive relationship, and they had been living together in temporary accommodation since the violent break-up of her marriage. As a result of the violence, the woman suffered a nervous breakdown and had had to go into psychiatric care. Nevertheless, neither of them was accepted as being in priority need under the Act, and they were forced to separate.

In the framework of homelessness, 'dependence' is defined narrowly in terms of financial dependence alone and does not take account of the fact that parents and young people might quite normally want to live together, as they would expect to do if they were not homeless. The use of 18 years as the point at which 'childhood' ends takes no account of the great difficulties young people of that age face in being truly financially self-supporting even if they have employment, and they will often receive reduced or no income support if they do not. Nor does it relate clearly to the Children Act's concept of the duty of local authorities to children and young people 'in need', which lasts up to the age of 21. Thus, young people may be forced to cut themselves loose at a time when they are experiencing emotional turmoil and insecurity because of their experiences, particularly perhaps their experiences of violence and abuse, and in any case cannot be financially self-sufficient. We have met young people who felt that they had no alternative but to live, against their will, with their violent father. Their only other choice was to become one of the young single homeless.

Even if there are no difficulties in being accepted as a priority, similar problems of the piecemeal splitting up of families can arise because of the length of time rehousing takes, particularly for larger families, due to the current shortage of larger-sized council or housing association accommodation. This creates pressure, especially for the older children, to live elsewhere. In our research, this happened while families were waiting in a women's refuge or other temporary accommodation for rehousing. For example, the older boys in one family had to stay with relatives, partly because some refuges in this country have an upper age limit for boy residents and partly because of lack of space, with distressing effects and tensions for all concerned.

There were several other instances in our study where families became split in the process of seeking rehousing. Sometimes a woman was unable to take her child or children with her when she first left; and in some cases, even if she was very likely to be re-united with them, the separation could be used to deny that she was in priority need under the Act. This had the effect of making it almost impossible to get the children back. Additionally, the delays experienced by women in some authorities in being accepted for rehousing, and then even longer delays in being rehoused, could lead to children remaining with or returning to live with the violent partner:

> I feel very, very bitter, very bitter. I left because of the violence and I ended up losing the [two] children and not getting a house. . . . I miss the kids so much. They were my last ones, my babies. . . . It's like I'm held to be at fault because I left the family home - so I lost

everything - even though I'd left because of violence. I couldn't get him out of the house. I couldn't get the house back. I couldn't keep the kids. I couldn't get another house of my own from the Council. And it's all because of his violence and yet he gets off scot-free (White woman in a rural area).

Occasionally, courts decide that children should remain in their previous accommodation because a refuge or other temporary housing is thought to be unsuitable. Women's Aid has evidence of cases under the Children Act where children have been ordered to live with the securely housed violent father himself, on housing grounds, while their mother was insecurely housed in a refuge due to his violence (e.g. Barron et al., 1992, para.9.10).

GOOD PRACTICE

The good news is that some housing authorities and housing associations have recognised the serious nature of homelessness due to domestic violence, and have developed good practice guidelines and domestic violence policies to govern their practice. Developing and adopting guidelines of this type in conjunction with the local refuge network and other relevant groups, for example local organisations of Black women, is recommended by the Women's Aid federations and by research studies such as our own. Such policies are designed to improve and regulate local operation of the homelessness legislation in relation to women and children homeless due to domestic violence, while still allowing for officer discretion.

Domestic violence policies vary as to their contents (see Hague and Malos, 1993, pp.128-132). The sort of practice recommendations which they often contain include treating abused women and children with support and respect, prioritising domestic violence cases, and conducting minimal enquiries into the nature of the violence. Additionally, they may contain policy decisions to treat as homeless and in priority need women and children escaping mental and emotional violence, violence from outside - as opposed to inside - the home, and women without children. There may be particular commitments to address the needs of Black women and of other women facing discrimination, for example lesbians and women with disabilities, and their children. Importantly, domestic violence policies very often recommend that domestic violence training is provided for all front-line workers, and that such training should include discussion of the effects of domestic violence on children (see London Borough of Hammersmith and Fulham Community Safety Unit, 1991; Leeds Inter-Agency Project, 1993). Clearly, the development of such policy and practice guidelines will have a beneficial effect on the lives of the children of abused women applicants.

GOVERNMENT PROPOSALS

The shortage of public sector housing, brought about by central government policies, has led to the Government trying to do something about the increasing numbers of homeless people. What it is proposing to do is not, however, to improve housing possibilities; but, rather, to amend the legislation so that councils will no longer have a duty to secure permanent rehousing for statutorily defined homeless people under the 1985 Act. This will have the effect of blaming and penalising the homeless for the shortage of social rented housing. If the new proposals - which were issued by the Department of the Environment in 1994 with a view to amending the law in 1994/5 - go ahead, they will mean that the homeless compete for rehousing with everyone else on the ordinary housing waiting list (Department of Environment, 1994). The right to be placed by local councils in temporary accommodation will also be massively eroded, and will be time-limited. One effect of all this may be to force people to move again and again from one piece of temporary housing to another - the emphasis being on private accommodation - with little hope of gaining permanent housing.

The proposals will mean a virtual rescinding of the present homelessness legislation. Many commentators in the media have suggested that they will result in a turning back of the clock to the situation in the fifties when all the homeless, including children, were highly stigmatised and had few housing rights, as remains the case for the young single homeless today. The proposals single out women who have suffered domestic violence for special mention in respect of offers of temporary accommodation. However, the proposal to bar 'persons from abroad' from assistance of any type if they have access to property in another country could be disastrous for women and children fleeing abuse and violence who are immigrants, or even for those who have been settled here for a long period or indeed are citizens who have lived abroad and are returning to this country after experiencing domestic violence. And Government promotion of private rented accommodation as an option for councils to use in discharging their duties in regard to both temporary and permanent rehousing could have severe consequences for women and children, due to the lack of security (both physically and in terms of tenure) of this type of accommodation, its expense, and its frequent rules against taking children, as previously discussed.

If the suggested changes go ahead, they will mean a serious decrease in the ability of abused women and children to achieve permanent rehousing. At the time of writing, the Women's Aid federations and many housing bodies are campaigning against the proposals. We do not yet know what will happen but, in July 1994, the Housing Minister announced the results of the consultation process to the effect that, despite receiving many thousands of submissions condemning the proposals, the Government plans to press ahead, with relatively minor modifications. Fortunately, it is no longer proposed that local authorities will not be under a legal obligation to provide temporary housing until they have completed investigations, which could have affected abused women and children catastrophically in an emergency.

CONCLUSIONS

Large numbers of women and children who are homeless due to domestic abuse wait for months or years in refuges or other temporary accommodation before being rehoused, and many never find permanent and secure housing. Many children, as well as their mothers, suffer traumatic life experiences as a result. In addition to exposure to renewed and sometimes extreme violence, particularly if forced to return home against their will due to housing inadequacies, the distressing catalogue of problems experienced by women and their children include: continued homelessness; continued transience in the search for rehousing; further disruption to children's education and mental and physical health; behavioural and psychiatric disturbances in children necessitating intervention by the statutory services; and high levels of anxiety, fear, depression, and hopelessness for both the women and children concerned. It is particularly troubling that some women who have left home due to violence, but who are unable to secure permanent housing, face the loss of their children to their securely housed partners. That children may be returned to the woman's violent partner or separated from their mother purely on accommodation grounds is very disturbing, and is contrary to the spirit of both the homelessness legislation and the emphasis on the interests of children and young people in the Children Act.

Although good practice in regard to homelessness exists, and attempts by housing authorities and associations to introduce domestic violence policies and good practice guidelines are to be applauded, many local councils are instead introducing harsher and harsher rationing measures because of the lack of available housing. There is little evidence, despite government support and recent innovations and changes in housing management, that the housing association movement or the private rented sector can make up for the shortage of council accommodation. This housing crisis reflects serious shortcomings in national government policy in respect of social rented housing.

If the new Department of Environment proposals become law, as the Government proposes, the situation for homeless people in this country, including women and children experiencing domestic violence, will become infinitely worse. For abused women and their children, the current lack of safe, permanent accommodation seriously affects the future not only of the women involved but of large numbers of children and young people as well. To make their rehousing situation any worse could have disastrous consequences.

References

Barron, J. (1990) *Not Worth the Paper: The Effectiveness of Legal Protection for Women and Children Experiencing Domestic Violence*. Bristol: Women's Aid Federation England.

Barron, J., Harwin, N. and Singh, T. (1992) *Women's Aid Federation England Written Evidence to the House of Commons Home Affairs Committee Inquiry into Domestic Violence*, October. Bristol: Women's Aid Federation England. (Also published as Memorandum 22, submitted by Women's Aid Federation England, in Home Affairs Committee, 1993b, see below).

Bull, J. (1993) *Housing Consequences of Relationship Breakdown*. London: HMSO.

CHICL/London Housing Unit (1992) *Losing Heart: the Impact of Government Policy on Housing Association Development in Central London*. London: CHICl/LHU.

Department of Education and Science HMI (1990) *A Survey of the Education of Children living in Temporary Accommodation*. London: HMSO.

Department of Environment (1991) *Homelessness: Code of Guidance for Local Authorities, Part III of the Housing Act 1985*. Third Edition. London: HMSO.

Department of Environment (1994) *Access to Local Authority and Housing Association Tenancies: a Consultation Paper*. London: DOE.

Greve, J. (1991) *Homelessness in Britain*. York: Joseph Rowntree Foundation.

Hague G. and Malos E. (1993) *Domestic Violence: Action for Change*. Cheltenham: New Clarion Press.

Health Visitors Association and General Medical Services Committee (1989) *Homeless Families and their Health*. London: BMA.

Home Affairs Committee (1993a) *Domestic Violence*. Vol.I, Report together with the Proceedings of the Committee. London: HMSO.

Home Affairs Committee (1993b) *Domestic Violence*. Vol.II, Memoranda of Evidence, Minutes of Evidence and Appendices. London: HMSO.

Law Commission (1992) *Family Law: Domestic Violence and Occupation of the Family Home*. Law. Com. No. 207. London: HMSO.

Leeds Inter-Agency Project (1993) *Violence against Women by Known Men: Training Pack*. Leeds: Leeds Inter-Agency Project, Sahara Black Women's Refuge and Leeds Women's Aid.

London Borough of Hammersmith and Fulham Community Safety Unit (1991) *Challenging Domestic Violence: a Training and Resource Pack*. London: Borough of Hammersmith and Fulham.

Malos, E. and Hague G. (1993) *Domestic Violence and Housing: Local Authority Responses to Women and Children Escaping from Violence in the Home*. Bristol: Women's Aid Federation England and University of Bristol School of Applied Social Studies.

Malos E. (1993) *You've Got No Life: Homelessness and the Use of Bed and Breakfast Hotels.*. Bristol: University of Bristol School of Applied Social Studies.

Mama, A. (1989) *The Hidden Struggle: Statutory and Voluntary Sector Responses to Violence against Black Women in the Home*. London: London Race and Housing Research Unit.

Miller, M. (1990) *Bed-and-Breakfast: A Study of Women and Homelessness Today*. London: Women's Press.

Morley, R. (1993) 'Recent responses to domestic violence against women: a feminist critique' in Page, R. and Baldock, J. (eds.) *Social Policy Review 5: the Evolving State of Welfare*. Canterbury: Social Policy Association.

Muir, J. and Ross M. (1993) *Housing and the Poorer Sex*. London: London Housing Unit.

Murie, A. and Jeffers, S. (eds.) (1987) *Living in Bed and Breakfast: the Experience of Homelessness in London*. Bristol: University of Bristol School for Advanced Urban Studies.

Russell, M. (1989) *Taking Stock: Refuge Provision in London in the Late 1980s*. London: London Strategic Policy Unit with financial assistance from the London Borough of Southwark.

Select Committee on Violence in Marriage (1975) *Report from the Select Committee on Violence in Marriage*. London: HMSO.

Shelter (1991) *Urgent Need for Homes*. London: Shelter.

Stearn, J. (1986) 'An expensive way of making children ill', *Roof,* September-October.

Tunstill, J. and Aldgate, J. (forthcoming 1994) *Implementing S17 of the Children Act: The First 18 Months: A Study for the Department of Health*.

Victim Support (1992) *Domestic Violence: Report of a National Inter-Agency Working Party on Domestic Violence*. London: Victim Support.

SECTION IV

Children in Refuges and After

10

Work With Children in Women's Aid Refuges and After

Thangam Debbonaire

INTRODUCTION TO WOMEN'S AID

Approximately 45,000 women and children were given accommodation by refuge groups in England in the year 1992-3, of whom nearly 28,000 were children (Women's Aid Federation England, 1993). Additionally, over 100,000 women each year contact Women's Aid somewhere in the country for advice and support without ever living in a refuge. Consequently, the services of Women's Aid are affecting the lives of thousands of children each year. Most refuges are now able to employ a specialist children's worker and all aim to provide specific activities and services for children.

A majority of Women's Aid groups in England are affiliated to and receive services from the Women's Aid Federation of England (WAFE). WAFE is a national co-ordinating organisation for refuge groups who are provided with resources, networking, training and information. It also lobbies for changes in the law, and promotes the needs and experiences of women and children experiencing domestic violence to other relevant agencies such as the police and probation service. WAFE runs the only national helpline for women experiencing domestic violence - offering advice, a listening ear, and referral to refuges or other agencies as appropriate. Sister organisations for refuge groups in the rest of the United Kingdom are Welsh Women's Aid, Scottish Women's Aid and Northern Irish Women's Aid.

The need for specific services for children comes from a recognition of their experiences and of the particular effects violence can have on children. These include a significant link between the abuse of women and the abuse of children (see chapter by Morley and Mullender, this volume), which indicates a child protection dimension to the work of Women's Aid.

Women's Aid values and ways of working

Women's Aid has always affirmed that violence against women is linked to the unequal position of women and children in society compared with men. Other principles underpinning the work are contained in the

WAFE *Statement of Aims and Principles* (WAFE, n.d.). Supporting and empowering women to make choices for themselves is underpinned by giving accurate information about legal rights and local provision. Support and access to refuge services applies to women whatever choices they may make, and for as long as they need it. Mutual self-help and support amongst women are seen in refuges' strong tradition of working collectively. Policies and practice are developed through participatory discussion and consensus decision-making. The obvious commitment to ending discrimination against women has extended to working against discrimination of all kinds and creating equality of opportunity for all women involved in Women's Aid, whatever their role. Women living in refuges and ex-residents are often involved in running the group as volunteers, unpaid management committee members, or as members of staff.

The principle of an 'open door' operates in most refuges affiliated to WAFE and means that women and children should always be given somewhere safe to stay in an emergency. When a refuge is full, the staff there will help a woman to find other emergency accommodation and also provide information and advice. Specialist refuges are an exception to the open door policy because they cater for specific groups of women who have particular needs or who face additional discrimination from public agencies and society generally. Refuges exist for Black women, Asian women, white mothers with Black children, and Latin American women. More are being developed at the time of writing. A refuge is currently being set up in London by and for women with disabilities. Jewish women and Chinese women have also set up specialist advice services. These refuges will always make sure that any other women contacting them are referred on to a refuge that can offer help. All refuges operate with a commitment to anti-discriminatory working and opportunities for equality.

Values operating in Women's Aid work with children

There are two key principles underlying the work done in refuge groups with and for children. These are a commitment to promoting and developing the rights of children experiencing domestic violence, and a belief that play is healing for children and that all children can benefit from play activities. Play helps children's development, gives them a chance to express themselves, encourages social skills and can also be educational. Play and other child-centred activities can provide a setting for promoting mutual support between children and between children and adults. It can also be a focus for finding non-violent ways of resolving conflict.

Children still have very few rights in law. They are the only group of people whom it is not illegal to assault in this country. What rights do exist on paper are limited or frequently ignored. This country has been a signatory to the *UN Convention on the Rights of the Child* for two years. Work undertaken in the independent Children's Rights Development

Unit indicates that there is still much more to be done to make many aspects of the convention a reality for all children (Children's Rights Development Unit, 1994, p.10). It is easy to ignore the rights of people who do not have a vote, as they do not elect the legislators and usually depend on others for a voice. Children's rights therefore need to be given as high a priority as possible as a fundamental aspect of equal opportunities. The implementation of any rights that do exist will require advocacy and support from others; rights cannot be exercised unless the person concerned both knows of their existence and is in a position to be able to exercise them. In order to make children's rights a reality, therefore, children will need advocates within the whole refuge group - to promote and facilitate expression of their needs in all aspects of refuge organisation and work. This does not necessarily mean that children do not speak on their own behalf; an advocate can give young people a space for expressing their needs and feelings themselves. Acting as an advocate is one of the roles of a children's support worker.

WHAT WOMEN'S AID PROVIDES FOR CHILDREN

Women's Aid groups vary in what specific services they provide, but almost all provide a core service. The offer of emergency accommodation is generally available 24 hours a day, 365 days of the year. Virtually all refuges provide some activities specifically for children, usually including after-school play sessions. Most organise trips and outings in the holidays and at weekends, which give the children's workers a chance to talk to individual children and allow the children to spend time together away from the refuge and with the focus on their own needs. Services may vary, for example to cater for specialist needs such as those of Black women and their children. The amount of work done with children has always been to some extent limited by resources, in particular the lack of secure statutory funding. That it nevertheless continues to develop in imaginative and resourceful ways is a tribute to the immense commitment and energy of the women involved over the years. Ironically, some refuges have found that where their local authority is particularly slow at re-housing women (over a year in some London boroughs), they are able to offer longer term one-to-one work with individual children.

There is a chronic need for funding for outreach and aftercare work with children escaping domestic violence who have never been in the refuge or who have left. At the time of writing, some refuges are in the process of extending their outreach services to provide specific activities for children. In one area, child workers run an activity session once a month for any children who have left the refuge. The children attending have said how much they value being able to stay in touch with the children's workers and with each other after moving into new accommodation. Other refuges are planning how to offer a service for children escaping domestic violence who are living in other temporary accommodation such as bed and breakfast.

One of the fundamental services a refuge offers all children is contact, often for the first time, with other children in a similar position. Many children coming into a refuge will never have lived in a home without violence present in it. Many believe that they are the only ones ever to have lived in that situation. Coming into the refuge can give children an opportunity that cannot easily be achieved elsewhere of sharing their experiences and realising they are not alone. In a refuge, they can have their experiences heard, validated, and understood by other children and adults who have been through similar things and who understand how it feels. One of the primary means for facilitating this process is through the work of a children's worker.

Refuge children's support workers

Most Women's Aid groups now employ at least one specialist children's support worker (WAFE, 1993). Many groups also train and involve volunteers in activities and outings. There is great dedication and skill shown by the women working with children in refuges. Some are ex-residents of refuges, so have first-hand knowledge of refuge life. Most have some formal child care or teacher training, or acquire and develop new skills and knowledge through working with the children as a volunteer, initially under the supervision of a children's worker. With the help of funding from ITV Telethon, WAFE regularly provides organised training programmes commissioned specifically for refuge children's workers across the country. Evaluation of the training courses has shown them to be of great benefit.

What does a refuge children's support worker do?

Job descriptions vary between refuge groups but there are core functions carried out by most refuge child workers. If there is not a designated post for children, other staff and volunteers in the group will still provide most of these. A child support worker will typically organise play and activity sessions, holiday outings and play schemes, as well as group sessions for children to plan activities and discuss matters about refuge life; she also represents the interests of children at meetings of residents, of staff, of the management committee, and so on. Some workers carry out one-to-one sessions with individual children or special sessions for groups of older girls or boys. Some provide training programmes for volunteers working with children. This can be a positive way of including ex-resident women in the work as well as residents, and of providing them with the opportunity to increase their skills and confidence in themselves.

Refuge life can be very demanding on children. They have to leave behind their toys and other possessions. Keeping a refuge address secret generally includes not being able to invite friends round and families may have moved far away from existing friends to escape the violence. They may also have to lose contact with other members of the extended family. Many children also miss their father and feel confused about why they are there. Not only the children's worker but also the other children can help new arrivals to cope and to understand more about what is happening.

Children's support workers are there to support the woman and children as well as to provide activities specifically for children. Play is the central element in this work. Play can fulfil many useful functions: development of social skills and imagination, exercise and physical development. Play sessions can provide a more relaxed and informal opportunity for children to express their fears and problems, verbally or through other creative expression. Sessions can also provide the opportunity for testing out conflict resolution. A children's worker will encourage the children to learn how to deal with disagreements without violence or abusive behaviour. Providing specific services for children also gives a clear signal to all refuge residents and staff that children's needs are important too.

In addition to providing services within the refuge, children's workers develop and maintain good contacts with other agencies in the area. This can achieve several objectives: raising general levels of awareness about the needs and experiences of children experiencing domestic violence, developing ways of working together in the interests of those children, and being able to provide women and children with access to services that the refuge may not be able to provide. Agencies with which children's workers usually have contact include local schools and nurseries, counselling services, health visitors, child protection teams, family therapy centres, contact centres, and youth clubs.

Children's feelings about refuge life

In Autumn 1993, WAFE ran a competition for children living in refuges to design a greetings card entitled 'refuge life'. (The winning entries were printed up as cards for sale and are available from WAFE.) The entries all displayed the obvious pleasure and fun that the children had derived from living in a refuge. Other external researchers and evaluators (e.g. Ball, 1990) have also remarked on the degree to which children have visibly valued the presence of the children's worker and they have been able to observe the difference she has made to their lives. Children's workers often say that many children enjoy living in refuges so much they don't want to leave; this is one reason why refuge groups are so keen to be able to provide aftercare services. Once the children have left the refuge, they will often still have need of contact with other children in similar situations as well as the attention of the children's worker, but may become isolated from this in their new accommodation. Aftercare services could provide the bridge to help children and mothers settle into their new lives without becoming dependent on the refuge itself.

NATIONAL WORK FOR CHILDREN

Nationally, WAFE lobbies Government and national professional agencies to improve law, service provision, policy and practice affecting children who experience abuse in the home. The National Children's Officer works with other staff to promote children's specific needs in each case. Recent initiatives include working with the probation service on the policy and practice in court welfare work, and working with the Home Office and police forces on improving police responses. WAFE briefing papers are available on a range of topics concerning children's needs and experiences. Publicity and press work carried out by Women's Aid regularly highlights the needs and experiences of children. Women's Aid works jointly, both locally and nationally, with other child care agencies to promote children's interests and rights generally and specifically, developing ways of working that protect children but do not undermine the non-abusing parent.

Child work mailings are compiled by the National Children's Officer for distribution to refuges on a quarterly basis. These mailings contain information about anything relevant to the work with children in refuges, including changes in the law or policy, funding sources, resources for children's work, and so on. They act as a means of sharing information and experiences between groups. Additionally, the Children's Officer writes and updates information leaflets for refuge groups and the public on relevant issues. Another vital role is developing and running specialist training courses specifically designed for refuge children's workers, as mentioned above. In the last three years, WAFE has been able to provide courses on promoting alternatives to physical punishment in refuges, anti-racist work, working with social services in child protection, the 1989 Children Act, and much more. This has allowed children's workers to recognise and value the skills and knowledge they already have and to build on these.

WAFE national children's workers' group

Children's workers in groups affiliated to the Women's Aid Federation of England (WAFE) meet regularly to exchange and develop ideas about working with children and to give each other support when necessary. This is facilitated by the National Children's Officer, at different locations around the country in order to increase the opportunity for participation. Issues raised in these meetings have changed over the years as the work done with children has developed and become better respected, both within WAFE and from funders and others. For example, five years ago when the group was established, less than half of all refuges had a specialist children's worker and almost all of them were part time, working very much in isolation. Many of the issues raised at meetings of child workers were therefore focused on this isolation, and on how to provide consistent levels of basic services without enough staff to cover work during holidays or sick leave. Getting support from each other to try to go back to their own projects and improve the situation was one of the key objectives for many women.

In the time that the group has existed, this has changed. Over two thirds of refuge groups now have at least one specialist worker. Many have more than one. Most women attending meetings are therefore no longer working in isolation but more often in pairs of child workers, or sometimes even in teams. This means that the group is now able to spend much more time reflecting on what services are provided and how these can be developed. There is time for individual women to get help and support from the group with specific problems. For women who are still working on their own or without adequate local support, this remains a very useful source of strength and advice. Women also exchange information about resources they have found successful, particularly books and play materials that reflect a multicultural community and promote anti-racist working. Issues are also worked on in more depth, perhaps over the course of several meetings. These vary from a problem that is cropping up repeatedly and which triggers a piece of policy development or implementation, to a specific task like collecting resources to promote non-abusive discipline for children in refuges.

In the last year, the WAFE Children's Rights policy has been developed in this way. (The policy is reproduced at the end of this chapter.) This process entailed developing a shared understanding of what values were operating within work with children in refuges, through discussion and reflection as well as reference to the Women's Aid aims and principles. A summary of services, ways of protecting children, and methods of involving them in refuge life was then drawn together and forms the main structure of the policy, organised under the headings of protection, provision and participation. The final task was to identify the greatest possible range of different methods of achieving the individual elements of the policy so as to provide a basic framework for all work with children in WAFE-affiliated refuges whilst also allowing for differences between refuges and between children. The resulting policy was formally adopted by WAFE member refuge groups in 1993.

The development, acceptance and implementation of this policy has done much to focus refuge groups' attention on children's needs in a practical context. Children's workers have used it to argue for better funding as well as increased respect for their work. Development of this policy has continued since, looking specifically at the child protection dimension. Information about local policies and service contracts is being shared within the group, considering various alternatives and thinking about issues arising from each possible policy decision. This has been supported by training that children's workers attend, both within WAFE and from local sources.

Overall, children's workers' meetings are an invaluable forum for recognising and valuing the skills and knowledge of women doing innovative and often unique work in highly pressurised emergency situations.

WAFE refuge groups have adopted a policy of aiming to make the refuge a truly safe space by promoting non-physical ways of dealing with conflict towards and between children living there. WAFE believes that children should be afforded the same rights to protection from violence and abuse as adults, which currently in UK law is not the case. In the long term, changing the behaviour of the adults of the future has to start now by bringing up all children to choose non-violent methods of resolving conflict. It has to be acknowledged from the outset that within refuges this is an ongoing process that involves everyone - staff, volunteers, women and children residents.

Promoting this policy in any setting can expose painful and perhaps hidden emotions and deeply held feelings about child rearing. However, many refuges have found that discussing the issue from different points of view not only helps to widen general awareness of children's needs and rights, but can also be a powerful way of looking at women's experience. It improves communication between adults and children in the refuge. Additionally, it helps to reinforce feelings of safety for children, which for some can mean that they are able to tell about abuse they have suffered - perhaps for the first time. The importance of this facility should never be underestimated.

Children's workers have used play activities to stimulate discussion amongst children about violence, prejudice and bullying. Some have undertaken creative work with children to allow them to express their feelings non-verbally. The children's pictures, paintings, collages, music and poetry are then displayed in the refuge or used as a focus for further discussion with them and perhaps with adult residents. Children's workers also use creative activities as a way of encouraging children to value and respect difference and individuality, their own and each others'. Some have found that mothers have gained from these activities too. This is partly from the shared activity with their child and also from looking at their own sense of self, sometimes for the first time in years.

Child protection issues

Elsewhere in this book others explore the relationship between the abuse of women and the abuse of children (see chapters by Morley and Mullender, Kelly, this volume). Refuge staff are often aware of abuse children have suffered directly, as well as the distress caused to them by the violence towards their mother. Indeed, refuge workers were amongst the first to take disclosures of widescale sexual abuse seriously. Along with other women's organisations, they built up valuable experience of being open to disclosures from both women and children. They became skilled at undertaking healing work through listening to and accepting survivors, helping them to understand that they were not to blame for the actions of their abusers, and assisting them to rebuild their lives. It is only more recently that social services departments have made a specialism out of child sexual abuse and their work is often the poorer for lacking an effective response to the ways in which men abuse their power in contemporary society.

Recently, some Women's Aid groups have been forced to confront the tension between their empowering model of survivors needing to make their own choices and the more bureaucratic approach of social services staff because child protection has become linked to funding conditions from local authorities. Some authorities have insisted that service agreements or contracts with refuge groups contain a condition of adherence to their child protection procedures. This presents dilemmas for refuge groups which cannot always be satisfactorily resolved. The criminal justice system is not efficient at convicting child abusers. In itself, the court system can often be abusive for the child concerned - requiring her or him to go over and over deeply painful events, either in court where they will be questioned in front of the abuser, or on video tape which may be dismissed as inadmissible evidence. The child cannot have counselling until the trial is over. She or he may end up in the care system unnecessarily. Even if a case of suspected abuse never goes to court, reporting to social services inevitably means more investigations into the child's life at a very vulnerable time.

Many refuge groups worry that the benefits of reporting could be outweighed by these profound drawbacks when the child is not returning to live with the abuser. Reporting when the child is neither returning home nor under a contact order may seem like an unnecessary intrusion into the lives of both mother and child. It also effectively punishes children for the actions of their abusers if, following reporting, they are pressurised into taking part in a criminal investigation in order to protect other children. The decision may be more clear-cut where refuge staff feel a child is in current danger, or where the child wishes to have action taken, or where she or he is having contact visits with the abuser. Informing social services in any circumstances involves thinking and planning how the child's emotional needs can be met. It also always has to involve the mother of the child since, if Women's Aid is to be trusted as an organisation by women needing help, it needs to retain its non-judgemental approach to the woman's decisions.

There is no doubt that, for some children, seeing their abuser successfully prosecuted for what he has done to them is very important. A recent case highlighted the positive benefits of good liaison between agencies when Women's Aid staff, police officers from the child protection unit, and social workers all worked together to bring a violent abuser to justice and a custodial sentence. This was initiated on the child's strong request and with the mother's full support. However, cases are not always like that and for some children the pain of the court proceedings may be too much to bear - especially if it does not result in a conviction. These tensions and contradictions between children's needs, women's needs, and social service and Women's Aid policies are still being worked through.

This is an emerging problem but already groups are engaging with developing solutions that are effective for all the people involved and primarily for the safety of children. This means starting from the value that children are generally most effectively protected if they are living with a non-abusing parent, usually the mother. Empowering and supporting the mother to be able to create a safe life for herself and her children is good child protection. It is also cheaper than having to take a child into care. Some refuge groups have carried out extensive consultation procedures with residents, volunteers and others when jointly developing a policy with their social services department. They may prepare leaflets and other resources for the mother and the children as well as for staff and volunteers. The emphasis is on sharing knowledge. Whilst this in no way eliminates the power imbalance between an individual woman and a statutory agency, it does help to redress it. It also helps all the parties to understand the motives behind a child abuse policy and thus increases its effectiveness. It would be beneficial to all if social services departments could make an equal move towards valuing the expertise and the cogent analysis of male abuse which are held within the heritage of Women's' Aid.

PROBLEMS FOR CHILDREN LIVING IN A REFUGE

Education

New problems constantly emerge as public policy changes and public opinion shifts. One new difficulty for children living in temporary accommodation is obtaining a school place. A recent piece of research by Alison Clark for the SPACE trust (1992) highlighted the range of obstacles to an adequate education for children living in temporary accommodation, including refuges. It is generally assumed that the provision of free education for all children between the ages of five and sixteen is a right in this country. However, it is not a right that can be taken for granted under the present system. Current educational policy has persuaded many schools to 'opt out' of local authority control over the last five years. This has meant difficulties and delays, sometimes for months, in finding school places for children in some areas. Many women discover that no matter what efforts they may be making to ensure continuity and stability for their children, these efforts can be easily undermined by the lack of a school or nursery place. Education, social services, and housing departments need to co-ordinate their policies to ensure that they are not excluding children living in temporary accommodation. Children with special needs have these difficulties multiplied. If the family has moved to a new area to escape the violent partner, there are often delays and difficulties in getting the transfer of a statement of special needs from the previous local authority which, in turn, delays the allocation of a school place. Children's educational opportunities are being limited by the accommodation they have to live in, which compounds their distress and upset.

Even after a child has a school place, there may be problems getting to school, or finding space for older children to do homework. Children from refuges may also find themselves very isolated. They may be starting in the middle of term without feeling able to explain the reasons for this. They do not have their own space to bring friends back to. Some children have been teased or bullied for being different. Black children can find this compounded by racism. Older children, particularly, may feel uncomfortable with their friends or other peers while they are living within the refuge. The lack of anywhere private to spend time, and the risk to refuge security of letting others know the address and telephone number, limit the amount of social contact they can enjoy. This makes the need for support and information from within the refuge even more acute.

Refuge children's workers and school staff have developed ways of trying to deal with the problems outlined above. In one area, the refuge has a permanently designated number of places at the local nursery. In another, the educational welfare officer liaises with the refuge to try to ensure that enough appropriate school places are available. Some refuges liaise closely with the welfare staff at the school on the needs of children living in refuges. Others have provided talks or training sessions on domestic violence and refuge life for staff of schools to increase their awareness of the issues. Some schools now include elements of conflict resolution on their curriculum, which provides a setting and framework for exploring what is wrong with using force (see also schools chapter by Mullender, this volume). Many children have found that, on balance, the benefits of being in the refuge outweigh the disadvantages, especially if they are highly aware of the past violence and its effects.

Deportation

A few children face the additional possibility of deportation of their mothers and themselves. Under the 'twelve month rule', women can be deported if they have been in this country for less than a year when they leave their husband, even if they can show that they can support themselves and their children. Many of these families will find that they are not entitled to the same provision from the State as others. The inadequacies of benefits and of public housing provision are irrelevant to them as they can find that they face the alternatives of returning to the violence, or deportation, or destitution. However, in recent years several threatened deportations have been successfully fought by women supporting each other, within Women's Aid and elsewhere, and campaigning together on individual cases. Lobbying on a collective basis for changes in the law continues.

Racism

Many children have to deal with racism from multiple sources, including from other children. As refuges take in a wide range of women and children who themselves reflect many of the prejudices present in society, racism will certainly need to be confronted within the refuge; this is one reason for the existence of refuges for Black women and children only (see chapter by Imam, this volume.) The WAFE Children's Rights policy includes the child's right to safety from racism. It makes clear that no group can guarantee this right completely, but they *can* take action to promote anti-discrimination and refuge staff use a range of methods for this work.

Racism is an abuse of human rights as it allows for or produces the conditions for one type of person or group or organisation to intimidate, oppress and otherwise limit the freedom of others who are seen as in some way different. Freedom from prejudice is the first article in the UN Convention on the Rights of the Child. The struggle against racism is an integral factor in the struggle against the abuse of women and children. Therefore, refuges can and do try to work against it and to tackle its effects on all women and children. Promoting anti-discrimination in this context means actively striving to value and respect differences, whilst acknowledging that this also means people having to take responsibility for the effects their behaviour can have on others. The underlying principle is that working against violence and oppression is about seeking freedom from oppression, not the freedom to oppress others. Working with such a principle is not, of course, straightforward; both training sessions and child workers' meetings regularly examine how it can be actively promoted in refuges.

CHILD-RELATED LEGISLATION AFFECTING REFUGE WORK

Although this legislation was explored in earlier chapters (see chapters by Harne and Radford; Hester et al., this volume), it has had a particular impact on women and children in refuges which is worthy of special attention.

1. Children Act, 1989

Background

This piece of legislation reached the statute books after an unprecedented amount of public consultation and lobbying, and with all party assent. It was widely applauded, both during its passage through Parliament and since, as a positive development in terms of improving social services practice, increasing partnership with parents, and placing increased emphasis on preventive work. Other welcome innovations included requirements to be mindful of a child's race and religion, and other important elements of a child's needs and identity (s.22[5][c]). However, the consultation did not include consideration of the specific difficulties surrounding domestic violence. As a result, the Act unintentionally presents new dangers and difficulties for women and children leaving domestic violence, as well as for refuge groups.

Impact on refuge child care

The Children Act contains a requirement for local authorities to ensure that there are local services for 'children in need' (s.17). However, only a handful of refuges have found that this has made any difference to funding received from the local authority. Most are still reliant on charitable sources for funding children's worker posts. Some local authorities have expressed sympathy but have said that they do not have enough resources to fund even this desperately needed service. The Children Act imposes an obligation on local authorities to avoid the need for care proceedings where consistent with the welfare of the child (Department of Health, 1991, The *Children Act 1989 Guidance and Regulations,* vol.1, para.3.2). Many children in refuges would probably have had to be looked after by the local authority eventually (in care or accommodated) if their mothers had not had a refuge to go to or to contact, but this is impossible to prove or to quantify in financial terms. Overall, the impact of the Act on funding for refuge work with children has been almost non-existent.

In the last few years, children's workers in refuges have become more involved in child protection work and their skills and knowledge in this area have been better acknowledged by social services departments. This has usually meant an increase in workload and responsibilities for children's workers but, without extra funding, this increases the strain on a refuge group's limited resources.

Contact orders

Contact orders are presented in the legislation as intended to promote the child's right to have contact with certain people. In practice, little seems to have changed and the initiative remains with whoever feels they have a right to have access to a particular child. This has become even more apparent recently as absent fathers are receiving bills from the Child Support Agency towards the costs of providing for their children; many feel this gives them the right to have contact with the child, whether or not this is what the child wants or is in her or his best interests. Children expressing quite clearly that they do not wish to see their father or to have contact with him often have this feeling ignored, rubbished, or attributed to indoctrination by their mother.

If a contact order is made, the next problem to face is the lack of a suitable place for contact. Contact centres, providing a neutral meeting place with facilities for absent fathers to spend time with their children, are scarce. Those that do exist are generally underfunded and in great demand. Lack of adequate funding means in some centres that the contact between father and children cannot be supervised, putting mothers under added anxiety. Some refuge children's workers have been asked to help act as supervisors of contact visits, but they do not generally agree, as they are also under-resourced and may be putting their own safety at risk. Contact centres are a badly needed resource, in the interests of children's welfare, and of their and their mothers' safety (see chapter by Harne and Radford, this volume, for a different view).

Contact does not just mean visits. The guidance to the Children Act states that it may also mean contact by telephone or letter (*Children Act 1989 Guidance and Regulations*, vol.1, para.2.29). In effect, this means that a court can order access to the telephone number and address of wherever a child is living. This is obviously detrimental to the security of refuges and therefore of the safety of other women and children. Many courts now accept that it is not appropriate for men to have this information and make other provisions for enabling contact. However in other cases, women can find that, after all their efforts to conceal their whereabouts from a violent man, they are back to square one after a contact order has been granted.

The emphasis in the Act on the desirability of children having contact with both parents does not adequately protect the safety of women and children escaping domestic violence. The Act assumes that parents are a unit of two equal partners with equal input into, and equal responsibility for a child's care and upbringing. This idealistic picture does not reflect the reality of most women's lives. At the moment, this is presenting new risks for refuge security and for the safety of women and children.

Residence
In several cases in the last two years, women have been ordered by courts to return their children to live with their father, the judge expressing the opinion that refuges were not suitable places for children and that it was in the child's best interests to live in the family home. This displays ignorance both of the nature of refuges and of the needs of children. Refuges are places safe from violence, where a mother and her children can begin to rebuild their lives. They are not permanent homes for children. The current legal provisions mean that it is often impossible for a woman to force her partner to leave the family home so that she can live there with the children (see chapter by Hague and Malos, this volume). Women in this country still have unequal access to adequately paid employment in comparison with men, and the lack of decent affordable child care limits their options for improving this still further. This can restrict the quality of housing women can afford when they leave violent men. However, this should never be a reason for returning a child to live with a violent man. It also denies the gains that many children experience from refuge life and emphasises the material side of providing for a child over and above other aspects of a child's upbringing.

Court welfare
The Children Act has increased the role and workload of the probation
service (through its civil work teams) in the preparation of court welfare
reports. These are required where an application for contact or residence
is being disputed (see chapter by Hester et al., this volume, for a fuller
discussion). As domestic violence not untypically involves such disputes,
there has been a consequent increase in Women's Aid groups' awareness
of court welfare officers and of the wide variation in their practice. This
autonomy is presented from within the profession as a strength.
However, it can and does lead to damaging and dangerous
inconsistencies. Examples of bad practice include forcing women to have
joint interviews with men they are frightened of. In one area, the
(female) court welfare officer has told the refuge that she is there to be on
the man's side as the refuge is supporting the woman. Others have
refused to acknowledge the genuine fear a woman has of her ex-partner;
inappropriate recommendations for contact have put the woman and her
children at risk of, at best, distressing scenes and, at worst, physical
harm. At the opposite extreme, there are reports from refuges of officers
who have an excellent understanding of domestic violence and who
would never force a woman into attending a joint interview.

Women's Aid has begun to address this issue nationally in order to
challenge bad and inconsistent practice. National staff have provided
training and speakers for national conferences on these issues. In 1989,
the WAFE National Co-ordinator was instrumental in the development
of what became a *Position Statement on Domestic Violence* for the
Association of Chief Officers of Probation (ACOP, 1992). The statement
contains a commitment that women should never be pressurised into
having joint interviews and should, indeed, be actively informed of their
right to choose to be seen separately. Unfortunately, there is no
compulsion on court welfare officers to comply with the Position
Statement and internal monitoring indicates that practice continues to
vary (private communication). At the time of writing, the Home Office is
preparing final drafts of a good practice policy for court welfare work. It
is to be hoped that this has drawn on the Position Statement and that it
will carry weight with the probation service and its civil work teams. The
safety and welfare of women and children are at stake.

Schools
The Children Act and accompanying guidance imposed new obligations
on schools. Many head teachers have felt uncertain about their legal
obligations towards absent parents and some have jeopardised the
safety of women and children by giving information to abusive men
about their children, stating that they have no choice but to do so
(contrast with chapter by Loosley, this volume). For some children, this
has meant that access to schooling is further limited by threats to their
mother's or their own safety, particularly when there is a fear that the

man will abduct them. If the child has remained at the same school, it may be relatively easy for the man to find out where the family is living, by waiting at the school entrance and threatening or following them. This also jeopardises the safety of other refuge residents and staff. The governmental guidance is not in fact clear. The Children Act increases men's rights to have 'parental responsibility' and the guidance accompanying the legislation stresses the desirability of both parents having and maintaining this responsibility (Children Act sections 2-4 and *Children Act 1989 Guidance and Regulations*, vol.1, paras.2.4-2.5). It is not clear what it should consist of in practical terms.

In some cases, the court has decided that a man with 'parental responsibility' has a right to have information about the child's schooling even where he does not have a contact order. The law does not make clear what exceptions should be considered, such as domestic violence. Clarification is badly needed. Matters are made worse by the fact that the court does not have to take unto consideration the safety of the caring parent when making decisions about a particular child. In some areas, refuge children's workers have been able to liaise with local schools to ensure that appropriate measures are taken to keep details of the child from the abusive man, and that no one besides the mother is allowed to collect a particular child from school.

Principle of no order
Section 1(5) of the Children Act introduced the principle of 'no order'. This means that orders cannot be granted unless doing so promotes the child's welfare. Where there is no objection or counter-application to a mother's application for a residence order, this means that an order will not normally be granted. However, other legislation and local authority policy and practice are not compatible with this aim. Many local authorities still require women to obtain a custody (or residence) order in respect of their children in order to be assessed as in priority need under s.59(1) of the 1985 Housing Act. Some women have been able to get an order on those grounds alone. However, the Children Act Advisory Committee in its second report deplores the use of orders for this purpose, considering that it goes against the 'no order' principle of the Act (Children Act Advisory Committee, *Annual Report*, 1992/3). This is laudable in theory, but many local housing policies go against both the spirit and the letter of the Children Act by still requiring proof as to which parent the child is living with before allocating housing. Additionally, the framework for assessing payments under the Child Support Act does not adequately take into account the fact that there may be no legal 'proof' of which child lives with which parent.

2. Child Support Act, 1991
Passage through Parliament of this legislation involved far more direct lobbying from WAFE and from individual refuge groups than did the

Children Act. This was perhaps because the penalties for women and children experiencing violence were far more obvious in this legislation at an early stage. WAFE was represented on the lobbying groups formed around the main child care agencies during the passage of the Bill and drafted an amendment to allow women suffering domestic violence to be exempt from the obligation to co-operate with the Child Support Agency.

Refuge groups embarked on a period of letter writing and campaigning, making sure that their MP knew that this was an important issue for many voters and getting other agencies involved too. At a national level, alliances were built with the other child care agencies and with relevant peers in the House of Lords, who worked on re-drafting the original amendment. Government Ministers involved had proclaimed that 'it would clearly not be right to create a position in which a threat of violence could be seen as a way of escaping payment' (Tony Newton, MP in *Hansard*, 17 December 1990, line 84, and other occasions, reported in *Children In Parliament*). However, the lobbying paid off. As a result of the amendment proposed by WAFE, women are not required to authorise the Child Support Agency to trace their abuser if they have 'good cause' to fear harm or abuse to themselves or any of their children as a result of the claim being made (Child Support Act, 1991, s.6[2]). This was a wonderful victory for the refuge movement, though partial in the face of the overall impact of the legislation. However, implementation remained the true test and there was a prolonged period of anxiety before the Act took force.

The last year has seen many women finding that they were able to refuse permission for the Agency to contact their ex-partner, as a result of the amendment, without facing financial penalties. The process of getting to that stage has often been painful for individual women. The Child Support Agency information leaflets request women not to bring their children with them for interviews, ignoring the fact that many will have no one to leave them with. There is little provision for interpreters for women whose first language is not English or British Sign Language interpreters for deaf women. Many women who are not in contact with Women's Aid have been unaware that they have a right to refuse information. They have been pressurised into giving permission for their ex-partner to be contacted and then fear for their safety as a result. One woman was forced to come back into a refuge after years free from abuse when her violent ex-husband was given information about her whereabouts. Many women have been frightened unnecessarily because they were not given information about their rights. These are not articulated in the leaflets or forms distributed by the Agency.

A crucial issue to note is the variation in the quality of official advice women get from Benefits and Child Support Agency staff. Some information is partial or misleading, whilst some is plainly incorrect (Garnham and Knights, 1994). Women not in contact with a refuge group or similar advice service are often unaware of their rights. Some women are coming into refuges for the first time as a result whilst others, already in refuges, get more helpful treatment specifically because they are known to be living there. In some areas, living in a refuge is itself taken as sufficient proof of harm or distress.

Proof of harm or distress

A major issue is that of proof of fear of harm or distress. Guidance for the Agency states that: 'the parent with care has a right to be believed except when what she says is inherently contradictory or implausible' ('Guidance on the requirement to co-operate', Department of Social Security, 1993). Many women's experience of domestic violence may seem implausible to social security officers if they have no knowledge of the issue from experience and have not had training. Some women have found that they have had difficulty in being believed and have been asked to provide proof. Such proof is, by the very nature of domestic violence, difficult or impossible to obtain since the violence takes place behind closed doors and many women never call the police or do not have their calls to the police recorded. If women are forced to risk violence to have a claim made and then gain little or no benefit for their children this increases the stress for them and their children. One of the aims of the Agency is to save the taxpayer money. This aim should not be pursued at the expense of women and children's safety.

FUNDING AND DEVELOPMENT OF WORK WITH CHILDREN BY REFUGE GROUPS

The Children Act requires local authorities to fund work with 'children in need' as defined in s.17(10). Children in refuges are clearly in need, as they are temporarily homeless as a result of violence. Many have witnessed this violence and, as mentioned above, may also be suffering from abuse directed at themselves. With a few exceptions, local authorities in England still do not specifically fund the work done in refuges with children, despite the fact that it clearly comes under this definition. This has been highlighted in a recent evaluation of children's work in refuges commissioned by BBC Children In Need, one of the most consistent funders of new child work posts and resources. In it, the author states:

> Most children in refuges fit the description of children in need according to the Children Act 1989 . . . [but] funding support is very difficult to find at present. Eventually it is to be hoped that salaries in the refuge field will not need to be sought from charitable trusts. But given the current difficulties, support for children's workers in refuges is still a way to reach some very needy children (Ball, 1992, paras.9.2&9.5).

Local authorities tend to emphasise funding services that are likely to help prevent the need to take children into care. For many women coming into the refuge, the threat of having their children taken into care is powerful and very real. Social workers aware of the violence at home often tell women that unless they enter a refuge, care proceedings will be instigated in respect of their children. Whilst social services do have a statutory obligation to protect children, threatening care proceedings is not a useful way to empower women or support them in making a violence-free life for their children. It also calls into question the relative costs of local authority care as against employing a children's worker in a refuge. If refuges are being used as an explicit alternative to care, then the authority should clearly be meeting the costs of those services. Recent figures from the Department of Health show that, in 1992-3, the average cost to the public of keeping one child in care was nearly £13,000 (*Hansard*, 11 May 1994, Col.155-156, from *Children In Parliament*). The same amount of money could provide the salary and resources for one part-time children's worker in a refuge working with perhaps (in some refuge groups) hundreds of children per year who, as a result of the refuge existing, would not have to enter the care system.

WAFE is currently embarking on a research project to evaluate the work done in refuge groups and make recommendations for funding, including staffing costs. An experienced independent researcher is carrying out this work. The results should be known in Autumn 1994.

Mog Ball, in her first evaluation of refuge children's work (Ball, 1990) recommended a minimum of one children's worker to every six adult bed spaces. A spot survey at recent meetings of children's workers confirmed that many refuges are nowhere near so well provided. However, information from the WAFE Annual Survey indicates that more and more are getting to that point, and are even finding that this is a bare minimum. To provide the range of services that many refuges now provide for children, groups are recruiting, training and supporting volunteers with skills in children's work to help at play sessions and other activities. Children's workers need time to plan activities, write fund-raising applications, make contact with other agencies, and so on. This cuts down on the amount of time that can be spent face to face with children, but it is all essential work if a high level of provision is to be offered.

The National Council of Voluntary Child Care Organisations (NCVCCO) and Children In Need have funded various projects for children's work in refuges in the late eighties and early nineties with the intention of 'pump priming' for permanent local authority funding, once a clear need has been established by the initial project. Funding for children's work continues in the main, however, to be reliant on donations, fund-raising, revenue from the refuge rents, and funding from charities and other temporary sources such as Safer Cities.

Some refuges are now entering the contract culture. This means that the range of activities they carry out are audited and costed, and an agreement drawn up between the group and the local authority about what services must be provided, how these should be monitored, and any other conditions. Child protection procedures constitute just one area of work which has had to be negotiated carefully with the local authorities involved, and the issues have still not been fully worked through (see above). The national child protection policy for refuges, currently under discussion, should prove helpful here.

The Special Needs Management Allowance (funding for staffing from housing associations that replaced the Hostel Deficit Grant) does not take into account the costs of provision for children, not even basic housing costs, which limits the amount of space that can be given to children living in a refuge. All of this means that much time is spent fund-raising for children's work simply to continue; time which could be spent with the children. This is stressful for the children's worker, and frustrating for the children and mothers.

The need for additional services

A very few refuge groups have sufficient funding to be able to provide regular advice, support and other activities for children experiencing domestic violence who are not living in the refuge. Many of these children will be living in temporary accommodation such as bed and breakfast. They will live there until permanent accommodation is found, which in some local authorities can take many months. These children face all the problems of living in temporary accommodation, which can include health risks, safety hazards, dietary problems, lack of privacy, increased risk of accidental injury as well as stress (see Conway, 1988; Greve and Currie, 1990; see also chapter by Hague and Malos, this volume). Children (and their mothers) living in temporary accommodation are isolated from support services and are also likely to be missing out on school, for a range of reasons (see above and Clark, 1993). In some cities, there are projects which provide support and help for all families who are homeless, including those living in temporary accommodation. This provision is welcome. However, there is still a need for work specifically for children escaping violence, for all the reasons outlined above.

Outreach work by Women's Aid has funding in certain local authorities, usually those with a well developed domestic violence policy and funding for inter-agency work. There has not been any formal evaluation of the impact of this service. What is already clear from research is that the need for outreach work is vast. Refuges are always full, but the number of women and children escaping or needing to escape domestic violence who never come into refuges greatly outnumbers those who do. Observation and anecdotal evidence confirms that where outreach services *are* set up, the women and children involved gain a variety of benefits. Access to a support network helps decrease isolation which, in turn, can help decrease stress. The provision of ongoing advice and support helps women feel equipped to take their own decisions. Group activities provide opportunities for sharing experience and learning from each other, and so on. Outreach for children could include play activities outside the refuge, advice and support, in connection with work done with women.

Evaluations of work with children in refuges

Many local authorities and other funders require reports to be written about the work done in refuges with children as a condition of their funding. Additionally, two funders have commissioned independent evaluations of refuge children's work nationally: the NCVCCO in 1988 and 1990, and BBC Children In Need in 1992. These evaluations looked at the work done in each of a group of refuges which, between them, had many variations in location, funding, provision and specialism (i.e. some were for specific groups of women and children). These evaluations assessed the impact of the work on children and their mothers. The NCVCCO report of 1988 concludes: 'Often the children need another person to talk to about their problems, who is there specifically for them'.

The evaluation report of 1990 highlights the value of a children's worker in protection work:

> Other children were able to talk to the children's worker and nobody else. In the most graphic case to occur during the ten-month period, a four-year old girl showing physical evidence of sexual abuse, would not talk to police or social workers. On discovering this . . . the children's worker was involved in video interviews with the child, and these led to charges being laid against a man (Ball, 1990, p.14).

It also gives a useful example of the methods and value of an advocate for children:

> In order to act as an advocate for the children within the refuge, some [children's support] workers established regular children's meetings, from which recommendations were taken forward to house meetings of the refuge . . . the general impression, over the year, was that consciousness of children's needs was raised in the refuges. Several refuge workers noted this (Ball, 1990, p.14; see also chapter by Saunders, this volume).

There are many ways of working with children who have experienced domestic violence and other countries have adopted approaches that are different from the one outlined here. They all confirm the need for, and value of working directly with children. Some Canadian shelters for battered women have developed flexible programmes of children's sessions (see chapter by Loosley, this volume). These focus on the crisis state of the child, their special needs at the time of admission, and developing extensive programmes for long term recovery. That work includes helping children to develop their own safety skills and planning. Also in North America, structured groupwork programmes cover understanding violence, dealing with feelings and wishes about the family, as well as developing safety skills (see groups chapter by Mullender, this volume).

Some of this sort of structured approach to helping children is used in refuges in the UK: in small groups or on an individual level. It is also an approach that could be appropriate in an outreach setting. Again, the possibilities for extending this type of work are limited by inadequate funding and staffing levels in refuges. Additionally, the benefits, housing and legal systems in this country are constantly throwing up new problems for women and children leaving violence. Refuge staff all too often are spending time trying to sort out these problems, which limits the amount of time available to meet emotional and other needs.

WAFE has just allocated funds from its Educational and Relief Trust for a group of experienced researchers to identify the difficulties for children in refuges leaving domestic violence, and to evaluate and document the wide range of work done with children in refuges throughout England (see chapter by Morley and Mullender, this volume).

CONCLUSION

The work done with children in refuges is skilled, wide ranging and, above all, it makes a positive difference to the children involved. Children's workers have worked and continue to work hard and with great commitment and energy to meet children's needs. There is a great deal more that could be done but only if more adequate and more secure funding of work with children were to be made available, at a statutory level.

References

Association of Chief Officers of Probation (1992) *Association of Chief Officers of Probation Position Statement on Domestic Violence*. London: ACOP. Drafted by David Sleightholm.

Ball, M. (1992) *An Evaluation of the National Children's worker post and a report on children's work in seven refuges, funded by the BBC Children In Need Trust*. Unpublished.

Ball, M. (1990) *Children's Workers in Women's Aid refuges: A report on the experience of nine refuges in England*. London: National Council of Voluntary Childcare Organisations.

Children and Parliament (1991) issue 142. London: National Children' s Bureau.

Children and Parliament (1994) issue 201. London: National Children' s Bureau.

Child Support Agency (1993) *For Parents Who Live Apart*. London: Department of Social Security.

Children's Rights Development Unit (1994) 'No sign of Government plan to meet UNCRC duties', *Childright*, January/February, 103, p.10.

Clark, A. (1993) *Homeless Children and their Access to Schooling: A Bristol Case Study*. Bristol: SPACE Trust.

Conway, J. (ed.) (1988) *Prescription for Poor Health*. London: Shelter.

Debbonaire (Singh), T. (1994) *WAFE Briefing Papers on Children's Issues*. Bristol: WAFE.

Department of Health (1991) *Children Act 1989 Guidance and Regulations Volume 1: Court Orders*. London: HMSO.

Department of Social Security (1993) *The Application of the Requirement to Co-operate: Policy Guidelines*. London: DSS.

Department of Health (1989) *The Care of Children: Principles and Practice in Regulations and Guidance*. London: HMSO.

Garnham, A. and Knights, E. (1994) *Putting the Treasury First*. London: Child Poverty Action Group.

Greve, J. and Currie, E. (1990) 'Homeless in Britain', *Housing Research Findings*, 10, February. York: Joseph Rowntree Memorial Trust.

Women's Aid Federation England (no date) *Statement of Aims and Principles*. Bristol: WAFE.

Women's Aid Federation England (1993) *Annual Survey, 1992-3*. Bristol: WAFE.

CHILDREN'S RIGHTS IN REFUGES:

POLICY FOR WOMEN'S AID FEDERATION OF ENGLAND

Adopted by WAFE at Conference 1993

INTRODUCTION

Preamble

Women's Aid (WA) exists to give help, advice, support and refuge to women and children who are experiencing physical, sexual or emotional abuse in the home. This work is usually funded badly or not at all by statutory bodies and relies on charity funding and the work of volunteers. This country currently has inadequate benefit levels for women and children, lack of adequate suitable housing stock, little statutory child care provision, cutbacks in funding of voluntary play groups and nurseries and a society which is discriminatory to children. Thus this policy and the guidelines that accompany it should be read in the context of a country which is failing to meet the standards of the UN Convention of the Rights of the Child, as well as failing to meet the levels of provision for children detailed in its own legislation (Children Act 1989).

The policy is a statement of rights for children in WA refuges in England, accompanied by guidelines on how those rights can be met by WA groups, even without a specialist children's support worker.

Values it is based on

The policy has been developed from a particular perspective. The WAFE children's workers' group who developed it believes that children have very few real rights in law in this country, that this country and the way it is structured is discriminatory to children, and that there is still very little public understanding of the needs and experiences of children who live with or are escaping violence. Children are not usually in a position to gain their rights without the advice or advocacy of an adult, and they can never make use of rights without knowledge of those rights. Therefore children in refuges need particular consideration. WAFE constitution states that the organisation exists for the benefit of women and children so the policy was developed to promote that aim.

Implementing the policy

The children's workers' group feels that the policy is not a radical introduction, but forms a statement of the work that is already taking place in refuges and sets a minimum standard for all refuges to work with. It is hoped that most refuges will find that they already go beyond what is listed in the policy. It is not intended that groups who feel that they cannot yet meet all of the policy should disaffiliate from WAFE but instead plan how to meet it and be supported and helped to implement it. Support and help is available from the WAFE National Children's workers' group which meets six times a year around the country, from the WAFE National Children's Officer and from the publications and resources that WAFE has, particularly the childwork pack.

The policy is divided into three sections of rights: provision, protection and participation.

I. PROVISION

1. All children who come to the refuge have the right to be welcomed into the refuge, offered somewhere safe to stay with their mother and other brothers or sisters and continue to be welcome throughout their stay.

    Guideline

    A refuge can be empowering for a child as they can be helped to realise that there are other children who have had similar experiences, given space and support to start to come to terms with changes in their lives, develop peer group support systems, and make use of specialist advocate support if there is a children's worker. Recognising that even where employed, specialist children's workers are not always available when a child arrives at the refuge, a variety of methods can be used for welcome and it is important to be led by the child's own needs: the refuge office can be made more child centred with pictures and selected toys, leaflets or colouring books (depending on age), keeping a supply of toys so that any worker can give a child one of her/his own on arrival, encouraging children already living in the refuge to welcome new children and show them around, displaying information on the walls about what is on offer for children.

    Offering refuge on the 'Open Door' principle is one of the principles of Women's Aid, so a child should always be offered refuge with her/his mother when requested, or referred and helped with getting to another refuge if necessary. Refuges operating or developing policies on age limits for boys should consider and regularly review what impact the policy has on families with older children; children should be able to stay with their mother and siblings wherever possible. Development of refuges should make accessibility to refuges for children and mothers with disabilities a priority to ensure that children or mothers are not discriminated against at the stage of admission into the refuge, or once in the refuge do not have to suffer the extra stress of an environment that is not fully accessible.

2. All children living in the refuge have the right to live in an environment that is healthy, safe and adequate for her/his needs.
   Guideline
   Refuges should always meet Health and Safety requirements, and should be checked regularly for maintenance repairs. Local authorities hold guidelines on space requirements for work with children, these could be used as a good practice guide. Ideally, refuges should be built or adapted to meet the needs of children and mothers with disabilities. Funding applications and negotiations with landlord or Housing Association should make meeting children's health and safety needs a priority. Refuges should hold readily accessible information about Health Visitors, Doctors, dentists etc. Staff involved with working with children should be trained in basic first aid and record any accidents. There should always be someone on the premises with responsibility for each child, staff and mothers need to work out clear arrangements for responsibility during play sessions.

3. All children living in the refuge have the right to have access to good quality play and activity sessions which may include:
   • activities and play sessions organised by the refuge;
   • play, sport, youth and other facilities available in the area where appropriate.
   Guideline
   Play is one of the most crucial elements of this work as it can meet many objectives simultaneously. However, good quality play sessions and other activities take staff time to plan and run. One of the most effective ways of meeting this need is where possible to employ a specialist children's worker(s). Funding applications should reflect the need for work with children and those to local authorities should stress the statutory obligation the Children Act imposes to fund work with 'children in need'. Management members and other staff should be aware of the time that planning takes up. Play work also requires a separate space for children's sessions and ideally also a safe enclosed outdoor space. Ideally, the play area will not be used for anything else.

4. All children living in the refuge have the right to information where appropriate, in ways that she or he can clearly understand, on the following:
   • what a refuge is and what it is for;
   • what refuge rules are and why they are made and have to be kept;
   • what a refuge children's worker is (if one is employed) and what her role is;
   • their legal rights, in association with their mother and independently;
   • any court proceedings they are involved in, especially where they have to appear in court;
   • any Social Services investigations they are a subject of;
   • any relevant refuge policies e.g. child abuse.
   Guideline
   A variety of methods can be used for giving information to children; verbally when the child first arrives or in children's meetings with children helping each other, using written materials including posters or leaflets, with posters or other visual information, using information leaflets such as

the ones published by the Children's Legal Centre on legal and other rights. Sessions with individual children may also be necessary for specific needs to be met. Initially and subsequently, work on informing children needs to involve mothers, to check out what the child already knows and what wishes the mother may have about informing them. Work on informing children should involve mothers at every stage.

5. All children living in the refuge have the right to have access to space she/ he feels comfortable with in which to express feelings about her experiences.
Guideline
It may not always be possible for this provision to be offered directly by the refuge for all children. Contacts with and up to date information about local specialist support and counselling services for children and young people may be more appropriate. Some refuges may be able to provide a one to one counselling service for children; the specific training, support and supervision needs of a worker doing this work need to be identified clearly. It is also essential that the mother knows about any counselling or one to one support that children receive, or is helped to find other services herself or find space and time to talk to her child. Refuges may develop policies for older children that allow them more independence to choose to have these services. Holding workshops with mothers on children's experience of domestic violence can help mothers realise that children have separate needs and have the opportunity to discuss their own feelings about their children's experiences.

6. All children living in the refuge have the right to advice and support or to refuse this.
Guideline
Information and space may not be enough and some children or young people may require further advice or support from within the refuge. Again, refuges need to be clear about when and how to inform or involve mothers. A child's wishes may conflict or appear to conflict with those of her mother, or advice may be conflicting. Involvement of and consultation with a child's mother is vital throughout the process of advising and supporting a particular child.

II. PROTECTION

7. All children in the refuge have the right to safety from violence, which includes the right to safety from physical punishment.
Guideline
All refuges affiliated to WAFE have a policy of promoting non violent discipline in the refuge. In order for this to work effectively there needs to be information available about alternative methods of discipline, supportive work with mothers which acknowledges the value of different ways of child rearing and information for children. Work directly with children could also include promoting non violent methods of resolving conflict amongst each other.

8. All children in the refuge have the right to safety from racism and racial abuse.

9. All children in the refuge have the right to safety from discrimination on grounds of class, race, gender, ability, religion, sexual orientation or sexuality.

Guideline to 8 and 9
No refuge can guarantee either of the above rights for women or children, but they can ensure that their policies and work practices reflect the commitment to these principles. Children may experience discrimination from other children, staff or volunteers or women living in the refuge. Work with children should aim to be inclusive and supportive of difference, and children should be encouraged to develop their own sense of self worth. Staff and volunteers should ideally have training on non-discriminatory working and also have the opportunity to discuss together issues and problems that arise, regularly and in a safe environment.

10. All children in the refuge have the right to security within the refuge, which includes there always being an adult on the premises with responsibility for her/him.
Guideline
Information given to mothers about refuge play sessions needs to make clear who is responsible for children during sessions and whether or not the refuge requires mothers to be on the premises during sessions. For trips and outings out of the refuge there should be a parental consent form signed for every child unaccompanied by her/his mother.

11. All children living in the refuge have the right to be believed
Guideline
One of the principles of Women's Aid is to accept a woman's word for what she has experienced. This right applies also to children, even if this may sometimes seem to conflict with the mother's right to be believed. It is vital to remember that children don't lie about abuse.

12. All children in the refuge have the right to confidentiality: children should be given clear information in ways they can easily understand on what this means and what the limits are; children should know who will be told about any disclosure of abuse and why.

13. All children in the refuge have the right to have action taken if they are in danger of abuse: refuges should have clear policies for all workers about child abuse and Social Services investigations; a disclosure of abuse may well not mean an investigation is necessary if the risk of further abuse has passed.
Guideline to 11, 12 and 13
It is vital for children to have their privacy respected but also for staff not to make promises to children that they may not be able to keep. When talking or working with children on a one to one or personal level, the child should be helped to understand that not all secrets can stay secret, some may mean that the worker has to ask for help for both of them. In order to work effectively, children's workers also need clear policies about how they will proceed with any disclosure of abuse.

Policies should be drawn up in consultation with local authority Social Services. All staff, management members, volunteers and residents need to be aware of it and understand it.

The above three rights and guidelines also highlight the need for training for all staff on child abuse and policies and procedures for dealing with disclosure and/or SSD investigations. In addition, staff dealing with this work need to have regular supervision and support, particularly any staff working one to one with children.

III. PARTICIPATION

14. All children in the refuge have the right to have their needs considered in the following:
    - making, enforcing or reviewing refuge policies and work practices;
    - making, enforcing or reviewing the rules and tenancy agreement of the refuge.

15. All children in the refuge have the right to have their needs and wishes considered, and, where possible and appropriate to be enabled to have a say and be involved in any of the following that apply:
    - choosing and planning activities and play schemes;
    - any court proceedings she is involved in;
    - any Social Services investigations she is involved in.

Guideline

This may be done with the support and advocacy of a specialist children's worker or other worker or volunteer who is clearly identified to the child as having this role. Separate refuge children's meetings for children to develop peer support, help each other understand refuge rules and take part in planning activities are also a useful way of enabling children to have a voice. A role as an advocate for children within the refuge will from time to time present conflicting interests and contradictions with those of staff or women living in the refuge. Job descriptions for children's workers may therefore need to include a statement about the advocacy role for considering and raising children's issues and needs, spelling out clearly that part of this role may involve being responsible for raising children's issues in all areas of refuge development.

11

Hammersmith Women's Aid Childwork Development Project

Gina Higgins

INTRODUCTION

Hammersmith Women's Aid (HWA) is an independent voluntary organisation affiliated to the Women's Aid Federation England (WAFE). For seventeen years, we have run a busy and successful refuge for women and children who have been abused in their homes. We offer temporary accommodation, support and advice, and aim to empower both women and their children to rebuild their lives and to determine their own future.

CHILDWORK

Hammersmith Women's Aid has steadily expanded and developed the childwork aspect of its service over the past ten years. The refuge can accommodate approximately twelve children at any one time. Approximately ninety children pass through the refuge every year. A core of these will stay for around six months, others for a matter of days or weeks. Sixty resident and ex-resident children join in our activities every year: these include the summer playscheme, Diwali and Christmas celebrations, and so on. We provide a very full and exciting programme of activities and services for children, much of it innovative, and have used the experience gained to develop our policy and practice to benefit the children.

CHILDREN'S NEEDS

Coming into a refuge, becoming homeless, can be a traumatic experience for any child. In many cases, children have experienced abuse themselves. They have needs that are quite different from their mothers', and living in a crowded refuge is stressful. Six families share one living-room and one kitchen-diner. There is a small yard and a small playroom. There has to be structured play, with additional support from the childworker, or the refuge would not remain a safe place.

We have found that children who have suffered violence are slow to trust and therefore may need to be with other children similar to themselves and with adults who they know so that they can build up confidence and learn to co-operate together in groups. When a family first enters the refuge, the childworker will show the child around the house. The child will then be introduced to a resident child who will go on to do the introductions with other children over a space of time. The childworker will have a meeting with the child and explain what is on offer within the refuge and in the Borough. She will listen to the needs of the child, taking into account their age, gender, race, and cultural background. The playroom is a good place to talk as the child can make use of the space provided and feel comfortable in this setting.

WHAT HAMMERSMITH WOMEN'S AID HAS TO OFFER CHILDREN

We provide a crêche five mornings a week for children aged two to five years. The playroom is later used for after-school sessions for children over five years of age. The activities on offer are: drawing, painting, stained glass, candle-making, clay, cooking, library, music, relaxation and meditation. Teenagers can use the playroom to do their homework. Planned workshops for children are also held there.

Teenage children at times have different needs and we have met these by introducing them to other opportunities where appropriate. Examples include: a mixed abilities girls' group, girls' clubs, boys' clubs, youth clubs, and Irish dancing. The Black Education Centre serves resident and local ex-resident children with lessons in English, maths and African culture. Swimming is a regular and very popular activity whilst local parks provide the space to release energy. Depending on the funding, the resident children are taken when possible to the local cinema and theatre.

When there is a new influx of families the children meet and discuss ways of living in a positive way within the refuge. Rules of the house are discussed and written up; also issues are discussed around racism, bullying, and sexism. Working in this way empowers the children and they feel safe knowing their boundaries; they also feel it is a fair way of working. Children's meetings happen on a regular basis. They provide a space for the children to have a voice and the childworker has to constantly revise the timetable and the activities to suit the current residents.

NEW PROJECTS

Many aspects of the development work over the years have been innovative, but one of the largest areas of new work has been the structured work with individual children on the effects of violence. The aim of this work is to help children to recognise their experience in living in violent homes, to talk about it, to begin to understand it, and to deal with their emotions. The workers are there to help and support them, and to develop with them other ways of problem-solving and of relating to others. Before taking on this work, the groundrules have to be accepted by the worker, mother and child. It is vital for the children to have their privacy respected but also for the worker not to make promises to the children that they might not be able to keep. Each child is helped to understand that not all secrets can stay secrets; some may mean that the worker has to ask for help for both herself and the child. In order to work effectively, for example, workers have clear policies on how they will proceed with any disclosure of abuse.

The development of a comprehensive policy on child abuse for Hammersmith Women's Aid has continued with the help of the Standing Committee on Sexual Abuse of Children (SCOSAC), members of the HWA collective, refuge workers, residents and ex-residents, and with financial support from the Gulbenkian Foundation. This has been very challenging work for the collective - as individuals and as a group - trying to incorporate different interests, experiences and beliefs (see chapter by Debbonaire, this volume).

In order for the resulting policy to work effectively, information is made available about alternative methods of discipline avoiding physical punishments. Supportive work is offered to mothers which acknowledges the value of different traditions of child-rearing, and information is readily available for children. Working directly with children also includes promoting non-violent methods of resolving conflict between themselves.

ANTI-RACIST AND ANTI-DISCRIMINATORY WORK

HWA continues to develop policies and good practice on awareness of the effects of all sorts of violence and abuse. This is shown in the multi-cultural playroom and in ongoing work we do with mothers and children: providing positive books, cooking, songs and nursery rhymes; sharing languages and other cultures; and providing information which is displayed around the refuge. Race awareness is discussed in children's meetings and also in separate workshops for women and children held at least twice a year. We recognise the crucial role of mothers and involve them as much as possible. In the last two workshops on race awareness, for example, the mothers helped their children by watching *Malcolm X* at the cinema and also watching a video entitled *Caribbean Women in World War Two*. They discussed these with the children which gave the children the information they needed for their workshop, and a better understanding of the issues discussed. We also take advantage of cultural areas on offer outside of the refuge. Examples are Southall market, Chinatown, and visits to Aklowa (African) Village in the summer.

Some children experience discrimination from other children and/or from women residents from time to time. Our aim at HWA, when working with the children, is inclusive and supportive of difference and encourages children to develop their own sense of self-worth. All workers have had the opportunity of undertaking training specifically around non-discriminatory work.

Just as all the refuge workers will raise anti-discriminatory policies in house meetings with adult residents, so childworkers will use workshops and children's meetings to help children learn that women who love women, men who love men, Black and white people, children with disabilities and learning difficulties, are equally human and equally deserving of respect. Ignorance and prejudice have fed on the violence in these children's lives; the refuge has to be a place where they are challenged and refuted. Children are capable of quite sophisticated understanding: they can do quizzes on what the words gay and lesbian mean and learn not to be frightened of the unknown. They can also take pride in developing their own policies, such as the following actual examples, reproduced with permission:

Racism means a combination of white power and superiority over the ethnic minority. This is our Anti-Racism Statement!

1. Do not make fun of other people's accents.
2. Do not make fun of their religion.
3. Do not make fun of other people's food, and make noises about it.
4. Do not make fun of people's hair and what they look like, calling names etc.

Anti-Sexism Statement!

1. We want boys and girls to play together.
2. Don't make fun of boys when they play with dolls and stuff.
3. Boys are not to take over the playroom.
4. Girls for football and rugby.
5. Club for both girls and boys.

LINKS WITH CHILD CARE IN GENERAL

An essential part of the childwork project is to work with other agencies in the Borough and nationally: to increase awareness of the effects of domestic abuse on children, to develop policies and practice within the refuge, and to share that work with other refuges and agencies. HWA is an active member of WAFE and a valued member of their national childworkers' group. It has worked with the National Childwork Co-ordinator, Thangam Debbonaire, to prepare draft policies on childwork in refuges, children's rights in refuges (reproduced in previous chapter), and also a childwork pack full of information for refuges. In addition, our childworker has facilitated workshops at the WAFE national conference and shared her experience, training, materials, and workbooks with other refuges locally and nationally.

Strong links have been built with Addison Primary School over the years and we appreciate the good relationship with the staff there which eases the way for children being settled into the new school. This was further developed when the childworker, a volunteer, and an ex-resident woman gave a workshop for teachers on the effects of domestic violence on women and children. This was followed by a similar workshop for the helpers at Addison School and another local school. As a direct result of these workshops, a teacher with past experience of WAFE volunteered to offer private tuition once a week for resident and local ex-resident children.

HWA's work continued with a joint project on bullying as part of our anti-violence work. This resulted in a poster designed by the children and further involvement in local schools. The childworkers and a student also gave a workshop on positive images for young women for 14 and 15 year olds at Fulham School for Girls - once again raising the issues of race awareness, sexism, sexual harassment and domestic abuse, and giving advice that they may need for future reference.

The health visitor from our local clinic works closely with HWA. She visits regularly, once a week, to talk to the workers and mothers and to check new children who are under 5. She is also willing to listen to any concerns mothers may have regarding older children. Over the years, health visitors have come and gone but the last one was particularly enthusiastic and joined with the childworker in a workshop for resident and ex-resident women on child abuse. It emphasised the need for boundaries and discipline for children whilst avoiding physical methods of punishment.

HWA refuge raised the issue of the effects of domestic abuse on children at its local multi-agency domestic violence forum. As a direct result, Hammersmith and Fulham Safer Cities Project included this in its criteria, enabling the forum to obtain a grant for a seminar on children and young people who witness domestic violence. It was called 'Suffering in Silence', and was held in Hammersmith Town Hall in December 1992. (A report is now available: Holder et al. , 1994). Although aimed primarily at local agencies, the seminar's speakers, workshops and panel discussion attracted attention from all over the country. A Junior Minister was amongst the speakers. HWA ran a stall for sales and information and the childworker and three volunteers facilitated the workshop on children in refuges. The day itself led to increased interest from social services, teachers, and other professionals.

The childworker went on to train local police officers on awareness of domestic violence with the help of her colleagues, the Community Safety Unit of the Borough Council, and the police Domestic Violence Unit.

VOLUNTEERS

The childworkers alone could not provide a good quality service to the families of HWA without the support of the volunteers. We have involved volunteers in the past but in an ad hoc manner. Safer Cities funding enabled us to run a structured programme which produced a better deal for the volunteers: they feel better trained and supported and more confident, and are therefore able to give a better service to the children in the refuge.

Volunteers cannot replace a qualified and experienced worker. She provides the stability and continuity that children and the project need.

The childworker also recruits, inducts and trains volunteers and provides them with ongoing support and supervision. The worker has made links with the local volunteer bureau who make most of the referrals. HWA are very satisfied with the volunteer project because it is productive and beneficial both to the volunteers themselves and to the children in the refuge.

FUNDING

The London Borough Grants Unit makes a revenue grant towards the salaries of three full-time refuge workers. The balance and all the other running costs of the project are met by the rents which the residents pay. HWA leases the house, free of rent and council tax, from Hammersmith and Fulham Borough Council. We receive no statutory funding for the work with children and have fund-raised for the salary of a full-time childworker for the past five years because we believe this work is essential. In addition, we have raised money from the Inner Areas Programme, local companies, charities, and have organised fund-raising to provide children's activities all the year round. Grants and donations have therefore come from a wide range of sources, in varying amounts, in both cash and kind.

HWA is finding that fund-raising takes up an increasing amount of refuge workers' time and has been uphill work over the years. We have appreciated the support of the Safer Cities programme and were particularly delighted when the BBC Children in Need appeal agreed to meet the childworker's salary for two years. We aim to use this time to persuade the local authority that they have a statutory duty to fund work with children in the refuge, because we believe they are 'children in need' as defined in the Children Act (see chapter by Debbonaire, this volume).

References
Holder, R., Kelly, L. and Singh, T. (1994) *Suffering in Silence: Children and Young People Who Witness Domestic Violence*. London: Hammersmith and Fulham Domestic Violence Forum. Available from Community Safety Unit, London Borough of Hammersmith and Fulham, Hammersmith Town Hall, King Street, London W6 9JU.

12

Women's Community House
Children's Program:
A Model in Perspective

Susan Loosley

INTRODUCTION AND PERSONAL STATEMENT

Mark told his story during a 'violence awareness' presentation in a grade 3 classroom of 7 and 8 year olds led by the children's program staff of Women's Community House:

> 'Last night my dad chased after my mom, sister and me with a knife. We ran to the bathroom and locked the door. Dad smashed the knife into the door over and over and then he left. We had to wait. I was really scared'.

The presentation had started by asking the children if they thought it was necessary to set aside one full week to discuss violence. They all agreed. We then asked where they see violence. The lists each class suggests are similar: 'in the school yard', 'in cartoons', 'in the movies', 'in sports', 'at home'. We asked them what kinds of violence or abuse existed in people's homes. Some children talked about sibling rivalry, some mentioned child abuse, and others told of 'parents fighting'. When this kind of gender neutral term is used, we challenge it by talking about abuse in families and how most often the abuse is against the women and children. We explain the shelter as a safe place for women and children to go if the woman is being abused by her husband or common law partner. It was at this point in the presentation that Mark disclosed. We took the opportunity to put together a 'safety plan' with Mark to help keep him safe, and we taught him and his other classmates how to call the police. Two days later, Mark was at the shelter with his family. Carol, his mother, had not known that the shelter existed until her son came home from school and told her.

It is my belief that children can learn and spread the message that woman abuse is not acceptable, and that families can access resources to end the abuse. Children often come home from school and discuss what they have learned about - the environment, recycling, the effects of smoking - and, in the case of Mark and other children we have taught, the safe place for abused women and children. Child advocates have unique and numerous opportunities to reach children and their mothers through a children's program at a shelter. In this chapter, I will highlight the program at Women's Community House in London Ontario, Canada, and share with you some of the children who have touched my life.

BACKGROUND

Women's Community House (WCH) is a safe place for abused women and their children. Since 1978, this non-profit charitable organization has offered short-term shelter, a 24-hour help line, supportive counselling, and a children's program. In August 1992, a second facility was opened to accommodate the increasing demand for space. WCH operates within a feminist based framework based on a belief in dignity, self-determination, self-worth, and the awareness that violence deprives women of these basic rights. Service is provided in a non-judgemental, non-directive way to create the opportunity for self-growth and awareness. The shelter responds to the diverse needs of the women by being accessible to women with disabilities, providing a toll-free telephone line, a transportation fund, a TDD line (for deaf persons), and access to a cultural interpreter service. Women's Community House employs 50 staff members and has the capacity for 53 residents between the two shelters with a maximum stay of six weeks. (This is a typical policy in North America but differs from the open-ended stays in British refuges.) The $2.2 million dollar (£1.5 million) second facility was purpose built and includes such provisions as: a women's quiet room, children's play room, youth room, library, storage, and a complex security system. The annual operating budget of $1.8 million is funded by the three levels of Government - Municipal, Provincial and Federal - with a further twenty per cent raised through community and corporate donations. WCH is an active member of the London Co-ordinating Committee to End Woman Abuse (LCCEWA) and helped to develop its integrated response to prevention (LCCEWA, 1992).

WCH established its children's program in March, 1986. A child advocate was hired with an initial one-year grant to develop immediate crisis intervention for children and to create the children's program. This position became permanent and a second child advocate was added to the program in January 1987. Since then, the program has been a model for others (Rossetti, 1988), growing to include two full-time child advocates, one relief child advocate, one full-time parenting group worker, and three recreation staff.

CHILDREN'S PROGRAM STAFF ROLES

Child advocates

The child advocates address every aspect of a child's physical and emotional safety while at the shelter. Advocates assess the impact violence has had on the child; act as a liaison between the child, the mother and outside agencies; provide short-term crisis intervention and group counselling for children, as well as parental support and education; and supervise a recreational program. They also offer public education through school outreach and a violence awareness program.

Parenting group worker

The parenting group worker provides an integrated program for women and children with a specific focus on groups for mothers. The groups address such issues as: coping as a single parent, effective parenting, accessing community resources, the effects on children who witness woman abuse, and the identification and validation of women's needs as they differ from those of their children.

Recreation / child care worker

Recreation/child care workers co-ordinate a variety of residential and community activities aimed at building trust and self-esteem amongst the children. The program offers parent-relief and childcare during groups for women.

FOCUSING THE WORK

In April, 1994 the children's program embarked on a strategic planning exercise in order to determine the focus of the program, to put new ideas and plans into action, and to define more clearly the role of the child advocate. This resulted in a mission statement specific to the children's work and four primary goals, along with objectives and action plans designed to meet these broader objectives:

Mission statement

The children's program of women's community house offers leadership through education and networking by providing a safe place which recognizes and responds to the needs of children and their mothers.

GOAL 1

To be an innovative, pro-active and fully supported team both internally and externally, demonstrating leadership by promoting the Children's Program through written literature and local, national and international outreach.

GOAL 2

The Children's Program has a responsibility to provide education and links with the community through openness, clear communication and joint programs.

GOAL 3

The Children's Program provides a safe place that insists on a non-violent, respectful, non-discriminatory environment for all children, youth and their mothers by promoting learning and change.

GOAL 4

The Children's Program promotes non-violent intervention in the delivery of innovative individual and group programs that both recognize and support the individual and the mother/child relationship (WCH, forthcoming).

Some of the 'action plans' consist of:

1. developing a children's program reference manual;
2. conducting action research on the children's program and publishing the results; and
3. networking provincially, nationally and internationally with other shelter-based programs.

Some of the accomplishments over the last year have been:

1. the development and updating of a school violence awareness program specific to the issue of woman abuse;
2. participation in a committee which developed and implemented a community group treatment program for child witnesses of woman abuse (see the groups chapter by Mullender, this volume);
3. participation in a committee which developed a video and guide for anyone working in situations where children may disclose living with woman abuse; the pack is entitled: *Make a Difference - How To Respond to Child Witnesses of Woman Abuse* (Children's Sub-Committee of LCCEWA, 1994; the guide is reproduced in this volume); and
4. team development of the *Children's Program Guidelines* (WCH, 1993).

THE CONTENT OF THE CHILDREN'S PROGRAM

Shelters for abused women and their children have become an essential and integral part of community services in Canada. Much thought and planning has gone into the children's aspect of their role: 'The programs already developed suggest that children are an important client group that has shaped the design, staffing, and programming of shelters' (Jaffe et al., 1990, p.100). At Women's Community House, the work with children operates within overall guidelines which will be outlined below. Specific work by child advocates encompasses intake and assessment; support for mothers; one-to-one support and counselling for children; support, education and prevention through structured children's groups; safety planning; liaison with schools concerning individual residents; and public education. Each of these will be explored in subsequent sections.

Guidelines

The children's program has developed guidelines (WCH, 1993) which are intended to promote feelings of physical and emotional safety and security for children while living at WCH, as well as easing co-operative living for all adult and child residents. If the guidelines appear not to be consistent with meeting the needs of any individual, they can be adapted with the support of a member of the children's program team. Topics covered include health and safety issues; the expectation that mothers will develop age appropriate routines for their children (with help offered if this is difficult); guidance on levels of adult supervision for different age groups of children; and a clear policy on discipline. WCH does not support the use of any form of physical discipline, or the use of inappropriate or excessive verbal or emotional control. Acknowledging that this is a time of crisis - when children's behaviour may deteriorate rather than improve, and mothers may feel under stress - the child advocates are available to support women in exploring effective and realistic alternative means of non-violent discipline, and to facilitate parent-child communication.

Intake and assessment

Each family that enters the shelter is unique and is offered support on an individual basis. It is the responsibility of the child advocate, in consultation with other staff and with family members themselves, to decide how best to meet the unique needs and challenges of the children in each family. Within 24 hours of arriving at the shelter, a child advocate meets with a woman and her children together to explain the services provided by the children's program and to go over the guidelines referred to above. The child advocate inquires about the immediate concerns regarding the children with a focus on physical safety needs, custody and legal issues, school and/or medical issues. In this initial meeting, she discusses with the child/ren the reason for coming to the shelter. In some cases, this may be the first time that the 'secret' is told in their presence, and the abuse discussed openly. The child/ren are reassured of the safety and security of the shelter. They are informed about the individual and group meetings available with the child advocate and about the program of recreational activities.

As part of recognizing the uniqueness of each family and the diversity of their experiences, backgrounds and needs, WCH offers shelter and service to families with female and male children, regardless of age. The acceptance of older boys may be surprising to those familiar with British refuges and certainly poses particular challenges to the work of the child advocate. Careful assessment and monitoring are required to ensure that the experience is beneficial to the mother, the older child concerned, and any younger brothers and sisters, and not a problem for other residents. The way in which these factors are balanced by the flexible use of child advocacy skills will be explored through an example.

Case scenario

Dianne came to the shelter with her three children: Kirsten aged 4, Jamie aged 7, and Andrew aged 17. The child advocate provided immediate assessment upon arrival at the shelter. This included meeting with Andrew and exploring and validating his feelings about coming to the shelter, including embarrassment and ambivalence. He was worried that the women might think he was abusive and admitted that he had been verbally abusive to his mother in the past. The child advocate and Andrew put together a plan of action in the event that he was feeling angry and needed to talk, including a meeting scheduled to discuss anger and appropriate conflict resolution. Andrew was made aware of the co-operative living guideline of no violence or abuse permitted in the shelter. Residents were informed that the 17-year old male child of another resident would be staying at the shelter.

During his stay a resident confronted Andrew about his choice of language with his siblings. Andrew responded by telling the resident to 'Shut up!' in a loud voice. The child advocate addressed this with Andrew by reviewing the Co-operative Living Guidelines and the plan of action they had agreed. She discussed with him how his behaviour may have affected the other residents in the shelter, and drew out the parallels between this and witnessing woman abuse.

Support for mothers

All children are adversely affected by witnessing their mother being abused, though some survive more resiliently than others. The impact varies from child to child, depending upon a number of factors including age, developmental stage, role in the family, and the extent and frequency of the violence (Catholic Board of Education, 1994, p.7). Women who come to the shelter may experience their children engaging in disruptive, non-compliant behaviour, uncharacteristically passive or aggressive behaviour, or excessive attachment behaviour. The role of the child advocate is to assess the behaviour and, in co-operation with the mother, to decide on an appropriate plan of intervention with her child/ren. The advocate will often also undertake work with the woman on her own, focused on helping her understand what her children are going through and how she and shelter staff can best meet their needs.

Meetings with the mother on her own might cover such topics as: symptoms of a child in crisis, the effects on children who witness woman abuse, child development, alternative non-violent discipline and parenting techniques, her particular child's adjustment to the shelter, and any particular concerns she may have in relation to the child or their relationship. This work might also lead to referrals to community-based group treatment programs or children's counselling centres if needed.

Case scenario

Helen requested a meeting with the child advocate to discuss Emily, her daughter, aged six. Helen said she was having difficulty with her child at bedtime. Helen stated that at home Emily had maintained a consistent bedtime routine but, since coming to the shelter, she would get out of bed and seek out her mother. When Helen had talked to her about it, Emily had said she was afraid of being alone in the room at night. The child advocate described Emily to her mother as a child in crisis owing to the impact of witnessing woman abuse, the disruption of her routine, and coming to the shelter. The child advocate helped Helen to understand the dynamics around Emily's fears and explained that they are not uncommon for children in shelter. Together, they undertook a problem-solving process to find ways of helping Emily feel more secure at bedtime. Helen decided to stay with Emily until she fell asleep and then to leave a night-light on. Helen also said she would check on her daughter frequently, so as to be close if she woke up. They also agreed that the child advocate would provide individual counselling for Emily on a regular basis.

One-to-one work with children

Individual meetings with children often include: following up topics discussed in group meetings; concepts of violence and its definition; exploring feelings of separation, loss, blame, guilt and anger; exploring fears of the abusive father; and nightmares. Children in the shelter are encouraged to talk to the child advocates and do so frequently and spontaneously. Child advocates will also assist children with school work, discuss future plans, and engage in trust-building activities through recreation.

Case scenario

Alexandra, an eleven year old girl, expressed how she felt rejected and abandoned by her father because he did not try to come and get her, her mother or brother after they came to the shelter. The child advocate assisted Alexandra to identify, express, and cope with her feelings and encouraged her to write or draw them on paper. The result was a letter to her father which, although she never sent it to him, provided her with the opportunity to express herself and helped her to acknowledge her feelings and work through them:

> Dad, it's me. I just wrote to say I'm extremely pissed off at you. I've been gone for over two weeks and you haven't even picked up a damn 'phone to ask where I was! And I should have known. You always say you love us but I don't believe it! 'Cause, if you did, you would have found us. And I don't give a damn any more and I don't ever, ever, ever want to see you again!!!!!!!! And it isn't Mom's, or John's, or my fault why we left - it's yours! And we left 'cause you abused us in three ways: emotionally, verbally, and financially. And I couldn't care less if you come looking for me. And if you do, when I say 'Nothing's wrong' it means 'GO AWAY' and 'I HATE WHAT YOU DID' and 'I NEVER EVER WANT TO SEE YOU!' Signed,
> Your X-daughter'

Group work with children

WCH recognizes the impact of witnessing violence on children and so has been instrumental in the development of structured work designed to meet this area of need. The children's group program promotes a safe environment for children to begin discussing and thinking about issues of woman abuse. For many, this represents the first real opportunity to talk about the abuse in their family. Children learn in groups that they are not alone in tackling their confused and angry feelings, through meeting other children who have had comparable experiences. From them, and from the group facilitators, they learn coping strategies for the future.

Group discussions facilitated by child advocates have both supportive and educational goals which are met through activities like drawing, brainstorms, and discussion. Groups are run twice weekly and are planned with a rolling programme so that new children can join at any time. Work focuses on common and current house issues such as: understanding woman abuse, shelter awareness, conflict resolution, who is responsible for violence, personal safety, peer interaction and social skills, family issues, and feelings (WCH, 1993).

Group scenario

The 'abuse recognition group' for children is run frequently owing to the high turn-over of residents. The group material and presentation can be modified to suit ages four and over. It begins by discussing the common reason that all the children have for coming to the shelter. Group members are asked to provide examples of violence, which are listed on a chalkboard - separating physical abuse like kicking or hitting from emotional and verbal abuse like name-calling. Once the lists have filled the space on the board, the children are asked to look closely at them and to distinguish the differences between the two.

The concept of 'inside and outside hurting' (developed by child advocates at WCH in 1991 and used with great success since) is introduced to the group at this point. Emotional and verbal abuse hurt 'your heart', as many children put it - on the inside - while physical abuse 'where you can see it', hurts you on the outside. The children are asked to identify the feelings associated with being abused. For example, they may be asked: 'How would you feel if someone called you a name?' The feelings they mention are put beside the example of violence on the board, usually in the form of a drawn face. As the feelings are generated, the children learn that no one kind of abuse is worse than another because similar feelings are experienced regardless of the abuse. Thus, 'I feel scared when somebody swears at me' equates with 'I feel scared when somebody pushes me'.

At the end of the group session, the children are asked to draw a picture about what was discussed in the group. Many children draw pictures about a particular incident of abuse that they witnessed against

their mother, whilst others draw what they learned in group, and some draw the safe house they now live in. Individual time is spent with each child to discuss their picture.

The purpose of the abuse recognition group is prevention. Children gain concrete knowledge of abuse which helps them begin to identify and label abusive behaviour in others and possibly in themselves. Usually, children think of abuse as being physical so they underestimate the impact of emotional abuse. An important focus of the group is to teach children that all forms of abuse have the potential to be harmful. Children often disclose what they have witnessed at home and, through attending the group, can begin to work through their experiences.

Separate groups are run on the prevention of child sexual abuse. Sexual abuse is also discussed as one of the forms of abuse tackled in the group outlined above where it is given separate attention, informing children what to do if they are being sexually abused. Safety planning also always encompasses this area of risk.

Safety planning

An integral component of the children's program is developing safety plans with children. A safety plan is a simple, concrete plan devised to help children get out of a dangerous situation and reach safety. A school safety plan is developed for those attending school, while a general safety plan covers any other occasions when the child is outside the shelter and may encounter the abusive partner or in the event that the woman returns to her partner.

Initially, the child advocate will meet with the mother to establish safety considerations:

1. What is the child's custody status?
2. What degree of risk is there that the partner will attempt to locate and/or snatch the child?
3. How does the woman think the child would respond to a partner's attempt at contact?

The components of the plan take into consideration the emotional well-being of the child at the time, and acknowledge that children may feel confused and ambivalent about the abusive partner. The safety plan is to support the child in the understanding that the woman is choosing to live separately from her partner at the present time.

Each school safety plan is tailored to the specific structure of the school. The school is requested not to share any information with anyone about the child/ren, as well as not to allow anyone other than their mother access to the child/ren while she is living in the shelter. A completed 'School Information Sheet' is provided to the school outlining the partner's description, as well as the child's custody status, and other relevant information. The safety plan essentially involves identifying who the child's helpers in the school are: such as the principal, the child's

teacher(s), and possibly the school administration staff. Children are instructed that, if ever the abusive partner does try to visit them at the school, they should not talk to him but should immediately go and report to one of their helpers. Each child's safety plan is reviewed with the established helpers present, to ensure that the child has identified the process and the support system in place within the school.

Work with schools

The primary goal of the children's program team is to ensure that a level of structure and routine is established for all children living in the shelter as soon as possible after intake. This includes either reintegrating child/ren into their home school if safety is not a primary consideration, or temporarily registering them with one of WCH's established 'safe schools'. Safe schools are those where the shelter has provided information and professional development on the effects on children of witnessing woman abuse. Specialized procedures and policies have been endorsed at administrative levels which promote safety and confidentiality. These schools are well versed in implementing a safety plan (see above), should the safety of a student be in jeopardy. In all cases, prior to the child/ren returning to school, the child advocate meets with the child/ren and mother to discuss and develop a school safety plan; they subsequently attend a school meeting together where the safety plan is reviewed and confirmed by the woman and child, the child advocate, and school officials. Safe transportation is arranged by the school principal through the local Board of Education, as authorized by a special protocol. The transportation process is fully discussed in the safety planning with the child/ren and school officials.

In extreme circumstances, where safety is the foremost issue and the child would be at risk even in attending one of the established safe schools, she or he may temporarily be absent from school. In this case, a child advocate would support the child's parent in consulting with a contact person at the Board of Education to advise of the situation and be granted the child's temporary leave from school.

Public education: school based violence awareness program

It would be a challenge to find any book written on the topic of woman abuse that does not end with an appeal to school systems for prevention programs . . . . The appeal is usually expressed as a recognition that underlying societal attitudes condone violence and that only a major commitment by school systems to address this problem can lead to any meaningful changes (Jaffe et al., 1990, p.112).

The Women's Community House children's program has provided the educational system with a violence awareness program for five years, since 1989, which provides a good example of the involvement of child advocates in wider public education. In its early stages, the program focused on ages six to twelve, and covered a range of issues related to violence in society and keeping children safe. The program has now been expanded to include children aged four to eighteen.

Over the last few years, the violence awareness program has grown extensively and received wide recognition. The goal is to offer children and youth a broader understanding and awareness of the issue of violence in society, and of societal attitudes and beliefs about violence and abuse, with a specific focus on violence against women in relationships and families. Our belief is that, through facilitating a safe environment for the discussion of a very sensitive issue, we are enabling children to identify alternatives to power and control in relationships; we are also offering concrete strategies for them to keep themselves safe and free from violence in their own lives.

The program consists of a variety of presentations for different age groups which incorporate learning materials, open discussion, puppet shows and skits. Children are encouraged to identify safe and trusted adults in their lives to whom they can disclose if they are a witness to woman abuse in their home or if they themselves are abused. Safety planning is a key component of the program.

It is through mutual community efforts like this program, and the promotion of an open awareness and understanding of woman abuse and issues of violence, that those involved with children can make a difference in their lives.

CONCLUSION

The Women's Community House children's program has been developed through extensive collaboration within the staff team, with professionals in the community, and by using the latest resources available on child witnesses of woman abuse. We are committed to our goal of being a progressive and innovative program always striving to be responsive to the needs of our clients, the children.

We no longer view children as the 'forgotten victims' in violence against women, but instead as individuals in need of a full range of specialized services. Through offering an effective children's program, child advocates have the opportunity to intervene in a child's experience of violence, to provide a positive support system, and to introduce children to a feminist philosophy of non-conditional acceptance. Children given the opportunity to experience alternatives to violent behaviour, and to the abuse of power and control in relationships, will hopefully choose to live free from violence in their adult lives.

We do not underestimate the resilience of children, or their ability to make a difference in the world. Our role as child advocates in a shelter is to plant a seed - a seed of healing, growth, and change.

Acknowledgement

Women's Community House wishes to acknowledge the contributions of its Executive Director, Jan Richardson, for early leadership and continued support; the child advocates who have contributed to the children's program by developing or re-developing the program described in this chapter, and the community that continues to support our efforts.

References

Catholic Board of Education (1994) *Children Who Witness Woman Abuse - School Based Support*. London, Ontario: Catholic Board of Education.

Children's Sub-Committee of the London Co-ordinating Committee to End Woman Abuse (1994) *'Make a Difference' - How to Respond to Child Witnesses of Woman Abuse*. London, Ontario: Children's Sub-Committee of LCCEWA.

Jaffe, P.G., Wolfe, D.A., Wilson, S.K. (1990) *Children of Battered Women*. Newbury Park, California: Sage.

London Co-ordinating Committee to End Woman Abuse (1987; revised September 1992) *The London Co-ordinating Committee to End Woman Abuse - An Integrated Community Response To Prevent Violence Against Women in Intimate Relationships*. London, Ontario: LCCEWA.

Rossetti, M. (1988) *Crisis Intervention for Child Witness/Victims of Wife Assault: A Model for Shelter Workers and Child Advocates*. London, Ontario: WCH.

Women's Community House (1993) *Children's Program Guidelines*. London, Ontario: WCH.

Women's Community House (forthcoming) *Children's Program Mission Statement*. London, Ontario: WCH.

13

Asian Children
and Domestic Violence

Umme Farvah Imam

The aim of this chapter is to explore the impact of domestic violence on Asian[1] children from a Black[2] perspective: a perspective drawn from working with and supporting Asian women and children living with domestic violence in a Black-run project. It is expressly recognised that a specific focus on Asian projects can sometimes deflect the attention which needs to be paid to experiences of racism shared by all Black people in this country (Mama, 1989, pp.291-93). The present author inevitably writes from her own, Asian perspective but does so with a commitment to challenging racism in its widest manifestations and in the knowledge that other communities of Black women have different and particular experiences which offer crucial lessons for wider society.

The commitment to raise these issues comes from several years of working alongside other Black women - networking and working collaboratively to extend choices to Black women and children facing violence in the family. By illustrating this account with examples drawn from experience (the names and some specific details about individuals have been changed to maintain confidentiality), I intend to highlight the specific issues which compound the emotional and social trauma experienced by Asian children as the result of male abuse of their mothers.

Some of the issues raised relate generally to the oppression and discrimination Asian children face as members of Black communities. Others are unique to them. They arise from certain cultural traditions and practices of the communities originating in the Indian sub-continent which have been perpetuated in a 'collusive silence' (Mama, 1989, p.84) in ways that maintain male privilege and power. The objective of this chapter is to promote good practice - an increased sensitivity in working with Asian children who live with domestic violence - by developing a greater understanding of the specific issues the children face. It is *not* to perpetuate the myths and stereotypes which characterise the Asian experience of cultural racism in society at large (Ahmed, S., 1986).

A second aim is to highlight the tremendous courage and strength demonstrated by Asian women in confronting and challenging both the chauvinism within their communities and the restrictive practices and structures of British society. This is important both in order to challenge the myths of their passivity and docility, and to underline that any analysis of the impact of domestic violence on children must be undertaken in the context of the experiences of those who are the primary victims of that violence. The perspective adopted is rooted in the shared realities of the women and children. This is particularly significant because, unlike the Western philosophy of 'individualism', the philosophical traditions of Asian communities contextualise the problems and concerns of individuals against the background of roles and responsibilities within families and communities (Ahmad, 1990).

THE IMPACT OF RACISM AND MULTIPLE OPPRESSION

An aspect of the experience of family violence unique to Asian children (and other Black children) living with domestic violence is their experience of the violation of their sanctuary and shelter from racism - the home. Unlike other children, Black children grow up with the experience of violence and abuse outside the home. For most, this is an everyday reality and part of their experience of living in a racist society. However the home, family and community typically provide safety and security from this violence and when violence pervades the home also, it adds to their insecurity and vulnerability.

Furthermore, as they accompany mothers attempting to move away from abusive situations, they are exposed to the oppression and discrimination of individuals and structures outside the family and community, including those who are ostensibly there to help. For Asian women, violence in the home is further compounded by 'general societal racism and state repression, to create a situation of multiple oppression and further punishment for those bravely struggling to establish lives for themselves and their children, away from violent men' (Mama, 1989, p.xiii). The decision to leave the familiar, if not supportive, networks of family and community is a difficult one and often taken as a last resort. The choices from women in taking control over their lives by moving away from family and community are further circumscribed by the racism and oppression Asian women and children face from individuals, agencies and structures when they step outside this environment. The impact of racism on their children is a significant factor in women's choices between the options open to them and limits their possibilities of leaving home. For many who brave the consequences and attempt to assume control over their lives, the debilitating effects of racism may yet compel them to return to the abuse from which they had striven so hard to escape.

These negative effects may be found in agencies set up to help and protect, in both the voluntary and statutory sectors, as will now be illustrated with the use of case examples. Good practice for children depends on confronting such abuses of power and position, and replacing them with an empowering awareness of the difficulties women face in safeguarding their own and their children's safety.

EXPERIENCES IN REFUGES

In recent years, Black women have challenged the exclusionary and ethnocentric nature of welfare agencies and, through self-organising and networking, have extended choices to Asian women living with domestic violence through establishing specialist refuges. In the light of these challenges, as well as through developing awareness about the different needs and experiences of Black women, organisations like the Women's Aid Federation, England (WAFE) have reflected on their accessibility to Black women and adopted anti-racist policies to ensure that all refuges are accessible to and meet the needs of all women. This was essential since a lack of understanding of the issues faced by Asian women leaving home had in the past contributed to mainstream refuges disempowering them through inappropriate and inadequate services.

The case of Meena and Sameer who accompanied their mother into a local refuge illustrates this experience. Sheela left her home about ten years ago accompanied by Meena (8 years) and Sameer (6 years). Despite the lack of awareness within the refuge, she was determined to establish her life away from her husband. However, she surrendered to pressure from the children to return home after they had been consistently physically and verbally harassed at the refuge. As the situation in the home did not improve she made several suicide attempts, until some Black workers supported her in moving into temporary accommodation and obtaining a court injunction to stop her husband from harassing her and the children.

Several years later, Meena (then 15 years) spoke of their experience at the refuge:

> Although we were frightened of our father and hated what he was doing to Mum, we did not want to leave our home and the family. When we went into the refuge, the other children would not play with us . . . we were called 'pakis' and 'blackies' . . . the other mums would also pick on us when the workers were not around . . . Mum used to keep us locked in our room when the workers were not there. We missed our family and could not understand why we had to leave our home.

In the absence of the present policies, the racism experienced by Sheela and her family was not challenged and eventually forced her to return to her abusive husband.

Although the WAFE national policies have ensured access and provision for Asian women in mainstream refuges, the effective implementation of the anti-racist policies depends on individual workers and on local Women's Aid groups; progress is inevitably patchy. The research carried out by Amina Mama (1989) indicated that many Black women did feel able to challenge individual acts of racism, particularly where they were present in numbers and there was at least one influential Black worker employed (p.283); the anti-racist policies could also be used to challenge inappropriate provision or attitudes. The struggle for change in mixed refuges is crucially important since by no means all Asian women will prefer to be in an Asian refuge. Issues of confidentiality are particularly acute there and, as Mama notes (p.293), some women may still fear they will be more easily traced in such a setting. Younger women may find an Asian refuge too 'traditional' or older women too 'feminist'.

THE STATUTORY SECTOR

Although the voluntary sector has responded to the challenges and implemented policies and guidelines for Black women, the impact on the statutory sector has been quite limited. Good practice and sensitivity to the needs of Asian women continues to be more the result of individual commitment than policies developed to combat structural forms of racism.

The housing department is one of the first agencies women need to approach in moving away from abusive husbands. Although feminist challenges have compelled local authorities to develop policies on re-housing women and children made homeless by domestic violence, these still vary widely across the country (see chapter by Hague and Malos, this volume). Newcastle upon Tyne, for example, awards them high priority in housing allocations but the reality for many elsewhere is long periods of waiting in temporary accommodation or refuges. For Asian women, and other Black women and children, the situation is further exacerbated by limited choices of areas for resettlement. Some women wishing to remain in their own community face several months of staying in refuges until properties are identified. For others, considerations of safety dictate that they move out of their established communities into areas or regions with limited numbers of Black people. For the children involved, both situations are stressful: the uncertainty and lack of stability of long periods spent waiting in temporary accommodation, or the move away from family, friends and established Black communities into environments where they are more vulnerable to racism without the comfort and security of the support networks they have left behind.

Social services departments typically become involved with cases of domestic violence when children are deemed to be at risk. It can be argued that all children living with violent men are at risk, however this was not the view taken by some of the professionals who were working with this woman fleeing from her home: Sapna escaped from her violently abusive husband leaving Tima (11 months) and Sonu (4 years) and sought shelter in a local Black refuge. She attempted, with the support of the workers, to take the children to the refuge. The social workers involved indicated that they would not support her as they had visited her husband and were assured of his competence to look after the children. It was only when the issue was taken up with other professionals that Sapna was allowed access to her children.

The role of the police in colluding with the violence against women through their inadequate response to 'domestics' has been well documented (see, for example, Edwards, 1989; Mama, 1992, chap.6). With reference to Asian women, the behaviour of the police is influenced both by the racism of individual officers and the insensitivity of the organisation to the needs of Asian women. The oppression perpetuated by police officers ranges from reluctance to enforce the law and insensitivity to Asian women and their calls for help, to harassment of single isolated women living away from their communities (personal communications). Some children who have taken great personal risks to call out the police in order to try and protect their mothers from abuse have reported the collusion of individual officers with the men. This is particularly the case in situations where the women are faced with additional barriers of language, the police sometimes making no efforts to communicate with the victim when they are called out to investigate an incident of male violence.

An example of this insensitivity is the case of Amjad. Amjad (10 years old) attempted to help his mother by approaching the neighbours to call out the police while his father was beating her up. The police officer who came out spoke only to the husband and made no attempt to establish that his mother had been assaulted, particularly when he was told that she could not speak English. Amjad was physically abused by his father when he intervened and attempted to translate for his mother. By colluding with the male perpetrator, the professional obligation of investigating a violent situation was ignored. There are also examples where women, as victims, have been detained overnight at police stations 'for their own protection' or at the behest of their husbands, often leaving young and vulnerable children with violent partners. This demonstrates the harnessing of State power by husbands to coerce and abuse their wives.

Another example of men's use of the power of the State to coerce women to stay with them relates to immigration legislation (see Debbonaire, this volume). Mama (1989) cites several cases where men have used immigration legislation to maintain their power over women (e.g. pp.114-115, 177-179). There are examples of women being threatened with deportation and separation from their children when they have attempted to move away. Others, who escape without passports or proofs of identity and legal status, are subjected to additional pressures if they approach welfare agencies for benefits, and are required to provide evidence of their status.

Those working with Asian women and children work hard at explaining their rights to women with whom they come into contact but sometimes all are trapped by the system into living with harsh decisions, particularly where there are children involved. Selma had been married for just over a year, and was the mother of a very young baby, when she had to leave her home due to her husband's brutality. As she had only just completed the minimum period of one year required for permanent settlement, the Home Office required confirmation that the couple were still living together before she was given the right to stay. Her husband threatened to inform the authorities that they were separated, if she did not return. Although she feared for her baby's and her own safety, she was forced to return to him or else face deportation or a voluntary return to India without her child. Selma was supported by workers in her decision to go back to her abusive husband, just as they would support any woman in her decision-making but with the additional sadness and frustration in this case caused by the knowledge that she went with reluctance and fear. She suffered for several months more before she was given the right to stay indefinitely and moved out finally to set up home for herself and the baby away from the violence and abuse.

RELIGION AND CULTURE

Religion and culture have been used universally by men to maintain their power over women and to justify misogyny and chauvinism. Asian men are therefore no different to men from other cultures when they invoke subservience and subjugation from 'their' women in the name of tradition and culture.

Mama, in a comprehensive study of domestic violence within Black communities, reports its widespread prevalence across communities, cultures and creeds (Mama, 1989, chap.1). 'Asian' communities, as collectively classified by dominant British society rather than by themselves, have this in common therefore. Yet they also encompass people of very diverse languages, religions and cultures. The unifying forces within this diversity are not only the common experience of racism and colonialism but also their shared origin in the Indian sub-continent. All are firmly rooted in similar patriarchal societies with clearly defined gender roles. The extent to which male power is maintained in these communities varies between religious groups, however. In Hinduism, there are strong and ancient traditions of subservience and obedience to men. Islam clearly delineates gender roles and maintains the legal, social and institutional subordination of women (Ahmed, L., 1992); whilst in Sikhism there exist more liberal attitudes, with some moves to promote equality for women.

Although none of the major Asian religions sanctions violence, certain parts of the Qoran, like the Bible, can be manipulated to justify the abuse of women; both also contain passages which specifically condemn violence (Mama, 1989, p.300). The manipulation is made easier through the male domination of religious and cultural practices and traditions. Within Asian communities, the strong patriarchal traditions and male privilege and control over women have been upheld by widespread collusion and silence on the issues of domestic violence and sexual abuse. This has resulted in denial of the existence of domestic violence in Asian families or, when acknowledged, it is excused as resulting from the oppression of Asian men in Western society. It has been left to Asian women's organisations to take responsibility for shattering the silence and confronting the denial. Asian women, like women generally, dismiss simplistic explanations put forward to condone the exertion of male power. These include social factors like unemployment, the influence of alcohol, or the hierarchical interplay between oppressions so that sexist behaviour and sexual violence are justified as a consequence of men being 'brutalised by state repression' (Mama, 1989, p.84). Thus Asian women have had to challenge the male influence over religion which limits their lives and also the collusion in their own communities which contributes to 'the collective abdication of individual responsibility for brutal and anti-social behaviours' (Mama, 1989).

Certain cultural practices and traditions add to the multiplicity of the oppressions experienced by Asian women and their children. Significant among such these is the concept of 'izzat', or family honour, which must be upheld at all costs. Men have invoked this particular tradition in maintaining the subservience of their wives by linking it exclusively to women, who are considered the embodiment of their family's honour.

In recent years, Asian women in Britain have drawn on strategies developed by their sisters in the Indian sub-continent to challenge the exclusiveness of women's responsibility for upholding family honour. As violence against women is carried out behind a façade of respectability within the community, women have sought to shatter this façade. They have exposed and publicised male perpetrators of domestic violence and this, in turn, has obliged men to share responsibility for family honour - for izzat - because none of the cultures condones violence or brutal behaviour and none of the communities can be seen to do so.

Asian women have thus made small inroads into challenging traditions that adversely effect the quality of their lives. However izzat continues to exert a powerful influence on the choices and avenues open to women when faced with violence in the home. So insidious is this exertion of male power that its implications seriously limit the life chances of those socialised within the culture. Not only does the defiling of izzat affect women themselves but being seen to betray the family and community has serious implications for the future of their children in the community. The repercussions of any dishonourable actions are especially serious for female children. Izzat continues be a compelling force for women in determining their choices in dealing with domestic violence, and in moving away from family and community. The act of leaving home is viewed as a betrayal of the family and community and has motivated certain communities to go to great lengths to seek out and bring back women and children who have escaped from violent families. This aspect of the culture has been zealously reported by the popular media to perpetuate myths about 'oppressive Asian cultures'.

ISSUES PARTICULAR TO ASIAN CHILDREN

Drawing on earlier discussions, this section focuses specifically on the impact of domestic violence on the children concerned, and outlines the specific issues that are unique to them as young members of Asian families living in Britain.

The ethos of collective responsibility and ownership of all problems and issues by families and communities provides opportunities for the support of women and children. Evidence suggests that some families and communities mediate in such situations and are successful in influencing the actions of the male perpetrators (Mama, 1989, for example, p.86). However, the strong ties and sense of responsibility to community and family may also be manipulated to keep women in violent situations. Another significant factor which forces women to continue to live with the violence is consideration of the children's security and comfort. This means that very many remain in abusive relationships as long as the children are secure in the affections of the family.

Saeeda, 35 years old, arrived in this country 12 years ago following her marriage. She had no relatives or friends in Britain and, from the day of her arrival, lived with her husband and his family. She suffered physical and emotional abuse from both her husband and his family. Her two children grew up with this abuse and control of their mother; although they enjoyed love and affection within their extended family, the abuse of their mother nevertheless had a significant impact on them. Moin (8) and Saba (6) eventually took the initiative of talking about the violence suffered by their mother to teachers at their school who were able to facilitate contact with workers in the area. Saeeda was supported in her decision to move away and subsequently was supported by local workers to establish a life for herself and her children in another part of the same city.

Saeeda's story not only illustrates the complicity of the family in maintaining the abuse but also highlights the resourcefulness and initiative shown by young children in supporting their mothers and identifying help. It also raises issues around the ethnocentric concept of childhood whereby children are conceptualised as passive recipients of care. Though not unique in seeking to protect their mothers (see chapters by Mullender and Loosley, this volume), Asian children frequently find themselves in positions where they take on the responsibility of facilitating help for their mothers. This is particularly so in situations where their mothers have problems in communicating in English, and lack information about the support available. Asian women who have migrated to Britain often suffer great isolation as the extended networks of family and community that would have supported them in their countries of origin, are not available and they find themselves completely dependent on coercive husbands. When faced with physical and emotional abuse, they have limited choices; both language barriers and the lack of knowledge about structures of help limit their options in escaping from the violence. In such circumstances, children have often played an important role in supporting their mothers and facilitating access to services, frequently demonstrating great courage and initiative in identifying and procuring help.

A few years ago, I received a call from the social services department to go to a local telephone booth where 9 year old Sunil was speaking to a worker in the social services department and wanted someone to go out and support his mother. The worker kept him in conversation and contacted me on another line with the location of the telephone booth. Sunil then took me into his home to speak to his mother about his father's violence. Sunil's mother had migrated from rural Pakistan and had no family support in the country besides the family into which she had married. She did not wish to go into the refuge, but was supported in her home by outreach workers and other community workers.

AGE AND GENDER ISSUES

In addition to the issues relating to traditions and culture, Asian children's experiences of domestic violence are also influenced by factors relating to their gender and age, as well as the intersections of these with class and religion. Being socialised into their patriarchal communities with clearly defined gender roles and a certain amount of indulgence towards male children, impacts on their experiences of living with and witnessing violence.

Most of the male children I worked with reported strong feelings of empathy with their mother and a driving need to protect her from the violence. Some of those who had been separated for some years and were now young adults wanted nothing to do with their fathers, even when the latter had indicated their remorse and contrition about their actions. At the other extreme were a few incidents reported by women whose sons had joined in the assault, but this had always been at their father's behest.

Female children, as discussed earlier, are constrained by considerations of family honour and the traditions of subservience to males. For daughters accompanying their mothers, there are additional issues surrounding respectability. Moving out of the home is certainly not approved of within communities but the severity of the sanctions against women and children depends on the community's perceptions of the place where the woman takes refuge. By holding the power to define the degree of 'respectability' of refuges and hostels, communities and families exert control over women and over the options open to them - prohibiting, for many, this essential first step towards more permanent accommodation. One of the important areas of work for Asian women's refuges is in challenging the rumour and myths about refuges that are promoted within communities to control women. Collusion between males results in refuges assuming notoriety. Young female children accompanying their mothers into refuges, hostels and other temporary accommodation share the sanctions brought against their mothers; the impact on adolescent girls and young women of leaving the home and compromising izzat goes beyond censure into grave repercussions which could lead to their being completely ostracised by the family and community.

The case of Rehana outlines the particular dilemmas Asian women with older daughters face in moving out. Rehana (34 years) decided to leave her daughter at home with her violent husband as she feared reprisals within the community if she took 12 year old Nadia with her into the refuge. Not only did this involve leaving Nadia with her violent husband, who suffered from mental ill-health, but it also meant Nadia being separated from her mother and from her brothers and sisters. Nadia understood the need for the separation through the socialisation involved in her upbringing, but she was nevertheless extremely distressed by it. Although she had never suffered any direct abuse from her father, she was apprehensive - particularly as she had witnessed his abuse of her mother. Rehana made the following comments about her action:

> I had to leave Nadia at home because of what it would mean for her future in the community . . . . I had to think about her future . . . . I knew she would be safe at home because my husband did not ever harm the children. I would not be able to get her married if the family and community ostracised us for going into the hostel.

Rehana was later counselled about Nadia's vulnerability and decided that she would challenge the rumours about the lack of respectability of the refuge. She did this by publicising the safety and security for Asian women in the Black refuge where she was sheltering, and succeeded in dispelling some of the myths and lies about the refuge in the community. She took Nadia into the refuge to demonstrate its respectability and she challenged men and women in the community to provide alternative provision to the refuge.

Several years later, I made contact with Nadia to find out her views and feelings about the period when she was left with her father. It was interesting to learn that, at the time, she had come to feel quite secure and considered that the experience had brought her closer to her father. In retrospect, however, she recognised that this was because of her relatively young age and owed much to the fact that she did not challenge his authority and power. Now, at 16 years of age - when she was asserting her own individuality and behaving like a 'normal' 16 year old - she had been publicly humiliated and physically abused by him on several occasions.

Agency policy and practice with reference to age and gender can also have particular implications for Asian children. Most refuges operate age restrictions for older male children. As Asian children traditionally live with their families and do not move out in adolescence or young adulthood, they find it very difficult to live on their own away from the family if their mother goes into a refuge with specific age restrictions. Some men take advantage of this in compelling their wives to return.

Asha (aged 35), for example, was referred to a local refuge to escape from her violent husband with Ramesh (12), Kanta (9) and Nita (6). On arriving at the refuge she was informed that Ramesh would not be able to stay there. This raised great concerns within her family but she resolved to stay in the refuge and arranged for a relative to have Ramesh for a few weeks until she could arrange alternative accommodation. However her husband learnt of the arrangement and took Ramesh away. Through physically beating his son he was successful in forcing Asha to return to him. Asha drew on this experience several years later, when she herself was involved in establishing a refuge for Asian women and was able to negotiate special provision for women with older male children.

CONCLUSION

This chapter has attempted to throw light on the specific issues and experiences affecting Asian children living with domestic violence, with the aim of promoting more effective and appropriate work by relevant voluntary and statutory agencies. It is important that these specific issues be understood against the wider background of the universality of domestic violence highlighted in this book, rather than being focused on exclusively as if particular cultures had a monopoly on oppression. Male power and dominance exist in virtually all societies. Their expression differs according to religions and cultures, but Asian cultures are no more oppressive overall than Western society and oppression needs to be challenged by all those who experience it. It is not their culture as such that Asian women have challenged, but the practices and traditions within it which are perpetuated and manipulated to maintain male privilege and dominance. While these persist, they have an adverse impact on the lives of many children and their mothers which is compounded by living in a frequently hostile and racist society.

Notes
1. The term 'Asian' is used in this chapter specifically to refer to people of Indian, Pakistani and Bangladeshi heritage.
2. The term 'Black' is used in this chapter to refer to all those who suffer discrimination and racism because of their skin colour. In the context of British society, this includes African, African Caribbean, Asian, and Chinese people - and many others.

References
Ahmad, B. (1990) *Black Perspectives in Social Work*. Birmingham: Venture Press.
Ahmed, L. (1992) *Women and Gender in Islam*. New Haven and London: Yale University Press.

Ahmed, S. (1986) 'Cultural racism in work with Asian women and girls' in Ahmed, S., Cheetham, J. and Small, J. (eds.) (1986) *Social Work with Black Children and Their Families*. London: Batsford

Edwards, S.S.M. (1989) *Policing 'Domestic' Violence: Women, the Law and the State*. London: Sage.

Mama, A. (1989) *The Hidden Struggle*. London: London Race and Housing Research Unit.

Yllö, K. and Bograd, M. (eds) (1988) *Feminist Perspectives on Wife Abuse*. Newbury Park, California: Sage.

14

Children in Women's Refuges: A Retrospective Study

Alex Saunders

When a woman seeks refuge from violence, her children face equal crisis and disruption in their lives (Jaffe et al., 1990, p.96). Whilst violence against women is often trivialised or ignored in wider society, the children involved are in an even more vulnerable position having no independent voice. Although they represent over two-thirds of the refuge population (Ball[1], 1990, p.6; Women's Aid Federation England [hereafter: WAFE] 1991), in such a hectic and often emotionally fraught environment children continue to remain relatively invisible.

This does not mean that the refuge movement has been unconcerned with children's rights and welfare. From the very outset, refuges in this country have been aware of the practical and emotional needs of children entering refuges (see for example Pizzey, 1974; Binney et al., 1981, pp.54-63). In North America, shelter staff have documented the trauma experienced by child witnesses, and this material has played a significant role in highlighting the need for more intensive community interventions (Jaffe et al., 1990, pp.95-96). In Denmark, work with children of abused women is more developed and better resourced than in the UK (O'Hara, 1992, p.5; Hester and Radford, 1992; Hester et al., this volume).

Women's Aid has to cope with a wide range of children from babies to adolescents, all from a wide variety of cultural and social backgrounds. Similarly, the ages of children in the refuge from one week to the next may vary considerably. Two reports provide details of the numbers and ages of children in refuges, and although completed approximately ten years apart they produced similar findings (Binney et al., 1981; Ball, 1990). In both studies, over 80 per cent of children were below secondary school age. Similarly, the numbers of pre-school and primary age children tended to be roughly equal in both. Although the number of older children in refuges at the time of the two studies was comparatively small, they still constituted up to 20 per cent (Binney et al., 1981, p.64) of the refuge child population.

In addition, some children move in and out of refuges at very short notice, whilst others can stay for up to two years awaiting rehousing (McKinlay and Singh, 1991, p.5). Ball found that whilst 27 per cent of children stayed for a week or less, 36 per cent were in a refuge for six months or more (Ball, 1990, p.7). Charles asserts that a trend towards longer periods of residence for women and children is developing, often in accommodation which is not designed for this purpose (Charles, 1991, p.10). While refuges continue to lack adequate resources to provide the level of care and support required by abused women, children accompanying them will be particularly impoverished (Binney et al., 1981; Charles, 1991, p.85). Over the years, the voices of children involved in refuge life have gone largely unheard. Whilst individual comments and indirect references have been documented in some Women's Aid publications (see for example Binney et al., 1981; Scottish Women's Aid [hereafter: SWA], n.d.; WAFE, n.d. and 1989), comprehensive research into children in refuges is only just beginning (see chapter by Morley and Mullender, this volume) and there is still a great need to record and consider the perceptions and views of children who have experienced life in a refuge. This dearth of knowledge means that children's position of relative powerlessness and isolation within refuges is reinforced.

The specific experience of children from ethnic minority backgrounds, for example, remains relatively unknown (see chapter by Imam, this volume). Of the refuges given grants as part of a recent joint project between the National Council of Voluntary Child Care Organisations (NCVCCO) and WAFE, three catered specifically for women from minority groups: two for Asian women and one for Latin American women (Ball, 1990) but, regrettably, in her evaluation of this project Ball does not specify the cultural background of people quoted in the report. In a similar vein, the first comprehensive study to look specifically at Black women's experience of male violence in the home (Mama, 1989), including refuge provision, makes rather few references to the experiences of their children.

My research grew from my personal experience as a child in a refuge. I conducted interviews with four adults: three women and one man, all of white European origin. As children they, like myself, had lived for a time between 1978 and 1980 in women's refuges in London. All had lived in refuges which employed a part-time children's worker. Sophia, now aged 23 years old, was 8 when she arrived at the refuge where she stayed for 14 months. Clara, aged 21, was 5 and stayed for 9 months. John, aged 29, stayed for 18 months when he was 13 years old. Sandra, aged 25, was 9 and stayed for one year.

It is important to set these interviews in context: more than 15 years have elapsed since these adults were children in refuges. During this time, both refuges and work with the children of abused women have changed considerably - as charitable sources have funded improved staffing, for example. Nevertheless, the central message of these personal accounts remains relevant in understanding the need for continually developing children's work. The rest of this chapter is devoted to those with personal experiences to share of refuge life between 1978 and 1980. To a lesser extent, it also draws on published accounts of children's feelings and reactions to more recent refuge stays.

Arrival

Both Clara and Sophia vividly remember how it all began:

> I remember leaving home. Mum and me were walking down the road with a pram full of my toys . . . (Clara).

> I remember my mum saying to me that we were going up the launderette. She had two bags full of clothes and she kept saying that were going to do the washing. But we ended up at this strange house that was a right state (Sophia).

The diaries of children's workers quoted by Ball noted the arrival of frightened newcomers, and the length of time it took to gain their confidence:

> Today for the first time D. (2) did not seem so frightened and was happy to be on his own with me (this after nearly 3 months in the refuge).

> R. (3) was very tense for several days. I found that lots of cuddling and affection soothed him, and calmed him down. His mother has commented on the change in him (Ball, 1990, p.8).

My research uncovered similar feelings:

> It was scary. Frightening. Coming away from your home and going into this strange place, not knowing anyone. Different people, different place, different kids. I got very disturbed. I played up. In fact, I was a right little sod, so was Simon (Sophia's brother), but I reckon that was us reacting to what we'd been through. I think the kids suffer more because they don't understand these disturbing things. They know there is something wrong but they don't know what it is, do they? (Sophia).

Refuge life from a child's point of view

There are a great many advantages and disadvantages about refuge life, which clearly vary from child to child. On the benefit side:

> I like it here - my mum and me aren't frightened (SWA, n.d., p.6).

> Mum asked if I wanted to come, my mum was getting beaten up and I was scared at home, didn't bring my toys, but since I see dad sometimes I want to get some of my toys. I like living at the Refuge, outings and lots of people to play with, a playroom, toys and garden, big ones, big building and a lot more people make it different from home, lived in homeless families for a while and hated it couldn't play (Ben - South East) (WAFE, n.d., p.37).

Many children simply feel relieved to have left a violent situation and glad that their mother is similarly free from abuse. The company of other children can also be invaluable since isolation is a common state for both women and children experiencing male violence. In fact, the communality of experience that is at the corner-stone of refuge empowerment sometimes extends to the children:

> I remember some of the kids used to call my nan 'Nan' ! I couldn't understand why they called her nan when she was my nan. In fact, we all seemed to have two or three nans. It was like a big family. You could share other people (Clara).

There are also many disadvantages to refuge life. Children will have been uprooted from family and friends, moved away from familiar surroundings including toys, pets, clothes, and separated from a father they may love. Children may be too young to understand what is happening or resent the disruption in their lives (McKinlay and Singh, 1991, p.5). For some children the benefits of leaving a violent home may not be immediately obvious. Not only is there uncertainty about what will happen next, but the immediate conditions of overcrowding, a lack of privacy, and shared rooms add to the pressures.

Arrival at a refuge can bring great relief to children who have been frightened and who may have been abused. However, on some occasions, the move itself involves children in new and threatening situations. In the ten-month period of the Ball evaluation, she refers to seven instances of men attacking or besieging refuges. Such attacks affect everybody living there and, in these circumstances, restricted movement outside the refuge may be imposed on children out of fear of violence or abduction (Ball, 1990, p.9). Sophia described a particularly terrifying experience that we had both endured at our Essex refuge:

> Do you remember that night he (Sophia's dad) came looking for us? When he drove his Jag through the refuge door? That was very scary and frightening - everyone hiding under beds and tables. He was screaming out: 'If I can't have my kids I'll kill them' (Sophia).

Facilities

In the study by Binney et al. (1981), 56 per cent of refuges had no playroom. Charles' study of facilities in refuges affiliated to Welsh Women's Aid makes similarly depressing reading. Of 27 refuges whose facilities were listed, 17 had no playroom - although most refuges without a playroom had an outside play area (Charles, 1991, p.24). Playrooms themselves were often too small and poorly equipped, owing to a lack of funds or the constant destruction of toys.

Where the playroom did not also serve as the women's sitting room, emergency accommodation, storage space, or a thoroughfare to other parts of the building, it was often locked to prevent the destruction of toys during unsupervised play (Binney et al., 1981, pp.64-65; Ball, 1990, p.9; NCVCCO, n.d., p.3). The reality of this unpopular and often reluctant policy is all too clear for this young boy:

I like painting and drawing but they only unlock the playroom twice a week (Binney et al., 1981, p.71).

Many refuges have access to a small outdoor space but, in common with the playrooms, this is often too small or otherwise unsuitable for many activities:

> There was a concrete garden outside. You felt all walled up - twelve foot high it was. It should've been a bit more pleasant for the kids. Outside stuff, like a sandpit. And its not only to make it pleasant. I'm a nursery nurse now and I understand how children learn through play. Things like water, sand and so on can be very therapeutic. I know it's all money but we didn't have anything like that (Sandra) (see also Ball, 1990, p.9).

Most striking of all, few refuges have any space or facilities for older children (Binney et al., 1981; Ball, 1990; Charles, 1991). Only six of the refuges in Charles' study were able to offer older children the option of using a quiet room for privacy and retreat and, in most cases, this room was being used for the same purpose by women (Charles, 1991, p.24).

Reactions of others

The social stigma often attached to abused women extends to their children (WAFE, n.d., p.30). Sandra's story illustrates this point:

> I feel so angry at the way everyone was treated. People used to cross the road sometimes . . . I remember being treated like a thief in the local sweet shop near the refuge. The shop owner would be watching you to see if you nicked anything just because you lived in a battered wives' home. When we bought penny sweets in his shop other kids would just say to him: 'I've got 20 pence worth'. But with me it was 'One, two, three . . .', he would count them all out in front of all my friends - silly things like that. It makes you so *angry* (Sandra).

Most children are not able to talk to friends about being in the refuge and don't tell anyone (Binney et al., 1981; WAFE, n.d.).

> I never told anyone. I closed up completely. I never used to tell any of my friends what I was going through (Sophia).

> I remember a friend of mine phoned my dad to speak to me, so my dad gave him the phone number of the refuge! This caused quite a stir, but all I was worried about was that this friend might know where I was. I told him that I was at a friend's house who had a lot of noisy kids! (John).

> I think a lot about the Refuge but I cannot talk to friends and don't think I will ever want to (Peter - London North East) (WAFE, n.d., p.38).

When Sandra overcame her reticence and confided in her friend she was particularly bitter at her friend's parents' response:

They don't wanna know you. They think you're some kind of scum. They look down their noses at you. When I used to walk in the front door of my friend's house, they used to say: 'Oh, they live in there' (Sandra).

Feelings of pain and isolation can be heightened by a lack of awareness by others of the practicalities of life in a refuge:

People's idea of the refuge was dirty kids. Scruffy kids running around with dirty knees, dirty hands, scruffy hair and holes in their clothes. But it wasn't like that at all (Sandra).

Clara recounted the following story with a potent mixture of anger and amusement:

When I talked to my friends about the refuge they always said: 'Oh you poor thing'. It's like they thought we had all been chucked in this one room with a bucket for a toilet! And the things that kids at school used to think we did in there. They thought we were told when to eat dinner, forced to do the washing-up, not allowed to play. Someone thought we had one pair of shoes passed between the whole set of kids. They used to think that if there wasn't enough room in the refuge people used to sleep in tents in the garden! (Clara).

School

Where schools did know of a child's situation there were often reports of teasing. Some children may have to change schools whilst older children may be forced to travel long distances to remain at their existing school, due to the location of the refuge (WAFE, n.d., p.30). All of my research participants recalled negative responses from head teachers at a time when they were most in need of support:

I remember my mum kept me from school because she couldn't afford to buy me any shoes. The headmaster sent us £30 to buy some but as soon as I returned to school he kept me in detention for a month (John),

My dad used to come down to the school to try to see me. I would have to hide until he went away. That's why my headmistress didn't like me. She wanted the perfect school with the perfect mum, perfect dad, 2.2 children, and a nice house. So she picked on me instead. The headmistress was always making comments like 'Hasn't your mother cut your hair?' or 'Can't you afford to go to the hairdressers?'. And it seemed like she was always looking at my uniform for a fault or a crease: 'Couldn't mummy iron your uniform?'. Nothing heavy, just subtle digs at me. When I think of what my headmistress put me through when I was in the refuge, I think that's why I went into working with kids (Sandra).

Father

A number of publications from Women's Aid have recognised the potential loss a child may be experiencing through enforced separation from their father (WAFE, 1989; Ball, 1990; McKinlay and Singh, 1991; WAFE, n.d.). For some children, overcoming the struggle between missing or wanting to see their father, whilst simultaneously feeling a sense of guilt and betrayal over these emotions, is one of the hardest tasks they ever face. The issue is made more complex with the possibility that the father may have been abusing the child, or by the subsequent anguish continued access may cause the mother.

> I wanted a dad. I used to see my friends with a mum and dad and I used to dream about them. But I don't even know him, not really. I have no respect for him (Sophia).

> I really wanted to tell someone that I missed having a dad. Not the one that beat up my mum, but just having a dad. But I didn't feel able to. There were women all around me who were beaten up, bruised, scared and angry at what men had done to them. I felt that I couldn't say anything (John).

> My daughter didn't like the Refuge at all. She screamed her head off. I suppose she wondered where everything familiar was. After going to see her dad she had nightmares. She must have felt torn up the middle (Annette - South East) (WAFE, n.d., p.33).

Despite the intensity of emotions unleashed by these dilemmas, none of my research participants was denied access to their father by either their mother, the refuge or social services. In fact, the biggest problem was their fathers' not keeping appointments:

> We would get all excited, all dressed up, wait on the corner of the road and he wouldn't show up. I used to hate him for that (Sophia).

Mother

For some women, the strain of constant abuse means that they do not have the energy or resources to meet their children's needs (NCVCCO, n.d., p.4). Not only are women coping with their own emotional needs, they are also having to make arrangements for the future:

> My mum doesn't have time for me anymore.

> It's boring, all the mums sit round and talk about what happened (SWA, n.d., p.6).

> I couldn't really talk to my mum about any of it because she had worries of her own. In fact, I spent most of my time trying to stop her from drinking too much or talking her out of suicide (John).

However this was not always the case:

Any men that used to come and have a dig - and there used to be quite a few that would knock on the door - my mum tended to keep us away from it. And she didn't let us see any of the rows or the fighting going on. I think she thought that we'd had enough of that (Clara).

In the Ball evaluation, several mothers commented on how difficult it was to meet their children's needs immediately after taking refuge:

In the refuge it's the first time you talk to women who have been through what you've been through. You need that time to yourself.

You need a break, the drama of leaving is over . . .

The kids have handled it quite well, but they miss their house and friends. I wonder if I've done the right thing, uprooting them. The boy has gone a bit wild, and his school work has gone down, but I feel depressed and too tired to encourage him (Ball, 1990, p.8).

Child workers

The commitment to improving children's experience of refuge life is most clearly expressed by the employment of children's workers. Each Women's Aid Federation now employs national workers whose brief is to promote the interests of children in refuges and there is a widespread recognition that specialist children's work should be developed within refuges (Ball, 1990; Charles, 1991, p.82; McKinlay and Singh, 1991, p.5).

The numbers of children using Women's Aid refuges, and their predicament when doing so, demands specialist children's workers. General refuge workers do not have the time to carry out any aspect of this task (Ball, 1990, p.15).

Briefly, a children's worker is expected to provide educational and recreational activities for the children, to provide appropriate support to meet their emotional and psychological needs, to fund-raise for the children, to liaise with local schools, health and social services, and to provide some security and continuity for children at a time when their mothers are unlikely to be able to give them all the attention they need (Charles, 1991, p.25). Detailed information can be found in Ball (1990, pp.9-12; NCVCCO, n.d; Debbonaire and Higgins, this volume). However, as there is no statutory duty to fund children's workers, until very recently few refuges could afford to employ them. In 1989-90, for example, Welsh Women's Aid employed only 9 children's workers in 32 refuges (Charles, 1991, p.280). Charitable sources of finance have begun to change this picture (see below and Debbonaire, this volume) but children's worker posts are still invariably on short-term contracts and often part-time.

In recent years, WAFE has been campaigning to raise awareness of the crucial role played by children's workers in helping children come to terms with their experiences (McKinlay and Singh, 1991, p.5). For some children, their mother is the only person they trust - although this often adds further stress to a person who already has a great many unfulfilled needs of her own. Often, children's workers are able to act as facilitators in this process, involving joint co-operation and negotiation between the mother, her children and the children's worker. This kind of work builds upon a tradition of feminist oriented practice in the field of child sexual abuse (see for example Driver and Droisen, 1989). Programmes concentrate on the restoration of the mother-child relationship, recognising the extreme pressure the mother is under and ending once she is able to protect herself and her children (Parton, 1990, p.58).

Conversely, in their submission to the NCVCCO report, Durham Women's Aid commented on how many children were able to talk to children's workers about past experiences which they had not been able to express to their mothers (NCVCCO, n.d., p.4). These children were able to build up a relationship with someone they could trust and who was not personally involved with their particular situation.

Children's workers were well received by children themselves in the Ball evaluation. In all cases, children were happy with the child worker. Workers were greeted with warmth and enthusiasm, and the observed play sessions were generally calm and creative (1990, p.13). The response from my research participants towards the children's workers they had met fifteen or so years ago was more mixed. There was general agreement that the children's workers they had met were warm and caring, and that most children enjoyed their company and the activities they organised. Sandra thought they were 'absolutely fantastic, they made you feel really special', whilst Sophia remembers with real joy 'the way we used to have cocoa in the room before we went to bed, and then she [the children's worker] would read us stories' (Sophia).

However, there was less praise for the children's workers' ability to spend time exploring children's feelings in the aftermath of arrival:

> They didn't ask me anything about what happened to me. They didn't sit down and talk with the children about it, they were more interested in the adults. Sometimes it was simply 'Get to bed', 'Go and play somewhere'; it felt like they were saying: 'Get out of the way and let the adults get on with it' (Sophia).

> Everyone at the refuge thought I was so helpful. I was always helping out with the younger kids in the playroom, supporting my mum whenever she was crying, depressed or had got drunk to forget it all. But no-one seemed to have any time for me. So one day I tried to punch a hole in the wall so that someone would pay me some attention (John).

All of the children's workers in the Ball evaluation regretted the limited time they had available to listen to children alone, especially older children. One writes:

I feel very frustrated in the job. The more I do, the more I see how much needs to be done . . . I had a long talk with an 8-year old today. He has been here for two months and this is the first opportunity I have had to spend time with him on his own. This boy has lived in absolute terror in his own home. I thought by now I was unshockable, but he has taught me different. He has started to soil himself and show disturbing behaviour, and when we started to talk the floodgates just opened. After three-quarters of an hour I had to leave to go to a meeting. He said, 'I have got so much to say and you haven't got time' (Ball, 1990, pp.13-14).

This frustration was sometimes compounded by the attitudes of general refuge workers. Although refuge workers expressed support for the childcare work role, some children's workers did not feel this was supported in practice. Refuge workers were candid about their tendency to forget the needs of children. Consequently, many children's workers described their work as having a low status in refuges while they themselves often felt isolated (Ball, 1990, pp.12&14).

. . . providing for children was considered on a par with collecting statistics and taking minutes . . . Children's workers were particularly irritated when refuge workers attended case conferences about children without informing them - even when social workers or health workers had always liaised with the children's worker at the refuge. This happened on several occasions in different refuges (Ball, 1990, p.12).

Most worrying of all, four of the child workers had resigned their posts before the end of the project. The reasons put forward by these workers were: a feeling of lack of support for child-care work within the refuge; a feeling that it was not possible to do the job part-time; the anticipation of the end of funding (Ball, 1990, p.15). All of this points towards the need for longer-term and more secure funding for children's work in refuges.

In order to act as children's advocates in the refuge, some workers have established regular children's meetings when children raise and discuss issues in the refuge that are important to them. Where possible, these meetings are run by the children themselves (Charles, 1991, p.39) and recommendations are taken forward to the general house meetings of the refuge (Ball, 1990, p.14). Some children's workers have commented, however, that matters of importance to children are placed as the last item on the agenda at house meetings ((Ball, 1990, p.14). In one refuge in the Ball evaluation, refuge mothers were unhappy about the idea of a children's meeting feeling, for example, that it 'stirred up trouble' (Ball, 1990, p.13). This was not the case in all refuges, though, and the general impression of children's workers was that this and similar initiatives raised the collective consciousness of children's needs in the refuges (Ball, 1990, p.14).

The belief of even one woman that children's meetings 'stir up trouble', highlights the tension and difficulties involved in the delicate balancing of rights within refuges. This is perhaps most clearly expressed through children's workers' handling of acts of violence directed against children as disciplinary action by a parent. It is not my intention to expand upon this debate in great detail as discipline was not a primary concern of my research participants. Nevertheless, whilst refuge staff may view empowerment as offering women the skills to parent children in less punitive ways, some women do react angrily when they see workers trying to change them or the way they parent their children (and Schechter records the same dilemmas occurring in the USA, 1982, p.91).

Since violence against children is firmly established as an acceptable and necessary form of control in western culture and history (Freeman, 1983; Franklin, 1986; Frost and Stein, 1989; Violence against Children Study Group, 1990), this can create value conflicts and increase stress at a time when women are already under extreme pressure. According to Hoff, these factors have resulted in policy in America being offered in the form of positive role modelling of alternative parent-child interaction rather than direct opposition to physical punishment (Hoff, 1990: 203). Whilst this is a clear recognition of the need to work with parents in order to 'protect' children, seemingly absent in much of this debate is the notion of the right of children not to be abused. This omission is illustrated by Hoff's comments on how non-violent discipline techniques are used in some American shelters. The policy is not strictly enforced, even though this means that some children still get hit, because the workers are caught up in wanting to avoid a 'violence breeds violence' explanation for the rule:

> . . . rigid adherence to this policy implies that violence is transmitted intergenerationally, a position which weakens feminists' political interpretation of violence against women (Hoff, 1990, p.203).

There is cause for optimism, however, as child workers both in the USA and this country begin to raise the profile of children's rights and their needs in refuges (see for example Schechter, 1982; Ball, 1990; WAFE, n.d.; and WAFE's moves towards adopting a national policy on child abuse to accompany that on children's rights, see Debbonaire, this volume).

Although many advocates had to ferret out their own motivations, scrutinise middle class value systems, and face the difficulty of intervening in a family at a time when the mother is most vulnerable, gentle confrontations about child abuse have become a standard part of most program's policies. Nonviolence has been taken seriously as a way of living in most shelters, even as confusion reigns about its exact definition and parameters (Schechter, 1982, pp.89-90).

I have discussed the role of children's workers at length because of their critical importance for children. The level of care and support offered to children depends to a large extent on the availability of a children's worker. Most crucially, children's workers may provide a vital source of support for children trying to survive male violence.

Follow-up support

When children leave a refuge there is little chance of follow up support. This is an especially important time for children, who may not have the maturity or financial resources to keep in contact with other children from the refuge. Women are strongly encouraged to remain active within the refuge if they wish, and they are seen as an invaluable source of support and inspiration to other women still resident there (e.g. Charles, 1991). Unfortunately, cultivation of this mutually supportive relationship has not always been extended to children:

> When I went in the refuge I was ashamed. I thought that I wasn't normal, that I was a bad kid and a failure. Maybe if I'd seen kids who had been in the refuge and turned out alright, I wouldn't have hated myself so much (John).

Once again, improved funding would increase the possibilities of work with ex-resident children (see Debbonaire, this volume) and some refuges do already routinely involve them in activities, with positive benefits on all sides (see Higgins, this volume).

In retrospect

At the end of the interviews, I asked each person to voice one thought about their experiences that they would most like others to consider. Both Sandra and John wished to place their reflections within the larger framework of violence against women:

> I think there's too much of it [violence against women and children] and its all behind closed doors. We are in [name omitted] and it couldn't be more snooty. When our neighbour found out where we used to live it was 'Oh, how disgusting', and yet she's beaten up next door (Sandra).

> All the time I was living in a refuge it felt very much like us and them. The outside world didn't understand and so I felt very ashamed and isolated. But now I feel quite proud of it really, and in a funny sort of way I actually enjoy thinking that other people will never understand what I went through. It makes me feel strong and special. But in another way I hate that feeling, because it shouldn't be like that - it's going on everywhere [violence against women and children] and it should be brought out into the open (John).

Clara and Sophia concentrated on the kind of support they would have liked to see for children in the refuge:

> The children should have their own personal counsellor. Well, not exactly a 'counsellor', I don't like that word, but a sort of big brother

or big sister or mate who knows what they are going through and can help them (Clara).

You get through it by yourself, but it would be nice to have a bit of help because it's hard work on your own (Sophia).

FUTURE DIRECTIONS

Women's Aid are already struggling to support women in the way they consider best. In addition, key areas of work such as fund-raising, outreach work, aftercare, public education and campaigning are all competing for the limited time and energy of workers. There are increasing administrative duties owing to changes in central government funding, social security legislation, and an increasing involvement with housing associations and charities. The task of juggling these competing pressures is played out within the wider framework of local authority cut-backs and government hostility, resulting in uncertainty and insecurity for the refuge movement. Cutting across all these issues is the central difficulty of maintaining and improving services whilst continuing the political struggle against male violence. Amongst all these concerns, it would be easy for work with children to be neglected or relegated to a low place on the list of priorities. The increase in specialist childwork seems an important way forward.

There is also the potential for Women's Aid to link up with other service providers and community organisations, working in unison to promote children's rights and needs. This is not only important for children but for the movement as a whole. In the present, politically hostile climate, alignments with other progressive movements can help to consolidate existing achievements whilst building a wider and larger power base from which to move forward, both here and in an international context (Schechter, 1982, pp.300-304). However this will require co-operation between organisations who may adopt different perspectives and aims, which may cause some conflict.

This is especially problematic within a society whose dominant belief system alternately denies and blames female survivors of domestic violence, and which defines children's needs as women's responsibility. For example:

When applying to local authorities for funding for a children's worker, some refuges reported that the argument was put to them that mothers in refuges should look after their own children (Ball, 1990, p.15).

Focusing upon children who witness violence may draw attention away from the violence itself - and from issues of male domination, power and control. It may also further subordinate the issue of violence against women, and advance intergenerational theories about cause (Dobash and Dobash, 1992, p.141; Morley and Mullender, this volume). For example, Dobash and Dobash cite as evidence the passage of Federal legislation to fund shelters in the USA. The funding of shelters for abused women was not achieved explicitly for women but was attached to the more popular and acceptable cause of child abuse (Dobash and Dobash, 1992, p.141). Ironically, this has resulted in a far more comprehensive service for children of abused women in the USA.

In this country, refuges are becoming increasingly involved with charities and housing associations which may also have consequences for policy. Money received from charities is usually tied to specified forms of expenditure, such as the purchase of equipment or the funding of outings, play sessions and so forth for children. Statutory finance, similarly, is coming to be linked to contracted services and may also carry bureaucratic expectations of procedural uniformity (see Debbonaire, this volume). This could lead to a transformation of philosophy, policy and/or practice as, like the American shelters cited above, activist organisations attempt to meet the criteria of funding bodies.

Recent initiatives by WAFE, however, give cause for optimism that services for children can be expanded without compromising the political struggle. They are currently working in conjunction with two other national charities to improve the conditions for children in refuges. Telethon is funding a national training programme for refuge workers working with children. At the same time, Children in Need is part-funding the national children's worker at WAFE as well as being a major funder of staff and capital equipment for child work in refuges (McKinlay and Singh, 1991, p.5). Initially, seven pilot posts were funded; this number later expanded to over 30 and has continued to grow. The co-operation between WAFE and NCVCCO discussed earlier is similarly encouraging and other important developments around children's rights issues hold out further potential for joint collaboration. For example, the Children's Legal Centre is campaigning vigorously about areas of law and welfare practice that need to be reformed if children affected by violence against women are to be properly safeguarded (O'Hara, 1992, p.4).

It is evident from the information in this chapter that the negative experiences of children who witness violence against their mothers may either be reinforced or ameliorated according to the quality of the service they receive in women's refuges. Children's workers are striving against huge odds to make children's experiences of refuge life both enjoyable and therapeutic. However it is evident that children would benefit from substantially more input than is currently offered by this hard-pressed service.

Notes
1. Ball's 1990 study uses only a small sample of nine refuges but has been cited extensively in this chapter owing to the relative lack of data in this field.

References

Ball, M. (1990) *Children's Workers in Women's Aid Refuges: A Report on the Experience of Nine Refuges in England*. London: National Council of Voluntary Child Care Organisations.

Binney, V., Harkell, G. and Nixon, J. (1981) *Leaving Violent Men: A Study of Refuges and Housing for Battered Women*. Leeds: Women's Aid Federation England.

Charles, N. (1991) *Funding Women's Aid Services to the Community in Wales: Research Report*. Welsh Women's Aid.

Dobash, R.E. and Dobash, R.P. (1992) *Women, Violence and Social Change*. London: Routledge.

Driver, E. and Droisen, A. (1989) *Child Sexual Abuse: Feminist Perspectives*. Basingstoke: Macmillan.

Franklin, B. (ed.) (1986) *The Rights of Children*. Oxford: Basil Blackwell.

Freeman, M.D.A. (1983) *The Rights and Wrongs of Children*. London: Frances Pinter.

Frost, N. and Stein, M. (1989) *The Politics of Child Welfare: Inequality. Power and Change*. Hemel Hempstead: Harvester Wheatsheaf.

Hester, M. and Radford, L. (1992) 'Domestic violence and access arrangements for children in Denmark and Britain', *Journal of Social Welfare Law*, 1, pp.57-70.

Hoff, L.A. (1990) *Battered Women as Survivors*. London: Routledge.

Jaffe, P., Wolfe, D. and Wilson, S. (1990) *Children of Battered Women*. Newbury Park, California: Sage.

Mama, A. (1989) *The Hidden Struggle: Statutory and Voluntary Responses to Violence against Black Women in the Home*. London Race and Housing Research Unit.

McKinlay, C. and Singh, T. (1991) 'Giving peace a chance', *Community Care* supplement on 'Child Care', 6 June, p.5.

National Council of Voluntary Child Care Organisations (no date) *Women's Aid and Child Care: Under Fives Initiative*. London: NCVCCO.

O'Hara, M. (1992) 'Domestic violence and child abuse - making the links', *Childright*, July, 88, pp.4-5

Parton, C. (1990) 'Women, gender oppression and child abuse' in Violence Against Children Study Group (*op. cit.*)

Pizzey, E. (1974) *Scream Quietly or the Neighbours Will Hear*. Harmondsworth, Middsx: Penguin.

Schechter, S. (1982) *Women and Male Violence: The Visions and Struggles of the Battered Women's Movement*. Boston: South End Press.

Scottish Women's Aid (no date) *Working with Children in Women's Aid*. Dundee: Scottish Women's Aid.

Violence Against Children Study Group (1990) *Taking Child Abuse Seriously: Contemporary Issues in Child Protection Theory and Practice*. London: Unwin Hyman.

Women's Aid Federation England (1989) *Breaking Through: Women Surviving Male Violence*. Bristol: WAFE.

Women's Aid Federation England (1991) *Women's Aid Federation England Information Pack*. Bristol: WAFE.

Women's Aid Federation England (no date) *You Can't Beat a Woman: Women and Children in Refuges*. Bristol: WAFE.

SECTION V

Direct Work With Children
in the Community

15

Make a difference

How to respond to child witnesses of woman abuse.

HOW TO RESPOND TO CHILD WITNESSES OF WOMAN ABUSE[1]

A Practical Guide

INTRODUCTION

Woman abuse is a crime. It is a significant and serious problem in all our communities. We now know a great deal about the extent of woman abuse. We know the victims are women and children and that they suffer social, emotional, and psychological trauma. We are increasingly aware of the debilitating impact on children who grow up in homes where their mother is beaten or otherwise abused by her partner. Across the country, three to five children in every school classroom are living with this reality. Even if the children themselves are not direct targets of the abuse, they are profoundly affected by the violence, the attitude of the abuser, and their own feelings about what is going on.

"I am scared when they fight in the dark"

A range of services to respond to woman abuse has slowly developed for the women, their children, and the persons committing the abuse. Included in these services are emergency shelters, short term housing, victim advocacy, and counselling. Considerable effort has been put into developing prevention programs aimed at changing the social values and attitudes that perpetuate this problem.

Schools hold a unique position within communities. More and more, it is at school that children are demonstrating or acting out their anger, fear and hurt related to witnessing woman abuse at home. Schools present opportunities to identify many of these children, to create an environment that is safe and secure, and to begin chipping away at some of the root causes of woman abuse.

Community agencies and health care organizations providing services to children have a responsibility to recognize that woman abuse exists and has a major impact on a high percentage of the children with whom they work. These organizations can assess the occurrence of woman abuse (past or present) in a child's life and provide support and information to the child. Links among agencies that provide group programs for child witnesses of woman abuse, or implementation of this type of program within individual agencies, are important steps for helping children deal with the effects of woman abuse in their lives.

But it's not just to teachers, service agency staff, or health professionals that children may try to disclose the abuse they see and hear at home. **Anyone whom a child sees as a trusted adult** may find that child coming to them looking for support and understanding. That trusted adult might be a coach, a camp counsellor, a neighbour, another child's mother or father...it may be **you.**

When a child discloses to you that woman abuse is occurring at home, you may at first feel overwhelmed by your own reactions. You're not sure what to say or what to do. You may also feel puzzled if the child tells you about the abuse in a seemingly matter-of-fact way. If children have been living with woman abuse as part of their day to day reality, many will talk about the situation offhandedly as a way of protecting themselves from being overwhelmed by feelings of terror and anger. When dealing with a disclosure, you need to be sensitive not only to these feelings but to the child's own cultural background which may be different from yours.

But the most **important** thing you can do to help children cope with the effects of witnessing woman abuse is to **notice** when there are signs from a child that all is not well at home, and to **listen** when that child gets up the courage to tell you about it. You may not be able to change the child's home situation, much as you would like to be able to do that. But you **can help** her or him decide upon a safe place to go whenever the abuse occurs. You should also not hesitate to ask for help from community resources, such as women's shelters and counselling agencies, who deal with the issue of woman abuse.

"It's upsetting to hear that coming from a child. You don't want to think that those kinds of things go on. A child you care about, that you know—it's hard to hear it from them. I think you feel their fear for the life that they lead."

- Camp Counsellor, who received a disclosure from a young camper

219

WHAT IS WOMAN ABUSE?

The terms **wife assault** and **wife battering** usually refer to physical violence or injury. However, woman abuse is not always physical. Other forms of abuse can be just as harmful. Woman abuse includes assault and battering and all other forms of mistreatment and cruelty, including constant threatening and psychological violence (mind games). All types of abuse relate to the misuse of **power and control** in relationships.

DOMESTIC ABUSE INTERVENTION PROJECT
206 West Fourth Street
Duluth, Minnesota 55806
218-722-4134

220

SOME FACTS ON WOMAN ABUSE

1. A Canadian survey by Statistics Canada states that 51% of women over 18 have experienced at least one incident of physical or sexual violence since the age of 16. (**Statistics Canada, 1993**)

2. Past studies indicate that at least one in eight women is physically assaulted by her male partner (some have estimated one in four). (**Nuttal, Greaves, Lent, 1985**) More recent research reveals that, in fact, **one third** of married women have experienced violence from their current or previous partner. (**Statistics Canada, 1993**)

3. Approximately 99% of reported violence in the family is directed at women and children—74% at women, 25% at children. (**Dobash and Dobash, 1983**)

4. In Ontario, the number of school-aged children exposed to woman abuse in their homes is estimated to be 150,000 to 250,000. Three to five children in each classroom may be witnessing woman abuse in their homes. (**Kincaid, 1982**)

5. 40% of woman abuse incidents begin during the time of the woman's first pregnancy. (**Education Wife Assault, 1985**)

6. Woman assault is a crime. When police, rather than the victim, lay charges or arrest the abusers, the probability of new incidents of violence is reduced by half. (**Jaffe, 1985**)

7. Without community intervention, physical and emotional abuse tend to become more frequent and severe—57% of all women murdered in Canada in 1989 died at the hands of their male partner. (**Statistics Canada, 1990**)

8. Children are deeply affected by witnessing violence in the home. Serious behavioural problems are 17 times higher for boys and 10 times higher for girls who have witnessed woman abuse. (**Wolfe, 1985**)

9. In a Canada-wide study, abused women reported that their partners had abused their children physically (26%), psychologically (48%), and sexually (7%). (**MacLeod, 1987**)

10. Poverty does not cause woman abuse. Woman abuse is found at all socio-economic levels. (**Sinclair, 1985**)

11. Substance abuse does not cause woman abuse. Batterers often use alcohol and/or drugs as an excuse to avoid taking responsibility for violent behaviour. (**Sinclair, 1985**)

12. If an individual is abusive in a dating relationship, the violence will likely increase after the couple marries. (**Mulligan, 1991**)

"I've been cut with a knife five times... When I was pregnant, he beat me and I lost my babies...he's beat me up quite a few times."

- *"Elizabeth", mother of two—a past victim of woman abuse*

WHY DO MEN ABUSE?

Because they...

- have learned this behaviour in their family of origin (75%[2] of batterers have witnessed their father abusing their mother) (**Rosenbaum & O'Leary, 1981**)
- believe and are influenced by dominant male images reinforced by society and the media
- live in a society where there are few, if any, negative consequences for woman abuse
- believe it is an appropriate expression of power and control
- want their partner to remain dependent on them

"My oldest...he just has to hit a kid once and he hurts them...I know it's due to the fact that he's seeing what he's seeing and he's not talking about it...he walks around like a time bomb."

- *"Elizabeth", talking about her 12-year-old son*

WHY DO WOMEN STAY?

Because they...

- want their relationship to work and hope their partner will change
- fear reprisals from their partner
- lack money or housing (95% of women who have left their partner, live below the poverty line) (**"For Richer, For Poorer", National Film Board, 1988**)
- want their children to have a father at home
- feel guilt, shame, and responsibility for the abuse
- are not aware that help is available
- may have religious or familial beliefs that condemn a woman for leaving
- do not have personal or social supports
- fear losing their children

"I always stayed in this relationship because I'd sooner have him in front of me than behind me. I don't know if you understand that or not...it was better for me to know where he was than not to know."

- *"Elizabeth", describing her fear*

HOW DOES WOMAN ABUSE AFFECT HOW CHILDREN VIEW RELATIONSHIPS?

Child witnesses of woman abuse may believe...

- it is acceptable for men to hit women
- violence is an effective way to solve problems
- it is okay to hit someone if you're feeling angry or upset
- men are powerful, women are weak
- inequality in relationships is normal—men have power and control over women
- there are few, if any, negative consequences for abusive acts
- they are responsible for the abuse and should therefore feel guilty
- they are responsible for stopping the abuse by "defending" mom or "confronting" dad

 (Strauss, Gelbs, & Steinmetz, 1980; Jaffe, P. et al., 1990)

"That's what you have to do to make the bitch pay attention—she doesn't listen to me."

 - 7-year-old "Andy" explaining to the principal why he punched his teacher in the stomach

"When he [step-father] hits my mom, and I'm there and I start crying, he yells at me that if I don't stop blubbering, he'll give me something to cry for too...and the more I cry, the harder he hits her...he says she's raising a 'blubberface'...so now I try never to let him see me crying in case mom gets hurt again."

 - "Lily", age 11

Witnessing woman abuse diminishes children's sense of self-worth and keeps them in a constant state of anxiety and fear that the world is an unsafe hostile place. Depending on a child's age and stage of development, she/he will try to cope with witnessing woman abuse in many different ways.

The most important thing you can do to help is to take the time to **LOOK** and **LISTEN** for clues that something is wrong at home, and then support the child in the context of her or his own reality.

EFFECTS OF WITNESSING WOMAN ABUSE ON PRESCHOOL CHILDREN

"Daddy, stop! Please don't hit mommy! Stop it, please stop!"
- "Jonathan", age 5

A preschool child often cannot describe the abusive episodes to you in great detail. As adults we need to look for other clues from very young children. These may be:

- physical complaints, such as stomach aches or headaches
- excessive separation anxiety
- bedwetting
- tendency to whine or cling, showing anxiety
- sleep disturbances (insomnia, heightened fear of the dark, resisting bedtime)
- failure to thrive
- withdrawal
- lack of trust/ability to relate appropriately to adults
- fear of a particular person or gender
- self-destructive behaviours/aggression
- predominant theme of power and control in interactions
- being overly helpful or eager to please
- fear or rejection of non-threatening touch

HANDLING A DISCLOSURE BY A PRESCHOOL CHILD

If you get a disclosure from a preschool child, the following are some hints to assist you in talking with the child. Your goal is to help the child feel supported and safe.

- Use short sentences, only 3-5 more words than the child's average sentence.

- Use names rather than pronouns (e.g. What did Bob (stepfather) do next?)

- Use the child's own terms. If the child says that "Daddy bops Mommy", use the word "bops" to talk about what the man does.

- Rephrase questions the child does not understand. Repeating a question may be interpreted by the child that she/he has given an incorrect answer and the child may change the answer.

- Be careful in interpreting answers to very specific questions. Children are apt to be very literal.

- Do not respond to every answer with another question. Merely acknowledge the child's comment. Take care not to overwhelm the child with too many questions.

- Preschoolers may not "disclose" intentionally but rather are describing their family life. You can continue talking about their family and add general questions such as: "All families fight at some time. What happens in your family when someone is mad?" Attempt to convey the information that the child is not alone, that this happens in other families, but that **woman abuse is not okay.**

- Attempt to assess the child's safety needs. Don't be afraid to ask questions such as "What did you see? What did you hear? What did you do?"

- Acknowledge and explore the child's feelings—e.g. scared, angry, confused, sad.

- Young children may disclose information over a longer period of time—be patient.

- Young children may spontaneously verbalize incidents of abuse in full detail, especially if they are in a safe, nurturing environment. Safety planning can be done at these times.

SAFETY PLANNING WITH A PRESCHOOL CHILD

A **safety plan** is a simple, concrete plan devised with the child to help her/him get out of a dangerous situation and get to safety. The safety plan is based on the belief that the child's priority is to keep herself/himself safe when mom is being hurt. Children cannot stop abuse, although they often try by distracting the abuser or directly intervening in the abusive episode. The best thing she/he can do for mom and the family is **to get out of the way.**

Points to consider when developing a safety plan with a preschool child (preschool children learn best through repetition over a period of time):

1. Have the child identify a safe room or place in the house, preferably one with a lock on the door and a telephone. The first step is for the child to get out of the room where the abuse is occurring.

2. Teach the child how to call for help. Make sure the child understands that she/he should not use a telephone that is in view of the abuser. This puts the child at risk.
    - Teach the child how to contact Police at the emergency number.
    - Ensure that the child knows her/his address and full name (rural children need to know the Concession and Lot number).

- Rehearse what the child should say (something very simple, such as "someone is hurting my mommy").
- Try using puppets to role-play different scenarios and then move on to "real" rehearsals.
- Teach the child about Block Parents and how to use them.

I HIDE UNDER MY BED
WHEN DADDY HITS MOMMY.
I AM SCARED.

- "Jonathan", age 5

EFFECTS OF WITNESSING WOMAN ABUSE ON ELEMENTARY SCHOOL-AGED CHILDREN

Depending on the level and frequency of the abuse children have witnessed, and their position in the family, school-aged children may exhibit some of the following behaviours:

- continuing physical complaints
- approval-seeking behaviour
- withdrawn, passive, compliant
- low frustration tolerance or infinite patience
- acting too frequently as "mother's little helper" or "teacher's little helper"
- temper tantrums
- fighting with siblings and classmates
- bullying

Some children demonstrate one extreme:

- impaired concentration spans
- poor attendance at school
- clumsy, accident-prone behaviour
- fear of attending school
- being labelled an underachiever at school

Others will demonstrate the opposite:

- excellent academic work
- perfectionistic standards (harbouring a tremendous fear of failure)
- being overly responsible (the "parentified child"), especially the oldest child

School-aged children may believe that woman abuse is their fault because they are "bad" and so, may act in a manipulative manner in an attempt to reduce the tension. Some children believe their presence will protect mom while others feel their presence causes the conflict, and they may avoid being at home. Children may experience fear that they will be abandoned or killed, and many are afraid of their own or others' anger. Some may have difficulty responding appropriately to women in positions of authority. Eating disorders such as overeating, under-eating or hoarding food, and sleep disorders are also possible clues pointing to an abusive home situation. If there are frequent and unpredictable parental separations and children are not informed about this, they may become even more insecure and distrustful of their environment.

HANDLING A DISCLOSURE BY AN ELEMENTARY SCHOOL-AGED CHILD

"My mom was lying on the floor and my dad was jumping on her head and kicking her in the back. Me and my brother were trying to stop him."
                                                 - "Jennifer", age 11

Your goal is to help the child feel supported and safe. Remain calm. Believe the child and be supportive without judging. Give the child reassurance: "I'm glad you told me; you did the right thing." "It's not your fault." "You are not alone; other children have also seen their dad hurting their mom."

Some hints:

*   Maintain eye contact.

*   Help the child discuss her/his feelings. Many children have legitimate fears about what may happen. You can't make these fears disappear but you can offer to help the child deal with them.

*   Follow your instincts. If you feel a child is trying to tell you something, ask a direct question.

*   Let the child know exactly what you are prepared to do. Will you be available if she/he wants to talk again?

*   Be realistic and honest. Don't make promises that can't be kept.

*   Attempt to find out what the child does during the violence in order to assess her/his safety needs.

Also consider...
*   the child's developmental level
*   the child's feelings: guilt, anxiety about "telling a secret", shame, fear of consequences
*   your own feelings about woman abuse

After the disclosure...

* talk with someone you trust about your feelings—disclosures bring out many emotions for which you may need support
* continue to be open to communication with the child—telling you is a huge step
* respect the child by not disclosing her/his identity to uninvolved colleagues

SAFETY PLANNING WITH AN ELEMENTARY SCHOOL-AGED CHILD

It is our responsibility as adults to let children know that the best way they can help their mothers is to go somewhere safe, away from the fighting. Children need to learn how to call the Police. Impress upon children that the Police believe woman abuse is a crime; it is against the law. If there are reasonable and probable grounds to assume an assault has occurred, the Police are mandated to lay a charge of assault. Intervention by the Police decreases the severity and frequency of assaults.

1. Emphasize the importance of being safe and that it is not children's responsibility to make sure their mother is safe.

2. Role-play calling the Police. (Children should only call the Police if they are separate from the fighting.) Teach them to give the 911[3] operator or Police the basic information:

   "Hello, my name is _____. I live at _____. Send the Police. Someone is hurting my mom."(Rural children need to know their Concession and Lot number.)

It is important for children to leave the telephone off the hook when they are finished talking. The Police will call the number back if they hang up. This could create a dangerous situation for the child if the abuser discovers the child has called the Police.

"Chris", age 9

229

EFFECTS OF WITNESSING WOMAN ABUSE ON ADOLESCENTS

Adolescence is a particularly vulnerable and stressful stage of life, the time when children are approaching the threshold of adulthood. Young adolescents are struggling for a sense of their own identity and place in the world. Although all teenagers from time to time indulge in escapist, sometimes self-destructive behaviour, adolescents who witness woman abuse are at far greater risk. They may themselves become a more likely target for physical abuse, since the tensions that arise from the adolescent's struggle for independence can lead to physical violence from parents who resent their loss of control over their children. For young males who have witnessed woman abuse at home, one of their greatest worries may be the fear of becoming like the abuser. Given the reality that many abusers were raised in abusive environments, this is not an irrational fear.

The following characteristics should not be viewed as exclusive to adolescents who witness woman abuse. However, if some of these characteristics are present in a young person, it is possible that woman abuse is a contributing factor and needs to be considered as part of your inquiry and assessment.

- escape into drug or alcohol abuse
- running away from home (or almost never being at home)
- suicidal thoughts and actions
- homicidal or violent thoughts and actions
- criminal activities such as drug dealing or theft
- poor self-esteem—pessimism that their basic needs for safety, love and belonging will not be met
- difficulties in peer relationships
- expressing decreased empathy for victims
- difficulties in cognitive and academic functioning
- escape into early pregnancy

"HE TOLD ME TO STAY OUT OF IT

BUT I WANTED TO HELP MOM.

HE'S SUCH A JERK!!!

I'LL NEVER BE LIKE HIM!"

"Bob", age 14

HANDLING A DISCLOSURE BY AN ADOLESCENT

If you are a teenager, friend or classmate...

- listen calmly

- take the concern seriously

- reassure your friend that nobody deserves to be abused

- support your friend in looking at the risks of more abuse

- reassure your friend that the abuse at home is not her/his fault

- suggest talking to a trusted adult: teacher, school counsellor, or a person in a community agency that deals with woman abuse

- realize the situation will not change overnight

If you are an adult...

- listen without judging, expressing shock, or making critical comments

- find a quiet private place where you will not be interrupted

- help the adolescent understand that she/he is not to blame for the abuse

- let the adolescent know that this type of problem exists in other homes and that she/he has the right to tell someone and seek help

- let them know that no one has the right to assault or abuse another person

- inform the adolescent that there are safe places to go with her/his mother

- help them develop a safety plan for themselves and younger siblings, and to know how to call for help for their mother

- let them know also that there are places where men who are abusive can go for help.

As caring, responsible adults, we must...

■   become informed about the facts of woman abuse and the community resources

■   work for change by recognizing and challenging sexist attitudes

■   understand and promote non-violent conflict resolution skills

■   acquire the necessary skills in order to recognize signs of abuse

SAFETY PLANNING WITH AN ADOLESCENT

The primary aim of safety planning with adolescents is the same as for pre-school and elementary school-aged children—to get them away from the dangerous situation and avoid injury. This may be problematic for teenagers who may feel that because of their "almost adult" size that they should intervene by threatening or "taking on" the abuser. Stress to adolescents that their best recourse is to seek outside help.

Assist them to map out an action plan to ensure their own and younger siblings' safety. Begin by exploring what they currently do when abuse is occurring in their home. Based on this information, you can determine how appropriate the existing plan is, what revision it needs, and how it can be improved.

Make sure that the young person is familiar with the use of 9-1-1, and emphasize that she/he should seek an area away from the violence when placing the call. Also, familiarize the young person with the available community resources who are experienced in dealing with woman abuse.

Above all, continue to emphasize that the best and the most important thing they can do for themselves and their mother, is not to try and defend their mother physically, but to get out of the way and seek help.

SUGGESTED QUESTIONS TO ASK WHEN YOU SUSPECT A CHILD
IS WITNESSING WOMAN ABUSE

If you have become aware that a child is manifesting behaviours or characteristics suggestive of witnessing woman abuse at home, or if a child directly discloses to you, you may initially feel at a loss for words and uncertain of what type of questions to ask. Here are some suggestions:

1. What happens in your house when there are disagreements?
   - between you and your brothers and/or sisters?
   - between your mom and dad (mom and stepdad, dad and stepmom)?

2. What does your dad do when he gets angry?

3. Did you ever hear your dad hurting your mom?

4. Did you ever see your dad hurting your mom?
   - What did you do?
   - How did you feel?

5. What things bother you or make you unhappy? Whom do you tell?

6. What kind of things make you scared? angry?

7. Do you worry about mom and dad?

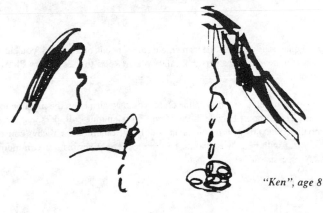

"My dad punched my mom in the nose"

"Ken", age 8

ASSESSING RISK

When a child discloses witnessing woman abuse, it is important to assess their level of safety in the home. You may need to ask questions to have a better understanding of the level of abuse the child is witnessing. Here are some suggested questions:

1. How recently did the abuse occur?
    -   Have the child explain the most recent incident of abuse.
    -   It is important to assess whether the child will be returning to a potentially dangerous situation. For example: Were weapons used? Was the mother locked in a room? Did the abuser stop the mother from leaving the house? Was substance abuse involved?

2. How often does abuse occur?

3. Have the police come to your house before? What happened then?

4. Has the abuser ever used or threatened to use weapons?

5. What does the child do when the abuse is happening? Did the child intervene? What was the outcome? Would the child intervene again?

6. Where were the child's siblings during the abuse?

Once you have asked questions to assess the immediate safety needs of the child, you can more effectively provide further support in developing a personal safety plan. (Refer to the **"Safety Planning"** sections in this information guide).

Based on the context of your relationship with the child, you may also be in the position to provide support to the child's mother. This support may be in the form of a telephone call, personal contact, or whatever most easily fits into the context of your relationship with her. Remember to always consider the woman's safety in making contact with her. What would be the most effective form of communication with her, based on your safety assessment?

CONTACT WITH THE WOMAN

In communicating with the woman, it is important to relay to her that:

- it is not her fault
- you are concerned about her and her child(ren)
- you are willing to help by giving her information and resources
- witnessing abuse is having an impact on her child(ren)
- there are places to go, and people who can help

"My dad was yelling at my mom and he was crashing the door with a knife, and then he smashed the bar. I was afraid he was going to kill her."

- "Chris", age 9

SOME SUGGESTED VERBAL COMMENTS

- At school (Brownies, baseball practice, etc.), we've been noticing that _____ has been upset, angry, very quiet, withdrawn, etc.
- Today while speaking with the teacher, _____ talked about what happens when there are disagreements at your house and her/his fears about your safety.
- I am concerned about you and your safety. I want to let you know that there are places where you can get help.
- No one deserves to be abused. There are people you can talk to and shelters where you can go to be safe.

During the conversation with the woman, attempt to assess...
- her access to outside contacts and her degree of isolation
- if she has a personal safety plan

Discuss with the woman a personal safety plan, that she can:
- call the Police
- use friends, neighbours, family members, for check-ins and a safe place for the children and/or her to go to
- store important documents and papers in a spot where she can get them if she has to leave quickly
- call the crisis shelter, 24-hour crisis line, and other counselling centres

MAKE A DIFFERENCE

"If kids reach out for help, but nobody's there to help them...when they find an adult...and look at them as an authority figure or someone that's all grown up and is supposed to help you...and you're supposed to be able to turn to an adult and ask the adult anything...and they don't do it for you—where are they supposed to turn, what are they supposed to do?"

- "Elizabeth", mother of two—a past victim of woman abuse

It's not easy. You may be afraid of doing or saying the wrong thing. You may feel you are not equipped to deal with the situation. Yet you do want to help.

For a child living with violence in the home, you can be a "safe person" who listens with acceptance, compassion, and encouragement. If you are a caring person, you're going to do the "right thing" by just being there for the child.

REACHING OUT...JUST A LITTLE...CAN MAKE A DIFFERENCE.

The text of this manual has been reproduced with permission of The Children's Subcommittee of the London Coordinating Committee to End Woman Abuse.

Notes

1. This is the text of the manual from a pack of the same name which also contains a video. The video needs to be adapted to UK use. The pack can be obtained at a cost of $50 (Canadian) from Children's Aid Society of London and Middlesex (Attention Larry Marshall), PO Box 6010, Depot 1, London, Ontario, Canada N5W 5RD.

2. The editors do not recommend readers to repeat or rely on this statistic but to concentrate on the other causes of abuse listed here and to read Chapter 3 for a fuller understanding of research findings in the field. Although inevitable in a popular publication like this manual which aims to make a strong impact, reducing complex and as yet incomplete research to simple statistics carries dangers since they are liable to be misinterpreted and misapplied. In Chapter 3, we deal in depth with the so-called 'cycle of violence' and do not find it to be sufficiently upheld by research to be a useful concept in practice. Blaming the family of origin can be a diversion from tackling safety needs and unacceptable behaviour in the present. It is because of its strengths in these areas that this excellent manual has been reproduced here.

3. 911 is the equivalent of the British 999 call.

References on Woman Abuse

Dobash, R.E. and Dobash, R.P. (1983) *Violence Against Wives*. New York: Free Press. (This edition is a USA reprint of the 1980 edition referred to in the Bibliography.)

Education Wife Assault (1985) *Fact Sheet on Wife Assault in Canada*. Toronto: Education Wife Assault.

Jaffe, P. et al. (1985) *A Research Study to Evaluate the Impact and Effectiveness of the Policy Directive That Police Lay Charges in All Domestic Violence Incidents Where Reasonable and Probable Grounds Exist*. Toronto: Provincial Secretariat for Justice.

Jaffe, P., Wolfe, D. and Wilson, S. (1990) *Children of Battered Women*. Newbury Park, Sage.

Kincaid, P.J. (1982) *The Omitted Reality: Husband/Wife Violence in Ontario and Policy Implications for Education*. Concord, Ontario: Belsten.

MacLeod, L. (1987) *Battered But Not Beaten: Preventing Wife Battering in Canada*. Ottawa: The Canadian Advisory Counsel on the Status of Women.

Mulligan, S. et al. (1991) *A Handbook for the Prevention of Family Violence*. Developed by the Family Violence Prevention Project of the Community Child Abuse Council of Hamilton-Wentworth. Section 2, p.11.

National Film Board (1989) *For Richer, For Poorer*. Film

Nuttal, S., Greaves, L. and Lent, B. (1985) 'Wife battering: an emerging problem in public health', *Canadian Journal of Public Health*, 76(5), September, p.138.

Rosenbaum, A. and O'Leary, K.D. (1981) 'Children: The unintended victims of marital violence', *American Journal of Orthopsychiatry*, 51, pp.692-699.

Sinclair, D. (1985) *Wife Assault: A Training Manual for Counsellors and Advocates*. Toronto: Ontario Government Bookstore.

Statistics Canada (1993) *The Violence Against Women Survey*. Centre for Justice Statistics (also Statistics Canada data on violence against women, 1990).

Strauss, M.A., Gelbs, R.J. and Steinmetz (1980) *Behind Closed Doors*. Doubleday, Anchor.

Wolfe, D.A. et al. (1985) 'Children of battered women: the relation of child behaviour to family violence and maternal stress', *American Journal of Clinical and Counselling Psychology*, 53, p.657.

16

Groups for Child Witnesses of Woman Abuse: Learning from North America

Audrey Mullender

One of the most striking aspects of North American intervention in the field of men's abuse of women is the existence in the more advanced programmes of an integrated range of services for various family members at different stages in the process of seeking safety or change. Groupwork intervention with children who have lived with the violence against their mothers - who are often referred to there as 'child witnesses' - forms a central plank of this raft of provision[1].

Groups offer a particular advantage in this area of work (as in many others) since, by bringing children together, they make it plain to those participating that they are not alone in what they have experienced. This helps to 'break the secret' of the stigma (Peled and Edleson, 1992, p.331); it also provides peer support for children in coming to terms with what has happened. Being with others helps them to recognise that they do not bear any personal responsibility and provides an excellent context for learning ways of being safe in the future.

Without groups, there can be a tendency for parents and professionals to assume that children are unaffected because they do not talk directly about living with abuse or its impact on them. In fact, though, they often do not have the *opportunity* to talk because no one asks them about their experiences. One girl was able, in an intake interview for a group, to give a vivid, blow-by-blow account of an attack by her father upon her mother with a baseball bat three years earlier, of which she had never spoken but the memory of which had been bottled up inside. Her mother wished the girl had had the opportunity of a children's group to deal with the issues at the time they happened. Another mother claimed her daughter had not been upset by the abuse which had ended seven years before but, within 20 minutes, the child was crying about it in her intake interview. Children are often surprised to learn that there will be, say, seven or eight others in the group who have also witnessed woman abuse. This is because they have existed in an atmosphere of secrecy and silence, thinking they were the only ones ever to have lived with such events. Discovering that this is not true helps them to speak out and to develop new awareness.

It is absolutely crucial in this work to have a basic understanding of violence against women and its effects on children (see chapters by Mullender and Morley, Morley and Mullender, Kelly, this volume). In Britain, most child care agencies are unaware of the issues and consequently do not see the need for specific programmes of work. Even a project which made particular claims to be responding to the needs of children living with domestic violence (Moore, 1975; Moore et al., 1981), demonstrated a lack of appropriate analysis. Though it took place some years ago, this project is still sometimes referred to - perhaps because so little targeted work has taken place here. It in no way constitutes a recommended model: the published accounts of the project (Moore et al., 1981) make no mention of helping women or children to be safe, their tone is blaming and dismissive, and the language used completely veils the fact that the subject at issue is men's violence to women.

Child care professionals who want to develop direct work with children which takes seriously the impact on them of living with abuse need to look further afield for appropriate ways of working. (They can also learn from work in refuges: see chapters by Debbonaire, Higgins, this volume.) The children's groups run in Canada and the USA over a number of years provide a useful model for direct work which both heals and empowers children. The predominant messages conveyed in these groups are that men are responsible for violence in the home and that children have a right to be safe. The development of this groupwork approach, together with the detail of two of the most advanced programmes, will be explored in the remainder of this chapter.

BACKGROUND - THE ORIGINAL CANADIAN MODEL

In Canada, groupwork stemmed from the research by Peter Jaffe[2], Director of the London Family Court Clinic, and his colleagues there and at the University of Western Ontario. Their empirical studies indicated that children who had witnessed violence against their mothers were at risk of problems in emotional and behavioural adjustment even when they had not themselves been directly abused (see, for example, Wolfe et al. 1985; Jaffe et al., 1990 ; and the summary in Morley and Mullender, this volume). Out of this work was developed a groupwork manual (Wilson et al., 1986, building in turn on work by Alessi and Hearn, 1984) outlining an interventive model for use with groups of children in any appropriate setting.

The Wilson et al. manual (1986) covered the detail of a ten-week programme, with activities and games outlined which conveyed the desired messages and information. It was aimed at children between the ages of eight and thirteen, sub-divided at ten or eleven, with up to ten participants in each group. Groups were run by one male and one female counsellor who were seen as 'role models for appropriate male-female interactions' (p.181). The model was pioneered by workers serving five communities in South Western Ontario. Its chief goals were prevention

and education since the groups were not long enough to offe
therapy or behavioural change. Groups could be run in any s
there were suitable staff who were knowledgeable about w.
such as child care and family agencies, or schools - but not where .
children were currently in crisis, such as shelters (refuges). Parents were
asked to give the children permission to talk about their family in the
group, in order to break down the secrecy which may have bound the
child into the abuse. The overall aims were:

> . . . to help children develop adaptive responses to experiences they
> have already encountered, learn effective and safe problem-solving
> techniques to confront future difficulties, focus on attitudes towards
> relationships and responsibility for behavior, examine the use of
> violence as an effective method of resolving conflict, and develop
> self-esteem (p.181).

Group content

The groups focused on the following issues over the ten weeks:

1. confidentiality in the group, apart from the workers' policy on not
   keeping disclosures of child abuse secret, including between children
   and parents;
2. naming and understanding feelings;
3. dealing with anger in healthy and unhealthy ways using role play
   and relaxation techniques;
4. safety skills, including child sexual abuse and the right to say no;
5. the use of current social supports and the network of community
   resources for a child or young person who feels scared, upset or
   suicidal;
6. self-concept and self-perceptions in different contexts of daily life and
   in relation to the family;
7. responsibility for violence lying with men, not the women and
   children they abuse, drawing on specific incidents and on children
   writing stories which can be read out, acted or videoed;
8. understanding family violence, exploring myths around blaming
   alcohol, job stress or mothers' behaviour as causes and elucidating
   the stages of violent incidents;
9. family issues including separation, visitation (contact), conflicting
   loyalties, step-parents, ambivalence, desire for the family to be back
   together, fantasies that this cannot be their real family, the ways
   that children feel and are treated or used in these situations;
10. review and termination, with an emphasis on new learning,
    strategies for children to empower and protect themselves, and the
    control they can exercise over their own lives.
    (Based on Wilson et al., 1986).

Critique

The model included an acceptance of the inter-generational transmission of violence, as did the research on which it was based (see chapter by Morley and Mullender, this volume, for a critique). It did not appear to offer much in the way of a wider understanding of gender power dynamics, either in relation to woman abuse or to group process, even though it was based on a clear analysis that the abuse is men's responsibility (despite a slip into mentioning 'parents fighting' in Meeting 7). For example, there was no option for group members to object to the presence of a male facilitator in a group dealing with memories of male violence, and an apparent assumption was made that the male facilitator available would automatically provide a positive role model. The approach did, however, offer the opportunity to help children confront social prejudices against abused women. For example, they may learn to utter statements that it is not acceptable for women to be abused but then, in the course of further discussion, reveal underlying and entrenched attitudes that violence *is* still acceptable if the woman does not clean the house properly, or if she stays out late or drinks, or if the conflict cannot be resolved in any other way, or if the abuser feels strongly in the right (Marlies Sudermann, personal communication). Such assumptions would all have been challenged in the groups. Issues of class, sexuality and ethnicity were not raised in the model; for example, there is mention of a christening as part of the normal celebration for a new baby. There are, however, two situation cards encompassing disability in an exercise on feelings.

The groupwork was always intended to form only one part of the work undertaken with any particular child in the context of a wider response to the family. There was no mention in the manual, however, of co-ordinated work with child and non-abusing parent to make sense of, or pursue the issues further together. This became an interesting feature of later variations of the model.

BUILDING AWARENESS: CHILDREN'S GROUPS IN LONDON, ONTARIO

Deriving from this earlier work, an impressive impetus has built up around children's issues in the context of co-ordinated work on woman abuse in Ontario[3]. The London Co-ordinating Committee to End Woman Abuse, a grouping of 25 public and non-profit agencies, has a Children's Sub-Committee. It conducted a survey (Pavlic et al., 1991) to estimate the numbers of children exposed to violence against their mothers in London and Middlesex County. Fifty social service agencies and all schools were circulated, with a 70 per cent return rate indicating that over 7,000 children of school age have witnessed woman abuse, from a total of 50,000 (14 per cent, or around 1 in 7). Ten agencies were by that time offering individual counselling and six, group treatment.

Following the pilot project undertaken under the auspices of the London Family Court Clinic (using the model outlined in Wilson et al.,

1986), groups for child witnesses began to be offered by Madame Vanier Children's Services, the Children's Mental Health Centre and London Children's Aid Society (the agency holding child protection responsibilities). Various attempts to establish a co-ordinated intake system and a method of sharing referrals have recently been rewarded with success: a proposal for a group treatment worker to manage this system and co-run groups was accepted by the Ministry of Community and Social Services in early 1993.

The resultant 'Community Group Treatment Program for Child Witnesses of Woman Abuse', is based at the London Children's Aid Society (LCAS) and has seven agencies as members. The programme is a community-based, co-operative model and is committed to being accessible to all abused women and children. It is overseen by an advisory committee made up of representatives from agencies connected to the Children's Sub-Committee of the London Co-ordinating Committee to End Woman Abuse. A standardised referral process and information leaflet have been developed, the former including a risk assessment of the child's current degree of danger from the mother's abuser. A total of 100-125 referrals a year are accepted from social service agencies and also from mothers in the community. The Community Group Treatment Worker co-facilitates the groups with workers from member agencies; the children in any one group will not necessarily all have links with the same agency. The programme is based on the LCAS model of groups which, in turn, is an extension of the Wilson et al. model (1986).

Group composition
One key way in which the groupworkers have reshaped the Wilson et al. model (1986) over several years of running groups for child witnesses is to extend the age range and, at the same time, to sub-divide it further so that the approach can be age-appropriate. Originally, groupwork was offered for eight to thirteen year olds but individual work revealed the same stories about their families coming from five and fifteen year olds, with the latter also talking about abuse in their own dating relationships. Consequently, the service and the model were extended to meet their needs also, with perhaps five sub-divisions across this range. The pooling of all referrals means that groups can now be very specific to children's developmental stage with, say, just five and six year olds grouped together, or seven to nine year olds. The younger the children, the smaller and more activity based the group: with the youngest there will only be five or six in the group and maybe three or four leaders (including social work students on placement) to work with the children on activities designed to open up the key themes. Teenagers can cope with up to nine in the group as they are more used to a discussion-style forum.

Staff aim for roughly equal numbers of boys and girls in each group and will not run with only one boy or one girl because they are working with essentially gender-based issues and this would leave the child concerned feeling very exposed. The programme has progressed to operate within a feminist framework. Although it is based at the LCAS, where sometimes feminist philosophy and child protection conflict - for example in removing children from women who stay with their abusers - this tension does not temper the philosophy operating in the groups. Throughout the entire group process, sexism is exposed and attention brought to the gender power dynamics.

One further aspect of group composition relates to siblings. In the past, when they have been in a group together, they have either interrupted each other's stories with their own memories and interpretations, or acted as rivals in the group, or felt unsure of confidentiality at home if one has talked more than the other. As a result, there is now a clear policy to separate them, even though it might mean the custodial parent driving twenty miles and back on two different days in the week with the accompanying expense. The focus of workers and parents is kept firmly on the question: 'Whose needs are we meeting?'.

Referrals and assessment

The programme accepts referrals from the LCAS' 1,900 open cases and from member agencies of the London Co-ordinating Committee to End Woman Abuse. There are some external referrals outside of the Committee, including from women themselves, but these are not actively sought.

Allocation to a group is not solely determined by chronological age; for example, if a child had a developmental delay or poor concentration they might cope better with a more activity-based group aimed at a slightly younger age-group. Great weight is placed on a pre-admission interview to assess this and sometimes a child will be asked to switch group after one or two meetings. The pre-group interview was originally designed to undertake the pre-testing in the evaluation of the Wilson et al. model (1986) but it has now been transformed into a practice tool. It includes a developmental assessment and an assessment of any other trauma currently occurring in the child's life which might make group membership unwise. A child who had recently disclosed sexual abuse would be needing to talk about that and would be referred to a group with that as the main focus; a child recently removed from home for child protection reasons or whose parents were in the middle of a messy custody battle might not be settled enough to benefit from the group either. Nor is the group aimed at those currently going through the crisis of living with abuse; rather, it focuses on recovering from its impact.

The child's mother or primary carer has always been expected to attend the pre-group interview to help set goals and to learn about the aims of the group. More recently, the joint Community Group Treatment Program has added to the model a parallel group for mothers where they spend a decreasing amount of the first four sessions together with their children and then go into their separate group; they also share part of the eighth and the last group sessions. This model is aimed at keeping mothers informed about issues raised in the children's group. The work undertaken may peel back the child's defences and make him or her act out in what could otherwise appear to be naughtiness.

The mother's presence at the pre-group interview gives the child permission to talk about the violence and what have been family secrets - not necessarily because anyone has insisted on secrecy (as in child sexual abuse) but because no one else comes to school talking about such things which leads children to conclude that they are not acceptable or 'normal' to discuss. Typically, in the interview, a question directed to the child will initially elicit a minimising response, the mother will add more detail, and then the child will pour out how it really was for him or her. For all these reasons, the treatment starts during the pre-group interview. Essential facts also begin to be conveyed then, such as the estimated number in the child's own class who have lived with abuse, in order to defuse the stigma before the group even starts. There is open acknowledgement of what it may feel like to come to the group: 'If I were you, I'd be nervous too. It's painful - that's normal'.

Aims, structure and content

The group is seen as primarily an educational group aiming to give children information and knowledge about woman abuse and to change their attitudes in certain key regards. Workers have largely stayed with the Wilson et al. (1986) 10-week life for the group. In the school summer holidays, they alter this to a group meeting twice-weekly for five weeks which they find very successful owing to its more concentrated impact. The teenage group has occasionally had a couple of weeks added when it was slow to cohere or had unfinished issues.

All groups are highly focused. From the first meeting there is discussion of children's understanding of why they are attending. 'You are here because you have seen your mother and father fighting, you've seen black eyes, you've seen blood'. As with the original Wilson et al. model (1986), there is an agenda for each week and the facilitators take the lead in pursuing it. The content stays very close to the original manual. The first week includes introductions, issues of confidentiality, group goals and establishing group rules, as well as definitions of violence. The members like the confidentiality in the group and say to parents: 'It's my group, I don't have to tell you'. In the session on identifying and expressing feelings, the children need considerable help in learning to differentiate between good and bad feelings and display a tendency to bring out more of their depressed feelings. This is followed up by a whole week on anger, which the children tend to avoid or to see as inherently bad. Workers want to convey to the children that anger is normal but that it is best dealt with through non-violent conflict resolution. This can include bringing back into the group a way that a particular child has tried to tackle an angry response.

The work on safety is a big issue in the group and the one where workers feel they perhaps make the most impact. Before the group, children have often felt they were the only ones who could stop the violence and have been injured as a result. The group teaches the children not to get involved in abusive incidents, to go to a safe place in the home, and very specifically how to ring the police: with information on how to dial 911 (the equivalent of 999), how the system works, who will answer, and what to say. This builds on a model from the local shelter which advises the caller to say 'There is someone hitting my Mom'; this has been found to obtain a more rapid response than naming the father as the aggressor - probably because that allows prejudices against 'just a domestic' to creep in. The advice also includes not hanging up the telephone because the police department will call back, giving the man the opportunity to answer and deny there is any problem. Also, the longer the 'phone is off the hook, the more likely the emergency operator is to hear screaming or other sounds which may increase the urgency of the response. Group members rehearse making calls in the group in front of the 'experts' - the other children - who comment on any possible improvements. Parents are told to expect children to make these calls. Children are helped to work out an individual safety plan: who they can trust when they leave the group and who they can tell in the event of further incidents. Safety skills include how to avoid or how to seek help in relation to child abuse, including sexual abuse.

The work on self-esteem is also a crucial part of this and similarly needs to be fed back to parents. The groups empower children who have previously felt they had no control over their own lives and no impact in the family. They are now prepared to confront attitudes there and to state what is unacceptable. Workers recognise that the child who comes back from the group sessions has changed a good deal and that the family needs educating to expect this or the child could be in danger of being reprimanded for answering back.

Although it is not particularly stressed in the original manual (Wilson et al., 1986), the children find themselves dealing with confused feelings about both parents throughout the group, including anger with father for his violence and with mother for believing his promises - as well as with brother or sister for siding with Dad, which may happen particularly if that child did not witness the violence. All these issues are dealt with as they arise; the groupworkers now have the experience not to try and pursue the agenda at a fixed pace.

Challenging myths and stereotypes through the group

Learning about violence in the group includes challenging stereotypes. Children and young people often hold the same myths as adults, for example that alcohol causes violence. These are challenged in the group with cartoons and question and answer quizzes. Children are encouraged to see the realities behind the myths: that their mother provokes the abuse, enjoys it, or could leave if she wanted to; that only poor women get beaten; that men do it because they are mentally ill or drunk; and so on. Older groups also look at wider societal issues such as where attitudes about violence come from. Workers stress that they are inculcated through television, sport, popular music and videos.

In addition to addressing underlying societal beliefs that oppress women, group facilitators also take opportunities to address discrimination of other kinds. For example, a groupworker suggested an exercise to enhance the children's feelings vocabulary; one child said: 'I don't want to - that's gay'. The workers took the opportunity to discuss the child's choice of words as discriminatory, in a way that was educational for all group members. There has been some ground for workers to cover in relation to anti-oppressive issues. For example, a few years ago one group ran with just one Black and one Native American member. During the session on feelings, a groupworker talked in an ethnocentric way about going red when we feel embarrassed; the Black child said 'I can't turn red' and everyone laughed. At that time, this was not picked up either in the group or out of it.

Overlaps with child abuse

Material in the group on personal safety planning and saying no to abuse may access memories which lead to disclosure of direct abuse. Either the child will say: 'That happened to me', or there will be an observably strong reaction to the material. The custodial parent is told of any disclosure, as is the family's social worker. He or she will work out the next steps with the family and the child; this might include involving the police and the LCAS in its child protection function, and will certainly cover current safety issues. Since disclosure accords well with the whole message of lifting the lid on secrets, the child can stay in the group and be given positive messages that he or she is still accepted, in a context where all the children are surviving what have been family secrets.

Follow-up

The groups are assessed weekly so that, at the end of the ten weeks, workers are very clear about the relationship between the reason the child came into the group and any change that has occurred or may still need to occur. As most are already clients of an agency, their individual social worker, as well as their mother, can follow on from the work undertaken with them.

CHILDREN'S GROUPS AT THE DOMESTIC ABUSE PROGRAM, MINNEAPOLIS

Another North American setting for these innovative groups for child witnesses is Minneapolis, Minnesota. The Domestic Abuse Program (DAP) was established in 1979. It is a large agency with approximately 35 staff offering women's groups, men's groups, open-ended self-help groups, individual counselling, couple and family work after the violence has ended, and advocacy with police and courts, as well as children's work. Like the Canadian agencies, it offers a 10-week curriculum for age-specific groups: this time for four to twelve year olds, in three sub-divisions. There are also other kinds of groups for adolescents and adolescent perpetrators.

DAP Children's Program[4] has served almost a thousand children (Domestic Abuse Project *Research Update*, 1993, 5, Summer, p.3) in a programme running since 1981 but, compared with the potential need, only a small minority of the children of adult clients go through the groups. A manual for the DAP children's groups is available (Peled and Davis, 1992, to be published in book form by Sage in late 1994), combining practice and research findings (Peled and Edleson, 1992). The Canadian and United States influences linked up when DAP mounted a national conference on children and woman abuse in July 1992 at which Peter Jaffe was a keynote speaker. This was the germ of the forthcoming book referred to in Chapter One (Peled, et al., forthcoming in 1994).

Intake and assessment

Any child joining a group must have a parent in a programme at this or another agency; there are concurrent parenting groups available. As with the other groups, there is an initial assessment; in this case, the workers go through the family history with the parent or parents there and then see the child alone. They look for any history of physical abuse, neglect and/or sexual abuse of the child, as well as the degree of emotional impact from living with violence. A child known at intake to have been sexually abused would normally be referred on to a suitable group in another agency (partly because it might be inappropriate to stay with a male and female therapist) but a child disclosing in the group would be able to stay. As happens elsewhere, some children are screened out so as not to set them up to fail or make the group less enjoyable for others. For example, a child too withdrawn to speak in the group, who sat under the chair and rocked, or a child who was out of control and who would make the group an unsafe environment for others, would not be accepted. Even then, individual play therapy might be used to work through issues with those who could be ready for the group later on. The educational model underpinning the group means that children are not pathologised but seen as needing to relearn the inappropriate things life has taught them.

Like the Community Group Treatment Program in London Ontario, outlined above, DAP has learnt from experience that there are dangers in having siblings in the same group because their family dynamics intrude. In one group, a girl of seven repeatedly stopped her six-year old brother from finishing his sentences; in another, a boy pounded his fist on the floor when his sister started to disclose the nature of the violence in their family - they 'shut each other down', as the worker put it. One DAP groupworker, on the other hand, reported two instances when including siblings together was successful so it may be that careful planning and debriefing can manage the tensions involved.

The leadership team and engaging with gender issues

As in preferred models elsewhere, group facilitators in DAP children's groups are one man and one woman. This is seen as giving the children a choice of a male and a female to relate to, and offering a positive model of a man and woman working as a team. Conscious efforts are made to counteract the gender stereotypes the children have seen at home: for example, here a woman shares control and a man is nurturing and softly spoken; the therapists take turns to lead the sessions and to lay out the snacks. It is considered important for the boys to see a positive male role model because they may have absorbed enough of the transgenerational idea to fear growing up like their fathers. Their mothers may also have remarked: 'You're just like your father'. Permission is expressly given to boys to cry in the group, to talk about fear and hurt, to help mum with the baby at home.

A conscious gender analysis is apparent. Grusznski et al. (1988, pp.440-41) explain that women's lower social status is seen as a major factor in male abuse and therefore is directly challenged through the structure, process and activities of the groups. Leadership and power in the group are deliberately shared, gender stereotypes are challenged, and positive messages are conveyed about women. In the agency's teenagers' group, one exercise asks members to brainstorm a list of heroines, heroes and others they most admire. They are then asked to draw out and explore what qualities are being admired by the boys and by the girls. Gender role analysis has also been undertaken using the same exercise for occupations, adjectives or animals; or by cutting out magazine advertisements, or considering fairy tales, films, television or books. Members discuss how they perceive their own roles in their family and peer group. Older groups undertake activities and discussions which challenge double standards and sex role stereotypes of submission and domination, together with the use and abuse of power.

Group content and process

Early in the group, after dealing with personal and group safety through establishing ground-rules and limits, the groupworkers ask the children what they think is abusive and help them to develop a vocabulary to describe abuse which they will be able to use throughout the group. 'Feelings education' (see below) is similarly, and as with groups elsewhere, an early topic so that the children can give names to their emotions. They move on to learning to assign responsibility and understand that the violence is not their fault; as this work progresses, they are encouraged to bring their own experiences safely into the open. Work on 'protection planning' has to be age-appropriate.but includes reading the cues that violence may be near, sharing actions used in the past which helped with safety, thinking about the safe places at home, learning emergency telephone numbers and what to say, planning escape routes and safe people to go to. With teenagers this is called 'power planning' since they often like to present as fearless and may prefer to feel empowered rather than needing protection. Eliminating the feeling of helplessness is a strong theme of DAP children's work (Grusznski et al., 1988: 437-8). There is also work on controlling one's own anger, on conflicting loyalties (not having to choose between Mom and Dad), on confronting stereotypical images, building communication and assertiveness skills, and developing self-esteem.

Play with a purpose

DAP groupworkers consider it crucially important to get the atmosphere right in the groups so as not to deter children from seeking further help with this or other issues. As before, there is a wide use of play activities. These include puppets and drawings with the younger children, and psychodramas and plays with the eleven and twelve-year olds. No manual or written description can convey the element of fun, magic and energy which the groupworkers create; they regard it as crucial to be able to play to do this work. Although the subject matter is deadly serious it does not have to be dealt with in a dry, adult way. This seems to be a particular part of the agency's ethos. For example, work on not being responsible for the violence may include the group writing and recording a chant or a song with the refrain 'It's not my fault!', then playing it back at key points in later sessions (Grusznski et al., 1988, pp.434-35). The room lights are turned on and off to discuss how things are scarier in the dark than the light, when kept secret rather than shared (p.436); analogies of volcanoes and overfilled balloons are used to demonstrate the pressure building up in a family (pp.436-37).

As well as being skilled groupworkers, staff need to be able to relate well to children and to meet children's individual needs through the group process. Debriefing includes checking how each child is coping in the group, and how much attention each has sought and received. If one child has been dominating the discussion, for example, the workers will plan to say 'It's important for you to talk but also important for other people to do it'. It will often be a child who is ignored at home who takes a great deal of space in the group. A favourite device is to go round the group giving each person a turn to speak, always starting with a different person.

Feelings work

British child care workers, for example in fostering and adoption, will be accustomed to feelings work. Ideas in use here (pp.438-39) include matching opposites on index cards, cutting out or colouring faces and figures, matching faces to scenes, a game of freeze tag (where the child who is 'It' has to guess the feeling conveyed by the expression of the child who is caught), and charades where the others mime a feeling taped to the child's back. 'Weather reports' describe how the children are feeling this week (sunny, thunder and lightning); homework focuses on specific situations generating strong feelings; puppets and plays are used to stress positives as well as negatives. Self-esteem (p.442) is reinforced by others through throwing a ball or giving a cut-out word or symbol and saying something positive as the ball is caught or the cut-out accepted, and by the children in drawing or writing positives about themselves - most elaborately in a personal inventory by teenagers, with a collage of how they see themselves folded inside another of how others see them. Workers and members help to extend and reinforce the positives and to set achievable goals to tackle the negatives.

The most difficult aspect of this feelings work is searching for honest and positive examples of the children expressing their anger. They have learnt too well in violent homes how to suppress their own feelings and blend into the background. Gestalt-type 'anger letters' to father are used with 'head', 'heart' and 'stomach' sections to express: 'I think', 'I feel', 'I want'. These terms are also used in learning to convey and receive feelings clearly. The group leaders emphasise their awareness that the open expression of feelings may not be safe at home (p.439) but the evaluation of the group still warns of potential dangers in this, as with a nine-year old confronting her father over his behaviour - though shutting herself safely in her room when he is drunk (Peled and Edleson, 1992, p.337).

Process and pace

Process issues involve dealing with the feelings behind the group agenda and tasks. When members of a group of nine and ten-year olds were asked to draw their most violent incident, for example, one child developed a sudden abdominal pain and another thought he heard his mother calling him away. The workers perceived the link between the task and these reactions, giving each child individual attention. This is a key point at which two or three workers are needed: one was able to explain to the first child how we feel fear in our stomachs and how this is normal and natural, while another talked to the second about the scariness of doing a drawing like this. There was good learning content here, regardless of whether the drawings were completed. DAP workers stress that they go at the children's pace and do not push them into tasks they find too uncomfortable. Rather, they are providing the opportunities to break out of the secrecy and isolation which foster their fear.

Follow-up

A family meeting is held following the group to consider what the child has gained from attending and what else may be required. If a child is seen as having been particularly 'needy' of time and attention in the group, for example, individual therapy may be recommended. There may also be unfinished business from the group. Peled and Edleson (1992, p.335) note that children are being required to peel away their layers of defence and to revive repressed memories which may not be easy to handle. Their example from an evaluation interview - some time after the group - of an eight-year old girl who certainly has not completed this process leaves one aware that mothers, and sometimes follow-up work, are left to carry on supporting the children through quite a difficult adjustment process. Although it always has a parent in membership of a parallel group, DAP involves custodial parents far less than does the Community Group Treatment Program in the direct work undertaken with their children. This may be an issue worthy of detailed reflection by any professional intending to learn from the groupwork accounts given here.

EFFECTIVENESS OF CHILDREN'S GROUPS

There has been relatively little reported work testing this, although what there is is encouraging. In Canada, Jaffe et al. (1986) conducted a small pilot study which showed moderate improvements in children's safety skills, self-esteem, and attitudes about violence. The same authors (Jaffe et al., 1990, p.89) reported a study of 64 children based on interviews before and after the group and rating by mothers and children using a number of standardised measures. This indicated that groupwork with child witnesses significantly improved safety skills and perceptions of both parents but not adjustment. In addition, agency co-operation improved and a more integrated community response was made. Eighty-eight per cent of mothers reported that their children enjoyed the group, as did children themselves (p.89). The authors conclude that groupwork is best suited to children with mild to moderate behaviour problems, whereas others may require individual counselling. This accords with lessons from experience that some children cannot benefit from groupwork (see above), although several agencies have found that children can be helped by individual work to graduate to groups, or to participate in both in parallel. The Community Group Treatment Program, which draws together five agencies in London, Ontario to provide groups for children who have lived with woman abuse, is also planning a study of its work. From September 1994, data will be recorded on each child by an external evaluator, as the basis of a report to be published in 1995 at the earliest.

In the USA, a recent formal evaluation was the qualitative work undertaken by Einat Peled and Jeffrey Edleson of the University of Minnesota (Peled and Edleson, 1992), in respect of the children's groups at the Domestic Abuse Project (DAP)[5]. Its 'overall positive findings demonstrate the value of the Domestic Abuse Project's group program for children' (Peled and Edleson, 1992, p.340). Group facilitators looked for success in terms of children's ability to acknowledge and work on memories and feelings about living with violence. Peled and Edleson (1992, p.331) record that 'the most widely acknowledged group goal' was that of helping the children to 'break the secret' of abuse in their families and hence to break out of their own isolation. This subsumed three areas of change in attitude: 'abuse is not okay, it's not my fault'; 'it's okay to feel and express feelings'; and 'I'm not the only one'. Children made progress in all these respects - learning how to define violence, that they were not alone in having witnessed it, and were not responsible for it. In addition, they learnt some specific techniques for self-protection, were helped to express their feelings, and 'experienced the group as a safe, fun, and self-affirming environment' (p.340).

There are individual differences in how well children do in groups according to their personality, family circumstances, and personal and family history of abuse (Peled and Edleson, 1992, p.336). In the main, child sexual abuse is dealt with in separate groups both in the USA and Canada. Direct physical abuse perhaps receives less attention in groups, even though it poses a serious risk (see chapter by O'Hara, this volume) and even though workers would probably be safe in assuming that directly abused children are likely to be present in any group of child witnesses (see chapters by Morley and Mullender; Kelly, this volume). Peled and Edleson (1992, p.336) were worried by a girl who did not reveal her own physical abuse by her father until the family session after the group had ended because she felt different from the other group members. Although one could argue that the group *had* empowered her to share this, and that she made her own choice about where she felt sufficiently safe and supported to disclose it, there is an issue about helping all children to feel included in the group by conveying overt messages that some children will have been abused themselves and can talk about it safely in the group.

Issues arising from the above accounts also indicate that careful attention needs to be paid to group composition in relation to age, gender, race, and the involvement of siblings. The role of mothers is also crucial since they will have to 'pick up the pieces' and an effective group can paradoxically mean a temporarily more distressed child who may have been blocking out painful memories. Practitioners planning groups in this country would need to have regard to all these matters at the planning stage.

CONCLUSION

Although Ontario and Minnesota are considerably ahead of most other places in this field, even there children's work is still less developed than services for women suffering abuse and for tackling perpetrators. A most positive start has been made in the groups outlined above but its further progress is not ensured without increased funding. Not only do the agencies reviewed have the resources to meet only a fraction of the real need for groups, but they would ideally want to see these accompanied by a growth in other, related services for children. Peled and Edleson (1992, p.340), for example, cite preventive work in schools and community-based settings, child advocacy and therapy services, and joint groups for children and their parents. All of these need to be located within a comprehensive response to women, children and male abusers. Pavlic et al. (1991) show the way forward for children's services: proposing an information package, a training programme, a full range of treatment services, improved ways to identify children at risk, nominated personnel in every agency and school with special knowledge and training, and further research.

It would seem absolutely essential for such a response to build on whatever strengths already exist. In Britain, this would mean drawing on the expertise and commitment of the national network of Women's Aid children's workers as well as developing a better awareness of the impact of living with abuse in those child care professionals who already hold expertise in child protection, child welfare, and direct work with children. The growth of inter-agency forums might provide a useful platform from which to launch initiatives in children's groups and the basic model developed in North America would provide a starting-point for content and process. Women's Aid has been more consistent in tackling issues of race and homophobia with children than the North American work, and is more flexible in working with mixed age ranges over differing time-spans. It also has experience of working closely with mothers to meet their children's needs, whereas the groups outlined above are still grappling with the issue of parental involvement and the tensions raised at home by group participation. Women's Aid should be looked to, and funded, as an invaluable ally in planning or delivering any such endeavour. Above all, no children's group of this kind should be attempted without an adequate analysis of men's abuse of women since this would risk confusing children still further and leaving unanswered the questions that most frighten them. Our learning should not be at their expense.

Acknowledgement

This chapter could not have been completed without the invaluable help and advice of Susan Loosley. Thanks also go to Larry Marshall and others who read earlier drafts.

Notes

1. There are also groups running in settings where women reside with their children, such as shelters and second stage housing projects.
2. Although his name is the best known because of the 1990 book (Jaffe et al., 1990) and his profile in putting men's abuse of women on the criminal justice, educational and political agendas in Ontario, Peter Jaffe did not run groups himself and the agency he directs, the London Family Court Clinic, does not offer groups - being largely an agency preparing individual reports for the courts where it is a leader in openly raising and challenging the issues of male abuse in all its assessments. Peter Jaffe helped give the work momentum and involved interested professionals in learning about it. Susan Wilson did run groups, initially with shelter workers, and developed from this a curriculum of issues which is still broadly followed by a number of agencies.
3. Sources for this section were: a personal interview with Larry Marshall and Carol Echlin at London Children's Aid Society; information supplied by Susan Loosley of Women's Community House and the Children's Sub-Committee of the London Co-ordinating Committee to End Woman Abuse; and published sources as cited.
4. Source: interviews at DAP with workers and researchers; published sources as cited.
5. Sources: published sources as cited and personal interview with Einat Peled.

References

Alessi, J.J. and Hearn, K. (1984) 'Group treatment of children in shelters for battered women' in Roberts, A.R. (ed.) *Battered Women and Their Families*. New York: Springer (Referred to by Jaffe et al., 1990, p.87).

Domestic Abuse Project (1993) *Research Update*, 5, Summer. From DAP, 204 West Franklin Avenue, Minneapolis, Minnesota 55404 USA.

Gruszuski, R.J., Brink, J.C. and Edleson, J.L. (1988) 'Support and education groups for children of battered women', *Child Welfare*, LXVII(5), Sept-October, pp.431-44.

Jaffe, P., Wilson, S. and Wolfe, D. (1986) 'Promoting changes in attitudes and understanding of conflict among child witnesses of family violence', *Canadian Journal of Behavioral Science*, 18, pp.356-80.

Jaffe, P. Wilson, S. and Wolfe, D. (1989) 'Specific assessment and intervention strategies for children exposed to wife battering: preliminary empirical investigations, *Canadian Journal of Community Mental Health*, 7, pp.157-63.

Jaffe, P.G., Wolfe, D.A. and Wilson, S.K. (1990) *Children of Battered Women*. Newbury Park, California: Sage.

Moore, J.G. (1975) 'Yo-yo children - victims of matrimonial violence', *Child Welfare*, LIV(8), September-October, pp.557-66.

Moore, J.G., Galcius, A. and Pettican, K. (1981) 'Emotional risk to children caught in violent marital conflict - the Basildon treatment project', *Child Abuse and Neglect*, 5, pp.147-52.

Pavlic, A. et al. (1991) *Report on Survey Results Examining the Number of Children Exposed to Wife Assault in London and Middlesex County*. London, Ontario: London Co-ordinating Committee to End Woman Abuse, Children's Sub-committee (NB This report was actually written by Larry Marshall of London Children's Aid Society).

Peled, E. and Davis, D. (1992) *Groupwork with Child Witnesses of Domestic Violence: A Practitioner's Manual*. Minneapolis: Domestic Abuse Project (To be produced in book form by Sage in late 1994).

Peled, E. and Edleson, J.L. (1992) 'Breaking the secret: multiple perspectives on groupwork with children of battered women', *Violence and Victims*, 7(4), pp.327-46.

Peled, E., Jaffe, P. and Edleson, J. (forthcoming in late 1994) *Ending the Cycle of Violence: Community Responses to Children of Battered Women*. Newbury Park, California: Sage.

Wilson, S.K., Cameron, S., Jaffe, P. and Wolfe, D. (1986) *Manual for a Group Program for Children Exposed to Wife Abuse*. London, Ontario: London Family Court Clinic (Funded by the Ministry of Community and Social Services - Family Violence Unit).

Wilson, S.K., Cameron, S., Jaffe, P. and Wolfe, D. (1989) 'Children exposed to wife abuse: an intervention model', *Social Casework: The Journal of Contemporary Social Work*, 70, March, pp.180-84.

Wolfe, D.A., Jaffe, P., Wilson, S.K. and Zak, L. (1985) 'Children of battered women: the relation of child behavior to family violence and maternal stress', *Journal of Consulting and Clinical Psychiatry*, 53(5), pp.657-65.

17

School-Based Work:
Education for Prevention

Audrey Mullender

Earlier chapters in this book have dealt with secondary and tertiary prevention. Secondary prevention in this context aims at preventing *further* abuse once children have disclosed their experiences, or once their mother has escaped the situation; it includes the provision of refuges and disclosure work with children. Tertiary level work seeks to lessen the damage caused by violence which has already taken place, for instance when children have lived with violence over a long period of time and have kept the effects bottled up; groups for child witnesses are a good example. This chapter now turns to primary prevention - the prevention of violence *before* it happens by altering attitudes, values and behaviours. Although it should not be forgotten that primary prevention is ultimately about material and structural factors in wider society, to date preventive efforts at this level have mainly been developed in school settings - aimed at influencing the generations of the future. As Jaffe, Hurley and Wolfe have commented (1990, p.469):

> The final frontier in dealing with violence in our society which most often leaves women and children as victims is the potential role of primary prevention programs . . . . Hope may lie in primary prevention programs within school systems which ensure that children from the primary grades up to adolescents in the secondary system are made aware of this issue.

A number of countries have begun to undertake work which relates to teaching young people about non-violent relationships, about the existence and impact of violence arising from sexual inequality, and about ways to prevent and oppose it. Work of this kind in schools, and in developing educational packs and curricula, is far more developed overseas than in Britain. This chapter will focus mainly on developments in Canada but New Zealand and Australia have also been making strides while, in Papua New Guinea, teaching on violence in relationships has been integrated throughout the national curriculum (Bradley, n.d.).

In this country, some Women's Aid groups have given talks in schools and have joined with teachers to plan anti-violence work, sometimes in conjunction with work on bullying, racism or other abuses of power between pupils (see chapter by Higgins, this volume). Some local authorities are developing programmes of work opposing male abuse which include school-based work. The London Borough of Hackney, for example, is in process of setting five-year targets for work on sexual violence which will place considerable emphasis on curriculum development within schools (personal communication).

School-based work is of particular importance because it offers a rare opportunity to engage with primary prevention. It also overlaps heavily with the other levels of prevention, however, since it inevitably involves not only children who are currently living with violent fathers and who may need help to become safe, but also children and young people who are themselves being violent (not necessarily in the same families). This fact needs careful handling. One problem with public education or prevention campaigns (whereby a public body, such as a local authority, makes a commitment to oppose violence in its own policies and procedures and through adopting prevention strategies, for example in schools) can be that they may make children and young people in both these groups feel excluded and hence even less likely to disclose or to seek help to change. Such campaigns need to take care not to appear to crusade punitively or moralistically against the kind of life which is many children's present reality but, rather, to engage everyone in providing the supports which can bring an end to violence and to the silence which upholds it (Susan Loosley, personal communication). Consequently, they need to be planned to draw on a wide range of services and information. The remainder of this chapter will outline detailed work in Canada, where a comprehensive model for schools-based prevention has now been developed and where a new educational pack draws together relevant material aimed at all age groups.

ANTI-VIOLENCE WORK IN CANADA

Some of the most advanced preventive work in schools is being carried out in Ontario, Canada. An exciting amount has been achieved there and, as a general approach, it would be highly transferable to the British context. This makes the relative inactivity here look inexcusable and dangerous in comparison.

The work dates from approximately 1988. Peter Jaffe, best known in the UK for his book *Children of Battered Women* (Jaffe et al., 1990), was on the Board of Education for the City of London, Ontario and hence had an influence over curriculum matters in all local schools. A conference co-ordinated by the Board asked school students whether violence prevention should be addressed in schools; a positive response led to joint efforts by the London Family Court Clinic (a court-related child and family agency, of which Peter Jaffe is Director), the Board of Education, and the local community to raise the issue in a serious way (Marlies Sudermann, personal communication). Training was offered for school principals and key teachers. A pilot programme in five schools received funding for each to hold an 'auditorium': a large-scale, day-long event with films, plays and speakers - including survivors of abuse - leading into guided discussion in the classroom. This was facilitated by designated teachers and professionals from relevant agencies. Other professionals with counselling skills were available to pupils who found the material upsetting or who made personal disclosures (Board of Education for the City of London and London Family Court Clinic, *Violence Prevention*, newsletter 2, June 1991, p.6).

In October 1989, 680 secondary school pupils and staff from 21 area school boards in the south west Ontario region attended a family violence day workshop with speakers, videos and discussion groups. Topics included: rape and violence in teenage dating relationships; knowing you are not the only one, and where to turn for help; what you can do to help - supporting and helping others to speak up; saying the right things to them; directing them towards appropriate services; setting up student-run hotlines, clubs and groups; displaying notices about services within and outside the school; teachers showing more awareness and concern. The overall conclusion was that school *is* a context in which it is possible to 'break the silence and help prevent violence' (*Violence Prevention* , July 1990, p.2). The work quickly spread. The Ontario Ministry of Community and Social Services made a special grant and, with help from the London Family Court Clinic, by 1991 workshops had been held in all secondary schools in London. The Ministry of Education also funded staff development.

During this time, the subject of male violence towards women had taken on added poignancy and urgency in Ontario because of the Montreal massacre: on 6th December 1989, Marc Lepine shot and killed fourteen women engineering students at the École Polytechnique in Montreal shouting: 'You're all a bunch of feminists. I hate feminists'. He deliberately separated women students from men and killed only the former (Labatt, 1990-91, p.2). The fact that this took place in an educational setting reinforced the schools-based work, rather as the police in West Yorkshire became more open to women's views on combating men's violence partially as a result of the 'Yorkshire Ripper' serial murders (Hanmer, 1989, p.95-96; in both cases an active women's movement locally ensured that the links were made). The Federation of Women Teachers' Associations of Ontario newsletter carried a special memorial issue a year later (in December 1990/January 1991) on 'Violence against women and children' and dedicated it not only to the 14 women killed at the Polytechnic but also the 119 killed in domestic relationships in Canada in 1989 who did not receive the same widespread publicity.

Early aims and strategies

One of the three major objectives of the Ontario Government's wider family violence prevention initiatives is: 'to develop expertise among teaching staff about the causes of wife assault and the effect on its victims, particularly children' (*Violence Prevention*, July 1990, p.1). The Ontario Ministry of Education recognised some years ago that these effects include an adverse impact on learning, making this work the proper concern of educators. It has developed a Statement of Direction, a discussion paper, a bibliography covering both French and English publications, and a set of procedures to be followed when children disclose living with violence (a 'child witness protocol'). Its regional offices have distributed resource kits to every local school board and publicised the several videos available. Social workers attached to schools are also called on to work with those who have already suffered the effects of living with violence.

At a more localised level, the Board of Education for the City of London has also committed itself to furthering a violence-free environment and sees itself in both an interventive and preventive role, the latter particularly with the younger children. The Board, jointly with the London Family Court Clinic, began in 1990 to publish a monthly newsletter called *Violence Prevention* with the slogan: 'Silence Hurts . . . Education Helps'. The Board has also produced and distributed separate leaflets for students - *Violence in Relationships: Students Can Make a Difference* - and for teachers - *Wife Assault: An Educational Issue*. Both publications carry locally researched information, for example, that 150-250,000 school-aged children in Ontario are exposed to violence at home. Both leaflets offer sections on definitions of physical, sexual, psychological and emotional abuse; reasons why men abuse and why women are forced to stay; agencies to contact; and things readers can do personally to help abused and abusing pupils - through listening, not minimising, and seeking outside help, for example. The leaflets also outline common myths about wife abuse: that it only affects certain segments of the population, that it is caused by drink, that women deserve or enjoy the abuse. These are counterposed with researched facts: for example, that the abuse happens across all classes and cultures, that alcohol is a common excuse but not a cause since not all batterers drink or not every time, and that women feel demeaned if others do not recognise the violence as solely men's responsibility. The Board advises teachers, through the leaflet aimed at them, that they can assist prevention by learning more themselves and dispelling myths amongst pupils, teaching that violence is never the way to solve problems, and exploring better ways to deal with anger, as well as promoting alternative forms of conflict resolution. The teacher's leaflet also carries a section on the impact on children of living with violence:

> Children from violent homes end up believing that:
> it's acceptable for men to hit women
> violence is an effective way to solve problems
> inequality in relationships is normal
> there are few, if any, consequences for violent acts

they are responsible for the violence or for stopping it
men are mean and strong, women are weak and helpless
(Board of Education for the City of London, n.d., *Wife Assault: An Educational Issue*).

There has, then, been an impressive amount of activity and a head of steam building up in Canadian education over a number of years for measures which, in their impact, combine prevention and intervention. Browsing through the *Violence Prevention* newsletters for July 1990 and June 1991, other means of helping which were utilised in the quite early stages - and which could certainly be emulated here - included: a resource list; a 'Health Fair' including violence prevention amongst the topics; information sessions for individual classes or staff groups; a presentation in school for pupils, staff and parents; a workshop for a whole year group in their own school following attendance by a few pupils at a regional one; a school assembly on the topic, with discussion groups afterwards; a topic-based teaching programme; canvassing support amongst parents and public bodies to complain to, and boycott, television channels carrying violent programmes in prime time; a group committed to listening to friends and classmates who have suffered violence at home or elsewhere; a student assembly with a panel discussing aggression and sex roles. Other ideas included the use of films, videos, poster displays, theatre groups, 'magic circles' (basically discussion groups using pre-set exercises and Round Robin techniques to develop listening skills and self-esteem: Crippen, 1990-1991), and a violence awareness week in school.

The latter, at elementary school level, involved age-specific daily activities, exercises, and presentations on the topic of violence. Eleven year olds helped six-year olds draw anti-violence posters, while twelve-year olds cut violent photographs and headlines from newspapers and magazines to use in a collage, and kindergarten children were given instruction by shelter workers on how to call for help if their mother was being assaulted. The local newspaper reported daily on events in school and a range of community agencies and services offered support. Many other schools sought information on how to replicate the event, leading the original school to assemble a resource and information pack on violence for use elsewhere. The clear conclusion reached was that 'one school can make a difference !!'.

Teachers and teachers' organisations have joined in the efforts for change through raising each others' awareness (Labatt, 1990/91: 8-9) and also raising funds. The Federation of Women Teachers' Associations of Ontario gave $97,000 in 1992 for joint teacher-community initiatives and launched a two-year anti-violence campaign (Sudermann et al., 1994, pp.15&17).

Current initiatives
Since then, the impetus has been towards integrating the work more fully into the general school system so that it is increasingly 'owned' by

schools and not seen as an 'add on' inspired from outside. By the time of writing, in mid-1994, the work in London, Ontario, has culminated in a video and training pack called *ASAP* - an acronym for *A School-based Anti-violence Programme* (Sudermann et al., 1994) and no doubt also aimed at achieving change 'as soon as possible'. Crucially, the Ontario Ministry of Education and Training is promoting a policy of not tolerating violence and of partnership in prevention. Its new violence prevention policy for schools was released in June 1994 (Ontario Ministry of Education and Training, 1994). It requires school boards to develop and revise their own policies on violence-free schools during 1994-95, for official approval and implementation by September 1995. These will cover: staff development; the curriculum; a code of behaviour; the school environment; identification and prevention of violence (including threats and verbal harassment); student, staff and community involvement; and procedures for dealing with violent incidents with a specified reporting and recording policy. The violence-free school policies must also be linked by the boards to policies on anti-racism and ethnocultural equity. Meanwhile, the active co-operation with women's organisations continues, with Women's Community House in London (a shelter, i.e. refuge-based organisation: see Loosley, this volume), for example, providing speakers for parents' groups, for teachers' staff development events, and for children in the classroom. The *ASAP* pack has also been circulated to every Board of Education across Canada in the hope that it will be more widely adopted.

The loose-leaf folder in the pack, which runs to several hundred pages, looks at why schools need to be involved in violence prevention - at every level from students to trustees and involving the local community; what kind of work is needed at each level; how a safer school climate can be created and gender equality promoted; strategies that can be adopted in elementary schools and in secondary schools; positive responses to disclosures both from children (see *Make A Difference* text, reproduced in this volume) and from staff; handling resistance; and further resources to draw on.

In elementary schools, a key idea is to base activities around a violence awareness and prevention week. Activities can involve everyone, starting with professional development for staff. In school there can be plays, speakers from local women's organisations such as shelters and sexual assault crisis centres, videos, special assemblies for each year group, and classroom-based work integrated into teaching. There is a whole curriculum available from the USA for this age group (Petersen and Gamache, 1988) which covers learning about the different forms of violence and their effects, personal safety planning, expressing feelings, assertiveness and self-worth whilst also respecting others. There is some overlap with the material used in groups for child witnesses (see groups chapter by Mullender, this volume) but the schools work is more educationally focused, is aimed at whole classes, and uses a range of techniques including stories and written work, role-playing and problem-solving, music, games and art, videotaping and puppetry (cited in Sudermann, et al., 1994: 73). Ontario teachers have also developed their own materials, with stories based on non-violent superheroes used as a basis for work in art, literacy, environmental studies and mathematics (Lawson, 1992, cited in Sudermann, et al., 1994: 17). Parents are involved through attending assemblies, special events and information evenings, as well as receiving newsletters. In one event, they joined pupils and others in joining hands around the perimeter of a school to symbolise peace - in a way which will be familiar to British readers from Greenham Common days.

Work in secondary schools has an additional emphasis on pupils' own relationships, many of which are already violent. Date rape is a common part of our society's manifestation of male power and control and of widespread male assumptions about their rights over women. Some men who are court mandated to attend batterers' groups in North America have barely left school. (One young man of 17 in a group visited by the present author, for example, had pushed his girlfriend out of a moving car.) Of pupils completing questionnaires in five Ontario schools, 54 per cent knew someone who was abused in a dating relationship and 17 per cent of boys said enforced sexual intercourse was appropriate if the girl had led the boy on (*Violence Prevention*, June, 1991, pp.6-7).

Programmes for this age group tend to be focused around large-scale events using theatre or outside speakers, with greater use of the local media. Pupils themselves are more fully involved - with a student planning committee for the programme as a whole, and specific schemes for young people to offer peer mediation or peer counselling. The overall school climate is seen as crucially important; one imaginative idea is for a positively rather than negatively oriented sanction to apply when a young person breaks any non-violence code the school may have adopted: this is for an in-school suspension whereby, rather than being sent home, the pupil is required to attend sessions on conflict resolution and interpersonal skills. Another positive idea is to reward positive, sharing behaviour rather than simply punishing what is undesirable (Sudermann, personal communication). The training pack emphasises that anti-violence work can be integrated into many aspects of the school curriculum (Sudermann et al., 1994, pp.17, 97&99) and teachers have shown creativity in bringing the topic into every subject from history to maths. At secondary level, suggested materials in the pack again analyse the major forms of abuse but go into more detail about possible causes, including wider issues of patriarchal societies and the feminisation of poverty. Materials developed by women's organisations are also suggested as useful teaching resources.

EVALUATION

The work has been evaluated throughout. The first three years of incentive funding from the Ontario Ministry of Education were evaluated by 'before and after' questionnaires in the five schools where events had been held as part of the pilot programme. Although this follow-up revealed unacceptable attitudes on the part of a small number of boys towards date rape and violent relationships, it also showed significantly increased knowledge amongst a majority of pupils about the facts on abuse and the possibilities of getting help (*Violence Prevention* newsletter, June, 1991, pp.6-7). In another form of active feedback, school students, staff and community discussion groups have made suggestions for future workshops and professional development events for staff. Young people themselves are almost universally supportive both of the topic being broached and of the approach adopted (Sudermann et al., 1994, p.23). The *ASAP* pack recognises that further work is needed, for example in involving more than a few key teachers (p.19), overcoming resistant attitudes (section H), and increasing parental participation (p.23).

A CRITIQUE OF THE *ASAP* MANUAL

No model yet developed is perfect. This critique is offered in full awareness that Britain lags behind London, Ontario, but in the hope that the hard work there could lead to rapid progress here if we learn from what is best and push at the boundaries of what is less strong.

There are a number of weaknesses in the *ASAP* pack. Firstly, the original material in the pack devotes only two pages to 'ethnocultural issues' (though there are undeveloped references elsewhere to antiracist guidelines and resource guides from the Ontario Ministry of Education) and one page to aboriginal issues (referring to native Canadians including Inuit people). The latter section makes an overt statement about systematic abuse by the dominant culture but the awareness of racism is not as integrated into the rest of the pack as a UK audience would now expect, making only occasional mentions of the multiracial pattern of immigration into Canada (e.g. p.7) and of antiracist curriculum resources. Secondly, homophobia is never overtly mentioned. The terms of abuse on page 53: 'weak, wimpy, nerdy' by no means represent the only name-calling aimed at non-macho boys, and the 'rough-housing' referred to (p.41) is usually fiercely heterosexist. Sexual harassment in the school setting is linked in the pack to gender but not to sexuality, and the list of oppressed people victimised by violence does not mention gay men or lesbians (p.7).

The pack could also have included a greater recognition that schools themselves and their staff may be abusive. More space is devoted to discussing student-student and student-family abuse than teacher-student dangers, for example. The issue is not entirely avoided - a newspaper feature by a young woman commenting on verbal harassment and sexist teaching by male staff is reproduced (p.74) and an example of institutionalised sexual abuse by a religious foundation in Newfoundland is mentioned (p.5) - but 'safe schools' (p.11) are largely equated with reducing 'aggressive behaviour at school' (p.12), 'difficulties in classroom management', and 'disruptive behavioural problems' (p.13), rather than with teachers confronting their own abusiveness or that of the school system as a whole. The potential presence of perpetrators amongst school staff is acknowledged (p.21) but they are somewhat insultingly included with survivors as possibly needing an opt out from the anti-violence work, and nothing is said about how to confront or report them (p.33).

A final criticism would be that the pack displays an over-deterministic attitude towards the impact of violence: 'Trustees need information on the links between experiencing or witnessing violence at home and subsequent aggressive behaviour at school', for example (p.11). It is misleading to assume that the dangers of pupil-to-pupil or of dating violence are confined to those who have lived with direct or indirect abuse (see Morley and Mullender, this volume). The extension of prevention to young people's interpersonal relationships is important for its own sake - control and abuse start young and men take them from one relationship to another - not because they have a simplistic cause, any more than does the violence already shown by some very young children who may need specific forms of intervention (pp.73&75).

On the positive side, the pack does not fudge the recognition that 'violence is not gender-neutral' (p.7) and it makes an overt link between the non-tolerance[1] of violence and the promotion of gender equality (pp.45-49). Other pluses include the awareness that teachers need to be well linked to a range of community resources if they are not to be overwhelmed when they raise the lid on this topic, and the recognition that all levels in schools need to be involved: the British equivalents would be secretaries and caretakers, governors, heads and teachers, pupils, parents, education welfare officers or education social workers, and educational psychologists. The pack's emphasis on the need to start by raising the awareness of school personnel before undertaking work with pupils is, of course, essential.

CONCLUSION

All in all, the *ASAP* pack and the context in which it is being used in Canada constitute one of the most comprehensive approaches available to primary prevention of abusive relationships and certainly provide a model for others, particularly in terms of the official backing for the work and its widescale adoption. The sense of excitement generated by the work in schools - with newsletters talking of teachers and pupils working together for change, and schools discovering reservoirs of strength and expertise in their local communities - gives cause to believe that such work can sustain a good deal of its own momentum once it is launched with official support. If so, it offers real hope for the future.

Acknowledgement
Much of the material for this chapter was gathered during a trip to Canada funded by a Mia Kellmer Pringle Fellowship from the National Children's Bureau. Susan Loosley, Children's Advocate at Women's Community House in London, Ontario, gave invaluable help in up-dating this information.

Notes

1. The Canadian educational policy of not tolerating violence is referred to locally as 'Zero Tolerance'. It refers, in that context, to an integrated set of policies aimed at achieving violence-free schools within a comprehensive anti-violence policy. In Britain, the term has been applied to a specific anti-domestic violence community education programme by the local authority in Edinburgh, using posters and other forms of media advertising. This has been repeated in London (England) by the Association of London Authorities, with some modifications, and is being considered or implemented by various local authorities elsewhere in the country.

References

Board of Education for the City of London (n.d.) Violence *in Relationships: Students Can Make a Difference* .

Board of Education for the City of London (n.d.) *Wife Assault: An Educational Issue*.

Board of Education for the City of London and the London Family Court Clinic (1990) *Violence Prevention*, Newsletter 1, July.

Board of Education for the City of London and the London Family Court Clinic (1991) *Violence Prevention*, Newsletter 2, June.

Bradley, S. C. (no date) 'Wife-Beating in Papua New Guinea: Situation Report 1990', unpublished.

Crippen, C. (1990-91) 'The magic circle', *Federation of Women Teachers' Associations of Ontario Newsletter*, 9(3), pp.10-14.

Federation of Women Teachers' Associations of Ontario Newsletter (1990-1991) Special Issue: 'Violence against women and children', 9(3), December-January.

Hanmer, J. (1989) 'Women and policing in Britain' in Hanmer, J., Radford, J. and Stanko, E.A., *Women, Policing and Male Violence: International Perspectives*. London: Routledge.

Jaffe, P.G., Hurley, D. J. and Wolfe, D. (1990) 'Children's observations of violence: I. Critical issues in child development and intervention planning', *Canadian Journal of Psychiatry*, 35, pp.466-470.

Jaffe, P.G., Wolfe, D.A. and Wilson, S.K. (1990) *Children of Battered Women*. Newbury Park: Sage.

Labatt, M. (1990-91) 'Violence against women: an epidemic and a national disgrace', *Federation of Women Teachers' Associations of Ontario Newsletter. Montreal Massacre Memorial Issue: Violence Against Women and Children*, December/January, 9(3), pp.2-9.

Lawson, J. (1992) 'Non-violent superheroes like Paul Bunyan', *Federation of Women Teachers' Associations of Ontario Newsletter*, 11(2), Curriculum Insert.

Ontario Ministry of Education and Training (1994) *Framework for the Development of Violence Prevention Policies by School Boards*. Toronto, Ontario.

Petersen, K. S. and Gamache, D. (1988) *My Family and Me: Violence Free. Domestic Violence Prevention Curriculum*. (Unit 1 for grades kindergarten to 3, and Unit 2 for grades 4-6). St Paul, Minnesota: Minnesota Coalition for Battered Women.

Sudermann, M., Jaffe, P.G. and Hastings, E. with Watson, L., Greer, G. and Lehmann, P. (1994) *ASAP: A School-Based Anti-Violence Programme*. Revised Preview Edition. London, Ontario: London Family Court Clinic.

Notes on Contributors

Thangam Debbonaire has been the National Children's Officer for the Women's Aid Federation of England since the start of 1991. Before that, her work included working as a volunteer and Management Committee member for a refuge for Asian women and editing a book celebrating the hundredth anniversary of the birth of Jawaharlal Nehru. She has lobbied and campaigned on behalf of children experiencing domestic violence over many recent pieces of legislation. She co-ordinates the national training programme for refuge children's workers and also provides information, resources and support for work with children in Women's Aid. She has delivered keynote speeches and training workshops about children's needs and experiences relating to domestic violence at several national conferences for relevant professionals, and has also worked with staff from other agencies developing good practice in domestic violence and children's needs. This has included publishing articles in professional journals for social workers and court welfare officers. She has been involved in consultation on several major pieces of research and other publications on domestic violence, and has initiated the development of the first England-wide research into the experiences of children in refuges. She is currently co-editing the publication of Alex Saunders' work on the experiences of children living in refuges fifteen years ago.

Gill Hague has worked for many years in women's groups and projects, and has been employed as a social worker, community worker, social work lecturer and researcher in both North America and Britain. She has contributed to a number of books on domestic violence and has written a guidebook, *Equal Opportunities; Policy into Practice: Gender*. She and her co-author Ellen Malos are activists of long standing in Women's Aid and have been committed for twenty years to working towards ending male violence against women. They have produced various joint publications and are the co-authors of a major report, *Domestic Violence and Housing*, published in 1993 by the Women's Aid Federation (England) and the University of Bristol, and *Domestic Violence: Action for Change*, an overview of current issues in domestic violence work. They are currently researching inter-agency responses to domestic violence, supported by the Joseph Rowntree Foundation.

Lynne Harne has been an active member of the Women's Movement for over 20 years. She has been a member of Rights of Women since 1983, and is currently working as a free-lance researcher, and writer on women's social policy issues and contemporary feminist history. She has researched and written extensively on legal issues concerning single and lesbian mothers, including: 'Lesbian mothers and the new myth of the father' (*Trouble and Strife*, 1984, 3) partially reprinted in *Women's Studies: A Reader* (Jackson, S. ed., Harvester Wheatsheaf); *The Lesbian Mother's Legal Handbook* (edited with Barrett, M., Women's Press, 1986); 'Families and fathers: the effects of the Children Act (*Rights of Women Bulletin*, 1993). She is currently editing a book on the backlash against feminism to be published by the Women's Press. She has campaigned extensively around issues concerning women and domestic violence and is involved in a Rights of Women working group researching into the operation of the Children Act in relation to domestic violence and the legal system.

Marianne Hester is Lecturer in Social Work at the University of Bristol. She has carried out research into many aspects of violence against women and has for many years been involved in action around violence and work with survivors. Her publications include *Lewd Women and Wicked Witches: A Study of The Dynamics of Male Domination*.

Gina Higgins works as a children's development worker for Hammersmith Women's Aid. She has personal experience of domestic abuse and of life as a resident in a women's refuge; the help and support she received there gave her the confidence to apply for her present post. Since her appointment, in addition to one-to-one work with children she has developed a range of initiatives both within and beyond the refuge, including a child abuse policy and work on bullying and racism which includes links with a local school. Nationally, she is active within Women's Aid Federation (England) working with other children's workers to improve services for children and to give them a voice, as well as in a training capacity. She has led workshops at a number of national conferences including 'Suffering in Silence', the first British conference on children living with domestic violence which took place in Hammersmith in December 1992. Gina is the author of *All Children Should Be Safe*, an activity workbook aimed specifically at children aged from 6 to 12 who are living in refuges. It is hoped that this will soon be available from WAFE at PO Box 391, Bristol BS99 7WS.

Carol-Ann Hooper is a Lecturer in Social Policy at the University of York. She is the author of *Mothers Surviving Child Sexual Abuse* (Routledge, 1992), a study of the experiences of women whose children had been sexually abused by male relatives, and several articles on child abuse. She previously worked as a counsellor and researcher at the London Rape Crisis Centre.

Julie Humphries is currently working at the Roehampton Institute as a member of the Domestic Violence and Child Contact Arrangements Project. She is also a Lecturer in Research Methods at St. Mary's University College, London.

Umme Farvah Imam is at present Tutor in Community and Youth Work Studies at the University of Durham. Her background is in community development work, particularly with Black women. She has several years' experience, both in India (where she was born and educated) and in England, in supporting women suffering domestic violence - latterly through her work at Roshni Asian Women's Association in Newcastle upon Tyne. She has been actively involved in the Black struggle and the development and campaigning work of several Black women's projects in Newcastle upon Tyne - particularly in the establishment of Panah, the Black women's refuge in the city.

Liz Kelly is a feminist researcher and activist, who has worked in the field of violence against women and children for over 20 years. She has been active in establishing and working in local services including refuges and rape crisis centres, and in local, regional and national campaign groups. In the early 1970s, she worked as the 'playgroup' worker in the Norwich refuge, and on many holiday play-schemes. She is author of *Surviving Sexual Violence* and many articles: on domestic violence, sexual abuse of children, rape and sexual assault, pornography, and feminist methodology. Since 1987, she has worked - with other feminists - at the Child and Woman Abuse Studies Unit, University of North London (CASU). CASU (currently Sheila Burton, Liz Kelly and Linda Regan) exists to conduct research, training, consultancy and networking from a feminist and anti-oppressive perspective. Over the last three years, CASU has devised a series of training courses for WAFE children's workers, including developing child protection policies, direct work with children, and building an anti-violence ethos in refuges. In 1994, CASU completed an evaluation of work with children in a London refuge.

London Coordinating Committee to End Woman Abuse is a network of social, health, education and justice services, comprised of members from social service agencies throughout London, Ontario. The Children's Subcommittee comprises representatives from the following organisations: The Children's Aid Society of London and Middlesex, The Board of Education for the City of London, The London and Middlesex County Roman Catholic School Board, The Middlesex County Board of Education, Women's Community House, London Second Stage Housing, The London Family Court Clinic, London Victim/Witness Assistance Program, Women's Rural Resource Centre of Strathroy and Area, Atenlos Native Family Violence Services, Madame Vanier Children's Services, and London Battered Women's Advocacy Centre.

Susan Loosley was born in Dunstable, Bedfordshire, and emigrated to Canada in 1970 at the age of four. She began her work with child witnesses of woman abuse at a Second Stage Housing facility in London, Ontario, where she implemented a group treatment programme for the child residents. She joined Women's Community House in July 1992 as a Child Advocate. Susan is an active member of the Children's Sub-Committee of the London Co-ordinating Committee to End Woman Abuse. Through that committee, she actively participated in the development of *Make a Difference*, a video and information guide which was launched in January 1994. She also co-authored a recent protocol document, *Children Who Witness Woman Abuse - School Based Support* for the Catholic Board of Education.

Ellen Malos has been involved in women's and community groups, and teaching and researching in women's studies and social policy since the 1960s. Her publications include *The Politics of Housework* and an introduction to women's studies, *Half the Sky*, with the Bristol Women' Studies Group. She and her co-author Gill Hague are activists of long standing in Women's Aid and have been committed for twenty years to working towards ending male violence against women. They have produced various joint publications and are the co-authors of a major report, *Domestic Violence and Housing*, published in 1993 by the Women's Aid Federation (England) and the University of Bristol, and *Domestic Violence: Action for Change*, an overview of current issues in domestic violence work. They are currently researching inter-agency responses to domestic violence, supported by the Joseph Rowntree Foundation.

Rebecca Morley teaches women's studies, social policy, and social and cultural studies in the School of Social Studies at the University of Nottingham. She has researched and lectured on the topic of men's violence against women for many years in Britain, North America and Papua New Guinea. Recent publications include: 'Recent responses to "domestic violence" against women: a feminist critique' in Page, R. and Baldock, J. (eds.) *Social Policy Review 5: The Evolving State of Welfare* (Canterbury: Social Policy Association) and 'Wife beating and modernization: the case of Papua New Guinea', *Journal of Comparative Family Studies*, Spring, 1994, pp.25-52. She has recently investigated the knowledge and attitudes of professionals working in child protection to domestic violence and its relationship to child abuse. Her current research is focused on legal and social policy responses to domestic violence to women. She is completing a book entitled: *Men's Violence to Women in Intimate Relationships: Feminist Knowledge and Politics*. She is also involved in a number of local women's and community groups working on the issue of men's violence against women.

Audrey Mullender is a qualified social worker and Director of the Centre for Applied Social Studies at the University of Durham. In 1991/2, she held a Mia Kellmer Pringle Fellowship from the National Children's Bureau for a transatlantic trip to study direct work with child witnesses of domestic violence. With several other contributors to this volume, she is part of a research team studying refuge childworkers' experiences of children and domestic violence on an England-wide basis. She is currently writing a book on domestic violence called *Part of the Problem?*, aimed at social workers and probation officers, to be published by Routledge in late 1995 or early 1996. She is the author of over sixty social work publications; one of the most frequently recurring themes in her work is the use of groupwork as a means of empowering people to oppose oppression and achieve social change.

Rebecca Morley and Audrey Mullender are joint authors of:
'Hype or hope? The importation of pro-arrest policies and batterers' programmes from North America to Britain as key measures for preventing violence against women in the home', *International Journal of Law and the Family*, 1992, 6, pp.265-287;
'Preventing violence against women in the home: feminist dilemmas concerning recent British developments' in Farrington, D.P. and Walklate, S. (eds.) *Offenders and Victims: Theory and Policy. British Criminology Conference 1991. Selected Papers: Volume 1,* London: British Society of Criminology in association with the Institute for the Study and Treatment of Delinquency, 1992; and

Preventing Domestic Violence to Women, London: Home Office, Police Research Group, Crime Prevention Unit Series, Paper 48, 1994.

During 1991, they made joint research presentations on domestic violence to the annual conferences of the Socio-Legal Studies Association, the Social Policy Association, and the British Society of Criminology, as well as to the joint international conference of the Law and Society Association (USA) and the Research Committee on Sociology of Law of the International Sociological Association in Amsterdam.

Maureen O'Hara works at the Children's Legal Centre, where she is responsible for policy concerning child protection. She is currently carrying out a national survey of the policies and practices of social services departments, the police, and the court welfare service in relation to child protection in the context of domestic violence. She has worked on issues of violence against women and children from a feminist perspective for many years, and is particularly interested in the links between the oppression of women and that of children.

Chris Pearson is research assistant at the University of Bristol working on the Domestic Violence and Child Contact Arrangements Project. She is a qualified social worker and also worked as a refuge worker for a number of years.

Khalida Qaiser works full time for a Women's Aid refuge and part-time as a researcher for the Domestic Violence and Child Contact Arrangements Project.

Jill Radford has worked for Rights for Women, and as a part-time Women's Studies Lecturer, as well as being involved in feminist campaigning for a number of years. She has written widely on issues concerning women and male sexual violence, including 'Policing male violence, policing women' in *Women, Violence and Social Control* (Hanmer, J. and Maynard, M. (eds.), Macmillan, 1987) and *Femicide: The Politics of Woman Killing* (edited with Russell, D., Open University Press, 1992) as well as a number of articles in the *Rights of Women Bulletin*. She has campaigned extensively around issues concerning women and domestic violence and is involved in a Rights of Women working group, researching into the operation of the Children Act in relation to domestic violence and the legal system.

Lorraine Radford teaches Social Policy and Women's Studies at the Roehampton Institute, London. She is currently involved in research into domestic violence and child contact, violence and inter-agency initiatives and primary health care. For the past fourteen years she has worked as volunteer for a Women's Aid refuge group.

Alex Saunders took a Master's degree in social work at Sussex University and is currently with the Frances Taylor Foundation at St Marye's in East Sussex, where he works with people with learning difficulties. His interest in the subject of domestic violence stems from his own childhood experiences. At the age of thirteen he spent eighteen months in a women's refuge when his mother fled the violence she had suffered at the hands of his father. His book *Children, Domestic Violence and Refuges: Children Speak Out* is about to be published with the joint involvement of the National Institute for Social Work, ChildLine and the Women's Aid Federation (England).

Kandy-Sue Woodfield trained in research methods at the University of Surrey. She is currently working at the Roehampton Institute as a member of the Domestic Violence and Child Contact Arrangements Project. She has taught Politics at the University of the West of England at Bristol and at the Roehampton Institute.

Bibliography

Ahmad, B. (1990) *Black Perspectives in Social Work*. Birmingham: Venture Press.

Ahmed, L. (1992) *Women and Gender in Islam*. New Haven and London: Yale University Press.

Ahmed, S. (1986) 'Cultural racism in work with Asian women and girls' in Ahmed, S., Cheetham, J. and Small, J. (eds.) (1986) *Social Work with Black Children and Their Families*. London: Batsford.

Alessi, J.J. and Hearn, K. (1984) 'Group treatment of children in shelters for battered women' in Roberts, A.R. (ed.) *Battered Women and Their Families*. New York: Springer (Referred to by Jaffe et al., 1990, p.87).

Amato, P.R. and Keith, B. (1991) 'Parental divorce and the well-being of children: a meta-analysis', *Psychological Bulletin*, 110(1), pp.26-46.

Andrews, B. and Brown, G.W. (1988) 'Marital violence in the community: a biographical approach', *British Journal of Psychiatry*, 153, pp.305-312.

Armstrong, H. (1994) *Report of Area Child Protection Committees National Conference: 8 March 1994*. London: Department of Health. ACPC Series, Report No. 4.

Association of Chief Officers of Probation (1992) *Association of Chief Officers of Probation Position Statement on Domestic Violence*. London: ACOP. Drafted by David Sleightholm.

Bainham, J. (1990) *Children: The New Law. The Children Act 1989*. Bristol: Family Law Publications.

Ball, M. (1990) *Children's Workers in Women's Aid Refuges: A Report on the Experience of Nine Refuges in England*. London: National Council of Voluntary Childcare Organisations.

Ball, M. (1992) *An Evaluation of the National Children's Worker Post and a Report on Children's Work in Seven Refuges, Funded by the BBC Children In Need Trust*. Unpublished.

Barnett, O.W. and LaViolette, A.D. (1993) *It Could Happen to Anyone: Why Battered Women Stay*. Newbury Park, California: Sage.

Barron, J. (1990) *Not Worth the Paper: The Effectiveness of Legal Protection for Women and Children Experiencing Domestic Violence*. Bristol: Women's Aid Federation England.

Barron, J., Harwin, N. and Singh, T. (1992) *Women's Aid Federation England Written Evidence to the House of Commons Home Affairs Committee Inquiry into Domestic Violence*. October, Bristol: Women's Aid Federation England. (Also published as Memorandum 22, submitted by Women's Aid Federation England, in Home Affairs Committee, 1993b, see below.)

Binney, V., Harkell, G., and Nixon, J. (1981) *Leaving Violent Men: A Study of Refuges and Housing for Battered Women*. Leeds: Women's Aid Federation England.

Board of Education for the City of London (n.d.) *Violence in Relationships: Students Can Make a Difference.*

Board of Education for the City of London (n.d.) *Wife Assault: An Educational Issue.*

Board of Education for the City of London and the London Family Court Clinic (1990) *Violence Prevention*, Newsletter 1, July.

Board of Education for the City of London and the London Family Court Clinic (1991) *Violence Prevention*, Newsletter 2, June.

Booth, Hon. Mrs Justice (1985) *Report of the Matrimonial Causes Procedure Committee.* London: HMSO.

Borkowski, M., Murch, M., and Walker, V. (1983) *Marital Violence: the Community Response.* London: Tavistock.

Bowker, L.H. (1983) *Beating Wife-Beating.* Lexington, Massachusetts: D. C. Heath and Company.

Bowker, L.H., Arbitell, M. and McFerron, J.R. (1988) 'On the relationship between wife beating and child abuse' in Yllö, K. and Bograd, M. (eds.) *Feminist Perspectives on Wife Abuse.* Newbury Park, California: Sage.

Bowlby, J. (1953) *Childcare and the Growth of Love.* Harmondsworth: Penguin.

Bradley, S.C. (no date) 'Wife-Beating in Papua New Guinea: Situation Report 1990', unpublished.

Bridge Child Care Consultancy Service (1991) *Sukina: An Evaluation of the Circumstances Leading to her Death.* London: Bridge Child Care Consultancy Service.

Bromley, P. and Lowe, N. (1992) *Bromley's Family Law.* 8th Edition, London: Butterworth.

Brophy, J. (1985) 'Child care and the growth of power: the status of mothers in custody disputes' in Brophy, J. and Smart, C. (eds.) *Women in Law: Explorations in Law, Family and Sexuality.* London: Routledge and Kegan Paul.

Brophy, J. (1987) 'Co-parenting and the limits of "law": divorce and parenthood in the 1990s'. Response to the Law Commission Working Paper No 96 from Rights of Women, unpublished.

Brophy, J. (1989) 'Custody law, childcare and inequality in Britain' in Smart, C. and Sevenhuijsen, S. (eds.) *Child Custody and the Politics of Gender.* London: Routledge.

Browne, A. (1987) *When Battered Women Kill.* New York: The Free Press.

Browne, A. and Williams, K.R. (1989) 'Exploring the effect of resource availability and the likelihood of female-precipitated homicides', *Law and Society Review*, 23(1), pp.75-94.

Browning, D.H. and Boatman, B. (1977) 'Incest: children at risk', *American Journal of Psychiatry*, 134(1), pp.69-72.

Bull, J. (1993) *Housing Consequences of Relationship Breakdown.* London: HMSO.

Burghes, L. (1994) *Lone Parenthood and Family Disruption: the Outcomes for Children.* London: Family Policy Studies Centre.

Burgoyne, J., Ormrod, R. and Richards, M. (1987) *Divorce Matters*. Harmondsworth: Penguin.

Campaign Against the Child Support Act (1993) *Dossier of DSS Illegalities. Implications of the Child Support Act*. London: Kings Cross Women's Centre.

Casey, M. (1987) *Domestic Violence Against Women*. Dublin: Dublin Federation of Refuges.

Catholic Board of Education (1994) *Children Who Witness Woman Abuse - School Based Support*. London, Ontario: Catholic Board of Education.

Charles, N. (1991) *Funding Women's Aid Services to the Community in Wales: Research Report*. Welsh Women's Aid.

Cherlin, A.J., Furstenberg, F.F., Chase-Lansdale, P.L., Kiernan, K., Robins, P.K., Morrison, D.R. and Teitler, J.O. (1991) 'Longitudinal studies of effects of divorce on children in Great Britain and the United States', *Science*, 252, pp.1386-1389.

Chesler, P. (1987) *Mothers on Trial*. Seattle, Washington: Seal Press.

CHICL/London Housing Unit (1992) *Losing Heart: the Impact of Government Policy on Housing Association Development in Central London*. London: CHICI/LHU.

Children and Parliament (1991) issue 142. London: National Children' s Bureau.

Children and Parliament (1994) issue 201. London: National Children' s Bureau.

Children's Legal Centre (1992) *Children and Domestic Violence: Submission to the Home Affairs Inquiry into Domestic Violence*. London: Children's Legal Centre. (Also published in House of Commons Home Affairs Committee, Session 1992-93, *Domestic Violence. Memoranda of Evidence*, volume II, Minutes of Evidence and Appendices, London: HMSO.)

Children's Rights Development Unit (1994) 'No sign of Government plan to meet UNCRC duties', *Childright*, January/February, 103, p.10.

Children's Subcommittee of the London Coordinating Committee to End Woman Abuse (1994) *Make a Difference: How to Respond to Child Witnesses of Woman Abuse*. London, Ontario, Canada: London Coordinating Committee to End Woman Abuse. (Training pack with video and manual. Available from: Children's Aid Society of London and Middlesex, P.O. Box 6010, Depot 1, London, Ontario, Canada, N5W 5RD. NB Video needs to be adapted for UK use.)

Child Support Agency (1993) *For Parents Who Live Apart*. London: Department of Social Security.

Christensen, E. (1990) 'Children's living conditions: an investigation into disregard of care in relation to children and teenagers in families of wife maltreatment', *Nordisk Psychologi*, 42, Monograph no.31, pp.161-232.

Clark, A. (1993) *Homeless Children and their Access to Schooling: A Bristol Case Study*. Bristol: SPACE Trust.

Cockett, M. and Tripp, J. (1994) *Children Living in Re-ordered Families*. Social Policy Research Findings No. 45, York: Joseph Rowntree Foundation.

Cohen, B. (1990) *Caring for Children: the 1990 Report*. London: Family Policy Studies Centre.

Conway, J. (ed.) (1988) *Prescription for Poor Health*. London: Shelter.

Coote, A., Harman, H. and Hewitt, P. (1990) *The Family Way*. Social Policy Paper No.1, London: IPPR.

Crellin, E., Kellmer Pringle, M.L., and West, P. (1971) *Born Illegitimate: a Report by the National Children's Bureau*. London: National Foundation for Educational Research.

Cretney, S.M. (1979) *Principles of Family Law*. Third Edition. London: Sweet and Maxwell.

Crippen, C. (1990-91) 'The magic circle', *Federation of Women Teachers' Associations of Ontario Newsletter*, 9(3), pp.10-14.

Davis, G. and Roberts, M. (1988) *Access to Agreement*. Milton Keynes: Open University Press.

Debbonaire (Singh), T. (1994) *WAFE Briefing Papers on Children's Issues*. Bristol: WAFE.

Demo, D.H. and Acock, A.C. (1988) 'The impact of divorce on children', *Journal of Marriage and the Family*, 50, pp.619-648.

Department of Education and Science HMI (1990) *A Survey of the Education of Children living in Temporary Accommodation*. London: HMSO.

Department of Environment (1991) *Homelessness: Code of Guidance for Local Authorities, Part III of the Housing Act 1985*. Third Edition. London: HMSO.

Department of Environment (1994) *Access to Local Authority and Housing Association Tenancies: a Consultation Paper*. London: DOE.

Department of Health (1989) *The Care of Children: Principles and Practice in Regulations and Guidance*. London: HMSO.

Department of Health (1991) *Children Act 1989 Guidance and Regulations Volume 1: Court Orders*. London: HMSO.

Department of Social Security (1993) *The Application of the Requirement to Co-operate: Policy Guidelines*. London: DSS.

Dietz, C.A. and Craft, J.L. (1980) 'Family dynamics of incest: a new perspective', *Social Casework*, 61, pp.602-609.

Dobash, R.E. and Dobash, R.P. (1980) *Violence Against Wives: A Case Against the Patriarchy*. Shepton Mallet, Somerset: Open Books. (The 1983 edition referred to in Chapter 15 is a USA reprint of this work.)

Dobash, R.E. and Dobash, R.P. (1984) 'The nature and antecedents of violent events', *British Journal of Criminology*, 24(3), July, pp.269-288.

Dobash, R.E. and Dobash, R.P. (1992) *Women, Violence and Social Change*. London: Routledge.

Domestic Abuse Project (1993) *Research Update*, 5, Summer. From DAP, 204 West Franklin Avenue, Minneapolis, Minnesota 55404 USA.

Donnelly, D. and Finkelhor, D. (1992) 'Does equality in custody arrangement improve the parent-child relationship?', *Journal of Marriage and the Family*, 54, pp.837-845.

Driver, E. and Droisen, A. (eds.) (1989) *Child Sexual Abuse: Feminist*

Perspectives. Houndmills: Macmillan Education Ltd.

Education Wife Assault (1985) *Fact Sheet on Wife Assault in Canada*. Toronto: Education Wife Assault.

Edwards, S.S.M. (1989) *Policing 'Domestic' Violence: Women, the Law and the State*. London: Sage.

Eekelaar, J. and Clive E. (1977) *Custody after Divorce*. Oxford: Oxford Centre for Socio-legal Studies, Wolfson College.

Eekelar, J. and Dingwall, R. (1988) (eds.) *Divorce Mediation and the Legal Process*. Oxford: Clarendon Press.

Elliott, J., Ochiltre, G., Richards, M., Sinclair, C. and Tasker, F. (1990), 'Divorce and children: a British challenge to the Wallerstein view', *Family Law*, August, pp.309-310.

Elliott, J. and Richards, M. (1991) 'Children and divorce: educational performance and behaviour before and after parental separation', *International Journal of Law and the Family*, 5, pp.258-276.

Evason, E. (1982) *Hidden Violence: Battered Women in Northern Ireland*. Belfast: Farset Co-operative Press.

Ewing, C.P. (1987) *Battered Women Who Kill: Psychological Self-Defense as Legal Justification*. Lexington, Massachusetts: D.C. Heath and Co.

Families Need Fathers (1982) 'Children and family breakdown: custody and access - a code of practice', unpublished pamphlet.

Fantuzzo, J.W. and Lindquist, C.U. (1989) 'The effects of observing conjugal violence on children: a review and analysis of research methodology', *Journal of Family Violence*, 4(1), pp.77-94.

Federation of Women Teachers' Associations of Ontario Newsletter (1990-1991) Special Issue: 'Violence against women and children', 9(3), December-January.

Ferri, E. (1976) *Growing Up in a One Parent Family*. Windsor: National Foundation for Educational Research.

Finkelhor, D. (1986) *A Sourcebook on Child Sexual Abuse*. London: Sage.

Forman, J. (no date) *Is There a Correlation Between Child Sexual Abuse and Domestic Violence? An Exploratory Study of the Links Between Child Sexual Abuse and Domestic Violence in a Sample of Intrafamilial Child Sexual Abuse Cases*. Glasgow: Women's Support Project.

Franklin, B. (ed.) (1986) *The Rights of Children*. Oxford: Basil Blackwell.

Freeman, M.D.A. (1983) *The Rights and Wrongs of Children*. London: Frances Pinter.

Friedemann, M.L. and Andrews, M. (1990) 'Family support and child adjustment in single-parent families', *Issues in Comprehensive Pediatric Nursing*, 13, pp.289-301.

Frost, N. and Stein, M. (1989) *The Politics of Child Welfare: Inequality. Power and Change*. Hemel Hempstead: Harvester Wheatsheaf.

Furstenburg, F. and Cherlin, A.J. (1991) *Divided Families: What Happens to Children When Parents Part*. Cambridge, MA: Harvard University Press.

Furstenberg, F., Morgan, S.P. and Allison, P.D. (1987) 'Paternal participation and children's well-being after marital dissolution', *American Sociological Review*, 52, pp.695-701.

Garnham, A. and Knights, E. (1994) *Putting the Treasury First*. London: Child Poverty Action Group.

Gayford, J.J. (1975) 'Battered wives', *Medicine, Science and Law*, 15(4), pp.237-45.

Gladow, N.W. and Ray, M.P. (1986) 'The impact of informal support systems on the well-being of low income single parents', *Family Relations*, 35, pp.113-123.

Goldstein, J., Solnit, A.J. and Freud, A. (1973) *Beyond the Best Interests of the Child*. New York: Free Press.

Gondolf, E.W. (1988) *Battered Women as Survivors: an Alternative to Treating Learned Helplessness*. Lexington, Kentucky: Lexington.

Gordon, L. (1988) *Heroes of Their Own Lives:The Politics and History of Family Violence*. London: Virago.

Graham, H. (1987) 'Being poor: perceptions of coping strategies of lone mothers' in Brannen, J. and Wilson, G. (eds.), *Give and Take in Families*. London: Allen and Unwin.

Green, R. , Mandel, J.B., Hotvedt, M.E., Gray, J. and Smith, L. (1986) 'Lesbian mothers and their children: a comparison with solo parent heterosexual mothers and their children', *Archives of Sexual Behaviour*, 15(2), pp.167-184.

Greenberg, D. and Wolfe, P.W. (1982) 'The economic consequences of experiencing parental marital disruption', *Children and Youth Services Review*, 4, pp.141-162.

Greve, J. (1991) *Homelessness in Britain*. York: Joseph Rowntree Foundation.

Greve, J. and Currie, E. (1990) 'Homeless in Britain', *Housing Research Findings*, 10, February. York: Joseph Rowntree Memorial Trust.

Grillo, T. (1991) 'The mediation alternative: process dangers for women', *The Yale Law Journal*, 100, pp.1545-1610.

Grusznski, R.J., Brink, J.C. and Edleson, J.L. (1988) 'Support and education groups for children of battered women', *Child Welfare*, LXVII(5), Sept-October, pp.431-44.

Hague G. and Malos E. (1993) *Domestic Violence: Action for Change*. Cheltenham: New Clarion Press.

Hanmer, J. (1989) 'Women and policing in Britain' in Hanmer, J., Radford, J. and Stanko, E.A., *Women, Policing and Male Violence: International Perspectives*. London: Routledge.

Hanmer, J. (1990) *Women, Violence and Crime Prevention: a Study of Changes in Police Policy and Practices in West Yorkshire*. Violence, Abuse and Gender Relations Unit Research Paper No. 1, Bradford: Department of Applied Social Studies, University of Bradford.

Hanmer, J. and Maynard, M. (eds.) (1987) *Women, Violence and Social Control*. London: Macmillan.

Hanmer, J. and Stanko, E.A. (1985) 'Stripping away the rhetoric of protection:

violence to women, law and the state in Britain and the U.S.A', *International Journal of the Sociology of Law*, 13, pp.357-74.

Hardey, M. and Crow, G. (eds.) (1991) *Lone Parenthood: Coping with Constraints and Making Opportunities*. London: Harvester Wheatsheaf.

Harne, L. (1984) 'Lesbian custody and the new myth of the father', *Trouble and Strife*, 4, pp.12-15.

Hart, B. (1990) 'The further endangerment of battered women and children in custody mediation', *Mediation Quarterly*, 7(3), pp.278-291.

Health Visitors Association and General Medical Services Committee (1989) *Homeless Families and their Health*. London: BMA.

Hershorn, M. and Rosenbaum, A. (1985) 'Children of marital violence: a closer look at the unintended victims', *American Journal of Orthopsychiatry*, 55, pp.260-66.

Hess, R.D. and Camara, K.A. (1979) 'Post-divorce family relationships as mediating factors in the consequences of divorce for children', *Journal of Social Issues*, 35(4), pp.79-96.

Hester, M. and Pearson, C. (1993) 'Domestic violence, mediation and child contact arrangements: issues from current research', *Family Mediation*, 3(2), pp.3-6.

Hester, M. and Radford, L. (1992) 'Domestic violence and access arrangements for children in Denmark and Britain', *Journal of Social Welfare and Family Law*, 1, pp.57-70.

Hetherington, E., Cox, M. and Cox, R. (1978) 'The aftermath of divorce' in Stevens, J.H. and Matthews, M. (eds.) *Mother-Child, Father-Child Relations*. Washington DC: National Association for the Education of Young Children.

Hinchey, F.S. and Gavelek, J.R. (1982) 'Empathic responding in children of battered mothers', *Child Abuse and Neglect*, 6, pp.395-401.

Hoff, L.A. (1990) *Battered Women as Survivors*. London: Routledge.

Hoggett, B. (1993) *Parents and Children*. Fourth Edition. London: Sweet and Maxwell.

Hoggett, B. and Pearl, D. (1991) *Family, Law and Society: Cases and Materials*. London: Butterworths.

Holden, G.W. and Ritchie, K.L. (1991) 'Linking extreme marital discord, child rearing and child behavior problems: evidence from battered women', *Child Development*, 62, pp.311-27.

Holder, R., Kelly, L. and Singh, T. (1994) *Suffering in Silence: Children and Young People Who Witness Domestic Violence*. London: Hammersmith and Fulham Domestic Violence Forum. (Available from Community Safety Unit, Hammersmith Town Hall, King Street, London W6 9JU.)

Home Affairs Committee (1993) *Domestic Violence*, Vol.I. Report together with the Proceedings of the Committee, House of Commons, Session 1992-93. London: HMSO.

Home Affairs Committee (1993) *Domestic Violence*, Vol.II. Memoranda of

Evidence, Minutes of Evidence and Appendices, House of Commons, Session 1992-93. London: HMSO.

Home Office (1993) *Criminal Statistics: England and Wales 1992*. London: HMSO.

Home Office, Department of Health, Department of Education and Science, and Welsh Office (1991) *Working Together Under the Children Act 1989: A Guide to Arrangements for Inter-Agency Cooperation for the Protection of Children from Abuse*. London: HMSO.

Homer, M., Leonard, A. E., and Taylor, M. P. (1984) *Private Violence - Public Shame: A Report on the Circumstances of Women Leaving Domestic Violence in Cleveland*. Middlesbrough: Cleveland Refuge and Aid for Women and Children.

Hooper, C-A. (1992) *Mothers Surviving Child Sexual Abuse*. London: Routledge

Hughes, H. (1992) 'Impact of spouse abuse on children of battered women', *Violence Update*, August, 1, pp.9-11.

Hughes, H. and Barad, S. (1983) 'Psychological functioning of children in a battered women's shelter', *American Journal of Orthopsychiatry*, 53(3), pp.525-531.

Hughes, H.M. (1988) 'Psychological and behavioral correlates of family violence in child witnesses and victims', *American Journal of Orthopsychiatry*, 58(1), pp.77-90.

Hughes, H. M., Parkinson, D. and Vargo, M. (1989) 'Witnessing spouse abuse and experiencing physical abuse: a 'double whammy'?', *Journal of Family Violence*, 4(2), pp.197-209.

Jaffe, P. et al. (1985) *A Research Study to Evaluate the Impact and Effectiveness of the Policy Directive That Police Lay Charges in All Domestic Violence Incidents Where Reasonable and Probable Grounds Exist*. Toronto: Provincial Secretariat for Justice.

Jaffe, P.G., Hurley, D.J. and Wolfe, D. (1990) 'Children's observations of violence: I. Critical issues in child development and intervention planning, *Canadian Journal of Psychiatry*, 36, pp.466-70.

Jaffe, P., Wilson, S. and Wolfe, D. (1986) 'Promoting changes in attitudes and understanding of conflict among child witnesses of family violence', *Canadian Journal of Behavioral Science*, 18, pp.356-80.

Jaffe, P., Wilson, S.K. and Wolfe, D. (1988) 'Specific assessment and intervention strategies for children exposed to wife battering: preliminary empirical investigations', *Canadian Journal of Community Mental Health*, 7(2), Autumn, pp.157-63.

Jaffe, P.G., Wolfe, D.A. and Wilson, S.K. (1990) *Children of Battered Women*. Newbury Park, California: Sage.

Jaffe, P.G., Wolfe, D. and Wilson, S. and Zak, L. (1986) 'Family violence and child adjustment: a comparative analysis of girls' and boys' behavioral symptoms', *American Journal of Psychiatry*, 143(1), pp.74-77.

James, G. (1994) *Discussion Report for ACPC Conference 1994: Study of*

Working Together 'Part 8' Reports. London: Department of Health, ACPC Series, Report no.1.

Johnson, J. (1992) *High Conflict and Violent Divorcing Families: Findings on Children's Adjustment and Proposed Guidelines for the Resolution of Disputed Custody and Visitation: Report of the Project*. California: Centre for the Family in Transition.

Johnson, M. (1988) *Strong Mothers, Weak Wives*. Berkeley, California: University of California Press, Berkeley.

Judicial Statistics (1992) London: HMSO.

Kaufman, J. and Zigler, E. (1987) 'Do abused children become abusive parents?', *American Journal of Orthopsychiatry*, 57(2), pp.186-92.

Kelly, J.B. (1991) 'Children's post-divorce adjustment: effects of conflict, parent adjustment and custody arrangement', *Family Law*, February, pp.52-56.

Kelly, L. (1988) *Surviving Sexual Violence*. Cambridge: Polity Press.

Kelly, L. (1989) 'Bitter ironies: the professionalisation of child sexual abuse', *Trouble and Strife*, 16, pp.14-21.

Kelly, L. (1992) 'Disability and child abuse: a research review of the connections', *Child Abuse Review*, 1, pp.157-167.

Kelly, L. (1994) *Evaluation of Child Work in a London Refuge*. Report to Hammersmith and Fulham Safer Cities. Unpublished.

Kelly, L., Regan, L. and Burton, S. (1991) *An Exploratory Study of the Prevalence of Sexual Abuse in a Sample of 1200 16 to 21 Year Olds*. Final Report to the ESRC. London: Child Abuse Studies Unit, University of North London.

Kennedy, H. (1992) *Eve Was Framed: Women and British Justice*. London: Chatto and Windus.

Kincaid, P.J. (1982) *The Omitted Reality: Husband / Wife Violence in Ontario and Policy Implications for Education*. Concord, Ontario: Belsten.

King, M. and Piper, C. (1990) *How the Law 'Thinks' about Children*. Aldershot: Gower.

Kirkwood, C. (1993) *Leaving Abusive Partners: From the Scars of Survival to the Wisdom for Change*. London: Sage.

Koch-Nielsen, I. (1984) 'Vold i oploste parfold' in Koch-Nielsen, I and Moxnes, K. (eds.) *Vold I Parforhold*, Copenhagen: Nordisk Ministeraad.

Koss, M. and Harvey, M. (1991) *The Rape Victim: Clinical and Community Interventions*. Beverly Hills, California: Sage.

Labatt, M. (1990-91) 'Violence against women: an epidemic and a national disgrace', *Federation of Women Teachers' Associations of Ontario Newsletter. Montreal Massacre Memorial Issue: Violence Against Women and Children*, December/January, 9(3), pp.2-9.

Landau, B. and Sharbonneau, P. (eds.) (1993) *Report from the Toronto Forum on Woman Abuse and Mediation*. Toronto: Toronto Forum on Woman Abuse and Mediation.

Law Commission (1986) *Review of Child Law: Custody*. Working Paper No.96. London: HMSO.

Law Commission (1988) *Review of Child Law: Guardianship and Custody*.

Law Com No 172. London: HMSO.

Law Commission (1992) *Criminal Law: Rape Within Marriage*. Law Com. No.205. London: HMSO.

Law Commission (1992) *Family Law: Domestic Violence and Occupation of the Family Home*. Law Com. No.207. London: HMSO.

Lawson, J. (1992) 'Non-violent superheroes like Paul Bunyan', *Federation of Women Teachers' Associations of Ontario Newsletter*, 11(2), Curriculum Insert.

Leeds Inter-Agency Project (1993) *Violence against Women by Known Men: Training Pack*. Leeds: Leeds Inter-Agency Project, Sahara Black Women's Refuge and Leeds Women's Aid.

Levinson, D. (1989) *Family Violence in Cross-Cultural Perspective*. Newbury Park, California: Sage.

Lewis, C. and O'Brien, M. (eds.) (1987) *Reassessing Fatherhood*. London: Sage.

Lewis Herman, J. (1992) *Trauma and Recovery: From Domestic Abuse to Political Terror*. New York: Basic Books.

London Borough of Hackney (1993) *The Links Between Domestic Violence and Child Abuse: Developing Services*. London: London Borough of Hackney. (Available from the Women's Unit.)

London Borough of Hammersmith and Fulham Community Safety Unit (1991) *Challenging Domestic Violence: a Training and Resource Pack*. London: Borough of Hammersmith and Fulham.

London Co-ordinating Committee to End Woman Abuse (1987; revised September 1992) *The London Co-ordinating Committee to End Woman Abuse - An Integrated Community Response To Prevent Violence Against Women in Intimate Relationships*. London, Ontario: LCCEWA.

Lord Chancellor's Department (1993) *Looking to the Future: Summary of a Consultation Paper on Mediation and the Ground for Divorce*. Cm.2424, London: HMSO.

Luepnitz, D.A. (1986) 'A comparison of maternal, paternal and joint custody: understanding the varieties of post-divorce family life', *Journal of Divorce*, 9(3), pp.1-12.

Maccoby, E.E., Depner, C.E. and Mnookin, R.H. (1990) 'Coparenting in the second year after divorce', *Journal of Marriage and the Family*, 52, pp.141-155.

Maclean, M. and Kuh, D. (1991) 'The long-term effects for girls of parental divorce', in Maclean, M. and Groves, D. (eds.) *Women's Issues in Social Policy*. London: Routledge.

MacLeod, L. (1987) *Battered But Not Beaten: Preventing Wife Battering in Canada*. Ottawa: The Canadian Advisory Counsel on the Status of Women.

Maidment, S. (1976) 'A study in child custody', *Family Law*, 6, pp.195-200, 236-41.

Maidment, S. (1981) *Child Custody: What Chance for Fathers*. London: National Council for One Parent Families.

Maidment, S. (1984) 'Law and justice: the case for family law reform', *Family*

Law, 12, pp.229-32.

Malos E. (1993) *You've Got No Life: Homelessness and the Use of Bed and Breakfast Hotels.*. Bristol: University of Bristol School of Applied Social Studies.

Malos, E. and Hague G. (1993) *Domestic Violence and Housing: Local Authority Responses to Women and Children Escaping from Violence in the Home.* Bristol: Women's Aid Federation England and University of Bristol School of Applied Social Studies.

Mama, A. (1989) *The Hidden Struggle: Statutory and Voluntary Sector Responses to Violence Against Black Women in the Home.* London: London Race and Housing Research Unit.

May, M. (1978) 'Violence in the family: an historical perspective' in Martin, J.P. (ed.) *Violence and the Family.* Chichester: John Wiley and Sons.

Mayhew, P., Maung, N.A., and Mirrlees-Black, C. (1993) *The 1992 British Crime Survey.* Home Office Research Study No. 132. London: HMSO.

McFarlane, J. (1991) 'Violence during teen pregnancy: health consequences for mother and child' in Levy, B. (ed.) *Dating Violence: Young Women in Danger.* Seattle, Washington, USA: Seal Press.

McGibbon, A., Cooper, L. and Kelly, L. (1989) *'What Support?': An Exploratory Study of Council Policy and Practice and Local Support Services in the area of Domestic Violence within Hammersmith and Fulham.* London: Hammersmith and Fulham Council.

McKinlay, C. and Singh, T. (1991) 'Giving peace a chance', *Community Care* supplement on 'Child Care', 6 June, p.5.

Miller, M. (1990) *Bed-and-Breakfast: A Study of Women and Homelessness Today.* London: Women's Press.

Ministers Responsible for the Status of Women (1991) *Building Blocks: Framework for a National Strategy on Violence Against Women.* 10th Annual Federal-Provincial-Territorial Conference of Ministers, Responsible for the Status of Women. St. John's, Newfoundland, Canada. June 18-20.

Mitchell, A. (1985) *Children in the Middle: Living through Divorce.* London: Tavistock.

Mooney, J. (1994) *The Hidden Figure: Domestic Violence in North London.* London: Islington Police and Crime Prevention Unit.

Mooney, J. and Young, J. (1993) 'Criminal deception', *New Statesman and Society*, 17/31 December.

Moore, J.G. (1975) 'Yo-yo children - victims of matrimonial violence', *Child Welfare*, LIV(8), September-October, pp.557-66.

Moore, J.G., Galcius, A. and Pettican, K. (1981) 'Emotional risk to children caught in violent marital conflict - the Basildon treatment project', *Child Abuse and Neglect*, 5, pp.147-52.

Morley, R. (1993) 'Recent responses to domestic violence against women: a feminist critique' in Page, R. and Baldock, J. (eds.) *Social Policy Review 5: the Evolving State of Welfare.* Canterbury: Social Policy Association.

Morley, R. and Mullender, A. (1992) 'Hype or hope? The importation of pro-arrest policies and batterers' programmes from North America to Britain as key measures for preventing violence against women in the home', *International Journal of Law and the Family*, 6, pp.265-288.

Morley, R. and Mullender, A. (1994) *Preventing Domestic Violence to Women*. London: Home Office. Police Research Group, Crime Prevention Unit Series, Paper 48.

Muir, J. and Ross M. (1993) *Housing and the Poorer Sex*. London: London Housing Unit.

Mulligan, S. et al. (1991) *A Handbook for the Prevention of Family Violence*. Developed by the Family Violence Prevention Project of the Community Child Abuse Council of Hamilton-Wentworth. Section 2, p.11.

Murie, A. and Jeffers, S. (eds.) (1987) *Living in Bed and Breakfast: the Experience of Homelessness in London*. Bristol: University of Bristol School for Advanced Urban Studies.

National Children's Bureau (1993) *Investigation into Inter-Agency Practice Following the Cleveland Area Child Protection Committee's Report Concerning the Death of Toni Dales*. London: National Children's Bureau.

National Council of Voluntary Child Care Organisations (no date) *Women's Aid and Child Care: Under Fives Initiative*. London: NCVCCO.

National Film Board (1989) *For Richer, For Poorer*. Film.

NiCarthy, G. (1987) *The Ones Who Got Away: Women Who Left Abusive Partners*. Seattle, Washington: Seal Press.

Nuttal, S., Greaves, L. and Lent, B. (1985) 'Wife battering: an emerging problem in public health', *Canadian Journal of Public Health,* 76(5), September, p.138.

O'Hara, M. (1991) 'Child sex abuse and the re-assertion of fathers' rights', *Trouble and Strife*, 20, pp.28-34.

O'Hara, M. (1992) 'A mother's duty to care: are there no limits?', *Childright*, 92, pp.5-6.

O'Hara, M. (1992) 'Child protection and domestic violence: making the links', *Childright*, 88, pp.4-5.

O'Hara, M. (1993) 'Child protection and domestic violence: changing policy and practice' in London Borough of Hackney (1993) *The Links between Domestic Violence and Child Abuse: Developing Services*. London: London Borough of Hackney.

Okun, L. (1986) *Woman Abuse: Facts Replacing Myths*. New York: State University of New York Press.

Ontario Ministry of Education and Training (1994) *Framework for the Development of Violence Prevention Policies by School Boards*. Toronto, Ontario.

Pagelow, M.D. (1984) *Family Violence*. New York: Praeger.

Pahl, J. (ed.) (1985) *Private Violence and Public Policy: The Needs of Battered Women and the Responses of the Public Services*. London: Routledge and Kegan Paul.

Painter, K. (1991) *Wife Rape, Marriage and the Law. Survey Report: Key Findings and Recommendations*. Faculty of Economic and Social Studies University of Manchester, Department of Social Policy and Social Work.

Parton, C. (1990) 'Women, gender oppression and child abuse' in Violence Against Children Study Group.

Pavlic, A. et al. (1991) *Report on Survey Results Examining the Number of Children Exposed to Wife Assault in London and Middlesex County*. London, Ontario: London Co-ordinating Committee to End Woman Abuse, Children's Sub-committee (NB This report was actually written by Larry Marshall of London Children's Aid Society).

Peled, E. and Davis, D. (1992) *Groupwork with Child Witnesses of Domestic Violence: A Practitioner's Manual*. Minneapolis: Domestic Abuse Project (To be produced in book form by Sage in late 1994).

Peled, E. and Edleson, J.L. (1992) 'Breaking the secret: multiple perspectives on groupwork with children of battered women', *Violence and Victims*, 7(4), pp.327-46.

Peled, E., Shapell, B., Jaffe, P.G. and Edleson, J.L. (forthcoming 1994) *Ending the Cycle of Violence: Community Responses to Children of Battered Women*. Newbury Park, California: Sage.

Pence, E. (1989) *The Justice System's Response to Domestic Assault Cases: a Guide for Policy Development*. Duluth, Minnesota: Minnesota Program Development Inc.

Pence, E., Hardesty, L., Steil, K., Soderberg, J. and Ottman, L. (n.d.) *What About the Kids? Community Intervention in Domestic Assault Cases - A Focus on Children*. Duluty, Minnesota, USA: Duluth Domestic Abuse Intervention Project.

Pence, E. and Paymar, M. (1990) *Power and Control: Tactics of Men Who Batter. An Educational Curriculum*. Duluth, Minnesota, USA: Minnesota Program Development Inc. (Revised edition).

Petersen, K. S. and Gamache, D. (1988) *My Family and Me: Violence Free. Domestic Violence Prevention Curriculum*. (Unit 1 for grades kindergarten to 3, and Unit 2 for grades 4-6). St Paul, Minnesota: Minnesota Coalition for Battered Women.

Pizzey, E. (1974) *Scream Quietly or the Neighbours Will Hear*. Harmondsworth, Middsx: Penguin.

Popay, J. and Jones, G. (1991) 'Patterns of health and illness amongst lone parent families' in Hardey, M. and Crow, G. (eds.) *Lone Parenthood: Coping with Constraints and Making Opportunities*. London: Harvester Wheatsheaf.

R v. Emery (1992) 14 Cr.App.R. (S.).

Radford, J. and Russell, D.E.H. (eds.) (1992) *Femicide: The Politics of Woman Killing*. Buckingham: Open University Press.

Reder, P., Duncan, S. and Gray, M. (1993) *Beyond Blame: Child Abuse Tragedies Revisited*. London: Routledge.

Richards, M. (1982) 'Foreword' in Beauil, N. and McGuire, J. (eds.) *Fathers: Psychological Perspectives*. London: Junction Books.

Richards, M. and Dyson, M. (1982) *Separation, Divorce and the Development of Children: A Review*. Cambridge: Child Care and Development Group, University of Cambridge.

Rights of Women (1984) *Lesbian Mothers on Trial*. London: Rights of Women.

Rights of Women Lesbian Custody Group (1986) *Lesbian Mothers' Legal Handbook*. London: The Women's Press.

Roberts, M. (1988) *Mediation in Family Disputes*. Aldershot: Wildewood House.

Rosenbaum, A. and O'Leary, K.D. (1981) 'Children: the unintended victims of marital violence', *American Journal of Orthopsychiatry*, 51(4), pp.692-99

Rossetti, M. (1988) *Crisis Intervention for Child Witness/Victims of Wife Assault: A Model for Shelter Workers and Child Advocates*. London, Ontario: WCH.

Russell, D. (1984) *Sexual Exploitation*. London: Sage.

Russell, M. (1989) *Taking Stock: Refuge Provision in London in the Late 1980s*. London: London Strategic Policy Unit with financial assistance from the London Borough of Southwark.

Schechter, S. (1982) *Women and Male Violence: The Visions and Struggles of the Battered Women's Movement*. Boston: Massachusetts: South End Press.

Scottish Women's Aid (no date) *Working with Children in Women's Aid*. Dundee: Scottish Women's Aid.

Seligman, M.E.P. (1975) *Helplessness: On Depression, Development and Death*. San Francisco: Freeman.

Shelter (1991) *Urgent Need for Homes*. London: Shelter.

Sinclair, D. (1985) *Wife Assault: A Training Manual for Counsellors and Advocates*. Toronto: Ontario Government Bookstore.

Smart, C. (1989) 'Power and the politics of child custody' in Smart, C. and Sevenhuijensen, S. (eds) *Child Custody and the Politics of Gender*. London: Routledge.

Sopp-Gilson, S. (1980) 'Children from violent homes', *Journal of Ontario Association of Children's Aid Societies*, 23(10), pp.1-5.

Spender, D. (1983) *Women of Ideas (And What Men Have Done to Them)*. London: Ark.

Stark, E. and Flitcraft, A. (1985) 'Woman-battering, child abuse and social heredity: what is the relationship?' in Johnson, N. (ed.) *Marital Violence*. London: Routledge and Kegan Paul.

Stark, E. and Flitcraft, A. (1988) 'Women and children at risk: a feminist perspective on child abuse', *International Journal of Health Services*, 18(1), pp.97-118.

Stark, E., Flitcraft, A. and Frazier, W. (1979) 'Medicine and patriarchal violence: the social construction of a "private" event', *International Journal of Health Services*, 9(3), pp.461-93.

Statistics Canada (1993) *The Violence Against Women Survey*. Centre for Justice Statistics (also Statistics Canada data on violence against women, 1990).

Stearn, J. (1986) 'An expensive way of making children ill', *Roof,* September-October.

Steinman, S. (1981) 'The experience of children in joint custody arrangement: report of a study', *American Journal of Orthopsychiatry*, 51(3), pp.403-414.

Straus, M.A., Gelles, R.J. and Steinmetz, S.K. (1980) *Behind Closed Doors: Violence in the American Family*. Newbury Park, California: Sage.

Sudermann, M., Jaffe, P.G. and Hastings, E. with Watson, L., Greer, G. and Lehmann, P. (1994) *ASAP: A School-Based Anti-Violence Programme*. Revised Preview Edition. London, Ontario: London Family Court Clinic.

Sun, M. and Woods, L. (1989) *A Mediator's Guide to Domestic Abuse*. New York: National Center on Women and Family Law.

Thiriot, T.L. and Buckner, E.T. (1991) 'Multiple predictors of satisfactory post-divorce adjustment of single custodial parents', *Journal of Divorce and Remarriage*, 17(1/2), pp.27-46.

Thoennes, N. and Tjaden, P.G. (1990) 'The extent, nature and validity of sexual abuse allegations in custody/visitation disputes', *Child Abuse and Neglect*, 14, pp.151-163.

Truesdell, D.L., McNeil, J.S. and Deschner, J.P. (1986) 'Incidence of wife abuse in incestuous families', *Social Work*, March-April, pp.138-40.

Tunstill, J. and Aldgate, J. (forthcoming 1994) *Implementing S17 of the Children Act: The First 18 Months: A Study for the Department of Health*.

Victim Support (1992) *Domestic Violence: Report of a National Inter-Agency Working Party on Domestic Violence*. London: Victim Support.

Violence Against Children Study Group (1990) *Taking Child Abuse Seriously: Contemporary Issues in Child Protection Theory and Practice*. London: Unwin Hyman.

Walby, S. (1986) *Patriarchy at Work: Patriarchal and Capitalist Relations in Employment*. Minneapolis, Minnesota: University of Minnesota Press.

Walker, L.E. (1979) *The Battered Woman*. New York: Harper and Row.

Walker, L.E. (1984) *The Battered Woman Syndrome*. New York: Springer.

Wallerstein, J.S. and Corbin, S.B. (1986) 'Father-child relationships after divorce: child support and educational opportunity', *Family Law Quarterly*, XX(2), Summer, pp.109-128.

Wallerstein, J. and Kelly, J.B. (1980) *Surviving the Breakup*, New York: Basic Books.

Whelan, R. (1994) *Broken Homes and Battered Children*. Oxford: Family Education Trust, Oxford.

Widom, C.S. (1989) 'Does violence beget violence? A critical examination of the literature', *Psychological Bulletin*, 106(1), pp.3-28.

Wilson, M. and Daly, M. (1992) 'Till death us do part' in Radford, J. and Russell, D.E.H. (eds.) *Femicide: The Politics of Woman Killing*. Buckingham: Open University Press.

Wilson, S.K., Cameron, S., Jaffe, P. and Wolfe, D. (1986) *Manual for a Group Program for Children Exposed to Wife Abuse*. London, Ontario: London Family Court Clinic (Funded by the Ministry of Community and Social Services - Family Violence Unit).

Bibliography

Wilson, S.K., Cameron, S., Jaffe, P. and Wolfe, D. (1989) 'Children exposed to wife abuse: an intervention model', *Social Casework: The Journal of Contemporary Social Work*, 70, March, pp.180-84.

Wolfe, D.A., Jaffe, P., Wilson, S.K. and Zak, L. (1985) 'Children of battered women: the relation of child behavior to family violence and maternal stress', *Journal of Consulting and Clinical Psychology*, 53(5), pp.657-65.

Wolfe, D.A., Zak, L., Wilson, S. and Jaffe, P. (1986) 'Child witnesses to violence between parents: critical issues in behavioural and social adjustment', *Journal of Abnormal Child Psychology*, 14(1), pp.95-104.

Women's Aid Federation England (no date) *Statement of Aims and Principles*. Bristol: WAFE.

Women's Aid Federation England (no date) *You Can't Beat a Woman: Women and Children in Refuges*. Bristol: WAFE.

Women's Aid Federation England (1989) *Breaking Through: Women Surviving Male Violence*. Bristol: WAFE.

Women's Aid Federation England (1991) *Women's Aid Federation England Information Pack*. Bristol: WAFE.

Women's Aid Federation England (1993) *Annual Survey, 1992-3*. Bristol: WAFE.

Women's Aid Federation England (1993) *Briefing Paper - Domestic Violence and Child Abuse: Some Links*. Bristol: WAFE.

Women's Community House (1993) *Children's Program Guidelines*. London, Ontario: WCH.

Women's Community House (forthcoming) *Children's Program Mission Statement*. London, Ontario: WCH.

Woodcraft, L. (1992) 'Do families need fathers?' *Critical Eye*, BBC2, Dec.

Yllö, K. and Bograd, M. (eds) (1988) *Feminist Perspectives on Wife Abuse*. Newbury Park, California: Sage.

Subject Index

A School-based Anti-violence Programme (ASAP) 261-4; critique of 263-4; evaluation of 262-3

abusive men: characteristics of 7; and domination and control of women 7; *see also* violent men

access: after divorce 7, 96-72, 86-99, 104; by fathers 71-2; *see also* contact

adolescents 171; and effects of witnessing woman abuse 230

advocacy: children 5, 54, 144, 162, 176-86, 209; individual 4, 5; system 4

anti-violence work 256-65; content of 258, 260, 261-2; and funding 258; and gender 256, 261, 264; and homophobia 263; and racism 263; and sexuality 263; and training 257

Area Child Protection Committee (ACPC) 57, 59

Asian children 4, 27, 188, 195, 198; *see also* Black children

Asian women 108, 110, 112, 133, 188-98; and 'izzat' 194, 196-7; and religion and culture 193-4; and use of interpreters 112; *see also* Black women

Association of Chief Probation Officers (ACOP) 112-13, 156

Australia: preventative work in 256

barristers: training of 82

Black children 4, 27, 45, 188-98; and racism 153; and refuges 152-3, 201

Black families; and domestic violence 188-98; and housing 132-3; and use of interpreters 132

Black women: and domestic violence 188-98; and housing policy 135; and institutionalised racism 110, 132-3; and refuges 122, 143, 153, 188-98; *see also* Asian women

Booth Committee report (1985) 81

bullying 174, 256

Canada 3-4, 43, 49, 162; children's work in 176-86, 217-37; and preventative work in schools 256-65

care proceedings 63

child abuse: and continued contact with father 75, 107; and disclosure 247; and

divorce 86; and domestic violence 3, 4-5, 24, 26, 28-33, 43-55, 58, 82, 142, 247; establishment 48; and fathers 29-30, 31; and female empowerment 48; and mother's responsibility 48, 61-2; and policy in refuges 171; and training in refuges 174

child care: agenda and domestic violence 3; professionals and domestic violence 3, 4, 5, 240, 254

child deaths: and domestic violence 5, 32, 47, 57-65; inquiries into 58; and parents 57

child protection 4; agencies 57, 61, 63; and domestic violence 58, 59, 60-3; and gender 59; guidelines 58; and refuges 147, 149-51; and relationship between refuges and social services 150-1, 161; and work of Women's Aid 142

child psychiatrists: and response to domestic violence 4

child psychologists: and response to domestic violence 2, 4

child sexual abuse 6-7, 47, 49, 54, 61, 72, 74, 90-1, 108, 149, 208, 253, 263; and domestic violence 32, 33, 244

Child Support Act (1991) 5, 43, 69, 76-9, 80, 83, 87; and children in refuges 157-9; and domestic and sexual violence 78; and proof of harm or distress 159; racist implications of 77

Child Support Agency 77, 158-9; and use of interpreters 158

childhood: notions of 44

children: accounts by 17-22, 44; and advocacy 5, 144, 162, 176-86, 209; and age related responses 44, 49; and anti-discriminatory work 172-3; and anti-racist work 172-3; and anti-sexist work 173; Asian 4, 27, 188, 195, 198; and attitude to violence 4, 25, 44-6; behavioural problems of 25, 27; best interests of 82, 103, 105, 110, 116-17; Black 4, 27, 45, 188-98; and coping strategies 44-6; and developing identity 46, 49; direct work with 2, 3, 4, 5, 26, 38, 45, 142-63, 171, 176-86, 200, 217-37, 239-54; and disclosure 3, 4, 32, 47, 172,

Subject Index

239; and play 250; and prevention 240; and safety 245-6; and self-esteem 246, 251; and siblings 244, 248; and stigma 239; and structure 245-6
Guardianship of Infants Act (1886) 70
Guardianship of Infants Act (1925) 70
Guardianship of Minors Act (1971) 71

Hammersmith Women's Aid (HWA) 170-5; and childwork development project 170-5
health visitors: and refuges 174; and response to domestic violence 2
Hinduism 193
homelessness: and children 122-37; and larger families 134; and legislation 5, 43, 127, 130-2; and local connection 128-30; and older children 133-4; and proof of violence 126, 127-8
housing 122-37; authority attitudes 127-8, 135, 137, 191; and Black families 132-3, 135; and domestic violence training 135; emergency 122; and good practice 135; housing association 124, 132, 135, 137; and immigration issues 132-3; and legislation 5; options for abused women 127; and public sector 123, 124, 132, 136; and racism 132-3, 191; temporary 124-6, 130
Housing Act (1985) 127, 157

immigration: and domestic violence 192-3; and housing 132-3; see also deportation
inequality 10, 142; class 10; disability 10; gender 10; race 10; sexual 10
injunctions: use of 68, 111, 113,130-2
intergenerational transmission of violence 33; see also cycle of violence
Islam 193
'izzat' 194, 196-7

judges: and role of fathers 68-9; training of 82

law: and ability to influence behaviour 88
Law Commission 9
'learned helplessness' 8, 9, 13, 40
leaving 7-8; men's response to 8-9; violence after 8-9
legal practice: and protection of women and children 43; see also court, court welfare officers
legislation 5, 9, 63; child protection 63; and children in refuges 153-9; and children's rights 54; and the family 68-

83, 95; historical overview of 69-71; and homelessness 5, 43, 127, 130-2; and parental responsibility 68, 69, 88, 157; and protection of women 122; and violent perpetrator 130-2; see also Child Support Act (1991), Children Act (1989), Housing Act (1985)
lesbians 76, 77, 83, 91,135
London Co-ordinating Committee to End Woman Abuse (Canada) 242, 243, 244

magistrates: training of 82
male dominance: and Asian families 188; in the family 57, 76, 188; in society 57, 212
Matrimonial Causes Act (1857) 70
Matrimonial Causes Act (1878) 70
Matrimonial Homes Act (1983) 111
mediation 87, 98-9, 11-11, 112, 118-19; in Denmark 117
Mediation in Divorce 111
mediators: attitudes of 108, 109; and children's wishes 116
motherhood: see mothering
mothering: and ambivalence 52; ideology of 51; and impact of domestic violence 51-3, 54; 'patriarchal' 51; professional attitudes to 51
mothers 3, 44, 206-7, 208; and child abuse 48, 61-2; and Child Support Act (1991) 69; and contact 109-10, 118-19; 'deservingness' of 70-1; emotional abuse by 73-4; and financial situation 69, 77; and groupwork 244-5, 253; and leaving children 54; lesbian 76, 77, 83, 91; lone 87, 91, 96-7; and protection of children 51-3; and refuges 181-2; and relationship with children 51-3, 71; rights 69-71; single 71, 72, 76-7; and stress 25, 27; support for 2, 10, 181-2; unmarried 71, 72, 76; and use of children 108

NCH Action for Children: and domestic violence research 39
National Children's Bureau 59, 61
National Family Mediation 111
New Right: and family policy 75-6, 79, 80-1, 87, 91
New Zealand: preventative work in 256
North America: and advocacy work with children 5; and children's work 3-4, 162-3, 200, 217-37, 239-54; and impact of domestic violence on children 48; and research 24-40

291

Author Index